THE
UNCHANGING
ARTS

By Alan Gowans

THE UNCHANGING ARTS:
New Forms for the Traditional Functions
of Art in Society

THE RESTLESS ART:
A History of Painters and Painting 1760–1960

IMAGES OF AMERICAN LIVING:
Four Centuries of Architecture and Furniture
as Cultural Expression

ALAN GOWANS

THE UNCHANGING ARTS

New Forms for the Traditional Functions
of Art in Society

J. B. LIPPINCOTT COMPANY
PHILADELPHIA & NEW YORK
1971

To

DONALD DREW EGBERT

Friend, mentor, pioneer investigator

of social functions

in the Arts

CONTENTS

vii

CONTENTS

CONTENTS

PART SIX

1

A Definition of the Field

■

I

ART NOW—AND THEN:
A PROBLEM DEFINED, AND
REDISCOVERED

*How the changed character of what we call Art has implications
not at first apparent, for apes and artisans as well as what we
choose to call Artists.*

THE FIRST HALF of this study, *The Restless Art: A History of Painters and Painting 1750–1950* (1966), ended with some comments on the ironic implications of the fad for "pop" art, going on when the book was being written:

> if photographers now perform painting's old function of record-
> ing life, if people now turn to advertising or posters when they
> want life made more beautiful, and go to movies or read comic
> strips when they want it made more pleasant—if, in short, paint-
> ing means people talking to themselves and art for all practical
> intents and purposes means the popular arts, then anyone who
> still wants to be called an artist might as well recognize that
> situation by exhibiting stenciled letters and flags and cast bronze
> beer cans and fragments of comic strips instead of easel paint-
> ings in the old sense. But. . . . There is a constructive conclu-
> sion to be drawn from the spectacle of popular arts flourishing at
> the moment when easel painting is moribund as a useful or
> necessary activity in society, from the fact that industrial de-
> signers and photographers and commercial artists and cartoon-
> ists live dignified and rewarding lives while advance-guard
> painters are reduced to quarreling petitioners for government
> aid. It is simply this: the present dismal state of painting does
> not mean that art is dead. It means only that the particular line
> of evolution taken by advance guard painting over the last
> hundred years has run into a dead end. When and wherever
> artists have been content to leave the search for Reality to
> philosophers or physicists or theologians, and have confined
> themselves to their traditional function of providing society with
> Beauty (on whatever level), art is as vital as ever.

This is the point of departure for *The Unchanging Arts.*

These titles are not idly chosen. Painting is the "Restless Art" because its function in society has been steadily shifting over the last two hundred years, so that the activity we now call "painting" is a fundamentally different thing from what was called "painting" two hundred years ago; it not merely looks different, it *is* different. How and why this happened is the basic theme of *The Restless Art.* And in *The Unchanging Arts* I propose to trace what happened to the social functions painting abandoned, the history of those arts variously called "popular," "mass," or "commercial" that picked them up, one after the other, and perform them still—those arts, in a word, whose function has been changeless.

It may seem odd to need scholarly studies of something so recent: if painting has in fact changed its fundamental nature, if its traditional functions are now being performed by other arts, surely that would be obvious? Far from it. So gradual has been the shift, so subtle the takeover, that few people, practicing artists and critics included, even suspect it. When in the 1850s Gustave Courbet published his manifesto declaring Reality to be the artist's first and proper concern—the birth certificate of Modern Painting, in fact—there were still some who challenged the idea, who criticized Courbet and his Impressionist successors not so much for what as why they painted, who maintained they were not doing what painters ought to do. But by the 1920s such opposition was long in the past—so long, indeed, that when a few scholars began to demonstrate that art in the Middle Ages and Antiquity had different motivations from what was called Art in the 20th century, it came as a revelation. And it is at this point that understanding of the "Unchanging Arts" begins.

In 1924 J. Huizinga published a famous historical study of *The Waning of the Middle Ages.* In his re-evaluation of historical attitudes to this period in history, he thought it worthwhile to devote a chapter to the medieval concept of what art is and what it does. "Art in those times," he wrote,

> was still wrapped up in life. Its function was to fill with beauty the forms assumed by life. . . . Art was not yet a means, as it is now, to step out of the routine of everyday life and pass some moments in contemplation; it had to be enjoyed as an element of life itself, as the expression of life's significance. Whether it served to sustain the flight of piety or to be an accompaniment to the delights of the world, it was not yet conceived as mere beauty.

Consequently, we might venture the paradox that the Middle Ages knew only applied art. They wanted works of art only to make them subservient to some practical use. Their purpose and their meaning always preponderated over their purely aesthetic value. . . . The nature of the subject was far more important than the question of beauty. Beauty was required because the object was sacred or because the work was destined for some august purpose. This purpose is always of a more or less practical sort . . . worship at the great festivals . . . representations of famous judgements to decorate the law courts, in order to solemnly exhort the judges to do their duty. . . . In the Middle Ages portraits were ordered for all sorts of purposes, but rarely, we may be certain, to obtain a masterpiece of art.

As all art was more or less applied art, the distinction between artists and craftsmen did not arise. The great masters . . . were not above colouring statues, painting shields and staining banners, or designing costumes for tournaments and ceremonies. . . . We have generally lost the profane works of the great masters . . . the court costumes with their precious stones and tiny bells . . . the brilliantly decorated warships. . . .

A few years later, Frank P. Chambers in *Cycle of Taste* (Cambridge, Mass., 1928) published his discovery that the same conditions obtained in the ancient world. Beginning

with the assumption that, not in the tastes and controversies of modern art-lovers and art-critics, can a working theory of ancient aesthetics be discovered, but in ancient literature itself. . . . What had Classical Antiquity to say of its own arts?

he soon uncovered what he called an "Unacknowledged Problem in Ancient Art and Criticism":

Aesthetic self-consciousness was born late into ancient Greek culture. The Greek knew not that he was an artist, till his arts were well past their prime. The Parthenon and Propylaea were already built, and had become the accustomed sights of Athens, before it was dimly borne in upon the Athenians that they were works of Art. Prior to the fourth century A.D. there is no evidence that works of art were admired, except for their costliness and magnitude. In sculpture and painting, the first quality demanded was life and realism. . . .

Thereafter, a sense for Fine Art, as distinct from the art of making things, developed, and had its final flowering in the cities of Hellenistic princes and the Hadrianic age of Rome. The problem was, of course, that

5

during the Revival of Greek studies in the 18th century, Winckelmann divided the history of Greek culture into three periods: the archaic, the mature, and the decadent. The mature period was the 5th century B.C., the Golden Age of Pericles, when the dramas of Sophocles were performed and the Parthenon was built. Winckelmann fancied that to such heights has the genius of man never before or since risen, and that at no time before or since has the sense of beauty been so pure and so prolific. Winckelmann's doctrine was enthusiastically accepted. It has held good to this day. But no attempt has ever been made to reconcile such a doctrine with the complete absence of aesthetic references in such writers as Herodotus and Thucydides, and with the inadequate and disappointing aesthetic references to be found in later writers such as Plato and Aristotle. . . .

People since Winckelmann's time have come to profess aesthetic admiration for many other periods and styles besides the Golden Age of Greece, to be sure; if anything, there is a general preference for the earlier, archaic Greek works, for Egypt, for primitivism generally. But, far from settling the problem, this only accentuates it. For not only is there even less evidence for any notion of Art on the part of the makers of archaic and primitive work, but the times when a self-conscious Art did flourish were precisely those that produced the work most *dis*liked by contemporary taste: Hellenistic bathos, Imperial Roman realism, Late Renaissance paintings like Guido Reni's. Or in other words, what art history seems finally to prove is that the more consciously a man sits down to Create a Work of Art, the more surely he will fail to produce anything like one. So it seemed to Chambers; thinking of his own time, when the idea of Fine Art as a self-justifying activity had developed far beyond anything even in the Late Antiquity, he concluded: "May it not also be true that the modern sense of beauty [i.e., the validity of the concept of Fine Art], heretofore so universally unquestioned, should, like the ancient sense of beauty, be a changeable and evanescent myth?" It might indeed. And the very idea threatens that whole fabulous, imposing, multibillion-dollar edifice of Fine Art built by dealers, painters, museum directors, connoisseurs and art historians over the past century and a half.

Three fundamental premises are taken for granted and proclaimed endlessly by almost everybody connected with the Fine Art industry of our time. The first is that Fine Art is concerned with Beauty: Why "Should the Artist Come to the Campus?" asks James R. Perkins of Cornell in *Saturday Review* for July 17, 1965; and typically replies, because "only he can infuse a campus with a desire for beauty." The second is that at all times and places there has always been an activity comparable to what we now call Fine Art, with similar ends and means: or as E. B. Feldman put it when introducing *Art as Image and Idea* (1967), "Contemporary art professes essentially the same functions in modern life as did its historic antecedents in earlier epochs. . . ." And the third premise is that the Low, popular, commercial, or mass arts used in everyday life are inferior to the Fine Art produced by Serious Artists for Exhibition in museums, and always dependent on it for inspiration, direction, and character. Not one of these premises can be proven. Indeed, any serious investigation of them, such as is implicit in Huizinga's or Chambers's books, or explicit in *The Restless Art*, suggests that none are tenable at all. Fine Art in our time exists in fact without any theoretical foundations.

Up to now, collapse of its foundations has not made any apparent difference to the edifice Fine Art has built. Nobody has attempted to buttress them or deny that they are gone; people have simply gone on adding to the building as if its foundations were still there. Books destroying the basis of Fine Art were duly catalogued and shelved in the Fine Arts sections of libraries, and in succeeding decades thousands of others were piled up against them, as if they and their implications never existed—books about the Art of Egypt and the Art of Ancient Iran, the Art of the Parthenon, and the Art of Byzantium, as if what Egyptians and early Greeks and Sumerians called "art" were the same kind of activity that the School of Paris and the Royal Academy engaged in; as if Raphael and Rembrandt and Pollock and Warhol were all exactly the same kind of artists, differing only in the kinds of forms they used. Almost everybody, it seems, takes this identicalness entirely for granted. University presidents as distinguished as James R. Perkins of Cornell see nothing incongruous about bringing Artists to campuses on grounds that "the creative artist's process involves the explicit stamp of his own personality on his work, be he Giotto, Nijinsky, or Pablo Picasso." Art historians as distinguished as Alexander van Millingen see nothing incongruous in using terms appropriate to (say) the Ash Can school of American painting to talk about *frescoes in the Kariye Djami* in the Bollingen Foundation's catalogue:

> characterized by comparative freedom from tradition, by closer approximation to reality and nature, by a charm and sympathetic quality, and by a scheme of color that indicates the coming of a new age and spirit.

And so on. Only occasionally would a more perceptive writer acknowledge the existence of any fundamental problem, as when Edgar Preston Richardson noted, in his introduction to *Painting in America* (1956),

> Before the separation of the artist from the craftsman . . . stretches the "undisturbed, innocent, somnambulatory production" (to use Goethe's phrase) of ages when the artist worked undisturbed by the worship of his own genius or by the critics' curiosity to peer into his psyche. Art was intended for use or delight, no more. One has only to look at the achievements of those ages to be aware that aesthetic self-consciousness is not the all-in-all of art, nor an entirely unmixed good. . . .

But from this observation came little further issue than to mention illustration and cartooning's being indulged in by some American painters.

But foundations *are* necessary. No edifice can hang indefinitely in air. And I think it is the developments in Fine Art during the late 1950s and -60s that will bring the whole crashing down. For whereas during the 1920s the full solipsistic implications of the theory of Fine Art were only just appearing, in very small and limited advance-guard groups like Dadaists and Expressionists, by the 1950s what was happening had become clear to everybody. It had become plain that those earlier efforts to free painting from what were considered outmoded restrictions on imagination had led, in the process of diffusion throughout society, to a collapse of all critical standards. Everybody, man, woman, and beast, was painting, and it was hard to tell who was who, since *"everybody* has won, all shall have prizes":

Item: According to the Baltimore *American,* January 20, 1957, Betsy, a chimpanzee resident of Baltimore, who has sold $3,000 worth of paintings, finds a rival in Rajah Chandra, the "painting parrot," who has turned out more than seven hundred and fifty water colors in his career, holding brush "with beak or claw as the mood strikes him," and whose work was accepted for exhibition at the Municipal Art Commission in Los Angeles; when informed of the identity of the exhibitor, the general manager of the Commission declared that "the artist has a real feeling for color."

Item: The January 19, 1958, issue of *American Weekly* reports that an exhibition at the Institute of Contemporary Art in London features the work of Congo the Chimp, which is described by

8

Dr. Desmond Morris as "possibly the greatest source of information for us concerning the mysteries of visual patterning and composition."

Item: According to the *Delaware Review,* May 17, 1963, Mr. Theodore Saint-Amant Cunningham of Texas, brought to the campus of the University of Delaware by its president, Dr. John A. Perkins, to serve as artist-in-residence and his personal painting instructor, declares in an interview with a student reporter, "You have on this campus one of the greatest masters I have ever seen, as fine as Da Vinci—Dr. John Perkins. . . ." This is followed up in the Wilmington *Evening Journal:*

> "I hardly knew what to say when I heard it," Dr. John A. Perkins, the smiling President of the University of Delaware said . . . Dr. Perkins set up on a sofa for the press two recent oil landscape paintings and a pencil drawing of his grandmother's profile done when he was fourteen years old. Without a doubt, the pencil drawing showed considerable talent. . . . [June 1, 1963]

In the 1920s, it could be presumed that advance-guard painters were with few exceptions sincere, competent, and talented, abandoning objective form and overt meaning by choice, often running great risk thereby. By the 1960s, no such presumption was possible at all. Everybody had heard (and many could verify) tales of housewives winning awards with their first attempts at painting, of practical jokers entering old boards and paint-splattered bedsheets in exhibitions and getting by undetected. The "put-on," once an esoteric sort of joke for an "in group," had become a widespread habit of mind among critics and a neat means of avoiding risks by artists, something both consumers and conscientious critics have to be constantly on the lookout for. More and more, the whole business is coming to resemble an unending and gigantic con game.

Already in the 1920s the number of people willing to subsidize painters without obvious talents or social usefulness was understandably (to some) limited; by the 1950s and -60s it was proportionately no greater, and the demonstrable talents or usefulness of painters in general very much less, but both the numbers of painters and the scope of their claims for special status had increased beyond belief. In fact, the more impossible it became to define what Art might be or what Artists did in or for society at large, the more strident and extravagant were their demands on society at large for support and privilege:

Item: Jacques Villon at the International Conference of Artists, Unesco, 1952, demands government support for whomever it may be agreed upon to call Artists, in the name of whatever they may agree to call Art:

> In our times . . . the artist's struggle to earn a livelihood is becoming so desperate that it can no longer be ignored. . . . So it is that we call on the State for increased support for artists. . . . Not to ask the State to become our patron—for that would interfere with our freedom of conception and execution—but only to support us financially.

Item: By the mid-1960s many universities were substituting, for the traditional compulsory freshman courses in English literature from Chaucer on, compulsory freshman courses on modern literature. Such a development was foreseen a dozen-odd years earlier:

> Mr. J. W. Saunders . . . in an excellent article entitled "Poetry in the Managerial Age" [Essays in Criticism, iv, 3, July 1954] . . . faces the fact that modern poets are read almost exclusively by one another. He looks about for a remedy. Naturally he does not suggest that the poets should do anything about it. For it is taken as basic by all the *culture* of our age that whenever artists and audience lose touch, the fault must be wholly on the side of the audience. (I have never come across the great work in which this important doctrine is proved.) The remedy which occurs to Mr. Saunders is that we should provide our poets with a conscript audience; a privilege last enjoyed, I believe, by Nero. . . . All that we need do . . . is to make not just poetry, but "the intellectual discipline which the critical reading of poetry can foster" the backbone of our educational system. In other words, practical criticism or something of the sort, exercised, no doubt, chiefly on modern poets, is to be the indispensable subject, failure in which excludes you from the Managerial Class. . . . [C. S. Lewis, "Lilies That Fester," *The Twentieth Century*, April 1955]

Item: A "National Centennial Conference on the Arts and the University" at Kingston, Ontario, June 6–10, 1967, passes five separate resolutions with slightly variant wordings, urging universities to support the Arts and so be "patron and custodian of man's creativity" and demanding "more public financial support" for this purpose. No attempt to define the Arts is made, nor any acknowledgment that any criterion of artistic standards is needed, except obliquely in a resolution that universities should "provide instruction in the arts without examinations and supply institutional artistic experiences for all under-graduate students. . . . This will demand adequate financial support from government," and so forth, and so forth.

In the 1920s, the number of advance-guard works purchased from living painters by public museums and galleries was comparatively small, and their prices comparatively modest. By the 1950s and -60s, purchases by public institutions were the greatest single means of support for painters, and, despite their being based on a completely different principle from older Art, it cost more to buy a painting from a "recognized" painter than to buy the average Old Master:

Item:

> Traditionally art was valued, to use a homely analogy, like a fine whiskey. Just as you take some everyday grain and water, then refine and process and distill them until in the end you get a product far rarer and more valuable than the sum of these raw ingredients, so the painter . . . took the raw materials of nature, refined and distilled them, selected and abstracted from them until he had an end product much finer than his original materials; and that is what you paid for. But Abstract Expressionist paintings were not like that. Their primary function was fulfilled in the act that brought them into existence. . . . For just as the hypnotist's swinging watch is of no worth *as a watch*, so Abstract Expressionist canvases could have no value *as pictures*. They remained at best the shell of an experience. There is something illogical about pricing and exhibiting them in the same way as traditional paintings. . . . [*The Restless Art,* pp. 396–97]

In apologetics like Malraux's *Museum Without Walls* you will find the justifying argument that Modern Painting is to the 20th century what cathedral and temple art was to ages past. Yet who actually believes them equals in merit? On the one hand, nobody proclaims the Decline of the West and the degeneracy of modern civilization more fervently than painters, one of whose great claims to special inspired insight is supposed to be frank and fearless exposure of its decay and misery; on the other, however much cyclical historians may contradict each other as to the precise causes and pattern of Western decline, all of them—from Vico, Henry James, Danilevsky, Spengler, Toynbee to Parkinson in *East and West*—take for granted that one of the chief manifestations of that decline was the contrast between Europe's great art before 1750 and what has been produced since.

Separately, any one of these items could be explained away. Together, they add up to a confirmation of what writers like Chambers and Huizinga could only begin to suspect in the 1920s—that something is fundamentally wrong with the whole concept of what art is and what it is that artists should be doing in and for society, on which the Fine Art "system" is based. Fine Art has got into the state it is because it has become something art never was. The trouble is not with any particular means or forms Fine Artists use; no "return to likeness" or anything else will cure what is wrong with them. The trouble is with their fundamental purposes and presuppositions about art itself.

II

LOW ARTS, HIGH ARTS, FINE ARTS: SOME CRITICAL DEFINITIONS AND RELATIONSHIPS

The question "What Is Art?" cannot be answered in terms of aesthetics ("Works of Art are distinguished by aesthetic values." "What are aesthetic values?" "Aesthetic values are what distinguish Works of Art"). To know what Art is, you must define what it does. Some unexpected conclusions result.

FEW questions can have been debated so long as "What is Art?" to so little purpose; it is time this nonsense ceased. For in fact the question is unanswerable in this form; it is in the same category as Electricity, Light, or Instinct. And just as you can answer "What is Instinct?" only with something like, "Instinct is what makes birds fly south in Fall," so you can define Art only in terms of function.

Instead of asking "What is Art?" we need to ask, "What kinds of things have been done by that activity traditionally called Art?" And then we will find that that activity historically performed four functions: substitute imagery; illustration; conviction and persuasion; and beautification. (1) In cases where the appearance of something needed to be preserved for one reason or another, art made pictures that could be substituted for the actual thing. (2) Art made images or shapes (including pictographs) that could be used in whole or part to tell stories or record events vividly ("illustrate," "illuminate," "elucidate" all come from the same root "lux" = "light"). (3) Art made images which by association of shapes with ideas set forth the fundamental convictions or realized ideals of societies (usually in what we call architectural or sculptural form); or conversely, art made images intended to persuade people to new or different beliefs (usually in more ephemeral media). (4) Art beautified the world by pleasing the eye or gratifying the mind; what particular combinations of forms, arrangements, colors, proportions or ornament accomplished this end in any given society depended, of course, on what kinds of illustration or conviction or persuasion a given society required its arts to provide.

In Western culture up to about 1750, the activity that was called art always involved performing at least one of these functions, and what was called Great Art frequently involved them all. In *The Restless Art,* however, we noted that what is called Art today has come to perform none of these functions, except incidentally. It is concerned with something else, with a search for and definition of Reality, with an activity which was in the past and still is today the concern of priests, philosophers, seers, scholars, scientists. The functions Art used to perform are now done by "specialists"—photographers, illustrators, designers, cartoonists. They deal with Reality also, of course, but in the way artists of the past always dealt with it—not exploring or defining Reality themselves, but simply putting into the most attractive, convincing, and intelligible form whatever definitions of it may be current (**1a, b**).*

Distinguished from what is best called Fine Art today, which performs none of the functions performed by the activity called Art in the past, are the mass arts created by modern technology, which perform all of them. They are successors to the traditional Low Arts, in function, origin, and character.

Does it follow that such illustrators, designers, and the rest are actual or potential successors to the Great Masters art history

---

* Parenthetical boldface numbers in text and captions designate illustrations to which the reader is referred.

records? Not necessarily. In the first place, their function is usually too narrow; what we call Great Art commonly performed most if not all of these functions at once; universality was one measure of greatness. But historically, Great Art had another and much more fundamental measure. The mere performing of given functions in and for society was characteristic of all art; what determined Great Art was performing them with imagination, with inventiveness, with originality, and above all, with individual expression. In the ages before these qualities were isolated and became autarchic ends in themselves, their presence was always what distinguished great art from lesser, major arts from minor, and what can best be called High Art from Low. But these are not the qualities that distinguish illustration, cartooning, industrial design and the rest to any great degree now, nor can they ever; the very nature of the function these arts serve precludes more than a minimum of personal expression. They are necessarily mass arts, pitched to a lowest common denominator of taste and content. As such, they are successors not to Great or High Art, but to the Low arts of earlier times, to the ideational art of primitive ages and early civilizations, and the minor and folk arts of the medieval and Renaissance periods in the West. To understand them, we need first to understand what constituted Low Art throughout history, and how it was related to High.

How art began in history we cannot know; but we can guess, by analogy with the creative and mental growth of children. First comes a period when technical skill is too small for anything recognizable to be made—a period of scribbles on walls and scrabbling in mud, of primeval "macaroni" scratchings on rocks; call it pure self-expression if you will, but without any distinct self to be expressed, you cannot call it art of any kind. Art as such begins with a recognition that these activities can be a means of communication with the world, of preserving memories, of telling stories—a kind of language (**56a**). At this stage the child does not want to invent sounds of his own, but to master those which people around him make and attach meaning to; he wants other people to know what his pictures represent without asking. And in primeval ages it must have been the same. To all such artists anonymity was essential. Originality was the last thing desired, because what they wanted were symbols and shapes recognizable by all. And it remained so through the first centuries of civilization everywhere—in Egypt, Mesopotamia, China; in archaic Greece; when Byzantine and Latin Christian culture was first taking form. To

14

be sure, legend names early "artists"—Imhotep; Tubal-cain; Daedalus; Mêng T'ien, inventor of the paintbrush. But these were not individual creators, only collective mythical symbolic figures personifying those timeless generations of craftsmen and builders who learned how to make images and buildings bigger, solider, in more permanent materials. And theirs was no High Art. It was ideational art—an art concerned with perpetuating the basic values and beliefs of society through symbols collectively inspired, anonymously executed, everywhere and immediately understood. This was the first, the earliest, the most basic form of Low Art. As we shall see, it still survives among us, vigorous as ever—shifting in form, as Low Arts always do; unchanging in function, as Low Arts always are.

How High Art historically grew out of Low Arts, and why. How Great Masters could be distinguished from anonymous artisans responsible for Low Art.

When does it first occur to a child that two pictures may be equally good at conveying meaning or whatever else he wants them to do, but that one may be nicer to look at than another, and so "better"? Only after considerable technical mastery has been achieved, that much we can guess. But as to the precise moment, who can tell?—any more than the precise historical moment can be fixed when people began comparing one image or temple or vessel with another on grounds of Beauty as well as use. All we know is that such a moment comes, and came in history; and when it did, High Art appeared.

With High Art comes the first possibility for great individual artists. For only when two works can be compared on grounds that, while both perform the same function equally well, one does it more attractively, more impressively, more intelligibly than another, can there be recognizable individual expression; and only when one artist can be distinguished from another, can value judgments be made that distinguish great artists from lesser. These value judgments will of course be based not on kind but on quality. If the Middle Ages honored cathedral builders above playing-card cutters, for instance, it was not because the first were artists and the second not, but first because it took greater skill and longer training to do the one job than the other, and second because cathedrals were of deeper and broader value to society as a whole than playing cards. As between one cathedral builder and another, or one wood-block cutter and another, judgment depended on the degree to which the work fitted its function, how competently the job was done, how well it met set specifications. And so it is at this stage that the Great Masters begin to appear: Exekias and Phidias and Polygnotus, William of Sens and Pierre de Montereau, the Han and T'ang masters, Giotto and Masaccio and Michelangelo in their several generations.

Not that the Great Artist *must* appear at such a given stage in history; there is nothing deterministic about it. Man and moment must meet. We can imagine many ripe moments for a Great Artist to appear in history when no such man came forward, as well as many a potential flowering of genius "born to blush unseen" because the time was not ripe for it. A certain degree of freedom for individual expression is essential, and many societies that reached the point of recognizing one work of art as superior to another never went on to that further atage. Egypt is a classic example.

Freedom for the Great Masters of High Art does not mean, of course, that they were individualists in any modern sense of eccentric independent rebels against tradition. Far from it. They may expand and enrich the expressive possibilities of the artistic tradition they inherit far beyond anything their predecessors imagined, but they never break with it. Quite the opposite; they build on it; they "see so far," as a medieval writer put it, because they "stand on the shoulders of giants." They work always within their tradition; in the highest sense they can say,

> The trivial round, the common task,
> Would furnish all we ought to ask.

That is why they are not famous in the personal sense in which modern painters are famous; they excelled enough in their own time that people preserved memories of them, from which modern scholarship can reconstruct something of their careers, but it was their works and not their personalities that were admired. Their function was not to get fame, but to give it. It is because they performed this function so well, because they so successfully solved given problems within their own given discipline, that people still speak of the Great Masters as exemplars of the triumphs of the human spirit and name them, along with philosophers and seers and scientists who likewise succeeded in their proper spheres of work, as the great ornaments of the race (**2a, b**). This is something usually forgotten when people talk or write about Art today; they forget that, unlike these Old Masters, our professed Artists claim fame not for their work but for themselves: as philosophers, seers and prophets speaking through the medium of paint or clay or plaster—a very different matter (3c).

With High Art come, too, new forms of Low Art. Not that the old primeval ideational Low Art ever disappears until the end of the civilization whose ideas it carries; but alongside it appear what received art history chooses to call the folk and minor arts. These are characterized by forms dependent on the lead of High Art; they are the work of anonymous and provincial artisans, reproducing and perpetuating the innovations of the Great Artists with a time lag of years, generations, sometimes even centuries. When we speak of the "influence" of Great Artists on their times, it is to these forms of Low Art that we must look to find it; so we trace the influence of forms created by Phidias or the Master of Olympia out of ideational proto-types through successive monuments in remote towns of Italy and Hither Asia, for example, or the Hudson River school's influence through Currier & Ives prints to Grandma Moses. It follows that, through the function of these Low Arts will be constant, their media and forms never are. Generation after generation, century after century, they will express a low common denominator of taste and ideas, a dead level of generalized experience; to that extent André Malraux was right in describing folk art (in *The Psychology of Art*, III, 1950, p. 56) as "drawn on legendary lore, whose roots plunge deep in time." But by continuing with "all popular arts are vaguely Gothic, a combination of sentimentality and stiffness. . . ." he went off the track, for it is not by their forms that we shall know them, but by their spirit, their function alone. The media and forms of folk and minor arts vary with time, place, and, above all, with whatever is the preferred medium and style of the High Art they are following: if that be madrigals, they may be ballads; if fully three-dimensional marble sculpture, freestanding clay figurines; if painted panels, block prints on paper; if monumental Baroque altars of bronze and plaster, household shrines of tin and papier-mâché—and so on.

But one thing is plain: the better the High Art is, the better the Low Arts will be. Because 5th-century Greece had great painted sculpture, it had fine coins, and pottery that on occasion rose to High Art itself (4a); the High Architecture of Romanesque and Gothic cathedrals improved the quality of that Low Architecture of barns and chapels from which they sprang. The High Art of Renaissance painting inspired beautiful Low Arts of tapestry, majolica, prints, and metal-work.

Whereas traditional High Art could and did consistently provide forms for Low Arts, because both performed similar functions, Fine Art cannot, since it performs none of them. In fact, the reverse is true: for three generations now, Fine Arts has consistently appropriated forms generated in the mass Low Arts and, by taking them out of functional contexts, made Precious Objects for Exhibition out of them.

Such a state of affairs is one professed aspiration of Fine Artists today. They dream and preach of a world saved by Design—of everything modeled on the pure plastic form of Mondriaan, or raised to spiritual exaltation through the works of Kandinsky, or transfigured through Happenings. But there is no sign of any such thing coming to pass. Quite the opposite, in fact. As early as 1855 Charles Baudelaire in his *De l'Essence du Rire* sensed that cartoons were somehow becoming a distinctive form of art parallel to painting and no longer dependent on it for forms as they had been earlier; by the 1890s perceptive observers like the poet Hugo von Hofmannsthal were more and more aware that influences were now actively going the other way, and were rather condescendingly suggesting that art critics should take cartoons more seriously because advance-guard painters were so obviously borrowing from them. And in the years since, while Fine Artists continue to profess contempt for grubby commercial work, they have been even more continuously influenced by it, until it can now be demonstrated—as we shall do in following chapters—that every single new development in painting for at least fifty years back can be traced to a source in popular, applied, or commercial art. The role of the Low Arts has been completely reversed; where once they followed, now they lead.

And in all fields of artistic activity much the same has happened. Literature is typical. "I incline to come to the alarming conclusion," T. S. Eliot wrote in his ponderous way in 1936,

that it is just the literature that we read for "amusement" or "purely for pleasure" that may have the greatest . . . least suspected . . . earliest and most insidious influence upon us. Hence it is that the influence of popular novelists, and of popular plays of contemporary life, requires to be scrutinized. [*Essays Ancient and Modern*, p. 105]

John Steinbeck put it much more brutally a few years later in his 1953 introduction to Al Capp's *World of Li'l Abner:*

> How do we know what Literature is? Well, one of the symptoms or diagnostics of literature should be, it seems to me, that it is read, that it amuses, moves, instructs, changes, and criticizes people. And who in the world does that more than Capp? Recently . . . I was out of touch . . . for a matter of three weeks. When . . . mail could reach me, I found about thirty letters. . . . practically every one . . . began—"Have you heard that Daisy Mae and Li'l Abner are married?" It was the most important thing that had happened in America. Well, that seems to me to prove that Capp is literature. Nobody reports on the doings of Horace Hairlip the sad and decadent denizen of [Faulkner's] aristocratic but mouldy South. And yet he is discussed in our literary gazettes as though he were literature. . . . I think Capp may very possibly be the best writer in the world today. . . .

I would not go so far as that; but it is worth pointing out that of all writers in the 1930s and -40s the two still most influential and widely read today (outside of English literature course assignments) are George Orwell and C. S. Lewis, neither of whom literary critics at the time paid any attention to—Cyril Connolly in *Enemies of Promise* (1948) airily dismissed Orwell as a "colourless reporter"—and whose works are rarely ranked as literature by critical standards even yet.

Is this because Low Arts have changed and improved so much? To some extent they have improved, certainly; art like Capp's or David Low's is obviously far more sophisticated and technically mature than its precedents in Cruikshank or Gillray. But the Low Arts have not basically changed; they still perform the same functions as ever. The difference is that, whereas two hundred years ago there was still a High Art performing these functions also, only better—and in the process providing Low Art with forms to draw on—it has been replaced by the entirely different kind of activity we call Fine Art. Whatever forms Fine Art has at any moment will be irrelevant in the Low Arts, because their forms are always determined by what they do in society, while those of Fine Art are not. What happens in fact is that the Low Arts have to generate their own new forms to meet social conditions and demands as they arise; forms so generated naturally come to represent the "taste of the times"; in due course Fine Artists become aware of the new taste, "discover" the forms, rip them from their context of social function, and make Precious Objects for Exhibition out of them—so you have forms from simultaneous photography glamorized as Cubism, cartoonists' techniques for representing motion glorified as Futurism, urinals taken out of lavatories exhibited as "found" art, bits of comic strips blown up into "pop" art, dials torn from dashboards becoming "op" art, and so on.

Or put it another way: the Low Arts are still capable of creating new forms because they are still in touch with life. But Fine Art has become an organism having no perceptible interaction with its environment. For organisms in such a state coroners have a word. They call them corpses. Two hundred years' gradual shift in the concept of what art is and what artists do has resulted in our no longer having High and Low Arts. The two kinds of art we have are the living Low Arts, and the dead.

III

ARTS LIVING AND DEAD

How an art-for-art's-sake type of Fine Art developed in late classical times.

THE IDEA of a Fine Art divorced from life was no invention of our civilization, but one of the Renaissance humanists' borrowings—or, more exactly, resurrections—from classical Antiquity. Every known civilization, in fact, shows traces of art "decadent" in C. E. M. Joad's sense of "losing the object," "forgetting what it's all about"—of late periods when once self-evidently right ways of thinking and action freeze into conventional dogmas and artificial rituals to be trotted out on special occasions under the name of Religion, and the statues and temples and drama created as natural parts and products of those ways of thinking and acting consequently lose their relevance to life and turn into Precious Objects to be put on Exhibition at particular times for contemplation under the name of Art. Frozen Religion and

dead Art—this pattern is recognizable in the archaism of New Kingdom Egypt, in neo-Sumerian and neo-Babylonian phases of Mesopotamian culture, in Sung China and Mughal India; but by far our
best documented knowledge of it comes from the classical civilization
of Greece and Rome (**4b**).

Here Fine Art first appears in the 4th century, after the
breakdown of Greek city-state life, with writings about "art" like Duris
of Samos's *Lives of the Painters and Sculptors.* It accelerates in the
Hellenistic Age, in lands where Greek culture is more and more a
veneer, less and less a spontaneous way of life, whose rulers personally
acknowledge none of the old beliefs. Greek art was made to embody:
the way Attalus III of Pergamum and Ptolemy III of Egypt, Polycrates
of Samos and Dionysius of Syracuse raid the temples of Greece and
carry off their cult images as proofs of their "cultural interests" shows
how much they think of the old gods' powers. By the first century
before Christ, the old High Art of Greece is plainly dead to any practical intents and purposes; wealthy Roman plunderers take it home in
shiploads as ornament for their villas. Concurrently, Fine Artists have
been appearing, who play variants on classic High Art not because
they have anything new to say, but according to whims of taste:
Lysippus and Praxiteles, Apelles and Zeuxis and Parrhasius, each more
"arty" than the last; there is a "Renaissance" of the "Parthenon style" in
the 2nd century, and an "Archaic Revival" in the 1st; there are
"schools" famous for their special styles, collected by Roman connoisseurs: Rhodes, Pergamum, Alexandria, Antioch. And as if this were not
familiar enough, we even have the kind of "art appreciators" typified
by Strabo, who in his *Geography* marvels at what earlier ages in his
own civilization accomplished:

> Works were raised of an astounding magnitude, and inimitable
> beauty and perfection, every workman striving to surpass the
> magnificence of the design with the elegance of the execution;
> yet still the most wonderful circumstance was the expedition
> with which they were completed . . . built in so short a time,
> and yet built for ages. . . .

and wonders why his age seems unable to produce anything comparable. *We* may wonder why he seemed unable to recognize the living
art being created all around him—the triumphal arches and the
aqueducts, the basilicas and the mosaics that would soon carry the
ideational foundations of a new civilization; but we should not, for the
same thing is going on unrecognized all around *us.*

It seems astonishing to us how tenaciously intellectuals in Late Antiquity held onto the idea of Fine Art. As late as Constantine's time,

> Constantine, in harmony with contemporary taste, took fairly seriously . . . the most famous poet of the age, one Optatianus Porphyrius. . . . He was skilled in making verses having the same number of letters, and the verses could be placed under one another to form a square or an oblong. Then the initial and final letters of the lines were made to stand out in red ink, when they were seen to make another verse. Sometimes the words of a line could be read backward, with equal effect. Yet again, the poems were written on purple, probably with silver ink, many letters being brought out in gold. If the gold series were now read by themselves, they made a verse once more, or even a whole poem; and the lines in gold set forth among themselves figures as on a carpet, e.g., the monogram of Christ, or a ship. . . . The art of poetry had become a matter of clever manual dexterity, but without soul . . . Optatianus was long marvelled at in succeeding ages. . . . [Hans Lietzmann, *From Constantine to Julian: A History of the Early Church*, 1950, p. 179]

Surely by this time, we think, it should have been obvious how dead such Art was. But not at all. Poems like Optatian's and pointless displays of technical virtuosity like the Lycurgus Cup in the British Museum (**4b**) were still considered far above anything produced by those lowly carvers and mosaicists who in retrospect were at that very moment creating the living art of Byzantine civilization; Literary Artists like him long continued to ignore all the advantages of the codex format (the early bound book whose pages made it easy to find anything anywhere in the text) and went on using scrolls (which had to be constantly unrolled forward or back), because codexes had been invented to serve utilitarian needs and therefore lacked the prestige of Art:

> The humble origins of the parchment codex . . . probably militated against its acceptance for belles lettres. [C. H. Roberts, "The Codex," *British Academy Proceedings*, XL, 1954, pp. 176–80]

Only with the total collapse of classical civilization was the corpse of Fine Art finally buried, and the ground cleared for creation of new, living forms. It was this corpse that the Renaissance humanists disinterred.

How the idea of Fine Art was the only thing Renaissance humanists actually revived from classical Antiquity.

The more we learn about the Renaissance, the less inclined we are to accept the Renaissance humanists' own broad claims to have brought back to life the ancient world of Greece and Rome. We still talk about this "rebirth" and still absurdly call the centuries between classical times and it the "Gothic Middle Ages," but so far from anyone's still thinking these centuries a "barbarian interval," it is becoming clearer all the time how little Renaissance humanists really knew about Greece or Rome, how much of what they called their "rebirth" was a classicizing gloss on ideas actually derived direct from medieval precedent, and how much of what did go back to the ancient world represented a disastrous retrogression from medieval standards.

There was no Renaissance of classical music, for classical music was never known in the Renaissance. There was no Renaissance of classical technology; for despite the quotes from Roman authors that Georg Bauer under his Latin pseudonym Agricola scattered through *De Re Metallica,* the machines and techniques he describes there were all inventions of the Middle Ages and went far beyond anything the Romans knew. There was no Renaissance of classical agriculture, because again medieval agriculture had gone so far beyond it; the heavy plough introduced on monastic farms during the 9th and 10th centuries had in fact revitalized a European economy ruined by the Roman practice of farming with slave labor. There was no Renaissance of classical law, for the Justinian code that the humanists took to be Roman law was in fact a final compilation of new laws based on Byzantine principles that had been steadily superseding the old Roman code since the time of Alexander Severus and Caracalla. There was no Renaissance of classical mathematics, for the basic principle of mathematics as an abstract language was unknown in the Graeco-Roman world. There was no Renaissance of classical physics, for the Graeco-Roman world was equally ignorant of the principle of *impetus;* paying lip service to Archimedes and Ptolemy, Western mathematicians and physicists tacitly ignored their outmoded concepts of concrete quantities and static reactions to push forward along the lines established by their 13th- and 14th-century predecessors: so Leonardo da Vinci's science was actually based on the mathematics of Nicholas of Cusa, Fibonacci, and Albert of Saxony; Kepler acknowledged his debt to Cusa; Galileo cited the precedents of William

Heytesbury and Nicole Oresme; Newton and Leibnitz used the differential calculus formulated by Richard Swineshead. And there certainly was no Renaissance of a "classical spirit" in J. A. Symonds's typically orthodox sense of

> recovery of freedom for the human spirit after a long period of bondage to oppressive ecclesiastical and political orthodoxy—a return to the liberal and practical conceptions of the world which the nations of antiquity had enjoyed. . . . ["The Renaissance," *Encyclopaedia Britannica*, 11th ed.]

Lawrence Brown's comments on this passage in *The Might of the West* (1963) are decisive:

> Quite aside from what he obviously did not know about the Middle Ages, it would be interesting if he had told where in Classical antiquity he discovered "liberal and practical conceptions of the world"? In mass slavery, in licit and open homosexuality, in rowboats as seagoing vessels, in technological poverty and scientific shallowness, in the endless petty bloodshed of the Greek city states, in the mixture of short-sighted apathy, personal tyranny and civil war that is the history of most of the life of the Roman Empire? These . . . were far closer to the reality of that society than a careful selection of Classical poets and dramatists, Aristotle's theory of aesthetics, a few carefully chosen ruins and pieces of broken statuary. . . . [P. 491]

There was, of course, a Renaissance of classical Latin, and its ultimate result was to make Latin useless for any purpose other than writing elegant and pedantic imitations of Roman authors, and so destroy it as a living instrument of European unity. There was a Renaissance of classical medicine, and it took over three centuries to recover from this revival of the errors of Galen and Hippocrates and to relearn the principles of structural anatomy, the value of sterilizing wounds, the use of distilled water and fruit for travelers' diets, and isolation for contagious diseases like smallpox—all known and practiced by medieval physicians and described in the 13th-century treatises of Theodoric Borgognoni of Ravenna, Gilbertus Anglicus of Montpellier, and Henry de Mondeville, chief surgeon of the French armies under Philip the Fair and Louis X. There was a Renaissance of classical geography, and if Columbus had used the new translation of Ptolemy, America would never have been found—but of course neither he nor any other navigators of this period used the absurd Ptolemaic maps still popularly called "medieval" but in fact unknown before the Renaissance; they relied on accurate medieval portolano maps, on accurate methods of oceanic navigation by compass and astrolabe devised in the 13th, if not the 12th, century, and on accurate facts of the earth's size and roundness known to every educated medieval man and available in print by Columbus's day—the *Sphaera Mundi* that John of Halifax (Sacrobosco) wrote about 1230, for instance, was available in many manuscripts and had been translated into five vernacular languages before it was first printed in 1472 (there were more than 25 later editions, by the way, including two for use in schools as late as 1629 at Wittenberg and 1656 at Leiden). There was a Renaissance of classical astronomy, with the result that

> in their attitude to nature, men like Roger Bacon, Nicholas of Cusa, William of Ockham, and Jean Buridan, who preceded him by a century or two, were "moderns" compared to Copernicus. The Ockhamist school in Paris, which flourished in the 14th century . . . had made considerable advances in the study of motion, momentum, acceleration, and the theory of falling bodies . . . they had shown that Aristotelian physics . . . was empty verbiage; and they had come very close to formulating Newton's Law of Inertia. In 1337 Nicolas of Oresme had written a commentary on Aristotle's *De Coelo*—in fact, a refutation of it—in which he attributed the daily round of the heavens to the rotation of the earth, and based his theory on much sounder physical grounds than Copernicus, as an Aristotelian, could do. . . . a century and a half before Copernicus, a succession of men of lesser fame than he had shaken off the authority of Aristotelian physics to which he remained a life-long slave. [Arthur Koestler, *The Sleepwalkers*, 1959, p. 202]

And Koestler goes on to point out that because Galileo followed Copernicus instead of Oresme, he could have no proofs for the rotation of the earth, was still trying to make the revival of Ptolemaic heavenly circles fit what he observed through his telescope, and therefore had to recant and admit his statement about a moving earth was only hypothesis. And there was, finally, a Renaissance of classical art; but it too was hardly what convention supposes.

How the Renaissance in fact revived neither the forms nor the functions of Graeco-Roman art, but only disinterred the buried classical concept of Fine Art, an activity divorced from social functions.

25

To begin with, there was no rebirth of Graeco-Roman forms, properly speaking. For, while early Renaissance artists did copy various details from ancient monuments, they almost invariably either misinterpreted their function (using Apollos for Adam, Venuses for Eve, Hercules for Samson, etc.), or ignored their original character (forgetting or not realizing how ancient buildings had once been painted, how like oiled and polished waxworks ancient statues were), or so far mistook the character of classical civilization as to imagine that forms with such typically proto-Byzantine dynamic tension as the arch-on-column or the Pantheon dome could be expressions of the same culture manifested in the cause-and-effect clarity of Greek post-and-lintel structure.

Neither was there, properly speaking, a rebirth of the "classical spirit" in art. To be sure, Renaissance artists did introduce a new frame of reference which related art directly to individuals, and made it intelligible in terms of personal experience—as when Ghiberti moved from cosmic-present time in the first panel of the Gates of Paradise to humanly intelligible one-point-perspective time in the last, or when Masaccio transformed Adam and Eve in the Brancacci Chapel from generalized symbols of spiritual states into figures with whose human emotions individual spectators could personally identify. This great innovation has been called a reappearance of the classical spirit or the "classical mind," and with good reason, for what happened in early 15th-century Italy does parallel what happened in early 5th-century Greece; and the parallel does continue in succeeding stages of development—I have traced it at length in *Images of American Living* (1964) and shown how similar stages recur again as a classical tradition evolves in 18th-century American architecture and furniture. But this was nothing like a conscious or deliberate "rebirth" of 5th-century Greek art, for the simple reason that to all intents and purposes 5th-century Greek art was quite unknown to Renaissance artists. Almost all its great monuments were still undiscovered, known only from books. If the new spirit of humanly intelligible Order had any one source, it was the *ratio* of High Gothic cathedral art seen through the eyes of men to whom it came as something fresh and new—for in early 15th-century Florence an immemorial Byzantine tradition of flat limitless pattern had only within living memory been superseded by the commensurate spatial volumes and balanced iconographical schemes of the Gothic tradition from Northern Europe. This Renaissance "classical spirit" was the expression of a certain mood of confidence which

26

had nothing specifically to do with Greece, Rome, or anywhere else. What Renaissance humanists did consciously and deliberately revive from the ancient world was something altogether different.

Renaissance humanists knew Graeco-Roman civilization almost entirely from books. And in the writings of Strabo and Cicero, Pliny and Pausanias, they found an attitude to art new to them. These writers talked about Art as something remote from life, as something to be Contemplated and Appreciated, to be taken out of everyday routine and put away in Collections; they talked about Artists who made objects not for utilitarian use but for the delectation of connoisseurs, and who thereby were people different from ordinary mortals, exempted by their genius from the commonplaces of life:

> Pheidias . . . Polykleitos . . . Myron . . . Praxiteles . . . are now worshipped along with the gods [says the Spirit of Sculpture, speaking to Lucian]. If you should become one of these, how should you help but become famous among all men? You will make your father an envied man, and bring renown to your homeland. [*Enhypnion*, 6–9]

They talked, in fact, about Fine Art. And this idea is what the Renaissance humanists set about to revive.

How the concept of Fine Artists as godlike geniuses first reappeared.

First came the idea of the Fine Artist. You can see it generating in the early Renaissance, manifested by such things as Ghiberti's *Commentaries,* talking about Giotto and *trecento* art in the way Pliny and Vitruvius talked about the Fine Art of Antiquity, presenting a theory of Beauty as something abstract; but it is as yet mixed up with the medieval idea of the individual achieving greatness working for and in his society rather than outside and beyond it— Donatello's self-portrait as St. George on the Or San Michele may be "an image of the Renaissance" in its new independence from its surroundings, as conventional writers say, but it is not all that different yet from Jörg Syrlin the elder's "typically medieval" self-portrait as Virgil in the choir stalls of Ulm Minster. In the second generation the Fine Artist appears unmistakably; Alberti is one personification of it, playing the inspired genius in music, architecture, and painting alike, imposing his ideas of Art in defiance of patrons' wishes or functional needs. But the quintessential Fine Artist is Leonardo da Vinci. Leo-

27

nardo it is who proclaims the Artist a "god" among men; who in scientific invention and artistic innovation alike is obsessed with a vision of what power the Artist should command. His equestrian figures, for instance: traditionally an idealized knight serving the community, made by earlier Renaissance artists into a symbol of individuals attaining power and glory through reasoned control over nature, the type becomes in Leonardo's works a statement of the truth that whatever personal power an individual achieves by control over nature must be expressed, and can only be experienced, in power over other men; beneath his equestrian figures for the Sforza and Trivulzio monuments and his Battle of Anghiari drawing for the Florentine Council, he introduces a new symbol, the fallen foeman, cringing and beaten, in intimation of George Orwell's *Nineteen Eighty-Four* (1949):

> How does one man assert his power over another . . . ? By making him suffer. Obedience is not enough. Unless he is suffering, how can you be sure he is obeying your will and not his own? Power is in inflicting pain and humiliation. Power is in tearing human minds to pieces. . . . Do you begin to see . . . the kind of world we are creating? . . . A world of fear and treachery and torment, a world of trampling and being trampled upon. . . . [P. 273]

Long before it was taught in the Ministry of Love, Leonardo had come to realize that ultimate power is power over the minds of men; hence the precocious interest in psychological states epitomized in his *Mona Lisa* and climaxed in his transformation of *The Last Supper* from the traditional memorial of Christ offering his body a ransom for sin into a study of twelve psychological reactions to a Leader's dramatic announcement of treachery in the ranks. In his person Leonardo exemplifies the kind of "genius" Vasari and Van Mander wrote about in their *Lives of the Most Illustrious Artists;* from him the line of descent runs clear to Courbet and Gauguin and Picasso—and to Adolf Hitler, the inspired Artist who tried to mold a whole world to his will.

How the idea first reappeared of Fine Art, which, having no social functions, is above criticism by any ordinary members of society.

Next comes the self-conscious idea of Fine Art itself. Greek and Roman writers took the art of their own time to be a dismal regression from the Great Masterpieces of earlier classical ages; how much more degraded, their Renaissance admirers argued, how much more "barbaric" and "Gothic" the work of subsequent ages must be! Of course, they could not prove this argument, any more than they could prove that Cicero's classical Latin was superior to the language of St. Thomas Aquinas; indeed, any attempt to demonstrate such propositions would surely prove the opposite—Botticelli's *Calumny* is stiff and pedantic by comparison with his other works, to the degree that he tried literally following Lucian's description of a painting by Apelles given in Alberti's *De Pictura;* Alberti's architecture similarly suffers from his dogmatic attempts to follow "the precepts of the Ancients." But they did not attempt proof. They followed the example of humanist literary critics, who

> jeer but do not refute. The schoolmen advanced and supported propositions about things; the humanist replied that his words were inelegant . . . condemned not because they had no use but because Cicero had not used them. The growing, sensitive, supple language of Bede, Aquinas, the great hymns, or the *Carmina Burana* were labelled "barbarous," despite the fact that medieval philosophy is still read as philosophy, the history as history, the songs as songs, the hymns are still in use . . . so that the "barbarous" books have survived in the only sense that really matters. It would be hard to think of one single text in the humanists' Latin, except the *Utopia*, of which one can say the same. . . . We read the humanists, in fact, only to learn about humanism . . . is it not clear that in this context the "barbarous" is the living and the "classical" the still-born? [C. S. Lewis, "New Learning and New Ignorance," *English Literature in the 16th Century*, Oxford, 1954, p. 19]

So in just this vein we find Filarete, for example, arguing that

> Today writing in imitation of the classical style of Cicero and Virgil is the best usage . . . the man who follows the ancient practise in architecture does exactly the same thing. . . . All private citizens of knowledgeability build in that style . . . neither would the Duke of Mantua, a great connoisseur, use it if it were not what I say. . . . Pointed arches are modern and in bad style. . . . It is true that to one who does not understand design, they appear more beautiful. . . . But I implore whoever sees them, not to look at them and to turn . . . the mind to the ancient ones . . . appreciate the beauty the ancient things have and the crudity that is in the modern. [*Il Trattato d'Architettura*, in E. G. Holt, ed., *Literary Sources of Art History*, Princeton, N.J., 1947, p. 147]

29

A century later this kind of attitude will be second nature to writers; Sebastiano Serlio will simply take classical superiority for granted, and in his *Opere* will contrast stage sets with classical forms for the Art of Drama as connoisseurs understand it, with Gothic sets appropriate only for vulgar plays that appeal to the cloddish mob.

How the idea of museums and connoisseurship reappeared—setting Works of Art *apart in special places, to be subjectively judged by special "rules of taste."*

"Connoisseur"—that is the key word (3a). For with connoisseurs come collections; and with collections, museums—the third step in the development of Fine Art. J. Huizinga thought that the new Renaissance habit of collecting was an accidental by-product of the new Renaissance taste for classical forms:

> in the treasuries of princes and nobles, objects of art accumulated so as to form collections. No longer serving for practical use, they were admired as articles of luxury and of curiosity; thus the taste for art was born which the Renaissance was to develop consciously. [*The Waning of the Middle Ages,* p. 62]

But it had to be the other way around. Only when people have the idea of Fine Art, of preserving an object serving no function but aesthetic enjoyment, will objects be collected as Art. As long as people have no idea of Fine Art and think only of art in terms of function, objects will simply be destroyed when their usefulness is gone or their materials are needed for something else, and it matters not whether what is dead was once Low Art or the greatest of High Art. When the Athenian state decided the gold and ivory in Phidias's statue of Athena was more immediately useful to the state than his great cult image, they tore it apart without a thought for any destruction of Art. When times and spiritual needs and theological emphases changed, Romanesque churches were demolished to make way for Gothic ones, and only stones or glass or revered statues still useful were preserved, as unhesitatingly as old tapestries or worn-out playing cards landed on the rubbish heap. Pope Julius II did the same to Old Saint Peter's when he wanted a new kind of basilica to express different ideas; and so for that matter did the Bishop of Quebec in 1864 when he destroyed the old church of Saint Laurent on the Ile d'Orléans once its replacement was completed (5). Living art traditions characteristically destroy and rebuild in just the same spirit as this morning's comic page, having fulfilled its brief function of providing entertainment and instruction, wraps this evening's garbage. Nowhere in living art will you find any idea of preserving artifacts of the past simply as Art, as "classics." Healthy civilizations preserve pictures and statues, manuscripts and buildings *as historical evidence* when they can, certainly: not for their forms of "beauty" alone, but only because they embody ideas and records of the past worth remembering.

Once objects are saved solely as Art, you may be sure that for all practical purposes they are dead, and you may suspect that the civilization collecting them for only that reason has begun to die too. It was so in the classical world, and the same thing began to happen in the Renaissance.

Already in the early 16th century you can see the developed type of Fine Art collector in paintings like Bronzino's connoisseur (*Portrait of a Man*) in the National Gallery of Canada (**3a**). Here is the Amateur and Connoisseur—one who Loves and Knows about Art. Knowing Art does not mean, of course, that he practices any. That still demands enough technical discipline to keep amateurs in the dabbling arty sense well in the future. Knowing Art means, for connoisseurs like this, esoteric knowledge of things hidden from the common horde of men—specifically, that there are certain kinds of objects which are Fine Art and certain which are not; and that some of this Fine Art is "most beautiful," some "less beautiful," and some "poor" or "ugly." "Good" Art in this instance means the Aphrodite statuette on his table. Once, such figures were made to be worshiped, or at the very least to suggest some Idea or Aspect of Divinity to beholders, and whether the actual sculptor of this piece still worked wholeheartedly for this reason or was already more concerned with creating a beautiful work of Fine Art, he would retain at least some vestigial feeling for its proper meaning and function. But of this the Renaissance connoisseur could know little and feel nothing. For him, in a 16th-century Western society, such a work could have no vital function whatever. It is a totally rootless bit of debris from the past, kept and collected only and entirely because its forms and texture give him aesthetic feelings when he Contemplates it. And being such, when the connoisseur calls it "good" or "beautiful" Art, he is not judging it as High Art traditionally was judged, by how aptly or imaginatively its forms fit functions; it has no functions to fit. Instead, he judges it according to sets of rules and subjective reactions arbitrarily established by connoisseurs like himself, in reference to objects dead as itself.

31

Such a standard of judgment must inevitably affect the work of contemporary artists, and it does. If objects of aesthetic contemplation divorced from practical functions are what wealthy connoisseurs want, that is what they will get—not only the objects made functionless through the passage of ages that dealers supply, but objects made without function deliberately by contemporary artists.

With connoisseurship comes the Fine Artist, working to produce whatever Fine Art connoisseurs favor, and so absolutely dependent on their whims.

The more Fine Art is wanted, the more Fine Artists will appear, each generation more self-consciously aware of "style" than the last—Mantegna, Francesca, Correggio, Memling, del Sarto, Mabuse, Parmigianino, van Heemskerck. It takes some time for the old traditions of High Art to break down completely, so that even in Mannerist paintings like Bronzino's connoisseur you will see how, despite a new kind of self-conscious "style," its forms are not yet entirely ends in themselves—these elegantly calligraphic lines, glossy nuances of chiaroscuro and subtly elongated shapes still appropriately serve to depict their elegant, suave subject. But the line of descent is already obvious. Already obvious, too, is a new idea of Eclectic Art, art deliberately created by borrowing *ek lektos*—from the best—in the past.

Of course High Art must be and always was eclectic, too; the difference is that in High Art earlier forms and ideas are borrowed for usefulness first, beauty secondarily. Any new and better way of expressing ideas or constructing vaults, whenever or wherever discovered, must and will be borrowed, for to go on using inferior forms would be poor art—this eclecticism is simply the converse of abandoning forms when their usefulness is over. Eclecticism in Fine Art, by contrast, means borrowing forms primarily because they are considered beautiful by connoisseurs. Being in no way commensurate with or judgeable by any functional standards, such beauty must be absolutely dependent on the connoisseur's rules of taste; it follows that Fine Artists have no say in what they borrow, pretend what they will. To create what connoisseurs will call "most beautiful" Art, they must copy what connoisseurs call "most beautiful" forms, regardless of private choice. So begins the process that made advance-guard Fine Artists of all men the most complete slaves to current intellectual fashions; so begins the professed contempt of Fine Artists for Low

Artists, based on envy of their creative freedom to invent forms as need arises—for the lowest commercial drudge is freer to invent forms than the fashionable painter bound to dance attendance on the whims of connoisseurs and museum keepers.

Lacking any constant frame of reference in social function, "good" and "bad" are meaningless terms applied to Fine Art and Artists; they can never be more than "in fashion" or "out." The revolts of one generation against another that our Fine Art museums record are meaningless revolutions in subjective taste.

It has been so since Fine Art first appeared. When connoisseurs thought Hellenistic art the most beautiful form of all, Fine Artists had to follow Praxiteles and Pergamum; when connoisseurs changed their minds and decided Roman art was better, Pompeii and the Ara Pacis became mandatory models; and so on down to the "psychedelic" Art Nouveauish decorators and "Miësian" stylists of today. For of course connoisseurs will change their minds, regularly and often. However absolutely mandatory any "beautiful" form may be on Fine Artists at any one moment, no moment is absolute; when Taste becomes intellectual fashion divorced from practical use, one generation's likes will be the next's horrors, inevitably. Here starts the unending parade of styles that fills our museums today—records of how one generation liked Roman and the next Greek, how some proclaimed Gothic unsurpassable and others preferred Italianate, of Picasso following fifty years' twists in fashionable taste without missing a beat, and so on until finally if Abstract Expressionism lasts five years people talk of its "long dominance in the Art market."

"Parade of styles" is perhaps not quite the phrase; "funeral processions" would be better, for from the beginning Art Museums have been places to inter objects out of all contact with life—fragmentary shrines where nobody worships, patched-up images nobody prays to, furniture nobody sits on, manuscripts nobody reads to any practical purpose, paintings whose subjects nobody cares about—and essentially they still are. Hence the mausoleum atmosphere of marble, steel, and glass; the immortal and immutably finished "classics" laid out reverently amid ferns and piped music; the canned obituaries played by pressing buttons; the new corpses forever arriving from busy morticians outside, or brought up from vaults below. Hence the critics and scholars and docents in their shoals, industriously reading and

33

writing eulogies. Hence the curious practice of labeling works with subjects in tiny letters and Artists' names in screaming majuscules, of talking about owning so many "Rubenses," or "Picassos," or "Pollocks"—when objects have no function, titles are meaningless. Hence the spectacle of squabbling apologists all contending that Fine Art is Good for People, but totally unable to agree on what it is good *for*— Châteaubriand and Ruskin claiming Gothic Art should be preserved because its beauty proves Christianity true, Gibbon arguing just the opposite; Hitler and Goering posing as preservers of Western culture when they loot Fine Art from every ruined nation in Europe for their museums at Karinhalle and Linz; Marxists damning capitalism because its blighting materialistic influence made the 19th-century Art of Painting so bad, Ludwig von Mises contending to the contrary in *The Anti-Capitalistic Mentality* (1956) that the 19th-century Art of Music was very good; champions of "abstraction" and "free expression" versus defenders of "sanity in Art" (who want to go back to Bouguereau, presumably)—hopeless, endless, unendable arguments all, graveside wranglings over words like "goodness" and "badness" which, when applied to objects without any living function whatever, can have no possible meaning.

"Burn the museums!" Futurists roared in the years before 1914—clear away this dead litter, and something living will grow! But their argument was hypocritical and absurd. Only neobarbarians would want to destroy the records of past history that museum objects embody; what needs destroying is the habit of mind that sees museum objects as Fine Art. And to that, the Futurists were more deeply committed than anyone before them. During the Renaissance and well into the 17th century, all artists still preserved at least a vestigial obligation to be of use to something or somebody besides themselves; 18th-century exhibitions of uncommissioned pictures "with a few notable exceptions were assumed to be the last resort of the unemployed," as Francis Haskell wrote in *Patrons and Painters* (London, 1963, p. 6). But by 1900 the idea of Fine Art had made unemployment the advance-guard painter's normal condition; where for Masaccio or Michelangelo a patron was someone who hired artists to do some job that needed doing, now the very word "patronize" had acquired overtones of charity to deserving poor, given with no thought of commensurate return—and no artists exemplified this state of affairs better than the Futurists. What they really wanted was to clear the cemeteries of old corpses so there would be room for the new ones they had

made, introverted and solipsistic paintings which unlike their predecessors never even began with a pretense of living connection with the
outside world. But this aspect of the argument was apparently noticed
by nobody. By the early 20th century an idea once resurrected from
Antiquity by a few speculative humanists had become accepted dogma
everywhere. Fine Art divorced from life was taken as the self-evident
starting point for arguments, no longer a point of argument itself. But
it is in fact no more self-evident than it ever was; how and why a
proposition so patently dubious came to its present ascendency is a
major chapter in Western intellectual history.

*As introduced by early Renaissance theoreticians and dilettantes,
the idea of Fine Art is rejected by the Great Masters of the later
15th century and High Renaissance, who recognize its dictatorial
implications; reviving in Mannerism, it is condemned by both
Reformation and Counter Reformation.*

The idea of Fine Art did not prevail all at once, or without
a struggle. Far from it; almost immediately some were aware of both
its inherent menace and its inherent futility, and among them were
many of the great High Artists of the West.

Donatello was perhaps the earliest. Just as his *Gattamelatta*
had been one of the greatest symbols of the power that command over
nature could give an individual emancipated from social duty, so he
was among the first to realize the dangers in that power which Leonardo made explicit. And if Leonardo's equestrian figures glorify the
Power of the Creative Individual controlling masses of other men
through his command of natural forces, statues like Donatello's *Mary
Magdalene* in Florentine Baptistry show what happens to the masses
under the horse's hoofs. As Leonardo prefigures O'Brien, the inquisitor
of *Nineteen Eighty-Four*, so Donatello's gaunt and ghastly later works
prefigure O'Brien's victim:

> "We control life, Winston. . . . at all its levels. You are imagin-
> ing that there is something called human nature which will be
> outraged by what we do and will turn against us. But we create
> human nature. Men are infinitely malleable. . . . You are the
> last man . . . you are the guardian of the human spirit. You
> shall see yourself as you are. Take off your clothes . . . stand
> between the wings of the mirror. . . ."
> A bowed, skeleton-like thing was coming towards him
> . . . a forlorn, jailbird's face with a nobby forehead . . .

35

crooked nose and battered-looking cheekbones . . . his body was grey all over with ancient, ingrained dirt. Here and there under the dirt were the red scars of wounds . . . the legs had shrunk so that the knees were thicker than the thighs. . . .

"You are rotting away . . . you are falling to pieces. . . . Do you see that thing facing you? That is the last man. If you are human that is humanity. Now put your clothes on again." [Pp. 277–78]

Botticelli's last works—exemplified especially in the mystic *Nativity*—changed in the same dramatic way, ostensibly under the influence of Savonarola's campaign against worldly vanities, but basically, I think (for in this age intellectual and social movements tended to be cast in religious molds as a matter of course), as a reaction against Fine Art, a return to art with function and meaning apart from forms, putting message first and aesthetics last, rather than the other way around. It was a combination of classical forms and clarity with this re-emphasis on the traditional medieval functions of art that produced the synthesis we call the High Renaissance: adopting classical forms for the same reason their predecessors had adopted Gothic or Romanesque ones in their time—because they seemed more effective ways of saying and doing what their art was expected to say and do; building on their predecessors' work as the Great Masters of the Gothic and Romanesque had done, the Great Masters of the Renaissance produced a comparable High Art. So Raphael reinterprets the early Christian mosaic cycles of Old Saint Peter's for his tapestry cartoons; so his Madonnas and Michelangelo's *Pietà* are not different in meaning or function from Madonnas and *Pietàs* block-printed as souvenirs from popular shrines, nor the Sistine ceiling from the Romanesque vault of Saint-Savin-sur-Gartempe or the Besserer chapel windows in Ulm Minster—but they achieve their ends by richer, more powerful, more immediate Renaissance means of expression.

By the 1530s and -40s, however, Fine Art was on the rise again. Beauty and classical forms that in High Renaissance art had been subordinated to function began again to be made ends in themselves. Vasari's *Lives* cast Leonardo, Raphael, and Michelangelo in the classical role of geniuses—with some justice in Leonardo's case, possibly, but certainly giving no warrant for wild 20th-century exaggerations like Irving Stone's *The Agony and the Ecstasy;* whatever else Michelangelo may have been, he was certainly nothing at all like a 16th-century van Gogh. Mannerism became the rage in Italy, and spread rapidly north to Flanders, to France, to Germany, bringing with it those striking intimations of late 19th- and 20th-century attitudes which have made Mannerism the "in" field for fashionable art historians in the 1950s and -60s. But in the 1550s this process was abruptly checked, as both Reformation and Counter Reformation leaders threw their weight against it.

How, contrary to popular belief, the Protestant Reformers' iconoclasm was not directed against art in general; it was the idea of Fine Art that they detested.

It is conventional to talk about the Protestant Reformers' "opposition to art"; what is not properly realized is that their opposition was not at all directed against art as traditionally understood and practiced in the West. It was the new idea of Fine Art promoted by Renaissance humanism that they detested, and the Counter Reformers shared their feelings completely on this point. This is a distinction essential to get clear, for between them the Reformers managed to check the growth of Fine Art for a century and a half, and determined the character of Low Arts thereafter.

Though the basic Renaissance principle of looking back to the ancient world for imagined models of perfection in art and literature had originally paralleled and encouraged the Reformation principle of looking back to imagined religious principles in the ancient world, in practice the Reformation worked strongly against Fine Art, in two ways. First, the Reformers' Biblical literalism led them to take seriously the Second Commandment prohibiting "graven images." But this could never have been interpreted as a ban on all artistic activity, for immediately after recording the commandment, Exodus (35:30–33) goes on to tell how "the Lord hath called . . . Bezaleel the son of Uri . . . filled . . . with the spirit of God . . . in understanding . . . in all manner of workmanship . . . to devise curious works . . . in gold . . . in carving of wood. . . ." and describes him and Aholiab making not only decoration for the sanctuary but also representational works, including "two cherubims of gold" which "spread out their wings on high . . . with their faces one to another . . ." (37:7–9). It followed that artistic activity with a social purpose—preferably but not necessarily the glorification of God—was both permissible and laudable; the Reformers held exactly the medieval view on this matter that you find set out by the 12th-century monk

37

Theophilus in *De Diversis Artibus:* although man has "lost the privilege of immortality" through original sin, still his inheritance from Eden includes the

> wisdom and intelligence, that whosoever will contribute both care and concern is able to retain a capacity for all arts and skills, as if by hereditary right. . . . So it has come about that, what God intended to create for the praise and glory of His name [i.e., man's capacity to create Beauty], a people devoted to God has restored to his worship.

What Reformers considered abhorrent (as medieval scholars did too) was the idea of Fine Art, of beauty as an end in itself. Understanding this will clear away a good many misconceptions about art history in Protestant countries. If they had less painting and sculpture generally than Catholic lands, it was because these arts had less use in Reformed worship, not because the Reformation opposed them as such; if much medieval art was destroyed, it was far less in any spirit of iconoclasm (we have heard too much of Cromwell) than simply, again, because this art had lost its function and was discarded in the same way so much Romanesque art was discarded and lost when Gothic came in. The flourishing architecture and music of Protestant countries is ample proof that the Reformation meant no loss of High Art in those fields where art served a social purpose.

Inimical also to Fine Art was the Reformation doctrine of the priesthood of all believers. If no kind of work is more inherently sacred than any other, if it is not what you do but the spirit in which you do it that counts towards salvation, then the idea of the Fine Artist as a unique kind of workman, a godlike creator, must be at best silly and at worst blasphemous.

How the Counter Reformation, condemning Fine Art as useless and pernicious, imposed a discipline that prolonged traditional High Art two centuries more.

The Catholic Counter Reformation checked Fine Art just as severely, though on somewhat different grounds. A passage well-known in art history describes Paolo Veronese (1528–1588) being interrogated before the Inquisition concerning his *Last Supper in the House of Simon* for a refectory in Venice:

> Q. Are not the decorations which you painters are accustomed to add to paintings or pictures supposed to be suitable and proper to the subject and the principal figures or are they

for pleasure—simply what comes to your imagination without any discretion or judiciousness?

A. I paint pictures as I see fit and as well as my talent permits.

Q. Does it seem fitting at the Last Supper of the Lord to paint buffoons, drunkards, Germans, dwarfs, and similar vulgarities?

A. No, milords. . . .

After these things had been said, the judges announced that above named Paolo would be obliged to improve and change his painting . . . and that if he did not . . . he would be liable to the penalties imposed by the Holy Tribunal. [Holt, *Literary Sources of Art History*, pp. 247–48]

Plainly, inquisitors like these were not against art or beauty as such, but against artists' making their work less functional for its purpose than it should be, whether by idiosyncratic personal choice or in the name of artistic values as such. Michelangelo or Raphael would never have needed any such a reprimand as Veronese received, for they were not yet much infected by Fine Art; in the Sistine Chapel and the Vatican Stanze, for example, they did not attempt to paint what they liked but followed programs devised by Marco Vigerio, a theologian at the papal court—their job was what artists' jobs always had been, devising imaginative forms appropriate for their purpose. In his later works like the Ricetto and Medici Chapel at San Lorenzo or Saint Peter's dome and façade, Michelangelo did not hesitate to distort and break every canon of classical art when the changed times demanded a changed expression; his primary concern was not with "art forms" but with effective communication of ideas.

As long as such discipline was in force, Fine Art was restrained, and in due course there succeeded to High Gothic and High Renaissance the High Art of the Baroque age—great by the same objective standards of forms imaginatively invented to fit function, and therefore quite interchangeable with older forms serving comparable functions. So in church architecture you find innumerable examples of Baroque-forms going exquisitely together with Renaissance (as in the 17th-century churches of France, and as late as Thomas Baillairgé's 19th-century churches in Quebec), or with medieval (as at Santiago, or Worms, or the Riddarsholm in Stockholm).

How traditional concepts of art went increasingly on the defensive from the 18th century on, but survived until the mid-19th century; America a dramatic example.

But towards the end of the 17th century Reformation and Counter Reformation attitudes begin to weaken, and Fine Art revives in inverse ratio. The process is most rapid in France, England, and northern Germany, where by 1750 High Baroque art has degenerated into a frivolous Rococo and the idea of Fine Art is plainly ascendant; it is at this point that *The Restless Art* begins. Elsewhere, however, traditional concepts hang on. The best and most familiar example is the 18th-century church architecture in south Germany; here forms may have Rococo lightness, but the function they serve gives them sublimity—Vierzehnheiligen, Banz, Amorbach, Würzburg are quite as great as earlier churches anywhere. Less well-known is the comparable survival of traditional attitudes in America.

America throughout the first half of the 19th century was the scene of ceaseless, complex, and violent argument over art. As chronicled in popular vein by books like Russell Lynes's *Tastemakers* (1958) or in more scholarly fashion by J. Meredith Neil, Lillian B. Miller in *Patrons and Patriotism* (Chicago, 1966), and others, it sometimes seems a hopeless morass of conflicting statements from half-forgotten controversialists. Yet once realize that it is the last installment of an old and basic European controversy over the nature and purpose of the activity called art, and what people called artists are supposed to be doing in and for society, and two quite clearly distinguishable sides can be made out.

One side holds that art is an activity growing naturally and inevitably out of the needs of society—"democratic" is a favorite word for it—and that as the social needs to be served change, not only will the forms of any given art change accordingly—as style in painting, for instance—but also the relative importance of the various arts will shift: in one age the dominant art may be painting, in another sculpture, in another furniture or architecture or whatever. Its most characteristic spokesmen have been people concerned with practical affairs. Some were prominent citizens like Benjamin Franklin with his belief that "to America, one schoolmaster is worth a dozen poets, and the invention of a machine or the improvement of an implement is of more importance than a masterpiece of Raphael [i.e., the mechanical arts are properly the predominant art form for his time and place]"; William Tudor, who thought the "arts of design" applied to manufacturing and industry were America's natural art; and John Quincy Adams, insisting on an "obvious and intelligible" decoration for the Capitol, expressing "the duties of the Nation or its Legislators." Others were artists of practical turn of mind: Gilbert Stuart, who laughed at Benjamin West's "acres of heroes" and said that for American artists "the only job worth doing is portraiture"; Charles Willson Peale, the most representative figure of all, with his versatile willingness to turn his hand to anything need-ful—now designing public decorations like his triumphal arch for George Washington, now making prints and portraits of public figures to foster patriotism, now running a museum for public enlightenment; in later generations, J. J. Audubon, George Caleb Bingham, William Sidney Mount. Still others were patrons, who in the old manner com-missioned works of art useful to the public. Such were the sponsors of the American Art-Union, whose philosophy was that Great Art must grow from a broad base of public acceptance and use, that art only for "the rich and effeminate" is like wax flowers, and that even if most of the many thousand engravings and paintings distributed in the Union's heyday during the 1840s were admittedly aimed at a common denominator of taste, they were justified because "someone may arise by and by, and for *his* sake we are content to encourage a host of lesser lights." Such too was Luman Reed, willing to help Thomas Cole until such time as he could support himself, because his art gave a new and growing country useful historical perspective.

Obviously what this side maintains is the old traditional concept of High and Low Arts—a painter like Peale is clearly in the tradition of medieval craftsmen and Renaissance *bottegas,* while art intelligible to the people was a basic philosophy of patronage as characteristic of the Athenian state and the medieval Church as it was of the Art-Union. And until 1860 this side maintained ascendancy—a surprising survival of the traditional concept of art resulting from a unique combination of historical circumstances.

To begin with, most settlers in America before 1860 tended inevitably to come from areas and classes essentially untouched by either the High or the Low Arts of the Renaissance, let alone by any notion of Fine Art. Their natural medieval bias was reinforced by strong Reformation attitudes to art; nearly all the early settlers were Protestants, and a high proportion of them held Reformation attitudes in an extreme Puritan or Quaker or Pietist form—as arts like the Puritan "plain style" or Shaker furniture manifest. Influential, too, was the English origin of most early settlers, for until William of Orange introduced Renaissance art in Dutch Protestant form, both Renais-sance and Baroque were so generally associated in the English popular mind with the foreign and hostile powers of France and Spain that neither achieved any mass support, despite sporadic attempts to intro-duce new styles by fashionable courtiers and kings—indeed, Charles I's patronage of Inigo Jones and Van Dyck had been widely inter-preted as evidence for those subversive intentions on which the rebellion against him had been justified. Medieval traditions were further strengthened by the breakdown of European class and appren-ticeship patterns in the New World; in a society where everyone had to some extent to be a Jack-of-all-trades, any notion of an Artist's making Precious Objects solely for contemplation was absurd, and it long remained so; until 1850 most "artists" in America were still what they had been in the Middle Ages—men whose work was part art, part craft, part decoration: master masons who built fine houses and master carpenters who built churches and master shipwrights who built boats, but who also on occasion were simple stonecutters and sawyers and corders; metalworkers who as occasion demanded made jewelry and fine silverware, cut plates for engravings, or decorated guns and knives; painters who made portraits and prints and tavern signs indis-criminately; carvers who cut tombstones and wood blocks and crest-ings for chairs. And finally, there was a long American tradition of aversion to European follies and fripperies, which included Fine Art. It began with the first settlers coming to found new societies free from European corruptions; it colors all Jefferson's thinking about the new republic and Washington's Farewell Address; it was the heritage of Frank Lloyd Wright, whose ancestors came from Wales in 1850

> with no lingering sense of having been exiled from a great and glorious culture to something less, something provincial and poorer, but to some society soldier, healthier. . . . out of this attitude and this tradition a healthy art could grow, and in the case of this family, of course, it did. . . ." [Maginel Wright Barney, *The Valley of the God-Almighty Joneses*, 1965, p. 20]

Mark Twain in the 1870s and -80s is still an eloquent spokesman for it, in his *Connecticut Yankee* and his railings in *The Innocents Abroad* against the "smoke-dried old fire screens which are chef d'oeuvres of Rubens or Simpson or Titian or Ferguson or any of those parties. . . ." But by now there is a difference; Twain is not so much talking from within a dominant tradition but defending one under strong attack. Rubens and Titian we know, but who are Simp-son and Ferguson? They represent the other and ultimately trium-phant side in the raging controversy of the earlier 19th century.

For from the late 18th century on, the inherited American concept of art was increasingly challenged by people who hold that art is something Fine, something above the ordinary concerns of living, something spelled with a capital A. They are people who tend in consequence to believe also in certain ages as being "classic," and hold that whatever was characteristic of those "classic" ages—both the kind of art and the particular forms of it that then predominated—is good for all time to come, so that any age or culture which failed to produce similar things is therefore provincial, decadent, or barbaric as the case may be. In contrast to protagonists of the older view, they are chiefly Artists themselves, or practicing critics.

You find an early hint of the new attitude in John Singleton Copley's famous letter of 1776 to Benjamin West, complaining that "in this country as you rightly observe there is no examples of Art . . . I think myself peculiarly unlucky in Liveing in a place into which there has not been one portrait brought that is worthy to be called a Picture within my memory [i.e., not that America lacks pictures, but that it lacks a concept of something called Art, as distinct from socially useful objects]." It is also, unfortunately, an intimation of its ultimate re-sult—the decline from Copley's early promise of creating a great High Art of portraiture out of living Low Arts of printing and limning, to the stilted and artificial Fine Art of his last English period. John Vander-lyn's career is another example: infected by early Salon successes in France, he ignored Jefferson's admonition that painting was not a proper High Art for America, and spent his life in frustrated railings against American barbarity. John Trumbull, too, fought any idea that what America had was art worth having; he claimed that only paint-ings in a Grand Style like his own should be called Art, that only people who appreciated his concept of Art should belong to an Academy, and that the United States was a cultural desert because his Academy (the American Academy of Fine Arts) failed to flourish.

The loud complaints and conspicuous failures of Fine Artists like these have disproportionately colored most accounts of the state of art in the early Republic. More unbiased and better factually documented studies, like Lillian Miller's *Patrons and Patriotism,* pre-sent the very different picture of a unified, thriving, vital society supporting all sorts of living arts—painters in every city, anonymous builders and stonecutters and print makers working at a high level of Low Art; but because this was not the kind of art Renaissance humanists admired, a noisy little band of self-appointed cultural

43

leaders arose to denounce it as not Art at all. They created, and passed on to later historians, the image of a backward, provincial, "undeveloped" land, of a cultural desert, of "colossal public indifference" to artists. Above all, once the first flush of the Revolutionary break from Britain abated, they talked incessantly about how America was "behind Europe" in Art. Andrew Jackson Downing is a great case in point. Ingratiating writer, engaging personality, he makes a career of Elevating American Taste to the level of Europe, insofar as in this "unfortunately democratic" country it can be done. He detests the little white Greek Revival temple-houses ordinary folk are building, with their naïve associations with liberty and patriotism, and in his campaign he is not above slanting arguments by showing the worst-proportioned, most badly arranged examples of them he can think of. He wants to make America an "artistic" land, filled with picturesque Gothic villas, like Europe (so he says); when he finds the public rejecting his ideas as foreign, snobbish, un-American, he sets it down to Poverty of Taste, bred by insularity.

As Lillian Miller tells us, opponents of the American Art-Union take the same line. When Bingham's *Jolly Flatboatmen* is selected as the engraving for mass distribution in 1846, the Literary World deplores a choice "the very name of which gives a death blow to all one's preconceived notions of HIGH ART"—how can something that is intelligible and appealing to ordinary people be Fine Art? What does it matter if every kind of painter lost opportunities when these opponents managed to have the Art-Union declared illegal in 1851, if "these violent dogmatic decisions crush and wither the timid likings of plain people, which might have developed into cultivated taste [as the Art-Union's defenders lamented]"?

Far better that than to have the wrong kind of painters flourishing, or have the public imagine that its timid likings might be any basis for true and Fine Art! Think what "educated Europeans" would say about the Art-Union level of taste! How humiliating for the country that James Jackson Jarves can find no buyer for the collection of "Italian primitives" he brought to America in the 1850s, that he has to give it away to Yale University to cover a loan!

As the 19th century moves on, this depreciatory comparison between European and American "educated opinion" about Art gets shriller and louder. Indeed, the Europeans were far ahead. Already in 1830 Thackeray found the idea of Literary Art as a self-justifying activity so far advanced in Paris that "there is scarcely a beggarly beardless scribbler of words or poems or prose but tells you in his preface of the *sainteté* of the *sacerdoce littéraire;* or a dirty student sucking his tobacco and beer and reeling home with a grisette . . . who is not convinced of the necessity of the new 'Messianism' and will not hiccup, to such as will listen, chapters of his own drunken Apocalypse." [Quoted in Cesar Graña, *Bohemian Versus Bourgeois,* 1964]

He could have found the same in painting (**3b**). By the 1840s and -50s, painters in France were likewise commonly proclaiming that their superiority to "bourgeois materialism" entitled them to exemptions from ordinary codes of living and especially from the law of supply and demand, regardless of any fact that, as Cesar Graña points out,

> the claims of the dispenser of intellectual values were always made to rest on the contention that these were higher things which could not be rendered into utilitarian terms. And yet, of course, the pragmatic point of the artist's demand on the public was to obtain a predictable rate of reward for his work.

How dismally backward a country was America, where still in the 1850s, as Lillian Miller summarizes it,

> Artists may have complained about prices received, lack of patronage, neglect by the government, but seldom did they complain about being misunderstood in their intention or frustrated in their creative purposes. Not so much because they found economic profit in conforming, as because they participated in the same religious and social environment, did American artists of the mid-century paint the kind of pictures and sculpt the kind of statuary that found warm receptivity among American patrons.

Not until the Civil War shook self-confident faith in the uniqueness of American civilization would the protagonists of Fine Art triumph, and the misunderstood Artist become common; and it would take until the Depression of the 1930s and the One-Worldness of the 1940s for all vestiges of the old tradition to disappear, for the living American tradition to succumb entirely to the dead concept of Fine Art that had begun its final march to dominance in Europe almost two centuries before.

How in Europe too resistance to the idea of Fine Art was strong in the 18th century, but steadily weakened so that by 1800 Fine Art was in the ascendancy.

It was during the 18th century that Fine Art gained decisive ascendancy in Europe. A turning point was evident around 1700, when the last acknowledged Great Masters began dying off; though men like Boucher, Houdon, Tiepolo and Robert Adam were still High Artists, nobody has ever claimed them the equals of Rembrandt, Bernini, Velasquez, Poussin, or Wren. As yet, however, the theoretical basis of art remains unchanged. When Joseph Addison wrote *Cato* in 1703, he still followed the traditional principles of High Art which he himself summarized:

> Music, Architecture, and Painting as well as Poetry and Oratory, are to deduce their laws and rules from the general Sense and Taste of Mankind, and not from the Principles of those Arts themselves; or in other words, the Taste is not to conform to the Art, but the Art to the Taste. [*Spectator*, 71]

Addison's first concern was not to create a Work of Art, with authentic classical forms to please erudite critics, or formal stagecraft interesting only to other playwrights, but rather to communicate what he considered truths and beauties to audiences in terms intelligibly related to their life, as medieval and Elizabethan playwrights had before him. And so his costuming, like theirs, was contemporary—"Juba's waistcoat blazed with gold lace, Marcia's hoop was worthy of a duchess on the birthday, Cato wore a wig worth fifty pounds," as Macaulay records it. And his audiences, like theirs, responded to an art that spoke to them: in London *Cato* had twenty performances and eight published editions, and in America an influence so lasting that half a century later Washington and Nathan Hale habitually quoted from it, and the hero's concluding speech to his Senate (2. 4) still echoed in the Virginia House of Burgesses:

> The hand of fate is over us, and heaven
> Exacts severity from all our thoughts:
> It is not now a time to talk of aught
> But chains or conquest, liberty or death.

Still in the 1750s Samuel Johnson could declare that writing should be disciplined like architecture: "if an architect wants to build five stories and his patron chooses to have three, the patron is to decide." He could deride Gray's refusal to write poetry except when inspired on the same grounds as medieval rulers would have made short shrift of a troubador who could not sing on command or a navigator who piloted only when in the mood. But now he is on the defensive; the shift in theoretical foundations described in *The Rest-less Art* has already set in. By 1800 Jacques Louis David is leading an advance guard of Fine Artists imposing a Taste to conform to their Art—now Roman, soon to be Romantic—who proclaim that Artists alone know what Art is, and therefore Artists alone should decide what the public needs.

By the 1830s Fine Art is taken for granted: "What do you learn from *Paradise Lost?*" asks Thomas De Quincey rhetorically in *The Poetry of Pope,* and answers, "Nothing at all. What do you learn from a cookery book? Something new . . . in every paragraph. But would you therefore put the wretched cookery book on a higher level of estimation than the divine poem?" Common sense might reply that it depends on whether you want to make an omelette or have the ways of God justified to man; or that Milton did in fact hope readers might learn something from his poetry instead of merely admiring his phrasing, that its being Art was no end in itself but a means to present its truths more effectively, as it was in *Cato's.* But common sense seems now to evaporate when Art comes under discussion; the idea of Fine Art has become an article of faith beyond all argument. Its ascendancy proceeds with the inexorable quality of Crusaders marching on a Holy Land—and this is no mere figure of speech. It is, in fact, part of a religous movement.

How the traditional concept of art is only one of many traditional ideas and institutions on the decline and defensive in the 18th century, and the same force is at work on all of them—a new religion, preaching the possibility of bringing Heaven to earth, and transforming all human institutions in the process.

What brought the great age of traditional painting in the West to an end around 1700? Science is the most commonly cited villain—or, more exactly, the Scientific Mentality, which in some unspecified way destroyed the poetic sense on which great art is supposed to depend:

> Post-Galilean science claimed to be a substitute for, or a legitimate successor of, religion. . . . As a result of their divorce, neither faith nor science is able to satisfy man's intellectual cravings. In a divided house, both inhabitants lead a thwarted existence. . . . Art lost its mythical, science its mystical inspiration. [Arthur Koestler, *The Sleepwalkers,* London, 1959, epilogue 8]

47

But surely this begs the question. Traditional religion and traditional science, as Koestler himself points out, worked from the same *ratio* in the Middle Ages, and throughout the 17th century remained so compatible that Jesuits in Rome taught the Copernican system among others, 17th-century scientists including Newton were deeply religious, and Galileo's great fame was the creation of a later age than his own. What split science and religion, mind and nature, reason and spirit in the years after 1700 was a change in the basic character and goals of science, religion, and art—a change which by 1900 had transformed them all into fundamentally different and mutually competitive kinds of activity.

It was the same sort of gradual, subtle, almost unnoticed change which a thousand years before had transformed the Roman polity, law, and art of Augustus's empire into the Byzantine polity, law, and art of Justinian's, with hardly any change of outward forms or titles—and again, the basic change was in religion. We can see it beginning in More's *Utopia*, concurrently with the new concepts of science and art propounded by Leonardo. For all that the Utopian religion More describes is Christian in ethics, fundamentally it is very different. It contains none of those warnings against putting trust or lasting value in the things of this world which appear in every book of the New Testament and in every great Christian writing, because what these virtuous and benevolent Utopians inhabit is in fact a Heaven already, a City of God brought down to earth. True, "utopia" means "nowhere," and we may suspect from More's absurd Utopian names that he sees no serious possibility of any such radically new society or religion's actually being established in the world of time and history, and so spins his story mainly as a means of making life here and now a little less imperfect. But two hundred years later the idea was taken up by a very different sort of people, who took it most seriously indeed.

For two centuries following More, the cultural climate remained as unfavorable for utopias as for Fine Art. But around 1700 it suddenly improves. Suddenly utopias are all the fashion, manifesting a dramatic shift in the premises of thought that Paul Hazard called *La Crise de la conscience européenne, 1680–1715* (1935):

> Around 1680 . . . a turning-point becomes evident in the mind of Europe. Between the Renaissance from which it proceeds directly, and the French Revolution which it fostered, no period is more important in the history of ideas. For a civilization founded on the idea of Duty—duty to God, to rulers—, the

"new philosophers" tried to substitute a civilization founded on the idea of Rights: rights of individual conscience, of criticism, of reason, of man, and of the citizen. . . .

What had been the idle fantasy of a perfect society here and now becomes a practicable vision of the Kingdom of Heaven brought down to earth. The "new philosophers" set themselves to realize it, to transform into its image every traditional human institution.

How believers in the Natural Goodness of Man try to make all human institutions conform to their dogma and so transform the state, religion, and science.

Central to their vision was a new concept of Man. Rejecting the traditional Christian view of a human race warped by original sin and owing any goodness it manifests to divine revelation and redemption, they proposed as fact More's Utopian fancy of men naturally good, virtuous, benevolent, wise. From this everything else followed. No more dumb acceptance of imperfect human institutions as the inevitable consequence of human frailty and imperfection; human imperfection is something that stupid and evil institutions have created, something that will disappear once new institutions are framed on the assumption that men are naturally good. No more dumb acceptance of inequality, either; men of good will living under good institutions can and must abolish it, create a world where heredity, accident, and luck will have no influence, where it can no longer be said that "time and chance happeneth to them all." Suffering and disorder must go, too; where all earlier ages thought of peace and joy and order as infrequent blessings in this life (Christians prayed to "pass their time in rest and quietness" as the Greeks talked of the rare delight of *sophrosyne,* the spirit of discipline which occasionally and briefly tempers nature's wild chaos and the excesses of human passion), the visionaries conceived order and peace to be normal conditions, pain and danger and chaos occasional themes for "romantic" contemplation. Theirs was a world where everything was evaluated in new terms, all traditional institutions transformed in character and function.

No longer would the state be simply a mechanism for controlling the passions and regulating the inequalities of a fallen race through a complex of loyalties up and down, each individual in a set place performing set duties, beginning with rulers responsible not to but *for* their subjects; the visionaries transformed it into a romantically personalized Nation, a divine institution functioning like God in Heaven, to enforce absolute equality, assure absolute sinlessness, provide absolute security, giving exactly the same rights to all its citizens. Of course in practice what resulted was a Divine Right of States to overrule the rights of any individual citizen and demand unlimited service from him; but this transformed concept of what a state is necessarily affected the role of every institution within it.

Traditionally, the state's essential function had been to provide enough law and order that its citizens could go about their several appointed businesses in peace—that the Church could help souls through the trials and tribulations of this life and prepare them for the eternal joys of Heaven above; science acquire more knowledge about things on this earth; art makes the world more beautiful, intelligible, noble. But now that the state as envisioned by the new philosophers presumed to do all these things itself, all other institutions were judged simply as helps or hindrances to it.

The solace and hope offered by traditional Christianity was superfluous; its offer of redemption absurd to men good by nature; its acceptance of inequality and pain a "thing of infamy" which the philosophers could not tolerate. Frightened by the increasingly violent attacks of "atheists" (as believers in the new vision curiously insisted on calling themselves), deceived by specious similarities of aim, churches over the years steadily adapted to the new vision by talking less and less about the Kingdom of Heaven, more and more about brotherhood of man and justice for all on earth, until many of them were transformed into no more than agencies for assisting the divine state in its mission. To no avail; for even if national and international welfare agencies had not been available to promote earthly brotherhood and plenty with more efficiency and less cant, churches were certainly not the state's chosen instrument for achieving its aims. That role was allotted to science, likewise transformed. Originally no more than one among many techniques of knowledge, science came to be a divinely ordained means for achieving the new dispensation, perfecting the human condition, making men mighty as gods. Successive generations of believers—from Diderot to Spencer, from Wells to Huxley to Hoyle—gave science an ever more visionary role and mystic aura. They counted on physical science to make life steadily easier and safer, men steadily wiser and more powerful, until one day we shall fly through space like angels and make bread from stones; on social sciences to create governments capable of ending all want and sin and misery; on natural sciences to control life and death, and make us immortal.

Inevitably, science so conceived conflicts with churches so transformed. For now, instead of one dealing with this world and the other with Heaven, both profess the same function; it is no coincidence that their clash begins during the 18th century, as visions of Heaven on earth mature and begin their transforming work. Neither is it any coincidence that while science flourishes in the 20th century, churches grow steadily emptier. For, once they compete for the attention of human beings assumed to be naturally good, able to perfect themselves by unaided effort and attain Heaven with no suffering or mortification of natural instincts, the outcome is foregone. On one side lofty and confused professions of noble motive; on the other rockets carrying men to moons, income-tax computers enforcing equality, surgery reviving the dead, bulldozers changing the face of continents—there can be no contest here.

How the idea of Fine Art feeds and depends upon the new religion.

But science does have one competitor—and more than a competitor, an aspirant to the Church's old estate of being to the State as sun to moon: Fine Art. Generation by generation the divine state's apocalyptic promises have been matched by the messianic hopes of advance-guard Art: David's Roman Revival and the French Revolution; Courbet's realism and Proudhon's positivism; Morris's communal crafts and Marx's communism; Roger Fry's vision of artists in *The Great State* of 1912, glorified through *Vision and Design* (1924); Constructivism and the Soviet workers' paradise; anti-art and the New Left attacking the existing order together—it is this sense of participation in the crusading "religion of the irreligious" that gives *The March of the Moderns* (1949) that inexorability and inevitability William Gaunt so well describes. And each generation of Fine Artists more insistently claims to be doing in the new State that redeeming work Churches performed in the old—that is to say, expanding the human psyche, making men steadily wiser, more sensitive, more creative, closer to the state of divine spirits. In *The Restless Art* we traced the ever-broadening offers of Courbet and Gaughin, Picasso and Kandinsky, Klee and Mondriaan to redeem their less perceptive fellows through revelations of Reality in Art. It is no accident that the same De Quincey who proclaimed the Fine Art of *Paradise Lost* to be something quite above and apart from any utilitarian function also described in *Confessions of an English Opium-Eater* how drugs might expand the Artist's mind—the same claims made today for Art inspired by hallucinogens.

Unfortunately, they remain claims only. What the 20th century calls Art is no more serious a competitor to science than what the 20th century calls religion. Neither does anything that science cannot do far better. And all that dedicating Art to the service of Heaven on earth has accomplished is to take from it the last possibility of usefulness. For not merely is this service no more the proper business of Art than it is of religion, but it has no practical application. Nothing like a Kingdom of Heaven on earth exists. There are no signs of anything like one appearing. The idea has been since its 18th-century beginnings a gigantic game of make-believe, of let's-pretend-things-and-people-are-not-what-they-are, and it is no less so now. To serve it is to serve nothing. Like the Treaty of Versailles, Fine Art is therefore not a machine to propel any existing forces, but to propel forces better than any existing. If all men were naturally good, if all men were spiritual, extrasensorily endowed, and lived in a perfect world, then Fine Art would have some claims to significance. As things are, it has none; it is wholly dead. And so we arrive at our present state.

With the Low Arts it is very different. For the more Fine Art has retreated into an unreal world of utopian visions, the more functions Low Arts have acquired in the world of time and history, and the more important it has become to understand them. It is in them that we meet the evidence of living people wrestling with living problems in living situations; to study them is to study the real history of living art in our times.

Why any study of Low Arts has to be organized in terms of social function.

How can such a study be coherently presented? There seem to be so many kinds of Low Arts, such diversity of media. Suppose, for example, you take as a model histories of painting. There, a historical sequence follows naturally from changing forms—when art historians talk of the "historical development" from Renaissance to Baroque, from Rococo to neoclassicism, they refer essentially to a succession of

52

forms; and something very like the same succession appears, with a quite consistent cultural lag, in the Low Arts from the 15th well into the 19th century. But at that point any such sequence of forms dissolves, and by the 20th century has vanished entirely, so that this organization collapses—the reason of course being precisely that as painting and other High Arts changed into Fine Arts, all formal influences on the Low Arts were necessarily lost.

What about an organization along the lines of Frederick Antal's sort of *Kunstsoziologie?*

> Both form and content make up a style. . . . Moreover, it is the content of art which clearly shows its connection with the outlook of the different social groups for whom it was created. . . .
> ["Reflections on Classicism and Romanticism," *Burlington Magazine,* LXVI, April 1935, p. 159]

It seems logical, for in a curious parallel to the way Fine Artists borrow forms from these Low Arts, Antal in the 1930s was in fact only applying to the study of "serious painting" an approach initiated by Eduard Fuchs in the first major study of popular arts, his 1901 *Karikatur der europäischer Volker.* The strictly Marxist analysis Antal (and Arnold Hauser after him) employed could be modified into a categorization of Low Arts by and for intellectuals (e.g., Beerbohm's or Thurber's or Du Maurier's cartoons), middle classes (most comic strips, book illustrations, etc.), and "the people" (Currier & Ives prints, comic postcards, vernacular architecture, etc.). But in practice this scheme fails also, for no consistent pattern of styles related to social classes can be ascertained; in every one of these popular arts every sort of form can be found, from the most abstract to the most photographically literal.

Are these forms perhaps dictated by media? How about an organization based on the idea that prints, photography, comic-strip boxes, lithographs each have appropriately characteristic forms? The problem is, they don't. Forms once characteristic of prints migrate into book illustration, and thence into animated cartoons, a format of narrative easel painting migrates into motion pictures and thence into comic postcards; and so on.

But this very fact suggests what the proper and effective organization of such material must be. If forms in these arts depend neither on media, nor on subject matter, nor on particular social classes, nor on precedents in painting, but on what they are supposed to do, with new forms being invented for given purposes if none appropriate exist; if, furthermore (as we have seen), it is function that traditionally has provided standards for judging and evaluating High and Low Arts, then plainly it is by function that they should be organized.

Hence the chapter headings that follow. They are based on those functions the activity called "art" has traditionally performed in society: substitute image-making, which has become the special function of photography; beautification, comprising those arts which ornament and enhance man's artifacts and environment; illustration (storytelling), the particular function of narrative easel pictures, book illustration, comics, movies, and animated cartoons; and the arts of conviction and persuasion, among them political and social cartoons, certain kinds of sculpture and architecture, and advertising.

So this is not a history of new arts; it is the history rather of new forms assumed over the last two hundred years by those old arts whose function has been unchanging through all recorded time.

2

The Unchanging Arts of Substitute Image-Making: Photography

■

How there is no basis for the conventional notion of photography's being a "new art" that forced paintings towards abstraction, literal reproduction of tangible and visible objects being in fact one of the oldest functions of the activity traditionally called art.

> In the Victorian era photography made its effective impact on the world. Photography brought to all classes a prolongation of poignant and of delightful memories of the dead, of the absent, of past years, incidents, and associations. Its effect on art was of more doubtful benefit. Many thousands of painters had formerly lived on the demand for portraits of persons, for accurate delineations of events, scenes and buildings and for copies of famous pictures. Photography henceforth supplied all these. By reducing the importance of picture-painting as a trade, and surpassing it in realistic representation of detail, it drove the painter to take refuge more and more in theory, and in a series of intellectualized experiments in Art for Art's sake.

THIS VIEW of the matter, by G. M. Trevelyan in *English Social History* (London 1943, p. 571), is the common one; and it involves two common assumptions. First, that photography was a new kind of art; and, second, that its influence was what forced the High Art of painting towards extreme abstraction and nonobjectivity. Neither is correct.

Photography as a technique was new, certainly. Though an ancestor, the "camera obscura"—a "dark room" with a hole in one side through which images were cast onto the other—was being used by painters in the 17th century to achieve correct perspective, and the general principle of salt solutions darkening in light had also been known for a long time (Thomas Wedgwood's method of making "fugitive images" was published in 1802), wide knowledge and use of photography dated only from 1839, when a process for fixing solar images invented by Nicéphore Niepce (1765–1833) in 1827 was published by him in collaboration with Louis Jacques Mandé Daguerre (1787–1851); and technical improvements were still being made in the

20th century. But the basic artistic purposes that the photographic technique served were as old as history. Photography is only a particular modern form of the most primordial of all artistic activities—the making of substitute images.

From the beginning, forms representing things seen, known, or imagined have always been the raw material of art, as sounds have always been the raw material of speech. And from the beginning, the most basic of these forms has been a literal transcription or imitation of tangible objects. Unretouched color photographs, "magic realist" *trompe l'oeil* paintings that "counterfeit nature," waxworks ancient and modern, all perform the most primary function art has had in history. To understand the effect photography has had on our world generally, and on painting in particular, this is a fact that must always be kept in mind. It rarely is, however, for the whole climate of contemporary opinion obscures it.

We have been taught to think of waxworks or "magic realism" as rare exceptions in art, made for special and eccentric purposes, and of no importance anyway. Though they may agree on nothing else, all sides in the modern art world take it for granted that "art" has never meant anything like photographs and waxworks, and, consequently, the closer anything approximates literal naturalism, the less Art it has always been. But these conventions hardly stand up to investigation. Was this kind of "realism" always in fact rare? Of course not. Remember how Egyptian and Greek sculpture originally was painted, waxed, equipped with lifelike eyes of paste and glass, colored hair, real weapons and clothes; consider the implications of Plato and Mohammed's both taking for granted that artists were people whose lifelike replicas affronted God the Creator; recall that in our own civilization painted statuary was still normal in the 15th century, that white "abstractions" became customary only when the idea of Fine Art was revived, and it will be obvious that waxwork "realism" was far commoner than is generally supposed.

And further, does every departure from literal naturalism in fact represent a conscious and deliberate choice on some artist's part? Manifestly not in the case of children; all esoteric theory to the contrary, it is easy to show that in ordinary situations they instinctively want to reproduce nature exactly. Sculpture in snow or plasticine is what they most naturally do, because it provides the kind of "complete images" they need to grasp and define facts and ideas about their world (which is why they make art in the first place). Two-dimensional work begins as an inadequate substitute forced on them by necessity, and they try to compensate for its limitations in all sorts of ways—so when five-year-olds draw a truck, for example, they will usually add to a side view the two unseen wheels "on top" to make it complete. What they would really like to do, of course, is to make a literal replica of a truck, like the toys they can buy; they do not, only because it is technically beyond them. In prehistoric art, a comparable predilection for "primeval naturalism" is evident. There, too, the most satisfactory substitute image would be an entirely lifelike replica, but there, too, technical limitations prevailed. Cavemen could and did make small ivory replicas of human figures and horses, but anything near life-size was impossible: so at Tuc d'Audobert we find life-size figures of bison in clay that were laid on their sides and so became relief sculpture, simply because a fully three-dimensional clay figure would snap off at the ankles. Logic and such chronological evidence as there is suggests that, once forced to depart from literal three-dimensional images for reasons like these, early men soon went on to relief (**56b**), thence to two-dimensional paintings and ultimately to abstract symbols simply for reasons of convenience and economy; "art" had nothing to do with it. By extension, we may wonder too how much of the "abstraction from nature" so much admired in early Egypt, archaic Greece, or early China was the result of technical deficiency or technological necessity, how much was deliberate artistic intent.

How photography superseded only those Low Arts concerned with reproducing natural appearances exactly, and therefore could not possibly affect the High Art of painting, which by definition involves selection and abstraction from nature; its impact was on Fine Art, by definition concerned with Reality.

The point of such speculation is, very simply, that the kind of substitute image photography naturally produces is a literal transcription of nature, and it therefore makes obsolete most literal transcriptions of nature in other, earlier media. Conversely, only with the greatest difficulty can photography make images involving any marked degree of selection and abstraction from nature. But High Art by definition involves images selected and abstracted from nature. It follows that the vast expansion of photography in our society since 1839 does not mean that photography replaced or competed with High Art; it only means that our society has far more uses for images literally transcribing natural appearances than is generally recognized, that many arts thought to be abstract in essence were in fact abstract only by technical necessity. To establish what the true relationship of photography to High Art is, we need only consider systematically what uses photography serves naturally, and what it does not; and in each case we shall see photography supplanting not the High Art of painting, but other, earlier forms of Low Art that make the same kind of substitute image it does, but less efficiently, accurately, and well.

Photography easily and naturally makes literal images of the appearance of buildings and streets and landscapes—the first photograph in history was Nicéphore Niepce's view of a courtyard at Chalon-sur-Saône in 1826. It therefore has made obsolete art like Wenceslaus Hollar's engravings or Canaletto's paintings, insofar as they were concerned with literal topography and building records. It can also replace by aerial views the sort of cartographical representations of cities common in atlases and encyclopedias for six hundred years before 1839. But photography can never replace the romantic landscapes of a Turner or the classically constructed landscapes of a Constable; it could never create the allegorized personifications that made so much early topographical engraving come alive; it could never replace an etching like Rembrandt's *Six's Bridge;* not once in a thousand years could a photographer catch the exact configuration of forms and colors that Vermeer set down in his *View of Delft.* Photography, in short, can never compete with the High Art of landscape painting; it only replaces some forms of the Low Art of topographical illustration.

Photography easily and naturally makes literal images of detail—what painters call "still life"; Daguerre's first photograph was of just such an assortment of miscellaneous small objects in his painter's studio. It therefore has made obsolete a whole category of *trompe l'oeil* painting, from the flower- and fruit-pieces of 17th-century Flanders to the magic realism of Harnett and Peto in late 19th-century America. But only with enormous and ridiculous difficulty could photographers attempt the selection and abstraction that gives their quality to Luca della Robbia's garlands, to Rubens's foregrounds, or to Rococo ornament; in short, photography cannot compete even with what Reynolds declared to be the lowest category in the High Art of painting, nor is it any serious rival of decorative Low Arts.

Photography easily and naturally makes literal images of the human body, and so makes obsolete all sorts of pornography; the thinly disguised pornography of much 19th-century Academic nude painting is replaced by the even more thinly disguised pornography of photographic "art magazines." But it has nothing like the range of selection and abstraction necessary to compete with the classical nudes of Giorgione or Ingres; only with absurdly disproportionate time, trouble, and fuss can photographers suppress enough irrelevant detail even to approximate the kind of generalized beauty that figure painters produce as a matter of course, even today. Photography cannot, in short, compete with the High Art of figure-painting. And neither can it compete in this area with ideational Low Arts. No photographer could have replaced the Venuses of Laussel (6a) or Willemsdorf, for example, or even graffiti on modern lavatory walls, for the whole point of such images is to exaggerate parts important to ideas of fertility or concupiscence, to a point far beyond anything in literal nature and so far beyond the limited powers of selection and abstraction photographers have available.

Photography easily and naturally makes literal transcriptions of human faces. It therefore makes obsolete that whole category of ordinary portraiture our ancestors called simply "face-painting." By putting sitters' heads through painted boards, early photographers easily duplicated the efforts of those itinerant limners who added heads to canvases prepainted with hands and bodies and scenery, and it was also not difficult to arrange poses and lighting that approximated the effects of the more professional and conventional painted portraits, as Brady's portraits of Lee and Lincoln, Steichen's of J. P. Morgan and Karsh's of Churchill each in their several generations show. But beyond this point portrait photography goes only with results entirely disproportionate to effort. Portraiture in the grand dramatic manner of Van Dyck or Sargent is far better done by painters, and so is autobiographical portraiture like the 17th-century *Self-Portrait* by Captain Thomas Smith in Worcester (6b). Instead of putting the individual and his worldly achievements into a perspective of eternity ("Farwell World; Farwell thy Jarres, thy Joies, thy Toies, thy Wiles, thy Warrs"), literal photography would make him out the candidate for an asylum. You could say the same about El Greco's *Cardinal Guevara*, and folk carvings of kings and judges. Photography, in short, competes only with the poorer sort of portrait painting, never with the best of this High Art. Neither can it compete with ideational portraiture. You can blow up photographs of Lenin or Mao into huge placards, but these never have the impact of their spiritual predecessors, the great sculptured, painted, and mosaicked images of Roman and Byzantine emperors, exaggerated and abstracted for physical effect. Photography might substitute for the cranked-out replicas of George Washington that Charles Willson Peale made, but it could never create the aura of greatness that Gilbert Stuart gave his sitter in the Lansdowne portrait. Can you imagine photographs substituting for the funeral effigies of medieval bishops and kings, for Michelangelo's Medici dukes, Bernini's papal memorials, or even the gravestones or decorative sculpture of early America (**17a**)? To be sure, in some Swiss cemeteries tombstones are erected with little enameled photographs of the deceased set into them, but you need only take one look at them to see how absurd the whole idea is.

This kind of analysis could be prolonged indefinitely. We can show how photography can make literal transcriptions of the horrors of battle, but never convey its grandeur and heroism as paintings can; women and children but not Mother and Child; dead men but not Death; a man writing but never anything like the inspired evangelist of the Ebbo Gospels. We can show how photography cannot even illustrate, when any degree of imaginative invention or technical abstraction is required—it is as useless to convey the spirit of Sebastian Brandt's *Ship of Fools* as of Hugh Lofting's *Doctor Dolittle* (as the movie abundantly demonstrates), as useless to serve modern medical textbooks as it was for the purposes of Agricola's *De Re Metallica*, Kepler's *Astronomia Nova,* Newton's *Principia,* or Colin Campbell's *Vitruvius Britannicus.* And so on; but the point must be obvious. There have been many technical advances in photography since Fox Talbot published his *Art of Photogenic Drawing* in 1839, but what he foresaw as its proper sphere of usefulness is essentially unaltered: "outline portraits or silhouettes"; copying "complicated minutiae of Nature" which would waste an artist's time; enabling "the traveller in distant lands" who might be "unskilled in drawing" to assemble "a large body of interesting memorials with numerous details which he had not himself time either to note down or delineate"; to copy "sculpture and engravings." Charles Baudelaire in his essay on "The Modern Public and Photography" in 1859 added that photography could make superior pornographic pictures; otherwise, he agreed with Talbot that it would never be a serious competitor to the High Art of painting. And, as we have seen, it never has been.

What, then, is all the commotion about? Why do so many writers talk about the devastating effect of photography on painting, how it "drove painters to abstraction" and so forth? Because, of course, these writers are not talking about the High Art of painting, painting as traditionally practiced in the West, with beauty as its goal and imaginative selection and abstraction from nature as its means. They are talking about painting as Fine Art, about an activity whose ends, means, and social function are entirely different. And this activity, the Restless Art, did indeed meet with competition from photography, for its essential concern and goal was the same—Reality. Once understand this distinction, and remember how painting changed its character and purpose in the course of the 19th century, and the whole history and significance of photography appears in its proper perspective.

How imitations of painting by early photographers do not represent competition with the High Art of painting, but dependence on it—i.e., the traditional relationship Low Arts always had to High; competition from Fine Art, not photography, was what destroyed the High Art of painting.

Photography was and is a Low Art, as defined in Chapter II, Part One—an inferior, cheaper, anonymously mass-produced version of the High Art of painting, taking over certain functions of engraving, limning, and lithography as they in their turn had been more efficient replacements for manuscript illumination, block prints, and etchings. Like all Low Arts, it followed the lead of an appropriate High Art as long as there was one to follow—so for twenty years we find photographers imitating the forms of the High Art of painting, at the usual remove in time. They did so all the more naturally because so many of them were painters by primary profession who looked on photography essentially as a labor-saving device for eliminating long preliminary sketchings and portrait sittings. Furthermore, early photographs existed only in single copies printed on metal, and so appeared much more like paintings done by other means than did multiple photographs made from a common negative, which only appeared in large numbers towards the end of the 1840s—in 1838 the Edinburgh inventory Mungo Ponton (1802–1880) fixed solar images on paper that could be rendered transparent, but it was not until 1847 that the first negatives on glass coated with albumen were made by Niepce de Saint-Victor, nephew of Nicéphore.

By the 1850s, then, it became clear that the cheapness and speed of photographic portraits would result in their displacing painted ones entirely in the mass market; but wherever money and leisure were available, painted portraits were unquestioningly assumed to be superior, and photographic ones copied from them. So in everything from small *cartes de visite* to Mathew B. Brady's pretentious photographic *Gallery of Illustrious Americans* (1850) you find one of two formats employed, both of them borrowed from painted portraiture—either a formal theatrical setting with furled curtains and pedestals, descended from the Baroque tradition of Van Dyck and Reynolds's grand manner, or an arrangement at or around a table, descended from the 18th-century French Rococo and English conversation-piece tradition. Such photographers almost universally looked on the kind of quick candid representation their cameras produced naturally in the same way most painters regarded their preparatory sketches—a necessary preliminary, perhaps, but never something to exhibit. Of this attitude Julia Margaret Cameron (1815–1879) is perhaps the best example; though her blurred "candids" are what historians of photography now chiefly remember her for, in her own time she exhibited only pictures elaborately posed in the manner of Royal Academy paintings.

In every category it was the same; throughout the 1850s photographers produced Low Art versions of all the themes and forms characteristic of the High Art of painting in the earlier 19th century. Eugène Durieu pioneered in photographs of nudes laboriously posed to imitate the kind of classical Venuses and romantic odalisques traditional in painting. Complicated photographic versions of academic allegorical paintings were made by pasting together a number of positives, rephotographing the whole, and creating a combination print with dozens of figures in it—*The Two Paths of Life* that Oscar G. Rejlander (1813–1875) exhibited at London's Royal Photographic Society in 1857 is the best-known of many. Henry Peach Robinson (1830–1901) created a sensation in 1858 with a combination print made from five negatives entitled *Fading Away*, imitating the Pre-Raphaelite type of sentimental genre picture (**7b** is such a composite); in 1869 he published a book on *Pictorial Effect in Photography* which was quite obviously based on textbooks for Academic painting and urged photographers to simulate painterly effects by "any kind of dodge, trick, and conjuration." Anthony Samuel Adam-Solomon (1811–1881), a French sculptor, made a great reputation with photographs imitating the composition and Caravaggian lighting of Rembrandt's paintings by means of retouched negatives. And so on.

All this is generally dismissed by historians of painting as a false start, "a confusion of media," as Beaumont Newhall put it in his *History of Photography* (1949), that inhibited realization of the potentialities of "photography as art." But surely this is to underemphasize the most important point about the first twenty years of photography—which is that no one at that time imagined photography was destroying the High Art of painting. The impossibility of photography ever being more of a rival to painting than block prints or lithographs had been was manifest in every attempt, to the bitter chagrin of those who tried: "There can be no gain and there is no honor but cavil and misrepresentation in it," Rejlander wrote Robinson in 1859. Photography could never become more than a Low Art, and it never has; there simply is not enough scope for inventive imagination and personal expression in it. What destroyed the traditional High Art of painting was not the rivalry of photography; it was the rival concept of Fine Art.

How Fine Artists, so far from trying to retreat from photographic likeness when it first appeared, did just the opposite, deliberately borrowing photographic forms for their "realism."

As we saw in Chapter III, Part One, the concept of Fine Art had appeared long before photography was heard of. Photography had nothing to do with it, except insofar as it made reproductions of past art more widely available from the 1840s on and so encouraged the existing tendency to detach "art" from any living historical context. When Renaissance humanists discovered a classical sarcophagus serving as a font in some church or dug up a statue from some Roman ruin, they could not help knowing that it was no longer performing its original function, but when you look at neat and tidied pictures of such objects in books you could that much more easily ignore its setting and study it as pure functionless form—"art without epoch," as the absurd cliché has it.

On the practice of Fine Art in the 1840s and -50s, however, photography's effect was immediate and lasting. That effect was not at all what convention describes, however. So far from Fine Artists' retreating towards abstraction when photography revealed the futility of reproducing nature exactly, the very opposite happened. It was on High Artists that photography had that effect; they had never copied nature exactly, never advocated doing it, and insofar as photography

65

had any influence on them, it was towards abandoning David Wilkie's sort of simple genre scenes in favor of more historical and allegorical emphasis—Henry Peach Robinson's illustrations of Wilkie's paintings in his *Pictorial Effect* as the kind of work photographers could most successfully hope to emulate was surely no accident. But on advance-guard Fine Artists of the 1850s the effect of photography was direct and unequivocal. They copied it, cold.

In *The Restless Art* I pointed out how and why the 1850s were crucial formative years for the triumph of Fine Art in painting, how a new concept of painting dedicated to Reality and of painters as rebel individualists, seers, and leaders was formulated in England implicitly by the Pre-Raphaelites, explicitly by Courbet in France. In that process, photography and its new "realistic" forms had a decisive influence. Courbet, Hunt, Millais, Brown, all were in their twenties when photographs first became widely available, and we who have been surrounded by photographs since birth can only dimly imagine the overpowering effect of seeing for the first time natural appearances copied with absolute mechanical objectivity. But so far from the conventional theory that they immediately realized the pointlessness of copying nature exactly, and proceeded to experiment with ever-greater abstraction and nonobjectivity, they did just the opposite. The Pre-Raphaelite Brotherhood and Courbet in fact both seized on the photographic image as their model for achieving that Reality which they had just proclaimed to be the goal of art. Where artists in the older tradition either ignored photography or adapted it to their purposes, and where photographers themselves tried to imitate the old High Art of painting, as Low Artists always had, the new advance-guard Fine Artists tried to paint like photographs. For proof, you have only to look at their pictures.

How photographic realism, not Italian Quattrocento High Art, was directly and indirectly the primary influence on Pre-Raphael-ite painting.

The official goal of the Pre-Raphaelite Brotherhood as organized in 1848 was a return to the Realities of painting before the Grand Style of the High Renaissance had "corrupted" it. But except for a few stylistic mannerisms, most notably long Botticellian necks and jutting jaws, you find precious few reminiscences of 15th-century Italy in early Pre-Raphaelite painting. What you do find in the late 1840s and early 1850s is an overwhelming influence from early 15th-century Flemish painting, especially Jan van Eyck. There are specific borrowings, like the convex mirror from the *Arnolfini Wedding* (**7a**) that appears in Brown's 1851 *Take Your Son, Sir;* an obvious imitation of the general mosaiclike effect of minute Flemish detail; and even an attempt to simulate by means of a white underground the luminous jeweled precision van Eyck achieved through successive coats of extremely thin oil. To painters in the old High Art tradition (Reynolds, for example), van Eyck's work had seemed little more than a technical curiosity, so that the Pre-Raphaelites' enthusiasm for him suggests how photography already was influencing Fine Artists to look at earlier art in a new way; but I think an even more direct photographic influence on the Pre-Raphaelites can be demonstrated.

Pre-Raphaelite detail not only was achieved in a technically different way from van Eyck's, it was differently conceived. Van Eyck's detail is the pictorial counterpart of Late Medieval nominalism in philosophy. Like Duns Scotus and his followers, van Eyck composed on the principle that only the individual detail has reality, that no ideal or conceptual whole exists apart from the particular details that make it up; it followed that each detail in van Eyck's pictures is a visual entity to itself, so that in the last analysis they are reduced to immense collections of single details unrelated to each other, existing independently in time and space. Pre-Raphaelite detail is conceived quite differently. When you look at a Pre-Raphaelite picture like Ford Madox Brown's *Work* in Manchester (*The Restless Art*, p. 151), or Millais's *Ophelia* (**7c**), you are not drawn closer and closer, deeper and deeper into it until you are lost in a maze of individual minute elements, as you are when you look at van Eyck's *Chancellor Rolin* in the Louvre, say, or the *Arnolfini Wedding* in the National Gallery. Instead, you adjust your viewpoint until you find the precise spot where you can take in the whole picture and still see each detail—because there always is such a spot, and you instinctively find it. Or in other words, you find the spot from which the picture was "taken"—for that is exactly how it was painted: the painter "took" the picture from one precise point at one particular moment and related all the details to it. Pre-Raphaelite "realism," in short, is not the realism of nominalist philosophy; it is the realism of photography.

How photography not merely "influenced" Courbet, but was the direct source of both his early and his late forms, and of his theory of Reality.

That photography influenced Gustave Courbet has long been recognized—but not, I think, how much and how thoroughly. Obviously pictures like *The Stonebreakers* of 1849 (8a) or *Woman With a Parrot* owe to photographic detail that stark "realism" which so startled contemporaries. Less generally recognized, but still obvious enough, is the photographic basis of Courbet's concept of what painting is; when in his Pavilion of Realism manifesto he renounces imaginative and idealistic beauty as the painter's goal in favor of a realism defined as what can be seen, when he says "show me an angel and I'll paint you one," Courbet is quite evidently speaking more like a photographer confined to what can be set before his lens than like the traditional High Artist whose concern had always been precisely to go beyond the world of appearances into realms of imagination. Hardly recognized at all, however, is how thoroughly photography dictated even what seems to be Courbet's departures from natural appearances: the "clock-work, childish stiffness" in his 1850 *Peasants of Flagey Returning from the Fair* that his contemporaries made fun of (8b); the rigidly side-view pose in his 1849 *Stonebreakers;* the unnatural crowding of spectators in his 1850–51 *Funeral at Ornans* onto one line as if on the edge of a wall; his failure to integrate foreground, middleground and background in *The Village Maidens* of 1853 (9a). Once criticized as inept—the cartoon of the Flagey peasants "painted by M. Courbet at the age of eighteen months" is famous—they are now commonly admired as examples of how Courbet, truer to his vision of the Artist as one who sees beneath and beyond surface appearances than to his theory of Reality demanding photographic form, manipulated appearances in order to bring out Realities unnoticed by other, less perceptive, men; of his Painter's genius and insight revealing the robotlike conformity capitalism had imposed upon humanity. Great ingenuity has in consequence been expended on discovering the exact source of such inspired devices. Art historians have suggested that Courbet might have found precedents in illustrations of Assyrian art from archaeological reports, in early Marxist-inspired studies of child psychology, from Rembrandts seen on visits to Holland. Quite generally ignored has been the most obvious source, the one Courbet himself acknowledged. But you need only look at the kind of photographs Courbet could have seen in the late 1840s to find every one of these alleged "departures from photographic nature" over and over again. Until well into the 1860s figures photographed out of doors almost always were posed for long exposures in the full-front or full-side stiffness you see in Courbet's *Peasants of Flagey* or *Stone-breakers*. Until wide-angle lenses became well-known and widely available, photographers taking group portraits had to crowd their subjects together in tight rows, and because of the lighting they had available, these groups almost always give the *Funeral at Ornans* impression of lining up in a narrow foreground plane. Examples of pasting figures onto backgrounds comparable to the effect of *The Village Maidens* could be seen in any photographer's studio when Courbet was painting it. Even *The Studio* itself (*The Restless Art*, p. 171) shows many signs of being conceived in just the way Rejlander composed *The Two Paths of Life*—it can in fact be seen as a great assemblage of reproductions of Courbet's earlier paintings put together like a combination print.

So far from demonstrating any departure from Courbet's announced conviction that Reality in painting meant photographic exactness, early pictures like these demonstrate to what absurd lengths Courbet was prepared to push his own theory, following logic to illogicality, as Jacques Louis David had before him. And so far from demonstrating how photography forced painters towards abstraction, these pictures were simply early and specific examples of a general principle operating for the next hundred years: Low Arts, instead of borrowing forms from High Arts in the traditional manner, more and more became suppliers of forms for Fine Artists. Decade by decade, photography will generate new forms to meet expanding social functions; decade by decade, these forms will be borrowed by Fine Artists as their social functions correspondingly contract.

How developments in photography during the 1850s and early -60s had no effect on the High Art of painting, but as imitated by Fine Artists in the later 1860s and -70s provided Impressionism's basic forms and rationale, thus continuing the pattern of retreat into photography, *not* away *from it.*

The early photographs that so influenced Courbet and the Pre-Raphaelites were mainly still lifes and portraiture, tightly detailed close-ups by technical necessity; more ambitious subjects were handled by assembling composites. But in the course of the 1850s the scope of photography began to expand rapidly, as new techniques were developed. In 1855 outdoor photographs of Crimean battlefields by Roger Fenton (1819–1869) were put on display. In the same year, photographs by electric light were taken by Gaspard Félix Tournachon, called Nadar (1820–1910), in Paris; in 1856 Nadar also pioneered aerial photography, taking pictures from a balloon. And in the later 1850s Charles Marville (fl. 1845–70) demonstrated how photography could capture immediacy—"this is how things look *now*"—with his records of the old Paris that Haussmann's grandiose planning was in process of destroying forever. In the 1860s a similar demonstration was given in the American Civil War records by Mathew Brady (1823–1896), Alexander Gardner (1821–1882) and Timothy O'Sullivan (d. 1883); and by the 1870s it was becoming commonplace for exploration parties to take a photographer along for immediate on-the-spot recording.

As we have seen, these developments had no effect on the High Art of painting. A hundred traditional phrases and formulas leap to remind us that its concern was never with how things look *now,* always with the long view—*ars longa, vita brevis,* art is long and life is short; *sub specie aeternitatis,* in the perspective of eternity; Michelangelo telling critics of his Medici tomb effigies, "In a thousand years, what will it matter how they actually looked?" How could photography affect an art so conceived? Even traditional battle-painting, conventionally supposed to have begun declining when photographers began to accompany armies, in fact continued to be done in quantity down to 1918; and if it then ceased, photography was not responsible, but rather a combination of the development of motion pictures rendering battles with painterly sweep and scope (D. W. Griffith's *Birth of a Nation* [53b] was what marked the end of battle-painting, and not Brady's photographs), and a general retreat from the whole high heroic tradition of battle in revulsion against the squalors of trench warfare. From the beginning, traditional painters and photographers plainly and necessarily excelled in different things; between the photographer's worm's-eye view of actuality and immediacy and the High Artist's dramatic imagination and idealization there could be no conflict of interest. But Fine Artists, whose concern by definition was with Reality, were in a very different case. For them, each successive development in photography meant some new revelation in "realistic form" to be admired and copied; and that is what they did.

In the early 1850s "distance" photography began producing broad simplified forms without the minute detail of the earlier close-ups. The same forms begin appearing in Fine Art in the late 1850s.

Courbet's 1858 *Portrait of Max Buchon* (Vevey Museum) (**9b**) is one of the first examples. So different is this from the tightly detailed work he was doing earlier that for a long time it was not recognized as his, but in fact from then on Courbet never returned to his earlier manner, and it was this kind of form that he passed on to his protégé Edouard Manet. That Manet's paintings of the 1860s with their flat full-front lighting shadowed only around the edges were inspired by photography has long been acknowledged. It is less generally realized, however, that the sensation produced by the "realism" of paintings like *Olympia* and *Luncheon on the Grass* was also largely produced by the same sort of photographic effects that had startled and irritated viewers of Henry Peach Robinson's combination print *Fading Away* in 1858, a picture whose subject (father and mother by the bedside of a dying girl) was by comparison entirely innocuous. Critics complaining of "poor taste" in all these pictures meant not so much what was represented—deathbed scenes and nudes were not exactly rare in painting of the 1850s and -60s—as the literal way these subjects were depicted, without any pretense at imaginative or idealistic abstraction from nature; they resented artists so evidently using "intimate" themes as excuses for experiments in pictorial literalism regardless of public taste or sensibilities.

In the later 1850s, the new documentary camera work developed by Fenton and Nadar began to make a new kind of pictorial composition common. Once photographers were no longer dealing with objects or people close at hand that could be arbitrarily arranged, the earlier convention of composing photographs like paintings on a balanced stage, parallel to the picture plane, had to be abandoned; having no mind, the camera lens knew no frame and produced a free pictorial space that flowed freely and spontaneously in and out of the sides of the picture. Once again, we find Fine Artists imitating this form ten years or so later. In the early 1860s, Courbet, Manet, and Degas were all still composing according to the old formula. Courbet's series of hunting pictures, Manet's *Olympia* and *Luncheon*, Degas's *Belleli Family* and *Young Girls of Sparta* are all composed according to the old formula, but by the later 1860s Courbet has begun using the new photographic space in *Dressing the Bride* (**10a**), and in the 1870s it is common to all the Impressionists, heralded as a great innovation by their admirers.

The early 1860s bring a series of further innovations in photographic form; one by one they appear in Fine Art in the late

1860s and -70s. Photographers experiment with color, covering plates with large coarse crystals dyed various primary hues, and in due course pointillistic canvases appear similarly covered with dots and dabs of primary-color paint; this photographic inspiration has long been known. As photographers work more and more freely, with emulsions still fairly slow, blurred forms become commoner. Sometimes they result from the subject's moving, as in the ghostly street scenes of the 1850s and early 1860s where people and carriages have moved too fast to be recorded, leaving only wraiths behind (12a); sometimes they result from photographers' deliberately moving the camera for effect, as in the famous "candids" of Julia Margaret Cameron. In either case, you find the same blurred forms appearing in Impressionist painting five or ten years later, forms whose source is the more obvious because they are so natural to photography and so unnatural to painting; and it is particularly interesting to note how after emulsions get faster around 1870 and photographed streets are once more populated, Impressionist streetscapes follow suit—ghostly and empty as old photographs in the early 1870s, they begin acquiring people and carriages in their turn around 1880, as you can see especially well in the work of Pissarro.

Finally, the expanding range of photographic techniques in the 1860s vastly increases the kind and variety of objects photographed, and this too we see faithfully imitated in painting. It is in the 1870s that Fine Artists decisively proclaim their concern with form alone, irrespective of what the forms represent; that Manet paints the *Bar at the Folies-Bergères* and *Le Skating*, implying by such titles that though a human being may appear in the picture it is no more than one form among many, all to be impartially painted; that Degas reduces women's bodies to elements in a textural pattern; that Cézanne's coldly scientific experiments in "significant form" begin. They call it a search for Reality and consider themselves inspired explorers in new realms of pictorial form; in fact, they are only following where photographers lead—and in the next two decades photography will take them to realms as yet unimagined, as it begins its conquest of movement and worlds beyond the reach of human eyes and minds.

How forms never before seen and strictly speaking invisible, revealed by new photographic technology in the 1870s, provided vocabulary and rationale for the New Reality of Post-Impressionism in the 1880s and -90s.

72

It took photography more than thirty years to develop emulsions sensitive enough and lighting precise enough to make sharp images of fast-moving objects. Though Charles Nègre (1820–1880) had "stopped" action as early as 1851, and the relatively slow movements of pedestrians were being captured in stereoscopic views of city streets by the early 1860s, really fast motion was not stopped until Eadweard Muybridge (1830–1904) photographed the successive movements of a galloping horse at intervals seconds apart in 1877. This was a justly famous feat, widely publicized and quickly copied in the next few years, especially after the perfection of gelatin dry plates in 1878, which put action photography within the reach of everyone. For Muybridge had done far more than merely win Leland Stanford's bet that at certain moments in their gallop horses have all four feet off the ground at once. He had opened up a whole new area of social usefulness for the camera by making it an instrument for scientific investigation of phenomena invisible to the unaided eye, anticipating microphotography and astrophotography, and in the process he had revealed, even more dramatically than the first photographers, kinds of visual images the human eye had never seen before. Both developments had an immediate effect on Fine Art. This was in fact the decisive moment, when it became unmistakable how fundamentally different an activity "art" dedicated to Reality must be from what had been called "art" in the past.

For traditional painters, the new instantaneous and multiple images had no more effective interest or use than earlier photographic images. Joseph Pennell summed up their reaction in retrospect, in connection with the huge atlas of human forms "stopped" in every kind of action which Muybridge had made at the University of Pennsylvania between 1883 and 1885, and which he had just published with the expressed hope of its being "useful to painters." Pennell did not think it would be, and explained why by citing an early attempt to make use of Muybridge's instantaneous photographs of horses by Thomas Eakins, in his 1879 painting of *The Fairman Rogers Four-in-Hand* (11b):

> "If you photograph an object in motion, all feeling of motion is lost, and the object at once stands still. A most curious example of this occurred to a painter just after the first appearance in America of Mr. Muybridge's photos of horses in action. This painter wished to show a drag coming along the road at a rapid trot. He drew and redrew, and photographed and rephoto-

graphed the horses until he had gotten their action apparently approximately right. . . . He then put on the drag. He drew every spoke in the wheels, and the whole affair looked at if it had been instantaneously petrified or arrested. There was no action in it. He then blurred the spokes, giving the drag the appearance of motion. The result was that it seemed to be on the point of running right over the horses, which were standing still." [Quoted in Beaumont Newhall, *History of Photography*, 1949, p. 87]

In other words, if you want to paint action, instantaneous photographic images will do you no good, for they are the opposite of action; they stop action. Traditional painters and cameramen are trying to do quite different things.

But if on the other hand you do not want to paint any particular thing, but just paint—that is, if "realistic forms" are themselves the subject and object of your painting, then the new photographic image reveals a whole new dimension of Reality. It shows that the eye does not see "realistically"—and if Reality is your goal, then you must follow the camera away from nature. And that is what the advance guard at once does. Georges Seurat adds to imitation of coarse-grained color photography imitations of instantaneous photographic images, takes one "shot" after another of "good subjects"—cancan dancing, circus riding—like a photographer making samples, finally produces his masterpiece of "new Impressionism," the *Grande Jatte* (*The Restless Art*, p. 201). This painting is a landmark in at least two respects. First, because it demonstrates so clearly what will henceforth become standard practice in "modern art"—borrowing images from advanced photographic techniques, investing them with mystic significance as works of Fine Art, and then claiming social relevance for the result. (For who, without this mystique, could claim that the *Grande Jatte* is an effective piece of social criticism, that these frozen figures represent a powerful portrayal of the stultification and rigidity of bourgeois life? Even if that were a particularly deep or novel idea—which it certainly is not—the meanest social cartoonist could project it in his medium a thousand times more effectively than any painting, and especially Seurat's painstaking kind.) And second, because this rejection of early Impressionism in favor of the superior Reality of that frozen world beyond the limits of natural vision whose existence photography had revealed marks the beginning of the dramatic "retreat from likeness" that will culminate in another generation with Cubism and Expressionism. Plainly this is not now, nor ever will be, a retreat *from* photography, as convention declares; it is a retreat *into* photography, away from the world of traditional painters towards a world that "eye hath not seen"—nor mind revealed—a world of invisible plates bombarded by electrons recorded on mechanical dials.

That same retreat from likeness was being furthered in the 1880s by Paul Cézanne at Aix-en-Provence, under the same inspiration. In *The Restless Art* I pointed out at some length how Cézanne approached his work more like a scientist than a traditional painter; how he experimented to realize his motifs with as little concern for ultimate implications as scientists experimenting to solve a set problem, how his paintings were more like interim reports than ends in themselves—in the same way as Muybridge's individual pictures of horses are not ends in themselves as even earlier photographs had been. But this is only the most obvious of the photographic influences discernible in Cézanne's painting. Consider, for example, the "significant form" for which he is famous. Instead of simply recording light impressions indiscriminately on canvas, his announced goal was to refine away superfluous and transitory elements, leaving only the bare basic structure of nature. But nature's basic structure is three-dimensional; on the face of it, to simulate such a thing in two dimensions is impossible. Cézanne had therefore to resort to several kinds of visual tricks. One was a subtle gradation of hot and cold colors; another was overlays of thin paint; but the most obvious was to represent objects from several points of view at once—to show both the top and the side of a coffee cup, for example. When successful (and Cézanne was the first to admit this was not often), the results were startling; his two-dimensional canvases did indeed seem to have a three-dimensional structure, and his admirers were right in proclaiming his form something new in painting. Yet somehow we seem to remember seeing something like this before. Where? Ah yes—in stereoscopic photography. In the mid-1870s, stereoscopic viewing was all the rage; every parlor had its viewer and sets of photographs made by a twin-lens camera, and still today we are startled when we look at them to see how these old scenes snap to vivid life (**12b**). What makes them so vivid? Because, of course, the stereopticon gives us not one image but two, from slightly different angles, just as our eyes do. This kind of photography in fact "sees around" objects just as Cézanne "paints around" them. In the 1870s this was a new kind of "pictorial form" never seen in art before, much more "realistic" than anything preceding it. For a Fine

Artist dedicated to Reality, it is clearly a form to be imitated, no matter how pointless the toil and struggle of reproducing in such an unsuitable medium something so easy and natural in another, no matter how useless the result.

Cézanne's work marks another turning point also, the beginning of a rapid erosion of traditional Renaissance perspective from painting. Once again critics have called this a retreat from photographic naturalism, and once again they are wrong; for it is only another example of the retreat from traditional painting *into* photographic realism. One of the first things the camera demonstrated was that we do not in fact perceive space the way Renaissance painters depicted it; we only think we do, because we have been surrounded since childhood by pictures which organize space according to the principles of Renaissance pictures, and they have taught us how to see, so that we unconsciously interpret the light impressions our eyes receive in those terms. But cameras, having no interpreting mind, record things as we actually do see them. The very first photograph ever taken—Niepce's courtyard of 1826—showed how the sides of tall buildings do not appear as straight lines converging at a vanishing point in infinity, but curve towards a projected intersection much closer. Long recognized in practice by laws requiring tall buildings on city streets to incline inwards or be stepped back so that they will not seem to be toppling over on people looking up at them from sidewalks below, this fact has been so consistently ignored in visual theory that early photographers took great pains to avoid criticism for "false perspective" by distorting their images with special lenses and bellows, and generally their successors still do. Cézanne's perspective, to be sure, was not photographic; but neither did it follow traditional Renaissance laws of representation—and the point is simply that the justification for Fine Artists' breaking with the traditional theory and practice of painting was not that "photographic naturalism" had made the old perspective superfluous, but that it made a new and "more realistic" perspective mandatory for them. And the net result of all this, of course, was to steadily widen the gulf between Fine Artists and society at large; while each new form photography generated was broadening its social usefulness, Fine Artists were just as dramatically eliminating theirs with each imitation.

How 20th-century photography has produced forms further and further removed from the visible world, and 20th-century paint-

ing faithfully copied them, continuing its steady retreat into photographic likeness.

It took some time for Cézanne's painting to become widely known; until his retrospective in 1906, in fact, he and his theories were largely confined to the underground of the Fine Art world. Thereafter, however, things moved fast. If it is agreed that forms represented from two points of view simultaneously are more "realistic" than those seen from only one, then why not attain even more Reality by representing them from three, four, ten, or fifty points of view at once? So the theory of Cubism rapidly evolves. That by 1912 Cubist paintings had lost all resemblance to anything visible in nature was of no consequence, for had not the camera demonstrated that Reality was not what appeared to the eye? That the public was simultaneously losing interest in advance-guard painting of this sort could with equal simplemindedness be set down to ignorant prejudice; it never seemed to occur to anyone to trace public apathy to the fact that these painters were only doing badly what photographers had long been doing easily and well. Yet of course nothing should have been more obvious. For while Fine Artists were still busy imitating the stereoscopic and instantaneous forms of photography produced in the 1870s, photographers had been pushing forward to new forms, and were now rapidly approaching the point where their cameras could capture anything light could reveal. Already in the 1880s they were producing forms far more visually exciting than Cubism.

Sometime around 1880 a technique was perfected for taking successive pictures of a moving object seconds apart on the same plate, instead of on different plates in successive cameras as Muybridge had done. Possibly Muybridge's friend Thomas Eakins was the inventor; more probably it was Etienne Jules Marey (1830–1904), a French physiologist who had begun studying movement with a zoetrope in 1867 and corresponded with Muybridge. However that may be, the result was to confront the world with yet another new kind of image, capable of infinite variation, some of which Marey published in an article in *La Nature* for September 29, 1883 (11a). Among his more dramatic experiments was to dress a man in black, paint white light-reflecting lines on his arms and legs, and make successive exposures of him walking against a dark background, so producing an abstract image of essential lines of motion which Marey used in studying fundamental human movements.

There was an unusual lag in time between the appearance of these new forms and their imitation by Fine Artists, but in due course they in their turn gave rise to yet another new movement in painting based on photographic Reality. This time it was called Futurism, and as usual was hailed as a radical and brilliant innovation, a revelation of the Reality of lines of force, and so on. Critics then as now solemnly announced that simultaneous representations of the successive positions of swinging dog chains or flying birds (*The Restless Art*, p. 322) were forms never seen in the world before, and invested with deep significance for the human condition. Or they compared a painting like Duchamp's *Nude Descending a Staircase* (*The Restless Art*, p. 323) with the late Pre-Raphaelite Burne-Jones's *Golden Stair* to explain how fast and far "modern art" was moving away from "photographic likeness"—when in fact it was precisely the other way around, when it was Burne-Jones who was selecting and abstracting from nature as beheld by eye and camera, Duchamp who was literally reproducing what the camera revealed.

Also around 1880, emulsions became fast enough for truly candid photography, and a variety of special cameras were developed enabling photographers to take pictures of people unawares. This invention made possible the "social documentary," usually meaning unstudied pictures of lower-class life in cities. Such an activity lent itself naturally to socialist agitation. Charles Marville, who pioneered it with his back-alley views of Old Paris, had begun his career illustrating a sociological *Histoire des Français sous Louis XIV et XV* and had lithographed *Propagande Socialiste* in 1849 and 1850; this lead was eagerly taken up. Soon all sorts of photographers were making reputations as champions of the exploited proletariat: Jacob Riis (1849–1914) and Lewis W. Hine (1874–1940) in New York; Eugène Atget (1856–1927) in Paris; Paul Martin (1846–1942) in London. By the time social-documentary photographs became common in Paris, Fine Artists had generally gone on to more esoteric photographic forms; but of course Lautrec's absinthe drinkers and brothel scenes owe a good deal to such documentaries, and in New York they were faithfully imitated by the Ash Can school, who at great labor and trouble recorded in paint the kind of impressions of bars, tenements, and alleys that cameramen had been already recording so fast and surely for two decades (*The Restless Art*, p. 387).

In this perspective, the 1913 clash in the Armory Show between the Ash Can school and the New Painting typified by

Duchamp's *Nude Descending* was a combat of Tweedledum and Tweedledee—between the "realistic" forms revealed by one kind of speed photography and another. And, as we saw in *The Restless Art*, 1913 essentially marked the climax of evolution in the New Painting. Thenceforth there was little to do but ring nonessential changes and stage periodic revivals like the 1960s' psychedelic resuscitation of Dada. Of course photography did improve some techniques and so provide variant new forms for Fine Art to copy. Stroboscopic photography produced much subtler successions of images than Marey's, and in due course we see them appearing in painting—the head of the lamp-bearing woman in Picasso's *Guernica* is a famous example of such borrowing from stroboscopic form. Micro- and astrophotography likewise produced ever more incredible forms, images of remote galaxies and slices of leaf tissue never before seen by human eyes, let alone recorded; they duly reappear in Dada and Surrealist canvases. So did instantaneous photography; by the 1930s cameras were able to "stop" splashing drops of water and bullets in mid-barrel (**13a**); in the 1960s these images too were being reproduced in plastic, glass, and mud, solemnly placed in frames and on pedestals as profound revelations of painterly psyche and alleged spirit of the age.

Examples proliferate everywhere. In the 1890s halftone reproductions by photographing through screens was invented; in the 1960s we find painters solemnly using the same process to produce "pop" art. But better than in any specific instances, the complete dominance of photographic form in Fine Art is demonstrated in the two theoretical premises on which "spontaneous" or "action" painting is based. How the first of these derives from photography is perhaps obvious; the painter who merely "assists" the paint to flow onto his canvas and take its own form is of course simply the counterpart of the photographer who "assists" the sensitive emulsion to make an image by exposing it to light. Less obvious, but still plain, is the photographic inspiration of conceiving ultimate Reality to lie in the act of creating rather than in what is created, so that the "finished" nonobjective canvas can never be itself a Reality, only an indication of one. For what is this but another translation into an inappropriate medium of the principle of motion-picture photography? The image that you see on a screen, like the "action" canvas, is simply the record of a Reality that cannot in fact be tangibly captured; a succession of individual still frames create it, but they are none of them the Reality itself, any more than the "action" painting is. But of course this principle goes back

79

beyond motion pictures. You find its origin in revolving drums and wheels with a succession of pictures on them, coalescing into a single image when put in motion, that were a great fad in the mid-19th century; every proper parlor had a praxinoscope or something like it for the amusement of guests. In themselves these drums and cards were as meaningless as the advance guard today says all substantial forms are; they became meaningful only when revolved fast enough to "destroy" each single picture by dissolving it into a single intangible image. They were, in short, the original "anti-art" objects. But they are, and always were intended to be, toys and nothing more; something to gratify idle curiosity. And so, in fact, are the paintings based on their principle. To such a state has the search for "realistic" form reduced Fine Art.

It has not come about unopposed. In every generation there have been people perceptive enough to see what was happening, and what the end result must be. Among the earliest was Charles Baudelaire, in his essay on the Salon of 1859, "The Modern Public and Photography." Beginning with the observation that "the photographic industry is the refuge of every would-be painter," he went on to urge,

> let it [photography] enrich the tourist's album . . . adorn the naturalist's library . . . enlarge microscopic animals . . . corroborate the astronomer's hypotheses . . . rescue from oblivion tumbling ruins. . . . But if it be allowed to encroach upon the domain of the impalpable and the imaginary, upon anything whose value depends solely upon the addition of something of a man's soul, then it will be so much the worse for us. . . . Each day art further diminishes its self-respect by bowing down before external reality; each day the painter becomes more and more given to painting not what he dreams but what he sees. . . . Are we to suppose that a people whose eyes are growing used to considering the results of a material science as though they were the products of the beautiful, will not in course of time have singularly diminished its faculties of judging and of feeling what are mong the most ethereal and immaterial aspects of creation? [In Jonathan Mayne, trans. and ed., *The Mirror of Art, Critical Studies by Charles Baudelaire,* London, 1955]

And again in 1890 Peter Henry Emerson (1856–1936) published a black-bordered pamphlet entitled *The Death of Naturalistic Photography,* in which he formally renounced his earlier attempts to "elevate" photography into "art" on the grounds that photography simply could not provide scope for the kind of imaginative and inventive creation that he had come to see constituted the essence of art: "the goddess Science . . . has little to do with the goddess Art."

How confusion in critical judgment through failure to distinguish between High and Fine Art—not recognizing that the "search for Reality" has made Art something entirely different from the activity called art earlier—results in the absurd assumption that Fine Art forms imitating the "invisible world" revealed by photography are more "abstract" than High Art forms selected and abstracted from nature, and culminates in the absurdity of an "art photography" which imitates "abstract" forms from painting themselves originally taken from photographs.

But these warnings were misunderstood. In Baudelaire's time there was still a sound body of opinion opposed to the idea that Reality was the artist's proper concern and ready to agree with him that literal transcriptions of nature would kill High Art; but most then, and almost all since, equated photographic form with what the eye saw. They consequently failed to recognize that Impressionist and Post-Impressionist forms were in fact based on "photographic realism," assumed that because traditional painters produced more recognizable forms than the Post-Impressionists and Cubists they were the sort of artists "bowing down before external reality" that Baudelaire was talking about, and so lent their weight to that very "encroachment on the domain of the impalpable and the imaginary," that very campaign against High Art, that Baudelaire deplored.

Peter Emerson's argument did not even attain the dignity of being misunderstood; it was simply ignored. For by the 1890s the idea of Reality as the goal of artistic activity was everywhere gaining ground among intellectuals, and they consequently had no idea what he was talking about. Indeed, the only effect Emerson's renunciation had was to encourage Alfred Stieglitz (1864–1946) to promote "art photography." He and his associates in the Photo Secession, most notably Edward Steichen (b. 1879), started a movement for art photography which deliberately imitated the effects of Impressionist and Expressionist painting; in 1916 Alvin Langdon Coburn achieved fame with an exhibition proving that "the photographer could make abstractions as readily as the painter."

Over these absurdities we need not linger. Obviously photographers could produce abstractions as readily as Cubists, Expressionists, or Impressionists; it was *their* abstractions that these painters copied in the first place. It was from *them* that these painters' Realities behind and beyond natural appearances had been discovered. "Art photography" is indeed the classic example of Plato's "false art, an imitation of an imitation, thrice removed from truth" (**13b**). To be sure, it was discouraging to think Emerson might have been correct when he wrote that photography could never be more than the "handmaiden of Art and Science," that "the medium must always rank the lowest of the arts." No matter how meticulously Paul Strand selects appropriate photographic material from nature, his medium can never afford him the imaginative scope for choice necessary for great High Art; Edward Weston's previsualization of final photographs at the moment of releasing his shutter can never be more than a humble variant of that moment when the complete imagery of an epic or idea flashes into the High Artist's mind. But at least their Low Art communicates with people, arouses and pleases and moves them as the imitation of photographic forms as ends in themselves never can. It is an activity that still offers something to the human spirit; it is, that is to say, Living, Unchanging Art.

3

The Unchanging Arts of Beautification: Commercial Design and Decoration

■

How the Fine Art concept of ornament differs from the traditional function of ornamental arts in society.

POPULAR TEXTBOOKS and light scientific articles assure us that man's superiority over animals was first manifested when he began to make tools. Insofar as such assertions contain any truth (a doubtful enough proposition in this age which measures civilization by improvements in scaffolding, satellites, and soap powders), it is surely not in using or even making of tools that distinctively human qualities are demonstrated so much as in decorating them—in the powers of reason, abstract thought and feeling that "beautifying" them to suit their uses and owners involves. Of such beautification, involving mind, heart and eye, animals know nothing; from earliest times it remained distinctive of men, one of the first traditional functions of that distinctively human activity called Art.

That concept of decoration remained constant almost into living memory, as the piece of decoration illustrated here (14) shows very well. Still in 1854, when it was made for attachment by metal screws to a heavy safe manufactured by Evans & Watson of Philadelphia under the trade name "Salamander," the principles involved were the same as they had been for millennia past—simultaneous appeal to eye and mind. That it made the safe a more attractive object to look at, by setting polished brass against black metal walls, is perhaps obvious. Less obvious, but particularly significant in this case, is the precise sort of appeal to the mind that it involved. On the simplest level, it explained the object it decorated. Representing in high relief how Salamander Safes could be put into an open furnace amid 2000 cords of burning wood and emerge unscathed, like the legendary salamander (a process proudly described in Evans & Watson's catalogues), it proclaimed those fire-resistant qualities which gave the safe its name. But by implication the whole cultural pattern that produced such an object at such a moment in history is also involved. It is not by accident that the composition of this scene recalls the formal language of Christian art, for instance; that just as Tintoretto in painting the *Miracle of St. Mark* or Raphael the *Disputà* arranged figures in a semicircle psychologically related inwards to some supernatural revelation, so the commercial artist likewise composed a semicircle of witnesses graduated from high relief at the sides to low relief in the center, pointing towards the "miracle" taking place in the furnace. This is an unself-conscious revelation—all the more significant for that—of the 19th century's faith in the miracles of applied science; and those acute in matters art-historical could no doubt trace the progressive shift of miracles from supernatural to scientific realms through a chain of such intermediaries as Rembrandt's *Anatomy Lesson of Dr. Tulp*, which uses the supernatural Baroque formula to dramatize the miracle of medicine,* 18th-century pictures of scientific miracles in Caravaggian style like the *Experiment with an Air Pump* by Joseph Wright of Derby (in the Tate), or *The Iron Foundry* by Peter Hillestom (in Stockholm), or 19th-century counterparts like Asher B. Durand's figures experiencing the miracles of nature in *Kindred Spirits* (New York Public Library); one might even perhaps find this commercial artist's immediate model in some Low Art variant of these in prints or woodcuts—for of course in the traditional art of decoration, as in all traditional arts, Low Arts were derived from High. Nor is it merely amusing to discover that the scroll this American eagle carries in his beak does not read "E Pluribus Unum," but "26 South Fourth Street Philadelphia"—the manufacturer's address; this is an equally unself-conscious and so equally significant expression of the idea that whoever benefits himself and makes a superior product also benefits the country—the conviction which de Tocqueville described in 1840 as characteristic of *Democracy in America* (II, 45), that

> every new method that leads by a shorter road to wealth, every machine that spares labor, every discovery that facilitates pleasures or augments them, seems to be the grandest effort of the human intellect. It is chiefly from these motives that a democratic people addicts itself to scientific pursuits, that it understands and respects them. . . .

As late as the mid-19th century, then, the arts of decoration were still performing the function they had for millennia past. That

---

* His partially destroyed *Anatomy Lesson of Dr. Deyman* makes the point better, combining Caravaggian spotlighting with a Renaissance prototype (probably a print of Mantegna's or Holbein's *Pietà*), thus transforming an image of potential resurrection to Eternal Life into an image of human life potentially resurrected here on earth.

function could best be summarized as (1) identifying use, and (2) humanizing artifacts. Through a combined appeal to eye and mind, given objects were no longer simply mechanical, but made distinctively human, related to a human context, integrated with life at many levels.

If such a concept of decoration seems surprising, that is of course because what Fine Art schools now teach is entirely different. Just as they now see painting as a Restless Art, no longer concerned with Beauty or communication or any of its traditional functions, but with something called Reality revealed only to the Painter-Seer-and-Prophet, so the very idea of "adding" decoration to an object in order to beautify or give it meaning is repudiated with horror. Insofar as Fine Artists have any concern with decoration at all (and that is contested), they conceive it as something growing out of and accentuating the nature of materials and structure—a means of bringing out and expressing the Reality of brick or metal, plastic or concrete. Obviously, such ornament is not a Low Art deriving its forms from High Art prototypes; it is a Fine Art, and as such, a self-justifying activity related to nothing outside itself. And axiomatically, "applied ornament is everywhere and always bad."

How the Fine Art concept of ornament condemns all historic art and architecture.

Rarely if ever is the full implication of the Fine Art concept of ornament considered. Yet it is inescapable. It in fact condemns almost everything that men have ever made, beyond the simplest tools.

Consider mimetic decoration, for instance. The history of decorative arts begins with the principle of evocative mimesis—the universal practice of imitating in new materials, or with new techniques, forms characteristic and evoking visual memories of older ones. When pots made entirely of clay superseded wickerwork or grass baskets smeared with mud, the old forms and patterns produced by weaving were reproduced by incisions and paint in the new material (**15a**). Round the forecourts of Egyptian temples run stone walls reproducing on gigantic scale the shapes of papyrus palisades fencing courtyards of prehistoric Egyptian chiefs' houses to keep their barnyard fowl safe. Greek entablatures are marble perpetuations of structural forms originating in wood. And so on—examples are innumerable, E. Baldwin Smith's books alone providing dozens (cf. *Egyptian*

87

Architecture as Cultural Expression; The Dome; Architectural Symbolism in Imperial Rome and the Middle Ages). The purpose of mimetic design and decoration was plain and simple. By perpetuating familiar forms, the design helped identify use (clay pots serving the same purpose as mud-smeared wicker ones; Heavenly Rulers' temples as earthly chiefs' houses, and so on) and humanize artifacts by relating them to users' personal experience, their sense for the appropriate, and their whole complex of cultural values (**15b**).

Yet Fine Art dogma demands that all mimetic forms be condemned as "bad" ornament. Nor can the issue be evaded by technological determinism. Fine Art theorists are fond of pretending that just as Gropius's Fagus Shoe Factory took the form it did because of the structural and tactile qualities of steel and glass and concrete, so Gothic cathedrals derived their mature forms (however conceived originally) from the particular properties of rib-vaulting in stone, Greek temples from post-and-lintel construction in marble, and so on. Consequently, they maintain, ornament in such Great Works of Art was no longer mimetic and was therefore "good," in contrast to primitive mimesis and especially the ornament on Victorian buildings, which was not derived from structural properties or texture of materials, but eclectically copied and indiscriminately applied, and so "bad."

Unfortunately, this will not do. The facts bear no such interpretation. Just as it is nonsense to imagine (as such theorists must) that Gothic cathedrals *had* to replace Romanesque ones once pointed vaulting was invented, that once somebody discovered how to put a dome on squinches Justinian had to use this technique in Hagia Sophia, that therefore if only steel and glass and concrete had been known in earlier ages Parthenons and Rameseums and Sainte-Chapelles would all have looked like the Seagram Building on Park Avenue, so it is nonsense to go on perpetuating the delusions of Ruskin or Morris or Viollet-le-Duc that earlier men shared either the 19th century's notion of Great Artists or its passionate concern for technology. No modern scholar of medieval culture supports any such ideas any longer. All agree on the primacy of meaning in medieval architecture—so Robert Branner in *St. Louis and the Court Style* (1965) shows that the Sainte-Chapelle was conceived as a huge jewel box in the most literal sense (**57a**); Richard Krautheimer* explains that when

---

* In "Introduction to an Iconography of Medieval Architecture," *Journal of the Warburg and Courtald Institutes*, V, 1942, pp. 1–33.

medieval men said one building was copied after another they did not refer to its outward form but to its symbolism and liturgical meaning, so that buildings looking totally different to us were considered similar by them; Norris Kelly Smith demonstrates in his *Medieval Art* (1967) that medieval man could not have conceived his art in our spatial and formal terms; and so on. And that meaning was primarily conveyed, of course, by applied ornament. To an even greater extent, if possible, the same is true of Greek, or Baroque, or any other of the "great epochs" of Western art—let alone the arts of India or China or Persia. No; if steel and glass boxes in the International Style idiom or brute concrete expressions of Existentialist Reality seem dehumanized, if they seem to exist in a world with laws of its own remote from life as it is lived, one reason is their total lack of that ornament which in times past always identified use, humanized artifacts, put art into life and life into art.

Modern dogma necessarily condemns as "badly" decorated almost all tools, all armor, all useful objects man made in the past, except the most primitive. Yet applied ornament designed to identify use and establish human relationships was characteristic of all forms of arms and armor, not only from primitive or ideological ages, but from all times and all places up to the 20th century (**16a**). Elaborate chased and sculptured helmets from tombs in Ur of the Chaldees, the Treasury of Atreus, burial barrows of the Viking North; painted shields of Greek hoplites and medieval cataphracts; the intricately figured breastplate of Augustus Caesar's statue from Prima Porta, and the exquisitely worked armor from Renaissance Italian *bottegas;* cast-iron cannon dredged up from the *Vasa* in Stockholm harbor, and elaborately designed Kentucky rifles from colonial smitheries; Excalibur with its mystically inscribed blade and jewel-flashing hilt, and bowie knives of the American Southwest with their distinctive shapes and incised mottos and emblems—all in their several ways and forms carried decoration related to life (and death) of their owners and users. So related, in fact, was every kind of tool.

Candlesticks and keys and combs, axes and anchors, handles and hairpins—anything in fact that men have felt to be extensions of themselves and their powers has been lavishly decorated with applied ornament of extrinsic meaning. Medieval and Renaissance "minor arts" have always been the best remembered and the most admired, but the practice is by no means limited to objects intended for churches or palaces; comparably luxuriant figural ornament can be found on scientific instruments, for example, from the 16th well into the 19th centuries, as the most cursory glance through books like Henri Michel's *Scientific Instruments in Art and History* (1967) will show. Always and everywhere until our times, tools of any specialized nature whatever had their function identified by their design, their use humanized by decoration.

Yet modern Fine Art theory must dismiss all but bare tools as "bad"—cold steel, blunt wood, impersonal plastic about exhaust its range of possibilities. To advance-guard 20th-century theoreticians, no sight is so satisfying as a wall blank inside and out, preferably of sick gray concrete with raw form-holes in it. It speaks to them ineffably, and no doubt in so speaking also says something about the 20th-century intellectual mind. Our ancestors felt differently. They used art to decorate walls, in every sort of way and as a matter of course, and so to enrich life. Sometimes the decoration was figural—frescoes, tapestries, mosaics, pictures in glass—depicting scenes appropriate to given situations; Biblical in churches, secular in homes ("peintid or wouun in thine hall or chaumbre: 'here ridith King Arthir, and there fightith Iulius Caesar, and here Hector of Troie,'" as Reginald Pocock's 1449 *Repressor* put it in defending images), Last Suppers in refectories and Last Judgments in courtrooms, kingly deeds in palaces. Sometimes it consisted of abstract patterns—geometric, linen-fold, folk, as media and taste dictated. And of course throughout history outside walls were decorated as frequently as in, both representationally (from the Ishtar Gate in ancient Babylon, for example, to Hans Holbein's houses in Basel) and abstractly (rusticated stone, half-timber patterns in wood and plaster, checkerboard in brick). Sometimes the forms of this decoration followed High Art (on occasion, as in frescoes and mosaics, it could be a High Art itself), sometimes it was folk copying of ideational Low Arts. Through all variations, the principle of decorating walls is once again to identify function and humanize use. But since none of this helps express the Reality of walls, Fine Art theory must condemn it all as "bad" and "poor."

By the same arguments, no decorative sculpture is admissible in modern life. Fine Art dogma allows sculpture only if it is obviously unrelated to its surroundings, if it evidences a "creative act" independent of all crass social compromises. Anything else is "commercialistic," and those who supply even cast-concrete panels for modern buildings, however abstract, are vaguely suspect of not being "true artists." Reading this view back into history, orthodox Fine Art theory considers, for example, that American sculpture begins in the

19th century with William Rush and reaches its first great moment in the generation of Horatio Greenough. But this is absurd; in fact Greenough's cold, dead, white Fine Art marks the beginning of the end of a two-centuries-long tradition of living sculpture that with William Rush had just begun to move towards a High Art. Once realize that "sculpture" for our ancestors did not consist of Precious Objects for Exhibition, but simply a meaningful and accepted activity in everyday life, and it will be apparent that early America abounded with it. Even Puritan New England must have been full of carved figures on buildings. William Sewall's diary records having "our cherubims heads . . . set up" (on the doorgate of his house in Boston) on December 6, 1698, for instance, then how on January 26, 1724/5 one was blown down by the wind, and how he took down the other on February 1 next. G. F. Dow's *Arts and Crafts in New England 1704–1775* (Topsfield, Conn., 1927) mentions all sorts of carvers and their work, including a famous account of sparks from a chimney fire flying into the open mouth of "one of the carved lions, couchant upon the Top of the Brick Wall of . . . Colonel Dyer's house . . . the mouth of the wooden beast discharging smoke and fire. . . ." Still in the early 19th century, William Bentley's Salem diary is full of references to similar work, including the row of life-size statues erected by the eccentric Timothy Dexter in Newburyport. Newport, New York, Philadelphia all have similar and more voluminous references to sculpture. Its function was to give character and human associations to an environment, not to be admired for aesthetic effect. If it has now almost totally disappeared, that is not so much because its material was perishable as because, like all the Unchanging Arts of life, such work was normally discarded when its purpose became obsolete, destroyed with as little compunction as when statues of George III in New York and Boston were broken up after the Revolution made them meaningless.

Decorative sculpture was at least as common inside buildings as out. Chimney pieces and door pediments, newel posts, moldings all could and did frequently have figural or patterned decoration (**17b**). All other tools and devices were similarly identified and humanized as a matter of course. Stove plates are a typical case in point; perhaps the best idea of their numbers can be gained from the collections Henry C. Mercer assembled in his museum at Doylestown, Pennsylvania, and described in books like *The Bible in Iron* (Doylestown, Pa., 1914). Carrying on medieval traditions in 18th-century forms, they represent true Low Arts in every way—forms deriving from High Art (of the 17th century, in this case), makers anonymous except when chance has preserved a name or two, like the "carvers and guilders" Nicholas Bernard and Martin Jugiez, whose receipt for "Eight pounds for carving the Arms of the Earl of Fairfax for a Pattern for the Back of Chimney sent Isaac Zane, Jr." was discovered by Charles F. Hummel (*Winterthur Newsletter,* November 27, 1959) in the receipt book of John Pemberton, Philadelphia merchant who collaborated with Isaac Zane in operating a furnace in Frederick County, Virginia.

That ordinary gravestones constitute a body of sculpture worth studying is a fact so long obscured by Fine Art dogma as only now to be recognized within the last decade or so (e.g., Allan I. Ludwig, *Graven Images,* Middletown, Conn., 1966). Yet it should be obvious that, merely because the relief sculptures of the Resurrection on Judgment Day and of Adam and Eve in Eden that you find on the tomb of Mrs. Richard Bulkeley (**17a**) in old Saint Paul's burying ground at Halifax, Nova Scotia (say), happen to be datable 1775, they are not necessarily less significant than the Romanesque work of Guglielmo or Gislebertus or the master of the bronze doors at Hildesheim, whose forms they so parallel—in this remote outpost of New England such sculpture served exactly the same purpose as in the time of Saint Bernard and Bishop Bernwald eight centuries before.

Early American ship and furniture ornament belonged to the same living tradition of decorative sculpture. From the gold-and-ivory thrones in Tutankhamen's treasure to Renaissance *cassones* to American Queen Anne and Chippendale chairs, furniture was always ornamented in such a way as to identify use and be related to the total culture of its makers and owners (**16b, 17b**). Viking long ships, Maori canoes, Greek galleys, Chinese junks, Spanish galleons, American clipper ships, all bore carved and painted ornament that made them more than mere transportation machines. Our airplanes and cars and trains are still decorated in that tradition to some extent, though there are Fine Art fanatics who would like to abolish all such humanizing elements from our environment if they could, sit us on bare planks and skins and shiny metal tubes and transport us in stainless steel coffins, all under the sacred rubric of expressing Realities of material and structure.

How Fine Art design, by its own rationale, ultimately condemns itself.

Many champions of Fine Art are intelligent men; surely it disturbs them to think how their dogma has torn what they call Art out of living history, created a faceless mechanical environment, and denigrated all human achievements in visual arts but their own? Not as long as they hold as an article of faith beyond all rational proof or criticism that we live in an age different from all others; and they do. In *The Thirties* Malcolm Muggeridge noted how

> With pathetic tenacity men cling to the belief that changing circumstances change life. Can a world in which aeroplanes travel at 400 miles per hour, they ask themselves, be the same as one in which there were only steam-engines, laboriously attaining their mile a minute? If a voice may be carried across a wide ocean, is it conceivable that the words thus transmitted should have no greater significance than if spoken across a tea-table? "The world of everyday life is now so radically different from the world of the Gospels," a clergyman writes, "and the effort required to interpret the universal truths that derive from the Gospel, in terms that mean anything in a world of intricate social organization is so immense, that the whole thing appears remote from life as it has to be lived," not, perhaps, reflecting that the Roman Empire's "world of everyday life" was also radically different from the world of the Gospels, yet not, for that reason, blind to their significance. War has always been brutish and unprofitable, but not so brutish and so unprofitable as now; therefore, the angry passions which formerly brought it to pass, must have given place to a more reasonable temper. . . . In the same way, it might be argued that whereas hitherto it was legitimately complained that the wicked prospered, non-stop electric trains between Brighton and London have rendered such a complaint obsolete; or that though it unquestionably used to be foolish to lay up treasure on earth for rust to corrupt, the invention of stainless steel has made it unprofitable no longer. . . . [London, 1940, pp. 156–57]

In the sixties the same kind of people took for gospel Marshall McLuhan's contention that ideas purveyed electronically must be very different in effect and quality from ideas spoken and written, even when books and speeches were his chief media for saying so. Whence it followed, of course, that history was pointless, and the whole traditional function of decoration relating artifacts to life, absurd:

> Perhaps the most striking distinction between the New Tradition and all older ones was in the aversion to ornament as such. Any and every kind of applied ornament was rejected on principle— Sullivan's or Wright's quite as much as Georgian pilasters or

Victorian gingerbread. This aversion went beyond mere anti-Victorianism; it sprang from an approach to ornament fundamentally new in history. . . . the new, self-consciously "modern" men felt no such tie with the past. They used their knowledge of the past to free themselves from it. They felt they were not part of history; they *made* history. You can see this most obviously in the new totalitarian states of the 1930s, like Nazi Germany or Communist Russia, whose rulers busied themselves rewriting history to suit their own purposes, re-creating the past so as to control the present and the future; but a similar attitude to history appeared everywhere to a greater or lesser degree. The past as an objective fact with any real influence or claim on them ceased to exist for large numbers of people in the 1920s and 30s, particularly in "intellectual" circles. Scorn for an architecture that borrowed from the past or was in any way dependent on it, followed as a matter of course. [Gowans, *Images of American Living*, pp. 441–42]

Among proponents of this new attitude to ornament, none was more forceful or influential than Dr. Lewis Mumford. It was an event of unusual significance, therefore, when in an article curiously reminiscent of H. G. Wells's last "mind-at-the-end-of-its-tether" renunciation of everything he had preached and worked for all his life, this acute critic in the *Architectural Record* for February 1968 announced that "what . . . has gone wrong with our youthful dreams about a truly modern style in architecture, one which should express the realities of our own age . . . is: They came true!"

In our admiration for the entrancing constructive feats made possible by modern technics, we did not imagine what the world would look like if every part of it was made over into the exact image of the machine . . . modern architecture . . . has revealed the real nature of our civilization: its compulsive irrationality, its mechanized barbarism, its psychedelic fantasies. . . . Our generation . . . should be able to learn from and rectify the mistakes it has made in its one-sided exaltation of technology. We should at last understand that unless we preserve human continuity . . . our scientific and technical advances will be not merely menacing but meaningless. . . .

When he came to consider ways out of this impasse, Dr. Mumford suggested that

modern man must restore his own self-respect, his self-discipline. . . . Man, as Pico della Mirandola well said, is the maker and molder of himself. In that process, architecture has been one of the chief means, through symbolic expression and beautiful form, of transforming and making visible to later generations his ideal self.

Specifically how that might be done he did not suggest; yet it is obvious. The principal way architecture historically achieved this symbolic expression was in fact through applied ornament and mimetically derived shapes serving their traditional function of identifying use and humanizing artifacts. Some vernacular building still does (22b); Wright's work derives its power from the same source (22a), and largely on this account was damned as "Victorian," as we shall see later. Here it is enough to point out that, however ludicrous and embarrassing the efforts of those Victorian eclectics who swathed General Grant villas in layers of swags and spindles, perched Parthenons and Saint Peter's cupolas atop thirty-story office buildings, or modeled banks on Roman baths, they at least had the merit of recognizing the problem of relating their art to human experience and human history. Those who merely jeered at their ineptitude, or proposed to concentrate entirely on functional facts, in fact presented no solution to that problem at all, and left posterity a wasteland. What was wrong with High and Late Victorian ornament was not, surely, that it was "applied," but that it was concerned with picturesque effects and spurious "tastefulness" to the exclusion of meaning or even common sense. Rejecting the whole concept of applied ornament in favor of expressing only Realities of structure and texture led directly to the same quagmire Reality had dragged painting into: if "art" is determined by anyone's subjective definition of "realistic expression," if a bicycle rack can be just as much a work of architecture as a cathedral whenever anyone chooses to announce that he finds "aesthetic quality" in one, then "architecture" can end only in solutions to building problems defined by architects themselves, by turns abstract, mechanical, or meaningless, and frequently all three at once—as Dr. Mumford has confessed. Whence it follows that the whole question of the function of ornament needs to be reexamined.

How the Unchanging Arts of ornament have survived in commercial design.

Of course there will be some ready to argue that any such investigation is idle. However sympathetic to views like Dr. Mumford's on the sterility of the 20th-century concept of design, they feel it is the only one we have—that the old concept of ornament is dead, and nothing can bring it back. To them we need reply only, look around! Though what we call Art no longer performs its traditional functions of beautification, there are other activities which do.

Chief among them is what we can best call commercial design—that is, the design of industrially mass-produced objects of all sorts. Here every aspect of the traditional arts of decoration is to be found, performing its unchanging historical function. Here too are artists performing their traditional function of giving visual form to ideas given them, anonymous creators with no pretentious claims to prophecy or genius, but simply dedicated to "beautifying" the world in whatever capacity they can (18).

Here is perpetuated in full vigor the primordial mimetic principle of decorative arts, imitating in new materials, or with new techniques, forms characteristic and evoking visual memories of older ones and so humanizing artifacts by relating them to users' personal experience and cultural context. Mass-produced station wagons of the 1940s and 50s, for instance, reproduce in pressed steel the appearance of their wood-paneled custom-made predecessors of the 1930s—so representing mimesis quite as well as any prehistoric pot or Greek entablature. Similarly early automobiles generally reproduced the forms of horse-drawn buggies, even on occasion to whip sockets for nonexistent horses (19a). Early electric-light fixtures reproduced the shapes of gas jets, as they in turn had reproduced the shapes of candles. Heavy plastic plates and cups reproduce the forms of cut glassware. And so on.

Likewise, you could still find well into the 20th century mass-produced tools designed and decorated on traditional principles. I am not thinking so much of elaborate tools like sewing machines or electric motors, which were large and expensive enough to be thought of as Art Objects and so always decorated badly—first with meaningless applied floral decoration and the like, then treated with equal meaninglessness as abstract compositions—as of simpler tools that were never consciously "designed" at all. Spades and axes and bayonets, for instance, whose shapes were steadily refined to express their function; or mass-produced music stands cut out for lightness in the shape of a lyre; or mass-produced bookends which were not only entirely functional but also cast of plaster in the shape of an old man reading in a chair by the fireplace—once recognize the principles, and you will find countless examples. Or consider how the hood ornaments of automobiles, primarily functional tools to lift hoods by, also served to identify the function of the whole machine (like figureheads on ships) and relate it to human history through forms drawn primarily from classical mythology—goddesses moving forward through the air in flight, eagles, leaping stags, and the like—literally representational in early days, abstract later (19a, b); when about 1950 they disappeared altogether, it was not because they had lost their function, as anybody who has burnt a hand lifting a hood by the hot metal knows, but because around that time automobile design became an Art, lost its original design principles, and began ringing changes justified as expressing the nature of the material and structure, though in fact meaningless exercises in unrelated aesthetics.

Commercial design still decorates walls on traditional principles. Historically, the long change-over from frescoed or tapestried or paneled walls to plastered walls covered by commercially printed wallpaper made no difference whatever in terms of the function of ornament, as the history of wallpaper demonstrates. It begins in the 17th century, when "flock" wallpaper became common—a cheap mimetic imitation of the effect of tapestry made by dusting lint over a sticky pattern stenciled onto paper or cloth. At the same time, cheaper imitations of painted panels were becoming available in the form of easel-painted pictures of domestic scenes and landscape, provided especially by the "little masters" of Holland in what came to be called even then the "Dutch picture factory" appropriately enough, since both flock wallpaper and decorative easel pictures were products of that middle-class culture of which 17th-century Holland was the first great stronghold. Again, the humanizing function of such decoration is plain—it expressed either appropriation by a rising bourgeoisie of those tapestried walls so long a symbol of upper-class status, or a desire to relate buildings metaphorically to the world they belong to, or both. And when mass-produced block-printed wallpapers began to subsume both forms in the 18th century, they were obviously conceived on the same principles—sometimes resembling tapestries, sometimes resembling easel pictures, often mixing the two. That 19th- and 20th-century wallpaper performed comparable functions is obvious (21). Go through any sample catalogue of wallpapers today, and you will find that the great bulk of them still derive from tapestries or from easel pictures. Nor did the growing tendency to paint walls instead of paper them make any appreciable difference; it only meant that instead of having walls ornamented with designs printed on wallpaper, mass-produced framed reproductions were hung up instead—and despite all efforts "to educate the public," the kind of pictures preferred remained overwhelmingly the same kind of landscapes and still lifes and genre scenes they had been for two and three centuries back. The only real effect of all the propaganda for Fine Art was to make the middle and upper-middle class self-conscious about the choice of pictures, so that they would choose Gauguin or van Gogh instead of some anonymous moose in the sunset (but not, alas! to be initiated into mysteries of Reality, only because these painters were "decorative" —horrid thought to both!). And wherever walls were decorated unselfconsciously, without any thought of Art but only for pleasure—in teenagers' rooms, for instance, plastered with all sorts of mementos of dances and prints of rock groups and old posters—there you found the old concepts reigning unchallenged, performing for the compartments of suburban boxes their old functions of identification and humanization.

One of the most striking survivals of the traditional arts of decoration is in the racing cars, especially amateur stock cars (20). Contestants in colored helmets and cars painted to match doing their warm-up laps; the pre-race line-up for introductions; the race itself, with spin-outs and crashes and disabled contestants being towed away; then the winner coming forward for his prize and a kiss from some local beauty in suitable undress—what is all this but medieval jousting tournaments in modern dress? Metallic forms, each in distinctive colors, parading before the stands, then hurtling down a course, some to grief and some to glory; victors riding up to claim the trophy of some fair maiden's favor—here it all is, reincarnate. And here the medieval tradition of decorative arts lives on in full vigor too.

Amateur drivers and crews customarily choose their own design and colors and—if they don't do it themselves—have their cars rebuilt by some commercial body shop and decorated by a signpainter. Not that they would consider this operation as anything to do with Art! Art in their minds is an activity associated with pretentious freaks, frauds who do things nobody can understand or conceive any use for. By contrast, most of their commercial designers are anonymous, doing meaningful and cogent work.* Everybody knows what a

---

* A few have achieved at least local fame—e.g., Kenneth "von Dutch" Howard, subject of an article by Roger Vaughan in *True* for September 1967; but until our age can distinguish living from dead arts, it is unlikely "von Dutch" or anyone similar will ever make the *Art Index*, or any dictionary of who's who in 20th-century Art, where every obscurest painter is so meticulously recorded.

racing car is for, and what the designer and/or decorator of one is trying to do. Obviously, his job is first of all to make a better body for racing—lighter, faster, safer. Over and above that, he tries to make it look better—sleeker, neater, speedier—insofar as he can without affecting performance. This he does in part by modifying wheels and fenders and chassis where possible, and in part by painting the car in patterns suggesting sleekness and speed, like stripes running from end to end across hood and roof—in a word, he designs to identify function. And then he does something more: he paints on emblems, color schemes, and unique patterns that distinguish the car from all others, making it no longer just another machine, but an extension of the team, an expression of the team's personality. In a word, he humanizes it by decoration.

Between this kind of activity and the Artist creating Precious Objects for Exhibition there is nothing in common. But if these drivers and crews and the commercial designers decorating for them could meet the knights who competed in medieval jousts, and the armorers and painters who worked for them, they would recognize kindred spirts at once. They share the joys of courting danger in the lists for the simple thrill of it; they share the affection and personal relationship medieval knights felt towards favorite horses, swords, and armor, for they feel about their cars the same way; but most of all, they share the same concept of ornament—understand the same, unchanging functions of ornament designed to identify function and humanize artifacts.

How commercial design is descended from traditional decoration and differs fundamentally from "industrial design," a by-product of the Fine Art mentality.

This vigorously flourishing commercial design requires some explanation. It represents a survival of those traditional arts of decoration which as long ago as Ruskin's time were confidently pronounced to be expiring, if not extinct already. The evil of machine production, it was asserted, had killed them, by destroying the traditional craftsmanship on which they depended. And it was in reaction to this state of affairs, so the story further continued, that a new concept of ornament based on Reality had to be evolved. Such, with appropriate variations, was the justification for three generations of Fine Art theoreticians, from William Morris to Herbert Read, arguing in favor of a new integration of "craftsmen" and "artists" to produce one. "Today the visual arts exist in isolation, from which they can be rescued only through the conscious cooperative effort of all craftsmen. . . . Architects, sculptors, painters, we must all turn to the crafts. . . ." from statements like this, in the First Proclamation of the Weimar Bauhaus in 1919, grew what has come to be called modern "industrial design."

Yet from even such a cursory survey as the preceding few pages, it will be evident that the demise of traditional decoration, as Mark Twain said about reports of his own death, was grossly exaggerated. What we have here in fact is another of those Fine Art myths, like the notion of representational painting being driven out by photography, which everybody repeats and nobody examines. And it proceeds from a similar fallacy. Just as advance-guard painting was not a reaction against photography, but an imitation of it, so here—so far from being a reaction against the "art" of the machine or a restoration of declining traditions of craftsmanship, modern industrial design is a direct outgrowth of machine production and a primary cause of the eclipse of those traditional arts of decoration which the old craftsmanship embodied.

Traditional decoration was not and could not be in competition with or affected by machine production, because the basic rationale of these operations was quite different. Whether or not an artifact was so decorated as to identify use and be humanized by associated ideas had nothing necessarily to do with whether it was made by a machine or by hand. Nor did the anonymity of machine-produced design represent any conflict with traditional craftsmanship, which had always typically been anonymous—as commercial design is still. The real conflict was between this kind of anonymity and the Fine Art concept of designers as "form givers" of unique genius; what machine production actually competed with was not decoration in the old sense of identifying use and humanizing artifacts—which it self-evidently could not do—but objects created by Fine Artists, supposed to embody and reveal the Reality of things. Thus, when Morris or the Bauhaus theoreticians or Herbert Read talked about union of "artists" and "craftsmen," they did not at all mean that the "artist" should try to approximate the function and role in society of those older craftsmen who made and decorated objects according to the traditional concept of beautification. They meant just the opposite. They meant that design and craftsmanship should become Fine Arts. They meant that potters or furniture makers or textile designers should claim the same sort of inspired-seer-and-prophet prerogatives as painters, and similar freedoms from crass utilitarian pressure. It follows that, just as what Fine Art theorists call painting today is an activity entirely different in ends, means, and social function from the activity traditionally called painting, so what they call industrial design is similarly antipathetical to the traditional arts of decoration. It not merely *looks* different from them, it *is* different. But it is not different from machine work. The kinds of forms that the machine naturally produces—depending for their appeal wholly on the nature of structure or materials—are precisely what industrial designers are taught to create as "expressions of Reality." Whence it follows that as in painting, so in industrial design—what new forms this Fine Art allegedly invents turn out on examination to be variant imitations of forms invented originally for and in commercial design, borrowed and put on display as ends in themselves (**18**).

Not, of course, that industrial design can ever be entirely an affair of Precious Objects for Exhibition, like paintings. The industrial designer can never altogether ignore what the objects he creates are supposed to do—that chairs are meant to be sat on, faucets to be turned, and so on. But he can come very close to doing so, as any typical exhibition of industrial design will demonstrate all too frequently. There evidences of the Fine Art mentality are to be recognized in many ways: in works of leading designers being set up on stands, spotlit, supplied with biographical notes and all the typical paraphernalia of gallery-going; in strong tendencies to gimmickry— faucets or doorknobs given odd shapes and unorthodox turnings for no rational reason, chairs of bizarre materials and structure, spoons too flat to hold liquids properly, and so on—that is, to pointlessly eccentric innovation, emphasis on change for change's sake akin to the constantly shifting styles of the Restless Art of painting—and, cumulatively, in the tendency to more and more subjective judgments of "good" and "bad" design. Just as it is impossible to talk about "good" or "bad" work by a painter who claims to be revealing some entirely subjective concept of Reality, so in much industrial design it is not possible to do much more than register personal approval or dislike. In contrast to the traditional arts of decoration, which could be judged objectively in terms of their success in identifying use and humanizing artifacts, much industrial design is created outside any objective frame of reference. This is the real reason for the confusion, the pointlessness, and ultimately the dehumanized character which Dr. Mumford so properly deplores in modern architecture, and by extension all modern design.

Defining the problem also suggests the remedy. If architecture and the artifacts surrounding it are dehumanized because the concept of ornament and design they are based on is bankrupt, then that concept needs to be abandoned, and design needs to be based again on the unchanging principles of that art of decoration which identified use and humanized artifacts. Precisely what form such artifacts would take is not an historian's or critic's business to suggest—that, precisely, is what an artist's traditional business was, is, and must always be.

4

The Unchanging Arts of Illustration:
Narrative Painting and Prints,
Comics, Movies, Television

■

I

THE TRADITIONAL LOW AND HIGH
ARTS OF ILLUSTRATION

ILLUSTRATION in its broadest sense is the function of all those sorts of visual arts concerned with recording events, real or imagined. That is a very broad sense indeed—so broad that until around 1850 nothing much like an "illustrator" existed in the narrow modern sense of the word. Traditionally, illustration was simply one among the many things all artists might be called on to do as a matter of course, and there might be many reasons for doing it besides simply making records. Illustrating history can be a way of creating it; if it be true that "the important thing about history is not what happened but what people think happened," then traditional illustration has shaped the world, and is still doing so: movies like the Soviet *Stalingrad* and Cecil B. DeMille's historical epics shape history while depicting it, just as Velasquez' *Surrender of Breda* did, or Egyptian reliefs of Pharaohs forever smiting their enemies on the walls of tombs and temples. Illustration can exhort by implication: by commemorating the Horatii's patriotic oath (*The Restless Art*, p. 21), David hoped not only to edify audiences but also inspire them to emulation, just as medieval illustrators of saints' lives hoped to inspire theirs. Or illustrations may arouse "beautiful feelings" by imaginative association with past epochs and events: so Greek painters recorded Marathon and Issus, Turner Trafalgar, Delacroix the exciting deeds of German robber barons (*The Restless Art*, p. 83), Wilkie the vanishing pleasures of rural simplicity (*The Restless Art*, p. 115). Illustration is, in short, one of the great traditional functions of High Art: the Sistine ceiling is illustration; so is Tintoretto's *Last Supper* in San Giorgio Maggiore and Leonardo's in Santa Maria delle Grazie; so is Titian's *Danae,* El Greco's *Burial of Count Orgaz* and Rembrandt's *Night Watch.*

And always along with this traditional High Art of Illustration went a traditional Low Art dependent on it—illustration recognizably derivative from and so inferior to it in inventive imagination. In earlier times, in fact, this Low Art is one of our chief sources of information about vanished seminal masterpieces that set the course of art history. Only from copies on vases and mosaics do we have any idea what Greek mural painting looked like; almost all we know of the great recensions of Gospel illustrations invented by master mosaicists for early Byzantium's major shrines at Jerusalem, Bethlehem, Antioch and Constantinople comes from faithful copies of them in silverwork and manuscript illumination. And if the High Art of the Middle Ages, the Renaissance, and the Baroque were to be destroyed, we could get some idea of it in the same way, from generation after generation of copies in the Low Arts, with comparable variations according to distance from the source in time, place and social class.

Sometimes the cultural lag is short and the copying direct, as when second- and third-rank painters and print makers spread innovations from the High Art of Rome or Florence or Paris to provincial centers within a decade or so. Sometimes it is long and complicated, as when forms and themes from High Gothic stained glass and illuminations, first copied in 15th-century block-printed shrine souvenirs and playing cards, reappear in 18th-century chapbooks combined with Renaissance and Baroque forms picked up along the way. A spectacular example is the 1855 Currier & Ives print of *The Bad Man at the Hour of Death,* whose ancestry can be traced back through prototypes in every century to a theme invented after the Black Death of 1348 (**23 a, b, c**). But however complicated the time and cultural lag between High and Low Arts of illustration may be, their relationship and their respective functions did not vary, and were still clearly understood until well into the 19th century.

In many respects and for many reasons, illustration was the great art of the 19th century. Unquestionably the largest proportion of pictures then painted were illustrations; alongside them, an equally prolific Low Art of printed book illustration flourished. Quite often—in fact, normally—you find the same artist engaged in both. But throughout the period the distinction between the two remains clearly understood—the forms of High Art are judged according to standards of imagination and inventiveness, of Low by fitness for mass media. And since the standards and values of both are rooted in function, all illustration in this period grows out of life and is one of the great cultural expressions of its age. It represents not only the best single manifestation of the romantic nationalism then dominant in Western civilization, but also a potent force for molding it by implicitly defining "national character." Illustration was in many ways *the* typical art of the 19th-century England, France, Germany, and the United States, as sculpture was of 5th-century Greece, architecture of 13th-century France, painting of 16th-century Italy.

1. *The English Tradition of Illustration*

In England it was William Hogarth (1697–1764) who set the national character of illustration. Adapting the theatrical principle of 17th-century Baroque painting, he created distinctive little stage sets, immensely detailed, busy with gesticulating actors, all making a different and distinct contribution to a complex whole (**24a**). Scaling his pictures down in size from their Baroque precedents, cutting the grandiose and flamboyant elements out of them, Hogarth also set a precedent for predominantly domestic, intimate and unostentatious atmosphere. And in pictures like his series of the *Harlot's* or *Rake's Progress, The Lady's Last Stake,* or *Calais Gate,* he established a characteristically English tone of dry rather than vicious satire, of good-natured tolerance towards human foibles and follies, of condescending amusement at the vanities of heroic ambition.

For 150 years after his time, this remained the basic format and tone of English illustrative painting (**24b**). How expressive of national character this illustrative painting was, is suggested by its close parallels with successive trends in Victorian architecture: in it can be recognized a "classical revival style," of which an example is the 1858 *Past and Present* series in the Tate by Augustus Egg (1816–1863); a Gothic Revival style, represented by Francis Danby (1793–1861) or pre-Raphaelite illustration in general; a picturesque eclectic High Victorian style, typified by William Powell Frith (1819–1909) and the late work of John Everett Millais (1829–1896); and finally in the 1880s a parallel to Late Victorian academic architecture in the "grand stage manner" of painters like William Quiller Orchardson (1832–1910), Frank Brangwyn (1867–1956), Frank Bramley (1857–1915) and Stanhope Forbes (1857–1947).* Running as a leitmotiv

---

* Thanks to three generations of Fine Art propaganda, few galleries display their 19th-century anecdotal paintings any longer. Fortunately, books illustrating them are still to be found, both from the period itself (as late as 1928, for instance, the Amalgamated Press, Fleetway House, London, put out a lavish volume of "modern masterpieces of British Art . . . chosen mainly for their popular appeal," consisting almost wholly of narrative pictures) and from the 1960s (e.g., Graham Reynolds, *Victorian Painting,* London, 1966; Raymond Lister, *Victorian Narrative Paintings,* New York, 1966); sooner or later, once museums and galleries begin to recover a fuller sense of their historical function, the pictures will surely reappear.

through it all, too, is a curious and distinctive sort of domesticated mysticism; but that can be recognized and described best, I think, in Low illustration derived from it.

The first tentative manifestation of this quality is in Thomas Bewick (1753–1828), whose revival and improvement of woodcut techniques first made it possible to satisfy an expanding literate middle class's demand for cheap and prolifically illustrated books. Although in content and function Bewick's most typical work, like *British Birds* (1799) or *Quadrupeds* (1790), belonged in the ancient category of primarily informative illustration along with medieval bestiaries and 18th-century encyclopedias (**25a**), a few of his tailpieces and incidental ornament break away from the formal framed compositions characteristic of engraved prints to become free vignettes; in them, there is often a curiously haunting quality despite their tiny size and commonplace subjects (**25b**). Bewick's indication of how abandoning frames might promote a new freedom of expression and a new close relationship of pictures to text was fully exploited by the generation maturing in the 1820s and -30s, led by George Cruikshank (1792– 1878) and Edward Calvert (1803–1883).

Though temperamentally, Cruikshank and Calvert were very different—Cruikshank being a political cartoonist who went on to become his age's most famous and prolific book illustrator, Calvert an associate of William Blake whose output always remained small—they had in common a distinctively British sort of otherworldly fantasy. In Calvert it took the form of a low-keyed mysticism. His simple and freely drawn vignettes, quietly and unostentatiously evoking the numinous in Nature, are a Low Art version of William Blake's painting, the more effective precisely because he had the self-effacement of a good Low Artist and so avoided that tendency to self-conscious religiosity and messianic utopianism which mars all but a few of Blake's mystic flights (**25c**). Calvert's little illustrations spring not from some personal vision, but from the same atavistic source whence came visions like Logres, *The Faerie Queene*, and *A Midsummer Night's Dream* in their several generations, and which would later find comparable expression in George Macdonald's fairy tales, the encounter with Pan in *The Wind in the Willows,* or Christopher Robin's farewell to Pooh in "that enchanted place" in the Forest. There is the same indefinable domesticity about this mysticism that you find in English illustrative painting, a quality that comes naturally, I think, from the closeness of a civilization bred on a small island.

This same spirit, in a different dimension, characterizes Cruikshank's illustrations. If he was called the perfect illustrator for Dickens, it is surely not because he illustrated Dickens's text most literally, but because the curious elfin quality of his drawings so perfectly complements and brings out that aspect of Dickens's characterization exemplified by Sam Weller's calling Mr. Pickwick "an angel in gaiters." Plainly, Cruikshank's style is rooted in caricature; equally so, his best illustrations—to *Oliver Twist*, to *John Gilpin's Ride*, to fairy tales like *The Elves and the Shoemaker*—are not "funny" in a vulgar sense, but rather "odd" in the sense of otherworldly; their spidery line and free vignette form removes them from the stolid pedestrian ground of actuality into the light air of whimsical fantasy (**26a**). It is this quality that made Cruikshank so admired and imitated; and it is precisely this quality that his imitators usually missed. John Leech (1817–1864) came close to it sometimes, as in illustrating à Beckett's *Comic History of England* (1848) and Barham's *Ingoldsby Legends* (1837 ff.), but not often. Similarly, the illustrations of Dickens by Hablot Knight Browne (Phiz, 1815–1882) are "better drawn" than Cruikshank's and so look that much more like period pieces now. For the same reason we could very properly call "lifeless" the illustrations by Randolph Caldecott (1846–1886) for Irving's *Bracebridge Hall* or *Old Christmas*, for while they still follow the Cruikshank formula of spidery-line vignette, they are so correct as to be practically historical illustration. Of all Cruikshank's followers, the one who came closest to capturing his spirit of elfin unworldliness was also one of the last— Ernest H. Shepard (b. 1879), A. A. Milne's illustrator (**26b**).

One might be tempted to ascribe Cruikshank's distinctive light touch to his thorough grounding in the Low Art of caricature, in contrast to the more formal training of Leech, Phiz and Caldecott, who all began as painters (the first two indeed exhibited their paintings fairly regularly); but this will not do. Edward Lear (1812–1888), whose *Nonsense Songs* (1871) and *Nonsense Pictures* (1872) carry the Cruikshank tradition to its highest point of drollery and complete integration of pictures and text (**27b**), was a painter; his *Illustrated Excursions in Italy*, so admired by Queen Victoria that she asked him for drawing lessons, was published in the same year as his first *Book of Nonsense* (1846). So was John Tenniel (1820–1914); in fact, it was precisely Tenniel's painterly training that made him in some respects an illustrator superior to Cruikshank.

Tenniel's early ambition was to paint great murals like the Nazarenes' in the Casino Massimo in Rome, with the tightly structured formal compositions and Quattrocento Italian linear forms of Peter Cornelius, and in 1843 his "cartoon" for just such a fresco on the life of Saint Cecilia won a national competition for decorating the new Houses of Parliament. The executed work proved a dull failure, however. Possibly because of blindness in one eye, Tenniel was unable to invent painterly forms on a grand scale, and all that resulted from the whole project was a change in the meaning of "cartoon" from "preparatory drawing" to "funny picture" occasioned by *Punch's* jeering at the competition. Tenniel thereupon turned to book illustration, beginning with *Aesop's Fables* for John Murray in 1848; and here success was immediate. The very insistence on tight structure and precise line that inhibited his painting gave his illustrations a strength and structure Cruikshank's spidery style lacked. The very quaintness of eclectic Gothic form that made his mural stilted, gave his illustrations a blend of familiarity and distance from literal nature perfectly suited to the spirit of his text, the tastes of his public, and the general function of Gothic Revival forms as an image of 19th-century British nationalism. The emphasis on technical problems inculcated by mural painting led him to improve on Bewick's woodcut technique; instead of working with a knife on a flat side of softwood, he took to drawing on the end of a boxwood block hard enough for burins to follow his most delicate line, so that he could command all Cruikshank's sketchy freedom while escaping formal or compositional fuzziness. Such a style made him the perfect illustrator for fairy tales and fantasies, and in 1865 he found the perfect text—Lewis Carroll's *Alice in Wonderland.* It and *Through the Looking Glass* (1871) at once became and remained classic examples of inseparable pictures and text, fixing Tenniel's place as one of the great illustrators in art history (**27a**).

Like Cruikshank, Tenniel had wide influence and many followers—Charles Henry Bennett (1828–1867) copying his *Aesop* almost literally (1857); Richard Doyle (1824–1883) moving from Cruikshank's orbit into Tenniel's with his illustrations to Ruskin's *King of the Golden River* (1851), and following him thereafter (e.g., Mark Lemon's *Fairy Tales,* 1867); Arthur Hughes (1832–1915) modifying the Pre-Raphaelite manner of his 1850s painting with Tenniel's quick line and controlled whimsy (**28a**) to become the classic illustrator of George Macdonald's stories (*Dealings with the Fairies,* 1867; *At the Back of the North Wind,* 1871; *The Princess and the Goblin,* 1872). It is Tenniel, too, who is the basic influence on Kate Greenaway (1846–1901; **28b**) and even Beatrix Potter (1866–1943). They complement and balance the more bombastic and cryptic mysticism of later 19th-century English painting represented by Rossetti and Burne-Jones, and all together round out a cultural expression rivaled in its age only by the novel. English illustration is as distinctively English, as contrasted with French or German, as Dickens is English contrasted with Hugo or Keller, a fact which those critics who admire English 19th-century literature but lament that 19th-century England had no "art," only "illustration," would do better to keep in mind. When they complain that English illustrative painters lacked the "French sense of form," they forget that illustration was a living art whose forms derived from vital function, not only expressing but implicitly helping to create the national ideal that shaped the destiny of 19th-century Britain—to what an extent we realize best, perhaps, as we compare English illustration with traditions elsewhere.

2. *The French Tradition of Illustration*

Jean Baptiste Greuze (1725–1805) was Hogarth's counterpart in French illustrative painting. The differences between them are instructive, for they set divergent traditions. Both base their art on Baroque precedent; but Greuze being closer to the source and in a country where Baroque art was deeply rooted, his dependence on it is much more obvious. Compared to Greuze's grand operatic stage, with its Caravaggian spotlighting and movement flowing freely in and out of the picture plane, Hogarth's is the limited box of a Punch-and-Judy show. Both are concerned with fostering new social and political patterns, but where Hogarth plays to a local audience and deals with particular instances of folly or injustice, Greuze addresses the world. Ostensibly Greuze's characters in *The Paralytic Tended by His Children, The Punished Son*, or *The Twelfth-Cake*, or the happy crowd at *The Village Betrothal*, are supposed to be French middle-class; but no one believes this fiction for a moment. It is no accident that Greuze is the darling of visionary philosophers like Diderot and d'Holbach, or that he anticipates Jacques Louis David's neoclassicism with his Roman Revival *Septimius Severus and Caracalla*. For in fact Greuze is not picturing actual people, like Hogarth, but illustrating Everyman—or more exactly, the idealized middle-class Everyman who will stand revealed in us all once the wicked monarchical institutions that cloud our natural goodness shall be swept away. Greuze's sweet little girls with their rolling eyes and innocent dishabille do not exist here and now; they are visions of naturally good Rousseauan beings who are to be in the new millennium. Where Hogarth's messianic message comes cloaked in sly anecdote, Greuze parades his in flamboyant sentimentality.

In due course the Revolution comes, and of course the new man promised by Rousseau and painted by Greuze does not appear; the middle class idealized by 18th-century visionaries turns into the bourgeoisie so despised by their 19th-century successors. Greuze is swept into obscurity, but the tradition he established is not. Rather, it is taken up and developed by a greater than he—Eugène Delacroix (1798–1863), who becomes for French illustration the seminal figure Hogarth was in England. Like Hogarth, Delacroix is primarily admired by modern critics for his painterly forms, and they make much of his influence on the Impressionists. But as usual they forget that Delacroix did not hold the "modern" concept of what painting is; that he was still concerned to please and communicate with an audience and that therefore his forms were not yet ends in themselves, but means to present his subject matter more vividly, more imaginatively; and that consequently his primary influence was not on Impressionism or anything like it. He was an illustrator, and if you want to realize the extent of his influence and the measure of his greatness, you have to compare him with his followers and imitators in illustrative painting throughout the 19th century.

Already by 1830 Delacroix had established his basic themes and means for their expression: the intimate illustration of exotic Near Eastern life in *Woman with a Parrot;* the foreground-stage literary illustration in *Dante and Virgil;* the middleground-stage national battle epic in *The Massacre on Chios;* the background-stage historic drama in *The Murder of the Bishop of Liège;* and all his later famous illustrative paintings are developments and refinements of these categories: *Women of Algiers* of the first, *The Capture of Weislingen* (*The Restless Art,* p. 83) and *Hamlet and Horatio* of the second; *Crusaders Entering Constantinople* and *Battle of Taillebourg* of the third; his Saint-Sulpice frescoes and *Christ on Galilee* of the last. And by 1830 too he had perfected his basic forms: the theatrically posed and grandly gesturing figures, the rich colors and painterly brushwork, the panoramic scale and melodramatic landscape backgrounds, all so very different from the restrained content and linear style of English illustration, and all so superior too to the painters who imitated them in every country of Europe. Compare, for example, Delacroix's intimate Near Eastern illustrations with what Alexandre Décamps (1803–1860) or Eugène Fromentin (1820–1876) did with this theme. Or his literary illustrations with those by Paul Delaroche (1797–1856), like *Edward IV's Children in the Tower, Murder of the Duke of Guise,* and *Death of Queen Elizabeth; Hagar and Ishmael* by Jean Charles Cazin (1841–1901) in the Luxembourg; *Christ in Gethsemane* and *Young Jesus in the Temple* by Heinrich Hoffmann (1824–1911). Compare Delacroix's national battle epics with Wilkie's *Heroic Maid of Saragossa; The Dream* by Edouard Détaille (1848–1912); *Friedland* and *1814* by Ernest Meissonier (1815–1891); *Washington Crossing the Delaware* by Emanuel Leutze (1816–1868). Or his historic dramas with *Emperor and Pope* and *Excommunication of Robert the Pious* by Jean Paul Laurens (1838–1921); Thomas Couture's *Romans of the Decadence* (*The Restless Art,* p. 117); *Thusnelda Before Germanicus* by Karl von Piloty (1826–1886); *Charles V's Entry into Antwerp* by Hans Makart (1840–1884). All these were famous paintings in their time, but by comparison with Delacroix's work, how stilted, posed, bombastic and overdone they all look now. To be sure, they tell us a great deal about the rise of romantic nationalism in Europe; but they also remind us how, by the objective standards obtaining in any living art, Delacroix is plainly *the* Great Master of illustrative painting in Europe.

He had, indeed, only one peer—Gustave Doré (1833–1883), as towering a figure in the Low Art of illustration as Delacroix was in High Art. Not, of course, that Doré was a rival; so far from competing with Delacroix at inventing High Art forms, Doré borrowed unimaginatively from him. It was early in the 1850s, after making a precocious reputation in cartooning, that Doré made his famous resolution to "illustrate all the classics with woodcuts." Vestiges of caricature persisting in some of his earlier illustrations (Balzac's *Contes drolatiques,* 1855; Sue's *Juif errant,* 1856) soon melted away, and by 1861 Doré's mature style appeared in his illustrated Dante's *Inferno.* This large and lavishly illustrated volume represented an essentially new concept in book publishing, a mass-produced 19th-century version of the medieval "presentation book," and it had immediate and enormous success. In 1862 Doré (unlike Tenniel) ceased drawing directly on the wood block, and had his drawings transferred to it by a photographic process, thus making his production even more prolific; a whole battery of engravers—almost forty of them—worked for him on one great illustrated volume after another, translated into all sorts of languages and distributed all over Europe, with the original illustrations reproduced by zincography: *Don Quixote* (1863), the great Doré *Bible* (1866), Raspe's *Baron Munchausen* (1866), L'Epine's *Days of Chivalry* (1866), La Fontaine's *Fables* (1867), *Popular Fairy Tales* (1871), the works of Rabelais (1873). Thereafter, the volume of Doré's illustrations slacked off, as ambition misdirected him towards a High Art of painting, sculpture and engraving; his great years of accomplishment were over, but there remained from them one of the great expressions of the spirit of their time, place, and nation(29).

The "classics" that Doré resolved to illustrate in woodcut were those Delacroix illustrated in paint: themes of high heroism, noble resolve, romantic idealism. These were not themes that appealed much to the temperament of the English masses, as a comparison of Doré's illustrations with those of Cruikshank and Tenniel would show in a moment; but in France they corresponded perfectly to the central mood of the nation. So did his forms. Though borrowing from Delacroix, Doré complemented rather than competed with him, for whereas Delacroix subtly fused classical and romantic elements into a single personal imaginative expression, Doré preserved their distinct and potentially antithetical qualities. At once more literally classical in detail and more melodramatically romantic in composition, Doré's illustrations represented a balance and reconciliation of opposites which, combined with their themes, made them unrivaled expressions of the traditional spirit of France.

Historians talk of France's traditional dedication to the goddess Reason; but in French history this dedication has been expressed in two very different ways. One has been to Reason in the sense of logic pursued *à l'outrance*, swinging violently from one extreme to another: in polity Saint Louis is succeeded in a generation or two by the amoral Philip Augustus, France passes from anarchy in 1650 to absolute monarchy in 1700 to anarchy again by 1790; in culture, French Late Gothic is the most flamboyant, French 17th-century academic painting the most "academic," French 18th-century radical philosophers the most revolutionary, French neoclassicism the most neoclassic in Europe. But Reason in the medieval sense of *ratio*, of cool ordered balance of opposites, has also been manifested more perfectly in France than anywhere else; this distinctively French *sens de mesure* has long been recognized in the High Gothic of Chartres and Amiens, the painting of Poussin, the architecture of Louis Le Vau, the writing of Boileau, Racine, and Blaise Pascal. Few, however, recognize how this kind of Reason was again embodied during the 1830s through the 1860s in the High Art of Delacroix complemented by the Low Art of Gustav Doré, with illustration as its *raison d'être*.

3. *The German Tradition of Illustration*

Schwind and Richter have achieved—in fairly equal measure—the greatest popularity of all German artists, for their work expresses what Germans most respect, admire, and appreciate: love of solid creature comforts as well as intangible realms of fantasy, precision and imagination, bluff directness and deep introspection, disciplined order and hearty humor—in a word, the German spirit. It was of course because they themselves possessed this German spirit, that they were able to express it in their works. . . . [Friedrich Haack, *Die Kunst des XIX Jahrhunderts*, Esslingen, 1913, pp. 146–48]

This is not perhaps a description of the German spirit that would come most readily to minds formed in the 1920s and -30s, any more than Britain or France in recent times immediately recalls the spirit of Tenniel's or Doré's illustrations; but on reflection we can recognize in 20th-century Germany caricatural distortions of these older qualities, see in Die Brücke and Der Blaue Reiter and Der Neue Sachlichkeit a trick-mirror image of the 19th-century illustrative tradition in which a much better and deeper German national culture was expressed, and thereby begin to reassess the significance of its central figure, Adrian Ludwig Richter (1803–1884).

In Richter all the best qualities of his many German contemporaries were comprehended, balanced and controlled (**30a**). He had the dreamy romanticism of Moritz von Schwind (1804–1871) without all that paraphernalia of medieval melodrama to which Schwind, so typically South German, was prone: no croaking ravens and dank waterfalls, no gloomy forests, cadaverous sages or sexless saints. He had Christian cheerfulness without the bloodless and ostentatious piety of Nazarene painting: you could never imagine Richter doing anything as contrived as Schwind's early *The Arts in the Service of the Mother of God*, let alone the pallid Quattrocento pastiches of Peter von Cornelius (1783–1867) or Johann Friedrich Overbeck (1789–1869).

115

Richter had the same instinctive sense for historical illustration as Adolf von Menzel (1815–1905); as Menzel made his first reputation illustrating Kugler's *History of Brandenburg Prussia* in the 1840s, so Richter made his with a *Historical Picture-Gallery of Saxony* (1834–36) and illustrations for Duller's *History of the German People* (1840). But whereas Menzel in the capital city of Berlin went on to ever more grandiose illustration, translating book illustrations into great painted canvases of Frederick the Great's exploits and thence patriotic glorifications of contemporary German empire builders, Richter in the provincial backwater of his native Dresden lived and died a romantic to the end. No Fine Art search for Reality infected him, so that he was immune alike from the bombast of Anselm Feuerbach (1829–1880) and Franz von Defregger (1835–1921), and the sensual Wagnerian murk later German romanticism sank into with Arnold Böcklin (1827–1901) or Mihály von Munkácsy (1844–1900).

Richter had the same sense for simple outline and clear color that gave such power of romantic evocation to the painting of his older Dresden contemporary Caspar David Friedrich (1774–1840). How beneficial Friedrich's influence on him was we may realize if we compare Richter's 1825 painting of *The Harpist* with his 1837 *Crossing the Elbe at Schreckenstein* (both still in Dresden). Both deal with a theme of the romantic soul's pilgrimage through life inspired by Goethe; but the first still shows clear though vestigial reminiscences of Richter's early training with his father, the engraver Carl August Richter (1778–1848), and specifically his early admiration for the prints of Daniel Chodowiecki (1726–1801). *The Harpist* is fussy in detail and finicky in composition, rather like a painted print, whereas *Crossing the Elbe* has a breadth of vision, compositional balance and color sense that could come only from studying Friedrich and indeed rivals Friedrich's best work in many respects. This influence preserved Richter from the Biedermeier cuteness of anecdotists like Karl Spitzweg (1808–1885) but did not lead to any vaunting yearnings towards Fine Art. Richter never forgot either that his art had a function or what function his talents could best serve:

> If my art never entered among the roses and lilies at the peak of Parnassus [he once wrote], it did bloom beside the roads and on the banks, in the hedges and in the meadows; travellers resting by the wayside were made glad by it, and little children created wreaths out of its flowers. [O. Jahn, *Richter-Album, eine Auswahl*, I, 1855, p. 22]

Not much of an ambition, by modern Fine Art standards. Our age thinks more of an illustrator like Alfred Rethel (1816–1859), who used his illustrative talents to plunge boldly into the struggle to create a brave new world, keeps green the memory of Rethel's *Dance of Death in the Year 1848*, honors him for socially conscious art, even while deploring the *"retardataire* romanticism" of his Charlemagne legend murals in the City Hall of Aachen. Our age makes a game of poking easy fun at illustrations like Richter's Musäus's *Folk Fairy Tales* (1843) (**30b**), *Student Songs* (1844), *Folk Songs* (1846), *Bechstein's Book of Fairy Tales* (1853). But which artist, and which concept of art, did more for the world in the long run?

4. *The American Tradition of Illustration*

From the beginning, conditions in the New World favored arts of illustration. New flora and fauna had to be recorded, voyages' accounts substantiated, settlements described; and when towards the end of the 18th century a High Art of painting began to develop, illustration was natural to it:

> Writing in *The Earthly Paradise* of 18th-century painting . . . Werner Hofmann declared that "English historical painting had made its decision, set its face against the glorifying tradition and rejected the . . . 'universal human.' West's *Death of General Wolfe* . . . and Copley's *Boy Attacked by a Shark* are important documents illustrating this trend." The fact that these painters were American is not mentioned; yet it is immensely important, as illustrating . . . how early a distinctive American tradition was evident. For what characterize both these pictures . . . are . . . communication, reportage. . . . [*The Restless Art*, p. 385]

But "American" paintings like these remain as essentially provincial variants of British 18th-century painting as the first "American" book illustration, a frontispiece to *The Power of Sympathy* attributed to one Samuel Hill in 1789, is plainly a provincial variant of 18th-century British print-making; it took half a century of independent existence for a distinctively American tradition of illustration to take shape.

You see it appearing first in subject matter. In *Patrons and Patriotism* Lillian Miller has noted what a surprisingly large number of painters were active in America during the 1830s, -40s, and -50s and how many of them painted genre scenes in addition to portraits:

David Claypoole Johnson (1799–1865), John Quidor (1801–1881), David Blythe (1815–1865), George Durrie (1820–1863), Richard Caton Woodville (1825–1856), Eastman Johnson (1824–1906), Thomas Waterman Wood (1823–1903), to name only a few (**31a, b**). In this period also Felix Octavius Carr Darley (1822–1888) starts his career as *the* illustrator of American writers: Hawthorne's and James Fenimore Cooper's novels, Washington Irving's *Rip Van Winkle* and *Legend of Sleepy Hollow*, Longfellow's poetry. As yet these illustrators still compose scenes according to the English formula established by Hogarth, carefully balancing and neatly delimiting their stages, filling them with actors who make more or less stereotyped gestures. But already their subject matter is distinctively American. They portray an immense range and variety of episodes, people from all walks of life in all sorts of situations: New York gentlemen and California miners, staid matrons and jolly barmaids, gamblers and preachers and Negro field hands, comedies of manners and burlesque farces, Indians on the prairie and Yankee farmers, frontier brawls and duels for honor, fiddling in barns and minuets in ballrooms. They are concerned far more with people as people than with "class types." Their satire is characteristically broad and boisterous, seldom dry, almost never cynical. They are rarely if ever condescending; they illustrate as participants from within rather than commentators from above. In sum, they are no longer drawing subject matter from a small country with an old, firm, subtly nuanced social structure, but from a vast land affording room for every conceivable sort of social organization, comprising long-settled coastal areas preserving formalities already archaic in the Old World, as well as empty frontier hinterland having no fixed patterns at all, with everywhere ferment and unlimited scope for self-expression.

Hogarth's tight little stage, so admirably suited to the English scene, was never designed to contain such a panorama as this. New forms are needed to serve the distinctive function of American illustration; and as always in living art, those who create them are thereby recognizable as the leaders in their generation. That is why we can objectively say that the two best American painters of the first half of the 19th century were William Sidney Mount (1807–1868) and George Caleb Bingham (1811–1879).

Mount and Bingham, like the great masters of traditional painting in times past, excelled their contemporaries not by doing something original and different, but by doing superlatively what others did only indifferently well (**32a, b**). The nature of their accomplishment is admirably described in Edgar Preston Richardson's *Painting in America* (1956), when he says of Mount that

> all he required for his life's work was what he saw around him in his own little corner of the earth. This does not mean he lacked ambition in his art. He worked hard to discipline his hand and brush to an effective and distinguished style. . . . To expressive drawing he added the charm of luminosity and a transparent simplicity of statement. . . . In *Bargaining for a Horse . . . The Painter's Triumph . . . The Banjo Player . . . Music Hath Charms . . . Eel Spearing at Setauket . . .* a human being or a group of people act a passing moment of their lives before our eyes. They are not isolated figures: their lives are drawn together psychologically into the unity of an action which they feel and share. This is a very rare achievement in genre painting. Minor genre painters make up for its lack by sentimentality or exaggeration or obviousness of anecdote. Mount, like Irving, was never obvious. He was simple, natural, easy, with a lucidity of style that conceals his skill.

and of Bingham:

> his achievement is one of the mysterious phenomena of the age. [Raised in Missouri, to all intents and purposes never seeing an artist until he studied at the Pennsylvania Academy in 1837–38, by 1844 he] produced one of the most original and striking works of its age, *Fur Traders Descending the Missouri* with its archaic strength of drawing, its strange smoky yet brilliant color, its air of solitude and mystery. Bingham seems to have had, at a very early date in his career, the idea of becoming the painter of what he later described as "our social and political characteristics". . . . Bingham saw the grand meaning of the commonplace. What is more extraordinary, he was able to create out of his meager experience of pictures and his own sensibility, a style of great visual poetry . . . a mood of grandeur and solemnity in his work, as if he would say to his fellows: This is a heroic age. . . .

With such forms Mount and Bingham raised their subject matter to a new imaginative level. Both had the same distinctively American range and scope as their contemporaries; the two complimented each other, in that Mount's was drawn from the old settled region around New York, and Bingham's from the Missouri country where raw new villages like Mark Twain's Hannibal sat on the edge of empty lands stretching on to the Pacific, so that between them they covered almost every conceivable social situation. And they diverged from English precedents in the same characteristically American ways;

so, for example, the electioneering Bingham illustrates may be brawling and boisterous, but it is open and free from any of the cynical implications of underhand rigging and hypocrisy in Hogarth's *Chairing the Member,* John Leech's series on Mr. Bagges's campaign, or Ford Madox Brown's *Work.* So Mount's subjects, though never exotic, are never narrow, local, or particular either, but retain always intimations of universality. But in presenting these subjects, Mount and Bingham broke out of the little crowded boxes their contemporaries still employed. In their most characteristic works, like Mount's *Eel Spearing at Setauket* or Bingham's *Fur Traders Descending the Missouri,* they pushed their action into a middle ground and surrounded it with a vast undefined space, and so created a new kind of unlimited format, appropriate to the limitless country they were illustrating.

And with their format they were able to bring out the full imaginative significance of this American subject matter. Whereas the frantic and continuous activity for everyone on Hogarth's stages appropriately expressed the nature of competitive life on a small island, Mount's and Bingham's spacious compositions and statuesque figures illustrate a world with room, and therefore a possibility of leisure, for all. Theirs are images of a land where everyone can work at his own pace, or indeed not work at all, where people while away time whittling at barn doors, playing cards on rafts, dancing, dreaming, spearing eels, hunting, gambling, drifting down lazy rivers in the noonday sun. And if Mount and Bingham impart grandeur and monumentality to such subject matter, it is because they conceive it as symbolic of the American promise of a new kind and quality of life. The world they depict, as Alfred Frankenstein was first to point out (I believe) is something new in history, a paradisial world like Adam's before the Fall, where the curse of work is lifted and existence is no longer a burden but a joy.

Not, of course, that this is the literal Reality of American life in the 1840s and -50s. Then as now individual lives had their full share of misery, crime, worry, squalor, misfortune; but Mount and Bingham were not concerned to illustrate it. Assuming, like all traditional High Artists, that audiences could learn about Reality without help from painters, their concern was so to select and abstract from the world around as to bring out potential ideals, beauties hitherto unrecognized. And in so doing, they created more than mere illustration; they created images of conviction that were the counterpart in painting to what, as we shall see in Part Five, Thomas Jefferson conceived his Classical Revival architecture to be.

One traditional measure of the effectiveness of new High Art forms is the extent to which they are copied; and by this measure Mount and Bingham were unquestionably the leaders of their age, for in the next two generations their illustration became the model both for second- and third-rank painters working to meet popular demand, and for mass-distributed Low Arts. The first kind of influence we see represented best, perhaps, in the painting of J. G. Brown (1831–1913) and Thomas Hovenden (1840–1895), whose immense popularity attests to the lasting appeal of the Mount-Bingham tradition. Brown's success with paintings of the American Boy as a symbol of unbounded opportunity, related to Bingham's raftsmen and the Huckleberry-Finn-Tom-Sawyer image, was such that, as Richardson says, "when he began to paint the ragged newsboys of New York his pictures were so popular that he was never allowed to paint anything else, and so ruined his talent by repetition"; while Hovenden's *Breaking Home Ties,* a pure bit of Mountiana, still won the "most popular picture" award at the Columbian Exposition of 1893 by a wide majority (**24b**).

In the Low Arts, Bingham's and Mount's influence is even more strikingly evident; here the best examples are the mass-produced statuettes of John Rogers (1829–1904) and the lithographed prints mass-distributed by the firm of Nathaniel Currier (1813–1888) and James Merritt Ives (1824–1895).

John Rogers's place in American art history has been badly distorted by ill-considered attempts of contemporary admirers to make a Great Artist of him. We are amused and faintly contemptuous to read in his biography by Chetwood Smith (*Rogers Groups,* 1934) of James Jackson Jarves's praising his "dramatic power . . . picturesqueness of composition . . . naturalness, harmony . . . unity. . . ." of Ralph Waldo Emerson's applying to his statuettes Michelangelo's remark about Tanagra figurines, " 'were they but marble, woe to the Antique' "; of the writer in *Farm and Fireside* for 1874 who attributed to John Rogers "all the excellencies . . . of Hogarth . . . Canova . . . Michelangelo . . . Reynolds. . . ." For in fact Rogers was the archetypal Low Artist—and to give him credit, he himself knew it and rarely pretended to be anything else. Like all the greatest Low Artists—Bewick and Cruikshank, Tenniel and Doré—he was an innovator in technique, not an inventor of imaginative new forms. After a peripatetic early life wandering about his native New England and the Midwest, which included stints in railroad machine shops in New Hampshire and Hannibal, Missouri, Rogers did study sculpture a few months in Florence with Edward Spence, but on returning to settle in

121

Chicago he made no attempt to establish himself as a sculptor and continued working at mechanical jobs until, in 1859, a little plaster group of *Checker Players* made more or less as a hobby won a prize at a local fair, and he got the idea

> that if he could turn out the casts at an initial cost to himself which would permit of their being sold at a really cheap price, the public would buy them in large quantities. . . . He was determined that his visions should not be imprisoned in costly marbles and bronzes in the parlours of rich men, but that clothed in simple plaster of a lovely soft grey color they should adorn peaceful unpretentious homes. . . . [Chetwood Smith, *Rogers Groups*]

Moving to New York in 1860, he perfected a technique of casting intricate forms from clay molds, began advertising parlor statuettes by mail, and soon had a huge and thriving business operating out of a large studio on Broadway—for Rogers possessed in equal measure the other essential of the successful Low Artist, an infallible instinct for divining the highest common factor of public taste (33a). In forms that were three-dimensional approximations of Mount's and Bingham's illustrations, he cast the same distinctly American themes: leisure and the good life in the American Eden (e.g., *Peddler at the Fair, Frolic at the Old Homestead,* four versions of *Checkers Down at the Farm;* even Civil War themes like *The Town Pump* that first gave him national recognition were almost invariably leisure moments), self-reliant individualism (*Fetching the Doctor,* with the little boy as hero, *Fighting Bob*), simple self-sufficient Arcadian life on the Jeffersonian model (*School Days, The Mock Trial, Tap on the Window, The Favoured Scholar, Weighing the Baby*), and so on.

It is no accident that posing *tableaux vivants* of Rogers groups was a most popular parlor game in the 1860s and -70s, that Rogers was elected to the National Academy in 1863, and that his groups won medals at the Philadelphia Centennial of 1876 and the Columbian Exposition of 1893 in Chicago; for he plainly perpetuated the same traditional concept of what art is and artists do that inspired the American Art-Union in the 1840s and the illustrations of Mount and Bingham, and of course all the great illustrative art of history. In that sense, perhaps, admirers of Rogers's "greatness" were not wholly wrong, only misguided as to its level. And when the popularity of Rogers groups began to fade in the late 1880s and -90s, it was not because this kind of art had lost public appeal, but only that the appropriate medium for its mass dissemination was changing. For example, the Rogers group of Lincoln, Stanton, and Grant in *Council of War* (53a) was very obviously what D. W. Griffith used as the basic conception for his scene of Lincoln drafting the Emancipation Proclamation in his 1915 movie *Birth of a Nation;* Rogers groups, that is, did not die, but only moved—from parlor tables onto movie screens.

Quite as plainly, Currier & Ives prints embodied the same concept of what art is, and theirs is similarly archetypal Low Art—technical innovation, forms borrowed from High Art, taste more collective than personal (33b). Not that Nathaniel Currier, who founded the business in 1834, invented lithography (Aloys Senefelder of Bavaria had done that in 1798) or even first introduced it to America (it had appeared in Boston as early as the 1820s); his innovation was to use it for making pictures that could be framed and hung as a cheap substitute for oil paintings, instead of merely a substitute for broadsheets in woodcut or satirical prints engraved in copper. That innovation did not happen all at once, of course. Currier's first successful print, of the *Steamboat Lexington Disaster* in 1841, is plainly a variant of the kind of broadsheets put out to announce special events since the 16th century, and for the next few years a high percentage of Currier prints still consisted of similar topical subjects, along with what were essentially social and political cartoons, like the famous *Drunkard's Progress* of 1845. The next step was to what were essentially book illustrations printed as single sheets, some of them from recent books (*Uncle Tom and Little Eva* was a great success), others of truly hoary antiquity, like *The Bad Man at the Hour of Death* (23c).

In the course of the 1850s, however (possibly due to James Ives's influence after he became Currier's partner in 1852), lithographed reproductions of illustrative easel paintings became the firm's chief stock in trade. Sometimes existing paintings were copied, and sometimes paintings done especially for Currier & Ives by a stable of painters who made all or part of their living in this way, usually by serving a particular area of interest: so M. Louis Maurer (1832–1932) supplied pictures of racehorses and Arthur Fitzwilliam Tait (1819–1905) sporting scenes, James E. Butterworth (1817–c. 1870) marine subjects, George Durrie (1820–1863) New England genre and landscape, Fanny Palmer (1812–1876) domestic anecdote, Thomas Worth (1834–c. 1900) folk humor. In retrospect, perhaps the most important of them was Charles Parsons (1821–1910), who began his career as a

Currier & Ives contributor and went on to become art editor for *Harper's Weekly,* where he was instrumental in encouraging such major later 19th-century figures as Thomas Nast, E. W. Kemble, and Howard Pyle.

But whatever their source, all Currier & Ives prints were chosen on a basis of broad public appeal; and that is their special significance for American cultural history. For even better than Rogers groups they provide a record of what the average American thought beautiful, significant and valid in the years from 1850 through the 1880s; and they show that during all this time of urbanization, of labor unrest, of war and industrialization, his image remained rooted in the soil. If you knew America only through Currier & Ives prints, you would suppose that almost all Americans in those years lived on rural farms in picturesque old 18th-century or Colonial houses, there enjoying Adamite leisure to go hunting, fishing, camping, *Sugaring in the Bush;* that Washington was still as universally deified in the late 1870s as when he made his triumphal procession to New York in 1789 (Currier & Ives prints of his exploits and Rogers's statuette of him were best-selling items for years after the Philadelphia Centennial of 1876). The world of Currier & Ives is, in short, still the paradisial ideal of Mount's and Bingham's illustrations. This is evidence, of course, for the power of that imagery; but it also shows how tenacious was the American dream, how powerful and deep the conviction that America was a different sort of nation from others. And if the popularity of Currier & Ives prints dwindled steadily from the 1880s until the business was liquidated in 1906, that did not mean an end to the ideal represented, only that (as in the case of the Rogers groups) the ideal migrated to hoardings outside the new movie theatres, and to the movies themselves. One of the first of all American motion pictures, *Washday Troubles* of 1895, simply picks up on celluloid where Thomas Worth's *Darktown Antics* series for Currier & Ives left off in the late 1880s; and for twenty years thereafter you can trace the influence of Currier & Ives prints on American movie shorts, for the very good reason that the world of Currier & Ives was a world that the great mass of Americans considered a valid ideal down into the 1920s. No American political history can be properly understood without keeping in mind the culture expressed in Low Arts like Rogers groups and Currier & Ives.

But after the Civil War an increasing number of Americans began to call the validity of that ideal into question; how and why is recorded in the last generation of American traditional High Art illustration.

Elsewhere* I have described how the leaders of this generation, Winslow Homer (1836–1910) and Thomas Eakins (1844–1916), became psychologically and physically alienated from American society, and how this alienation was reflected in an increasing preponderance of themes of isolation and remoteness in their work. The same holds for others, such as later works of Eastman Johnson (1824–1906) or the "cowboy painters" Frederic Remington (1861–1909) and Charles M. Russell (1864–1926). Not that the subject matter of post–Civil War American illustration was basically different from the prewar years; essentially, it still has the distinctively American preoccupation with themes of leisure, of sports, of the free individual in a spacious land. The difference is in setting (32a, b; 34a, b; 35b). Now free individuals are on the defensive. To enjoy American freedom they have had to leave the mainstream and find backwaters of American society, areas distant from post–Civil War currents of urbanization and industrialization either geographically (remote prairies, seacoasts, mountains, Caribbean islands) or demographically (outlaws, Negroes, decaying genteel classes); and even there civilization is constantly creeping up on them. So Remington described (in *Collier's* for May 18, 1905) how he left upstate New York for Montana in 1880 to find the free life of the West, only to be told by an old wagon freighter,

> "There is no more West. In a few years the railroad will come."
> . . . He made a new point of view for me. . . . I saw men all
> ready swarming onto the land. I knew the derby hat, the smoking chimneys, the cord-binders, and the thirty-day notes were
> upon us in a restless surge. I knew the wild riders and the
> vacant land were about to vanish forever . . . and. . . . I began to try to record some facts around me. . . .

To express this subtle change of emphasis, High Artists in this generation employ new forms; in place of the serene classical clarity so appropriate to Mount's and Bingham's images of values and ideals central to their society, they adopt sketchy Academic Impressionist brushwork equally appropriate to images of values and ideals becoming increasingly peripheral and unstable. Any random comparisons of typical works will make the point. Look, for example, at *Raftsmen Playing Cards* (32a) or *Eel Spearing at Setauket* (32b) and then at Eakins's *Max Schmitt in a Single Scull* (34a) or Homer's *Gulf*

* *The Restless Art*, pp. 137–40; also "Nineteenth-century American Painting," in *The Arts in America*, II, Charles Scribner's Sons, New York, 1969, pp. 247, 273.

Stream (**34b**). In all of them, the same vast seas and skies; but whereas in the first pair the waters are tranquil, the skies sheltering, and everyone at ease in Zion, in the second the mood is hunted and haunted. So far from being pleasure craft, scull and fishing boats are means of psychological and physical escape. Temporarily they float in calm, like Huck Finn and Nigger Jim on their raft thinking how "it was kind of solemn, drifting down the big, still river, laying on our backs looking up at the stars"; but the world around is troubled and treacherous now, threatening them on all sides. Schmidt's river is hemmed in by the crisscrossing bridges of that urban civilization from which he can never long escape; sharks and shipwreck and starvation await the Negro, just as slavery waits on the banks for Jim, and the gentilities of Widow Douglas and Aunt Sally for Huck. In the world Homer and Eakins painted, like the world Twain wrote about in *Huckleberry Finn* (1884), all the old values were threatened (**34a**). As their traditional concept of what art is was being eaten away by the new ideas of Fine Art coming over from Europe, so Huck and Jim fell foul of the Duke and Dauphin, symbols of European culture with their superior airs and their fractured Shakespearean "art." Twain is the exact literary counterpart of Eakins and Homer. Like them he held that the artist's first duty is not to create a Work of Art but to meet public demand. Like them he dealt with traditional American themes of free individuals in a vast and varied world. Like them he revealed in his style how those old ideals were in flux—his short quick sentences and strings of spiky Anglo-Saxon words are the literary parallel to Homer's later sketches. Like them, he grew increasingly alienated from fashionable art trends. Like theirs, his characters are old American individualists fighting an increasingly difficult battle to preserve their old way of life against hostile odds, whether Huck Finn resisting shoes, *The Innocents Abroad* European "culture," or *A Connecticut Yankee* the whole feudal system. And all their characters, literary or painted alike, enjoy only momentary and illusory escape. Jim becomes a free man, but *The Gulf Stream* suggests what freedom will mean to him. Huck, in the last words of the book, announces "I got to light out. . . ." but where will he go? The world of Bingham and Mount, the world Twain and Homer and Eakins grew up in, is gone; and so too, with their generation, is the traditional High Art of American illustration. Illustration will go on, to be sure; but everywhere it will take new forms and be concerned with different things. That process begins in the 1890s.

1. TYPES OF LOW ARTIST

(a) The 12th-century German miniaturist Rufillus of Weissenau "wrapped up in his work"—an initial in his manuscript of "The Passion of Saint Martin," formerly in the Hofbibliothek, Sigmaringen. Ms. 9, fol. 244 recto.

(b) The 20th-century cartoonist H. C. (Bud) Fisher comparably involved in *his* work—a *Mutt and Jeff* strip for August 20, 1919.

Common to these and all Low Artists is a clearly defined but quite narrow function in society, and consequent anonymity; addressed to a lowest common audience denominator, Low Art affords little scope for expressing individual personality, "personal appearances" like these being rare and often as not whimsical exceptions, without bearing on intrinsic significance of the work.

My Goodness, but Isn't Mutt the Chummy Old Thing

2. TYPES OF HIGH ARTIST

(a) *The Building of Constantinople,* tapestry designed c. 1622 by Peter Paul Rubens for King Louis XIII of France. Philadelphia Museum of Art. The kneeling figure has been identified (by John Coolidge, *Journal of the Society of Architectural Historians,* XXIV, 1965, pp. 310–12) as a portrait of Salomon de Brosse (c. 1565–1626), and the scene (by Catherine Sweeney Scott, *ibid.,* XXV, 1966, pp. 212–15) as an allegorical allusion to Henry IV's making Paris into a "new Rome" as Constantine had Byzantium (the architect holds plans of the Pantheon, comparing them to the new Church of the Holy Apostles in the background).

(b) Thomas Cole, *The Architect's Dream* (*Homage to Ithiel Town*), 1840. The Toledo (Ohio) Museum of Art. Though Low and High Artists fulfill the same social functions, High Artists fulfill them more competently and imaginatively, invent newer and more appropriate forms, with more personal expression; so Rubens's painting and de Brosse's architecture are distinguished by "style" from comparable work by anonymous artisans or other High Artists. *The Architect's Dream* marks a transitional point. Though still serving society in the sense that the painter's purpose is to give fame rather than get it and the architect's to choose historical architectural forms for symbolic purposes according to their use, the Artist is already put on a pedestal, as a Great Man.

3. TYPES OF "FINE" ARTIST

(a) A connoisseur (*Portrait of a Man*), painted about 1550 by Agnolo Bronzino. National Gallery of Canada, Ottawa.

(b) *Triumphs of Art,* painted about 1840 by Paul Delaroche. Detail of "The Hemicycle" in the Palais des Beaux-Arts, Paris.

(c) Picasso posing in Paris some time after his liberation by the United States Army, 1945.

This connoisseur ("knowing one") is still only an *amateur d'art,* not yet the amateur artist his kind will become (Rowlandson's *Dr. Syntax,* 40b, exemplifies that type). But the statuette on his table already embodies a new concept of Fine Art divorced from function and valuable exclusively according to "rules of taste" defined by the connoisseur himself; by so defining what Art is, he dictates a new role to Artists—no longer primarily builders or carvers or doers of anything, but "knowers" like himself, admired more for their "genius" than for what they do. So by the 19th century Delaroche conceives Ictinus, Apelles, and Phidias on a dais, Gothic Art and Greek Art (L.), Roman Art and Renaissance Art (R.) all as immobile figures waiting for whatever laurels the capricious goddess of Art cares to bestow. And so too the contemporary Fine Artist, divorced from life and serving no social function, no longer giving fame by what he does but getting it for what he is, dances attendance on her whims. Wearing her laurels, today's favorite struts and frets upon his little stage; tomorrow's will be different —on grounds no better and no worse.

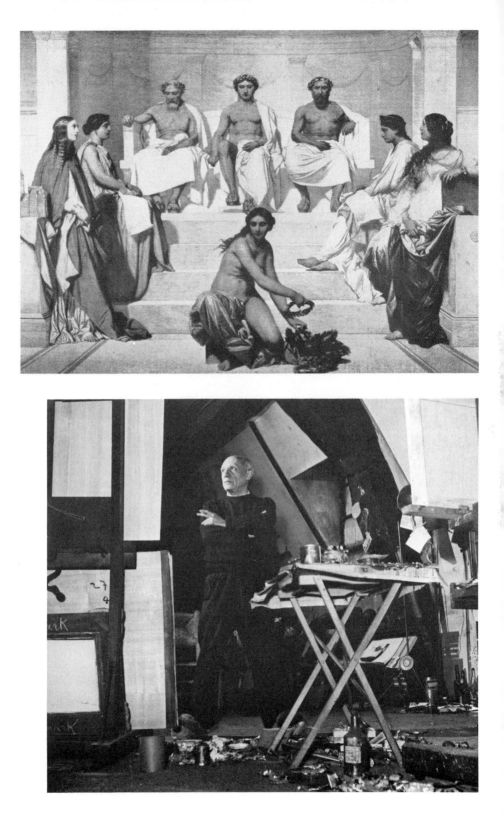

HERAKLES UND ANTAIOS
KRATER DES EUPHRONIOS
PARIS, LOUVRE

4. HIGH ART AND FINE ART IN ANTIQUITY

(a) Decoration of a 5th-century B.C. Greek *krater*, with scene of Herakles (Hercules) wrestling the giant Antaios, drawn unrolled. The Louvre. Typical High Art, fulfilling social functions comparable to those of prehistoric pottery, but in a manner distinctive not only of classical Greek civilization but of the particular artist who signed it—Euphronios.

(b) The Lycurgus Cup, 4th century A.D. British Museum. Insofar as this decoration has a "subject," Hercules may be represented. With iridescent body glowing green or red in different lights and intricate silver overlace, this piece requires more technical skill than the preceding; but having no discernible social function, cannot be compared with it or anything else except in reference to some purely subjective taste now long forgotten. Typical Fine Art of late Antiquity.

132

5. LOW, HIGH, AND FINE ART IN ARCHITECTURE

The local craftsmen who built the first church at Saint Laurent, Ile d'Orléans, Quebec, in 1695 (left) followed thoroughly traditional forms long established in France —spires and fieldstone walls like these appear on old prints of Charlemagne's 8th-century abbey church of Saint Riquier, for instance. Simply fulfilling a social function, without originality or invention, it is typical Low Architecture.

In the early 19th century this type of church was deliberately revived as a symbolic form to proclaim the idea of French survival in an English-speaking continent, and thus became a model for dozens of parish churches built during the 1830s and -40s in the diocese of Quebec by its official architect, Thomas Baillairgé (1791–1859). By subtle proportioning and judicious integration of details from other traditions in the Province, Baillairgé created original and distinctive

versions of this old type—typical works of High Architecture.

It was Baillairgé's follower Raphael Giroux (1804–1869) who built the new church of Saint Laurent in 1864, seen here beside its predecessor just after completion. Already in his work a shift of emphasis is apparent; far more interested in aesthetic effect through picturesqueness and scholarly detail than in fulfilling the functional need of making an image of French-Canadian ideals, Giroux's work is well on the way to becoming Fine Art. Its design thus becomes a matter of connoisseurs' taste and soon will be criticized for not being elaborate enough; then in the mid-20th century taste will swing around, connoisseurs will regret demolishing the old church, and will build replicas of it on the island as Precious Objects for contemplation.

6. LIMITATIONS
OF PHOTOGRAPHY

(a) So-called Venus of Laussel, presumed to be a fertility fetish from the prehistoric Solutrean period; height 17¾ inches. Bordeaux Museum. The nickname is indicative of typical confusion—whatever it was made for, this was certainly never a Work of Art like Roman copies of Greek Aphrodite figures.

(b) *Self-Portrait* by Thomas Smith, New England, second half 17th century. Worcester (Mass.) Art Museum.

Conventional notions of photography forcing art to "retreat from likeness" in the later 19th century are refuted by the fact of how few traditional functions of art photography could perform. Photographs of a nude could never serve the functions of the Venus of Laussel, for such distortion in relative size of parts to bring out an abstract idea of fertility would be impossible in photography. Even such Low Art versions of portraiture as Thomas Smith's attempt to represent "the whole man" are beyond photography's effective range. Photography could compete only with those literal transcript of nature which no High Art and only a few Low Arts (e.g., pornography, topography) ever attempted; it was Fine Art dedicated to Reality, that photography competed with, and so from the 1840 on Fine Art borrows forms steadily from it to keep abreast of "photographic reality."

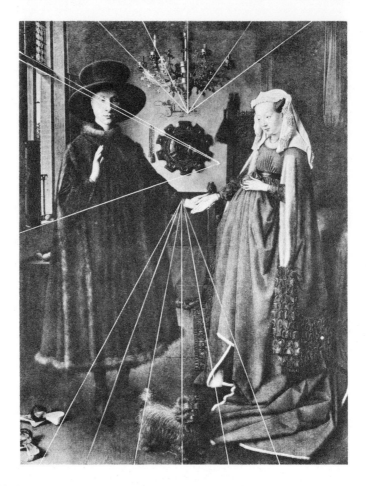

7. PRE-RAPHAELITE PHOTOGRAPHIC REALISM

(a) Perspective analysis of Jan van Eyck's *Arnolfini Wedding*, 1434. National Gallery, London.

(b) *Ye Ladye of Shalott*, composite photograph by Henry Peach Robinson, 1861. Gernsheim Collection, Humanities Research Center, University of Texas at Austin.

(c) *Ophelia*, a "composite painting" by John Everett Millais, 1853, figure and background being painted in entirely different times, places, and circumstances. Tate Gallery, London.

So far from Italian Quattrocento painting, the basic influence on early Pre-Raphaelite painters was photography. If they admired the minutely

detailed oil painting of 15th-century Flander it was because these Flemish "primitive: looked so "photographic," being not only "ph tographically detailed" but made up (as anal sis of the *Arnolfini Wedding* shows) like typic: composite photographs from the 1850s, of a semblages of objects depicted at different time and angles. It follows that while at first sigl Robinson's photograph might seem to be imitat ing Millais's painting, in fact only the subje: (if that) need have been borrowed, the tech nique of both works deriving from composit photographs of the 1840s—Robinson thereb typifying how Art Photography has alway imitated advance-guard painting forms then selves derived from earlier photographs, an exemplified Plato's "false art . . . thrice re moved from truth."

137

8. PHOTOGRAPHIC REALITY IN COURBET'S EARLY PAINTING

(a) Detail of *The Stonebreakers*, 1849. Formerly Dresden Gallery, destroyed 1945.

(b) Cartoon of Courbet's 1850 painting *Peasants of Flagey Returning from the Fair* mocking the curious stiffness of Courbet's new style as technical incompetence. Actually, its jibe at Courbet's *verité vraie* pinpoints the reason: his doctrinaire search for Reality is leading him to copy exactly the stiffly posed figures of early long-exposure photography.

9. PHOTOGRAPHIC REALITY
IN COURBET'S LATER PAINTING

(a) Courbet's *Village Maidens*, 1853. New York, Metropolitan Museum. As long as photographs lacked capacity for deep backgrounds, they commonly posed groups in one narrow plane against flat painted backdrops (when they did not resort to composite photographs), and it is precisely this effect that we see here —four figures and dog lined up in a narrow plane and "pasted" against a flat background, so that dog and cows, for example, are in no conceivable formal or spatial relationship to each other.

(b) *Portrait of Max Buchon*, 1858. Vevey Museum. If this seems less stiff and detailed, more like brush-stroke Impressionism, than Courbet's earlier painting, it is not because he was ceasing to employ photographically "realistic" forms, but because photography was developing new forms for him to employ—more relaxed poses and broader effects made possible by faster emulsions during the early 1850s.

10. (a) Courbet's *Dressing the Bride,* 1865–
70. Smith College Museum of Art, Northamp-
ton, Mass. Here is reflected, in its more spontaneous composition and rough forms (is it
really unfinished, as has been assumed?), effects from early instantaneous indoor photographs, such as Nadar's early experiments
with artificial illumination in the mid-1850s.

(b) *Grande Vague, Cette,* by Gustave Le
Gray (1820–1882), 1856. Courbet's series of
"impressionistic" wave studies in the early
1870s is almost indistinguishable (in black-
and-white reproduction) from such composite
photographs as this—necessarily composite, of
course, because with existing emulsions the
difference in light values between sea and sky
was too great for them to be photographed together.

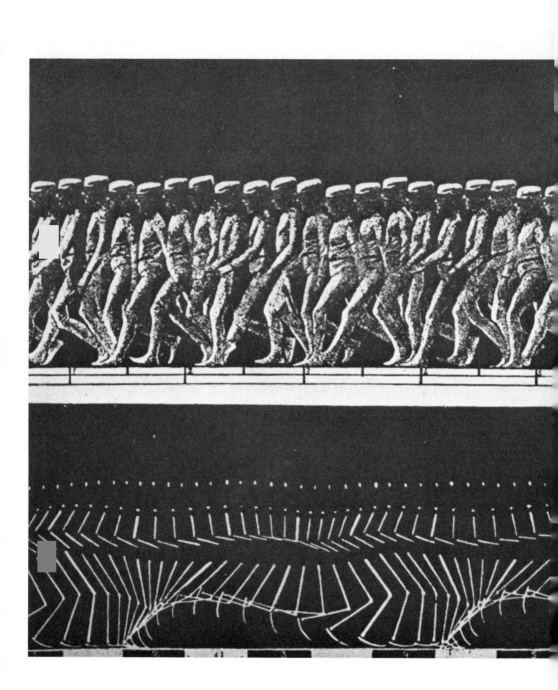

11. THE SEEN AND THE UNSEEN:

RETREAT FROM LIKENESS IN PHOTOGRAPHY AND FINE ART

(a) Study by Etienne Jules Marey, in *La Nature*, 1883. If advance-guard painting after Courbet seemed to move steadily away from what the eye sees, one major reason was that from the 1860s on, photography began to reveal forms never seen by the human eye before. In the 1870s photographers like Eadweard Muybridge and Marey were perfecting devices to "stop" motion, and by the 1880s were publishing them. Studies like these are examples.

(b) Thomas Eakins, *The Fairman Rogers Four-in-Hand*, 1879. Philadelphia Museum of Art. The horses closely followed Eadweard Muybridge's "stopped action" photographs. But on painting the wheels equally "stopped," Eakins discovered that, so far from suggesting motion, the new forms froze it; he therefore repainted them according to old High Art conventions (e.g., in Velasquez' blurred spinning wheel in his 1650 *Las Hilanderas*). Fine Artists, however, who had no purpose except the Reality of their paintings themselves, copied such forms literally—Seurat's frozen *Grande Jatte* (*The Restless Art*, p. 201) and Duchamp's *Nude Descending a Staircase* (*The Restless Art*, p. 323) being typical results.

12. UT PICTURA PHOTOGRAPHIS:
PHOTOGRAPHIC
POST-IMPRESSIONISM

(a) *City Hall, Toulouse,* daguerreotyped by Bathélemy-Urbain Bianchi, 1840. George Eastman House, Rochester. In these blurred motions and ghostly empty streets are intimations of Impressionism to come in the 1860s and -70s; in elimination of all but the world's most immobile and permanent aspects, of Cézanne's search for "significant form" in the late 1870s and -80s.

(b) "Significant form"—three-dimensional depth on a flat surface—being found by a young lady with a stereoscopic photograph viewer, c. 1875.

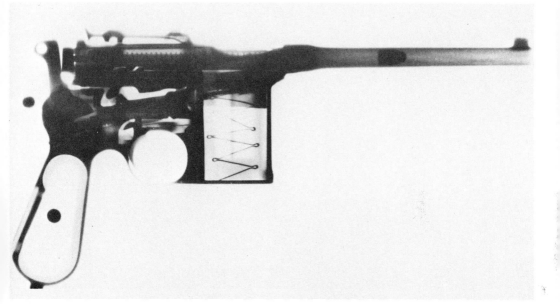

13. THE NEW VISION

(a) Bullet passing down barrel of automatic pistol, X-ray flash picture. Speed photography creates whole galleries of new images; in due course copied by Fine Artists as ends in themselves.

(b) Cecil Beaton's portrait of W. H. Auden, 1963. A typical example of Fine Art photography. Like Robinson's a century earlier (7b), it represents a Reality thrice removed from the real—inspired by Cubist paintings themselves based on Marey's and Muybridge's new photographic forms of the 1870s.

14. Brass relief ornament attached to Salamander safe manufactured by Evans & Watson of Philadelphia in 1854.

15. ARTS OF DECORATIVE IDENTIFICATION

(a) Colchester Jar, found near Colchester, Vermont. Though shape and decoration are determined by mimetic imitation of forms derived from a prototype in wicker, they serve to identify function. Such a mimetic design is universal; jars not very different from this pre-Columbian Amerind work can be found in prehistoric India, prehistoric China, primitive Africa, and so forth.

(b) Glass vessel with stamp of Thomas Great, apothecary and keeper of the Red Lion Inn, Colchester, England, c. 1720. The shape is determined by mimetic imitation of leather prototype; the seal provides personal indentification.

147

16. ILLUSTRATIVE DECORATION

(a) Knife sheaths made in Germany, c. 1570. Old and New Testament scenes on opposite sides, the narrow edges (not shown) bearing decorative panels of kings and queens in rinceaux. "Irrelevant" by modern doctrinaire design standards, but highly relevant in the sense of relating the object to life. Reminder of the basic nature and purpose of living (in this case, the Christian hope of Heaven), such decoration raises objects above the merely utilitarian and materialistic level, and by humanizing them enriches life.

(b) Cherrywood side table, made in Connecticut c. 1790, with inlaid patriotic and Masonic symbols. Decorations similarly enriching life, though with a different concept of its ultimate significance.

17. EARLY AMERICAN SCULPTURE

(a) Detail from sarcophagus-type tomb of Mrs. Richard Bulkeley, Old Saint Paul's burial ground, Halifax, Nova Scotia, 1775.

(b) Judge (?) carved in oak, from furniture or wall paneling. American, c. 1700.

18. Designs for salt and pepper shakers from the 1960s. One (salt) is mass-produced by machine, coldly utilitarian. Another (pepper), similarly mass-produced, is commercially decorated to identify function and humanize use. The other two are decorated in accordance with contemporary Fine Art fashion—its forms borrowed in this case from "pop" art. They thus become Works of Art, but also meaningless and misleading, for both have exactly the same decoration, and both are labeled "soup."

19. TRADITIONAL AND FINE ARTS OF AUTOMOBILE DESIGN

(a) The general design of this 1932 Chrysler is typical of the period 1931–34, still preserving strong vestiges of the first mimetic automobile design which reproduced in the new medium forms typical of the buggy.

(b) The 1946–48 Chrysler has unified many elements—headlights and hood ornament and fenders all flow together—but still the evolution is consistent, and there is plenty of chrome serving no strict functional purpose, simply suggesting speed and other qualities desirable in the user's eyes.

20. Stock-car team members posing behind the machine they have adapted for racing and decorated. However vigorously they might deny the fact, they are artists practicing the traditional arts of decorating to identify function and humanize artifacts.

21. Refrigerator designed c. 1928 in "colonial" style. Orthodox design theorists reject with horror the idea of a refrigerator resembling a Queen Anne chest. For them, one kind of object ought never to resemble another; decoration and shape must always grow out of Realities of physical function, structure, and materials. But this of course means that no object can possibly be made meaningful in any objective, communicative, or symbolic sense; all must be existentialist creations existing in, by, and for themselves alone. How then distinguish between mere artifacts and Works of Art? Erwin Panofsky in *Meaning in the Visual Arts* (*Papers in and on Art History*, 1955, pp. 2, 322) explains how there are "certain man-made objects to which we assign a more than utilitarian value," which "demand to be experienced aesthetically." What he does not explain is, who are the "we" that "assign more than utilitarian value"? On what grounds do "we" assign it? By whom and on what principle is the difference to be determined between objects that "demand to be experienced aesthetically" and those that do not? Extraordinary that on such shaky foundations the whole 20th-century theory of decorative arts should depend, and all historic decoration be dismissed as having no relation to modern life!

2. INTRINSIC AND EXTRINSIC DECORATIVE SYMBOLISM IN ARCHITECTURE

(a) While consistently maintaining that architectural forms grow out of and must retain meaning, Wright steadily moved from early intrinsic expression, influenced by Arts and Crafts aesthetics and "realism," to more extrinsically symbolic shapes. In his campus for Florida Southern College in Lakeland, designed in the late 1940s, and particularly in this Annie Pfeiffer Chapel, both kinds of symbolism are present—intrinsic suggestions of "spiritual" and "mystic" in the deliberately disguised structural system; a contrast of extrinsically significant shapes among a chapel so designed, an obviously geometric administration building ("rational" thought [!]), and between them a library combining elements of both.

(b) If this Chinese Village Restaurant in Victoria, British Columbia, recalls Frank Lloyd Wright, it is not because of any imitation but simply that, like Wright, the designer (Ted Bowers, 1967) was concerned first with a meaningful shape to identify his building's function, and secondly with forms typical of the region (in this case, the Arts and Crafts vernacular of the Canadian West Coast).

23. THE TRADITIONAL LOW ART OF ILLUSTRATION

(a) Printed page from the *Biblia Pauperum*, 2d half of 15th century. Devils confront dying man with his sins while saints comfort another (in "speech balloons," deriving from scripts carried by actors in contemporary plays). A Low Art version of contemporary High Art styles of Flemish masters.

(b) *The Wicked Statesman, or The Traitor to his Country, at the Hour of Death,* engraving from cover of the Massachusetts Almanack for 1774. Same theme, with Death figure interpolated from medieval *Three Living and Three Dead* imagery; but "sin" is now more political than moral, and the High Art model is 18th-century Grand Style portraiture.

156

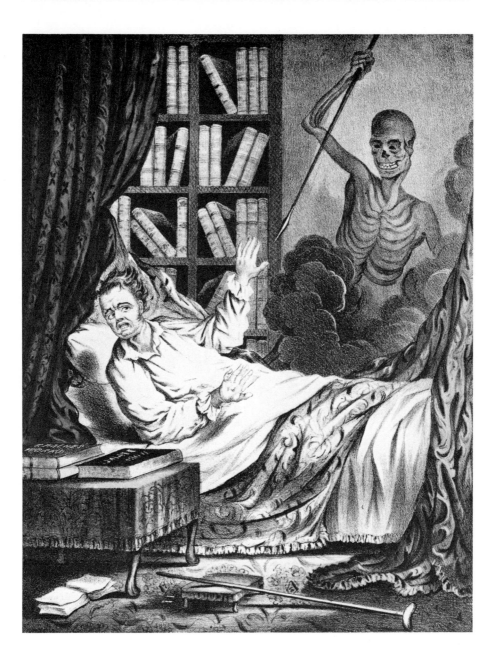

(c) *The Bad Man at the Hour of Death*, Currier &
Ives lithograph, c. 1858. Same theme, but intellectual
sin, apparently; a volume of *T. Paine's Works* is seen
at the bedside. The High Art model is something like
"Gothick" romanticism of Fuseli or Benjamin West.

24. THE ANECDOTAL TRADITION IN ENGLISH ILLUSTRATION

(a) *The Industrious 'Prentice Mayor of London,* plate from Hogarth's *Industry and Idleness* series. On a tightly balanced stage crowded with busy figures, Hogarth illustrates his familiar preaching of the politically just society where rank depends on merit, not birth.

(b) Thomas Hovenden, *Breaking Home Ties,*
1890. Philadelphia Museum of Art. Still this
late a popularity prize at the 1893 Columbian
Exposition in Chicago was won by this Irish-
American painter's work, typically Hogarthian
both in composition and theme—the "Industrious 'Prentice" in American costume, every figure
on stage acting busily. The tradition descended
through an innumerable series of intermediaries, and from this point went straight into the
movies.

(a) This *Brown Bear* from Thomas Bewick's illustrations to *General History of
Quadrupeds* (1790) shows the greater
accuracy of reproduction his new woodcut technique made possible.

(b) Characteristic of the little vignettes
scattered through books illustrated by
Bewick in the late 18th and early 19th
centuries, and a typical Low Art version
of romantic themes from High Art painting.

(c) A typical woodcut by Edward Calvert,
exemplifying his early creed, quoted in Raymond Lister's 1962 study of him: "I have a
fondness for the earth, and rather a Phrygian
mood of regarding it. I feel a yearning to
see the glades and nooks receding like vistas
into the gardens of heaven." Later Calvert
turned toward Fine Art, wrote endless
dreary treatises about form and color, produced little more of significance.

(a) George Cruikshank, illustrating "A Lay of St. Nicholas," from Richard Harris Barham's *Ingoldsby Legends* (1837 ff.): "The Fiend made a grasp, the Abbot to clasp / But St. Nicholas lifted his holy toe / And, just in the nick, let fly with a kick / On his elderly Namesake, he made him let go." In the *Ingoldsby Legends* the medieval past is adapted to serve as a symbol of British national continuity as it was in Gothic Revival architecture, or in *Punch;* both style and spirit here closely resemble *Punch*'s traditional cover by Doyle (65c). (For Cruikshank's typical genre illustration, see *The Restless Art,* p. 107).

AN ENCHANTED PLACE   175

"Well, it's not as grand as a King," said Christopher Robin, and then, as Pooh seemed disappointed, he added quickly, "but it's grander than Factors."
"Could a Bear be one?"
"Of course he could!" said Christopher Robin. "I'll make you one." And he took a stick and touched Pooh on the shoulder, and said, "Rise, Sir

Pooh de Bear, most faithful of all my Knights."
So Pooh rose and sat down and said "Thank you," which is the proper thing to say when you have been made a Knight, and he went into a dream again, in which he and Sir Pomp and Sir Brazil and Factors lived together with a horse, and were faithful Knights (all except Factors, who looked after the horse) to Good King Christopher Robin . . . and every now and then he shook his head, and said to himself "I'm not getting it right." Then he began

(b) Ernest Shepard, page from A. A. Milne's *The House at Pooh Corner* (1928). The medieval motif continued, with the same typical English whimsy in both text and illustrations.

27. PAINTERS TURNED ILLUSTRATORS

(a) John Tenniel, illustration from *Alice in Wonderland* (1865). Modeling his Duchess on a famous 16th-century portrait by Quentin Massys (cf. Martin Gardner's *Annotated Alice*, 1960), Tenniel mocks the pretensions of the Fine Art of Painting (including his own early efforts), just as Lewis Carroll's text mocks the pretensions of the Fine Art of Literature. It is no accident that the Mouse's tale from *Alice* is the best-known English example of emblematic or figured verse, that ancient kind of Fine Art which Optatianus practiced at Constantine's court.

(b) Edward Lear in his *Nonsense* books (here, *Nonsense Botany*) like Tenniel and Carroll satirizes not only the Fine Art of Painting he himself practiced, and of Poetry, but also the solemn pretensions of contemporary biology to comprehend all life and history through Darwin's *Origin of Species* and *Descent of Man*.

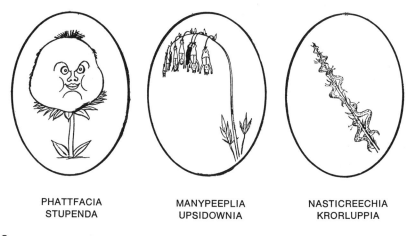

PHATTFACIA
STUPENDA

MANYPEEPLIA
UPSIDOWNIA

NASTICREECHIA
KRORLUPPIA

28. (a) Arthur Hughes, "Little Diamond Carried by Lady North Wind," from George Macdonald's *At the Back of the North Wind* (1870). As an illustrator, Hughes was forced by his medium to eliminate the excessive detail and sententiousness featured by the Pre-Raphaelites (North Wind's neck, jaw, and flowing line), giving his work distinctive style; what Auden says of Macdonald applies equally to Hughes's illustrations for him: "the gift of mythopoeic imagination . . . seems to have no necessary connection with the gift of verbal expression or the power to structure experience . . . his appeal transcends all highbrow-lowbrow child-adult differences of taste."

(b) Kate Greenaway, sketch from a letter to Violet Cunningham, c. 1890. The same elfin fragility and lack of inventive imaginative forms that made Kate Greenaway a minor anecdotal painter give her children's illustrations a genuine mythopoeic appeal like Hughes's, having freed her from the artfulness of her Arts and Crafts associations (her house at 39 Frognal was a major example of Norman Shaw's shingle style); where Walter Crane's illustrations for children were "meant to appeal to the eyes and artistic taste of the little ones" and be "educative," "Greenaway . . . sought for nothing but their unthinking delight" and so "pleased them far more" (M. H. Spielmann and G. S. Layard, *Kate Greenaway*, London, 1905, p. 72 and illustration).

29. *Samson Destroying Dagon's Temple,*
woodcut from Gustave Doré's *Bible,* 1861.
Antecedent of such illustrations is Delacroix's background-stage historic drama
type of painting; their descendants, in-
numberable movie "spectaculars" with
characteristic "cardboard" architecture, a
composite concoction from Assyrian and
Egyptian archaeological discoveries, and
typically French sense of *la gloire.*

30. RICHTER'S ROMANTIC ILLUSTRATION

(a) Adrian Ludwig Richter, *Crossing the Elbe at Schreckenstein*, 1837. Dresden Museum. Maturest of several versions of a theme from Goethe involving the harpist as a soul symbol, deepened and broadened through classical and romantic influences: here Richter is a great master of the High Art of illustration.

(b) Chapter heading from "Rübezahl" in Musäus's *Folk Fairy Tales*. Though Richter's characteristic "style" is evident, he skillfully abandons the monumental forms of High Art for the lighter ones appropriate to his theme—the spread of gossip through a small town, adapted from illuminated manuscripts. Typical of Richter also is the lack of political or social overtones—his is the traditional Christian view that if people would behave decently the world would be a decent place to live in, and if they don't, they will be miserable under any political or economic system.

31. TOWARD AN AMERICAN ILLUSTRATION

(a) John Quidor, *Ichabod Crane at the Ball at Van Tassel's Mansion,* c. 1845. Sleepy Hollow Restorations, Tarrytown, N.Y. Conceived, like Quidor's other illustrations of the Knickerbocker tales, in the Hogarth formula of a tight little stage with gesticulating actors, just as Irving's stories are really an Old World sort of story.

(b) Eastman Johnson, *Corn Husking*, 1860. Everson
Museum, Syracuse, N.Y. By now, distinctively American illustration has appeared, not only in the subject
—quite obviously these are not peasants, but North
American independent farmers, who work and play
at their own pace—but also in style: the tight little
stage has been opened out at both sides and back, so
that a sense of unlimited spaciousness suggesting unlimited possibilities develops.

32. GREAT MASTERS OF AMERICAN ILLUSTRATION

(a) George Caleb Bingham, *Raftsmen Playing Cards*, 1847. City Art Museum of St. Louis.

(b) William Sidney Mount, *Eel Spearing at Setau-ket*. New York State Historical Association, Coopers-town. Bingham and Mount can be called great on objective terms, measured against the many others who were doing the same thing. They also have the comprehensiveness of the traditional masters—while plainly belonging to the same era as, say, Richter (compare these boat scenes with 30a), just as clearly this is American and not German romanticism.

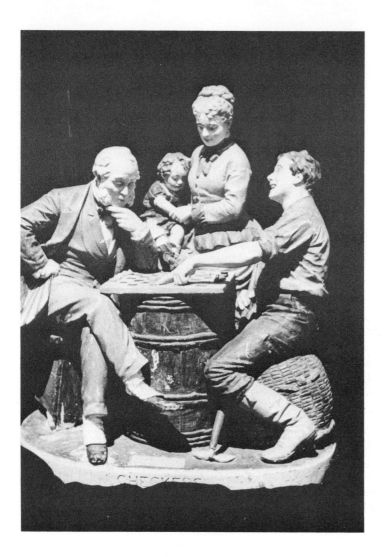

33. THE AMERICAN DREAM, ILLUSTRATED FOR THE MASSES

(a) John Rogers, *Checkers Down at the Farm,* 1870.
That four versions of this subject appear in Rogers
groups attests to the wide appeal of themes of leisure
in the American·Eden. Rogers groups were originally
monochromatic—white or buff—in deference to the
Fine Art convention in sculpture; some owner has
hand-painted this particular example, instinctively
following the older and more universal tradition of
lifelike-painted statues.

(b) *Catching a Trout* (*"We hab you now, sar!"*),
Currier & Ives lithograph of a painting commissioned
from Arthur Fitzwilliam Tait, 1854. Compared with
versions of similar themes by Bingham and Mount
(32a, b), it is less symbolic and more literal, less
original and more stereotyped (including the "Uncle
Tom" stereotype of the contented, faithful, humorous
"darkie" lasting in the popular arts right down to
Jack Benny's "Rochester"), and so adapted to a low
common denominator of mass appeal.

34. ALIENATION ILLUSTRATED

(a) Thomas Eakins, *Max Schmitt in a Single Scull*, 1871. New York, Metropolitan Museum.
(b) Winslow Homer, *The Gulf Stream*, 1899. New York, Metropolitan Museum. In contrast to the contentment expressed in similar themes three or four decades earlier, (32a, b, 33b), open water offers no haven to the typically harassed and tormented individuals Eakins and Homer paint.

(a) Illustration by Edward Windsor Kemble for *Huckleberry Finn,* written in the early 1880s, when the old individualism Bingham and Mount knew had somehow gone rancid, and catching that mood exactly: "Perfect!" Twain said on seeing Kemble's illustrations, "My dear immaculate family just as I created them!" "There was empty dry-goods boxes under the awnings, and loafers roosting on them all day long, whittling them with their Barlow knives; and chewing tobacco, and gaping and yawning and stretching—a mighty ornery lot"—direct ancestors of the inhabitants of Dogpatch, Kentucky.

(b) Charles M. Russell, *Watching the Settlers,* c. 1910. Montana Historical Society. Essentially a magazine illustrator, Russell's style and mood were clearly, though perhaps not directly, related to Homer. In a 1921 letter to Douglas Fairbanks he expressed nostalgia comparable to Twain's for the free and open America that had vanished, in comparable (though unstudied) prose: "The old time cow man right now is as much history as Richard, the Lion Harted or any of those gents that packed a long blade and had their cloths made by a blacksmith. . . ." But from this to Wild West movies is a short and logical step indeed. Both Will Rogers and William S. Hart were close friends of Russell's.

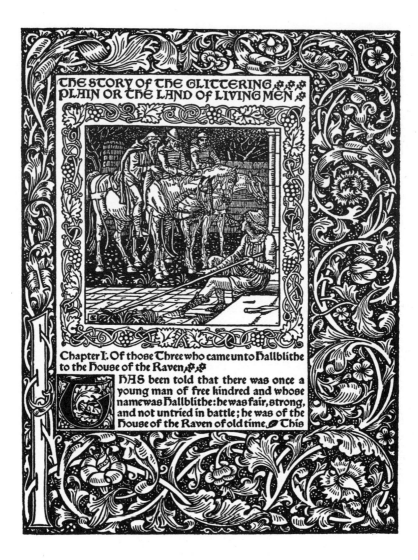

36. FINE ART ILLUSTRATION

(a) William Morris, page from *The Story of the Glittering Plain*, with the collaboration of Walter Crane. The Book as Precious Object, to be admired, not read.

MOST CURRENT FOR THAT THEY COME HOME TO MEN'S BUSINESS & BOSOMS. LORD BACON

CRITICAL & HISTORICAL ESSAYS BY THOMAS BABINGTON MACAULAY VOLUME TWO

LONDON : PUBLISHED by J·M·DENT·&·CO AND IN NEW YORK BY E·P·DUTTON &CO

(b) Standard *Everyman Library* title page for a series of "classics," following Morris's lead—"classics" here plainly being understood by Mark Twain's definition of "books everybody praises and nobody reads." Such a title page in fact screams: "Classic! To be admired and read if, when, and as Men of Taste dictate." A surer way of smothering any living content could hardly be devised.

Lynd Ward's 1930 *God's Man; A Novel in Woodcuts* is an archetypal example of the tacit assumptions behind Fine Art illustration.

(a) Conceived like a series of stills from an early 20th-century movie, complete with soulful eyes, it borrows a Low Art form obsolete a decade earlier, and a technique last used in living Low Arts in 18th-century chapbooks (40a). And it depends entirely on an unthinking and unquestioned assumption that there is absolutely no differentiation between the Fine Artist now and traditional artists of the past. So God's Man sees himself as the legitimate successor to the medieval illuminator (b), the Greek pot painter (c), and even an Egyptian sculptor;

and so, without the slightest suspicion that these predecessors worked strictly within the framework of what their society needed and wanted done, God's Man scorns the filthy lucre of his world, demands complete freedom and, of course, finds only frustration. Though naturally a modernist and a leftist, Ward's hero is no different from the "bourgeois" 19th-century Academic painter in his concept of Fine Art; both hold the same fallacious idea that Artists always were what they claim to be now, and so vitiate all possible understanding of what living art was and is—as is evident from the amusing and instructive comparison between (c) and (d) Paul Thumann's *Art Wins the Heart*, c. 1875.

a

b

c

d

177

(a) With illustrations like this from *The Wonder Clock* (1887), Howard Pyle introduced into American illustration Adrian Ludwig Richter's kind of homely medieval romanticism; like Richter (30 b), he catches less the letter than the spirit of naïveté found in illuminators like Rufillus (1a)—in this particular instance, he even employs the medieval cosmic present, representing goose and sausage four times in the same spatial frame.

(b) Pyle's influence on the Brandywine School is obvious in this illustration by N. C. Wyeth to Jane Porter's *Scottish Chiefs;* also the characteristic romantic theme of the Late Victorian Age in America, of a heroic individual facing a hostile world.

38. PYLE AND
HIS INFLUENCE

Chapter XXIII.
The Good Witch
Grants Dorothy's
Wish.____

(c) How pervasively Pyle influenced later American illustration can be demonstrated by this comparison of two illustrations to L. Frank Baum's Oz books. The first, by Baum's original illustrator, W. W. Denslow (to *The Wonderful Wizard of Oz*, 1900), is clearly in the Kate Greenaway manner; the second (d), by John R. Neill (to the 1909 *Patchwork Girl*), is much closer to Pyle, far more romantically evocative than cute.

(a) Maxfield Parrish, "Arithmetic," cover for *Collier's Magazine,* September 30, 1911. A collage before the term or the technique had been introduced to Fine Art by Picasso and Braque, as William S. Hecksher, who cites the parallels, observes in his "Genesis of Iconology," *Stil und Uberlieferung in der Kunst des Abendlandes,* III, 1967. The difference is that whereas "their collages started . . . as part of an intensified search for reality," Parrish employs the collage not as an empty formal device but to suggest how one generation passes to another the fascination of numbers and mathematical language.

(b) Norman Rockwell's "Rosie the Riveter," from an early World War II *Saturday Evening Post* cover, employs Michelangelo's *Isaiah*—albeit humorously—to show Rosie as the heroic and romantic symbol of women in wartime.

39. THE TIMELESS APPEAL OF ROMANTIC ILLUSTRATION

(a) *Dick Whittingdon and His Cat*, woodcut from an 18th-century chapbook. Such illustrations, with their balloon speech, grotesque drawing, and appeals to lower-class taste, provide some precedents but no real source for comic strips and movies, for they represent in fact not the start of a new art form, but the last survival of medieval illumination—text so far outweighing pictures in importance that many of these woodcuts were used for different stories indiscriminately if they seemed to fit at all; and the grotesque drawing is not caricature, but a survival of ideological bigger-the-better principles.

(b) Comic strips and motion pictures originated with the kind of close-balanced combination of words and pictures represented in the early 19th-century *Tours of Dr. Syntax* by Thomas Rowlandson, "texted" by William Combe. Among other subjects mocked is the Fine Art dilettante; Syntax affects to be a painter and loves talking about connoisseurship: "I wish to judge, by certain rules / The Flemish and Italian schools; / And nicely to describe the merits / Or beauties which each school inherits."

40. ORIGINS OF MOVING MEDIA

41. THE SEQUENTIAL NARRATIVE

(a) A professor of aesthetics at Geneva, Rudolphe Toepffer, in the 1830s put a series of pictures together to show successive moments in the same action, as here in this episode from *Histoire de M. Vieux Bois,* where the hero, a Swiss Dr. Syntax, forgets his resolve to hang himself on hearing his beloved's voice in the street.

(b) In 1847, at the precocious age of fifteen, Gustave Doré produced a series, *The Labors of Hercules,* obviously modeled on Toepffer's technique, but with much greater technical skill. Here, the Augean stables.

(c) By the 1860s Wilhelm Busch in Munich was using the new technique consistently for droll pictorial storytelling; this is a typical excerpt from one of the escapades of *Max und Moritz*.

Und schon ist er auf der Brücke,
Kracks! die Brücke bricht in Stücke;

Wieder tönt es: „Meck, meck, meck!"
Plumps! Da ist der Schneider weg!

Plötzlich will es Meier scheinen,
Als wenn sich die Straße hebt,
So daß er mit seinen Beinen
Demgemäß nach oben strebt.

(a) Two from Wilhelm Busch's eleven-panel narrative sequence *Der Undankbar*, 1876. As Herr Meier drunkenly staggers home, the road heaves and spins—not of course in reality but in Meier's drunken mind—just as in the late 1880s Van Gogh "expressionistically" painted his visions of Arles and Auvers. But of course Busch uses the technique not as an end in itself but to tell his story more effectively, as he does the simultaneous imagery of his *Virtuoso* (discussed and illustrated in *The Restless Art*, p. 229).

Schnell sucht er sich aufzurappeln.
Weh, jetzt wird die Straße krumm,
Und es drehn sich alle Pappeln,
Und auch Meier dreht es um.

"By Jove! it is slippery."

"Oh, hang these slanting pavements!"

"A man does have to have command of his feet on these bad spots."

(b) Such innovations as these, serving a direct and obvious purpose, soon became international lingua franca in cartooning. Typical are these three of a twelve-panel sequence *A Slippery Day*, drawn by A. B. Frost for *Harper's Weekly* in 1883. In Frost's own *Stuff and Nonsense* a year later he published the famous *Tale of a Cat*, a direct ancestor of animated cartoons.

(c) By 1904, when George McManus drew these two of his six-panel *Newlyweds* strip in the New York *Evening Journal* (ancestor to *Bringing up Father* and *Rosie's Beau*), such simultaneous imagery was commonplace in comics—though as yet so unheard-of in Fine Art that Duchamp's and Futurist use of it was called revolutionary. (Note, by the way, how in this early strip McManus still fails to get his balloons reading consistently from left to right.)

THE YELLOW KID TAKES A HAND AT GOLF.

43. COMIC-STRIP PIONEERS

(a) R. F. Outcault, strip (rearranged) of a Sunday page *Yellow Kid*, appearing in October 1897. Such elements as the dialect speech on the Kid's shirt front and the violence, incidentally directed at the Negro "straight man," betray the primary source of a comic like this in the lower-class burlesque stage.

(b) F. B. Opper, two panels from an *Alphonse and Gaston* comic page, New York *American,* 1904, with the collaboration of James Swinnerton and utilizing his *Little Jimmy.* Such collaboration was common enough in the days before syndication; on other occasions Opper's *Alphonse and Gaston* shares a strip with Dirks's *Katzenjammer Kids*—an example of the anonymity and common effort characteristic of Low Arts.

(c) F. B. Opper, two panels from a *Happy Hooligan* strip, New York *American,* 1905.

a

44. TWO COMIC-STRIP CLASSICS

(a) H. C. (Bud) Fisher, strip from *The Mutt and Jeff Cartoon Book*, 1910. Though in this first of all comic books the medium in still called a "cartoon," it actually consisted of collected strips from *Mutt and Jeff*'s first three years, mostly dealing with the pair's escapades betting on horse races and prize fights (especially the Jeffries-Johnson bout of 1909)—hence the direct descent of Segar's *Popeye*.

a

(b) George Herriman's *Krazy Kat*, July 14, 1929. The subtler burlesque of the 1920s, with even deeper roots in the past. King Features Syndicate, Inc.

45. *THIMBLE THEATRE'S*

IMAGES OF AMERICAN LIVING

(a) Popeye, as the 1930s version of folk heroes
Hercules and Samson, champions traditional Western
values in a May 13, 1936, panel.

(b) Popeye founds Spinachova, Great Society of the
1930s, and expounds some universal principles of
government in human society, January 11, 1935,
which E. C. Segar's readers understood if intellectuals did not.

(c) J. Wellington Wimpy, Popeye's (and Everyman's) alter ego, counts on the magic of Science (here exemplified by the Jeep's four-dimensional future-foretelling powers) to bring about Heaven on earth; Olive Oyl, Popeye's Delilah, abets him (June 11, 1936).

(d) Like those intellectuals who called Hitler a patriot and Stalin an agrarian reformer, Wimpy refuses to recognize that barbarians exist (panels from "Fountain of Youth" sequence, February 27, 1934).

46. *LI'L ABNER'S*
AMERICAN DREAM

(a) Al Capp's original basic imagery, a white-collar-class fantasy of untrammeled and uninhibited life in the American Eden—here in 1948 Li'l Abner, bearing a great resemblance to Tarzan (comparable figure from an earlier generation), is pursued by innumerable Janes in one of Dogpatch's annual Sadie Hawkins Day races.

(b) Capp's *Fearless Fosdick* satire on Chester Gould's Dick Tracy, employed as a device to get Li'l Abner married to Daisy Mae at long last (1951).

(c) This April 30, 1954, panel was from the original Shmoo sequence, Capp's elaborate satire on the Welfare State; Abner and Daisy are now married.

(d) Just in case people missed the point of the first Shmoo satire, Capp returned to it in early 1968; Moonbeam McSwine and friends receive Welfare State bounty here; Mammy Yokum comments.

47. A page from Robert L. Short's *The Gospel According to Peanuts* (Richmond, 1965). This book makes a major contribution toward understanding how living arts function in our society, not to mention understanding *Peanuts* and Christianity. In this typical passage Short discusses how *Peanuts* characters reflect the 20th-century religion of human self-sufficiency and visions of Heaven on earth, and how Schultz lampoons its absurd assumptions, in this case those of the "takeover generation." For Short, Charlie Brown with his "globe-like head and his T-shirt of thorns can be seen as a 20th-century representation of Everyman."

Good Grief! 71

serious questions that have caused many people—from Job to Camus—to rebel violently against the nature of reality. Lucy, who is noted for wanting to go "through life with the least possible effort on her part," in "sort of a spiritual jet-stream," again kicks against the pricks of reality by shouting, "By the time I'm eighteen, I expect this world to be perfect! Why should I have to live in a world somebody else has messed up?! *I'll give them twelve years to get everything in order!*" "What if they need more time?" asks Charlie Brown. "Tell them not to bother wiring for an extension! The answer will be, '*No!*'" On this side of paradise, the Church has no final answer to "the problem of evil." Paul addressed himself to this problem when he said:

> You will say to me then, "Why does he still find fault? For who can resist his will?" But who are you, a man, to answer back to God? Will what is molded say to its molder, "Why have you made me thus?" (Rom. 9:19-20).

© 1964 United Feature Syndicate, Inc.

"Where were you when I laid the foundation of the earth? . . . Who determined its measurements—surely you

193

48. A *Wizard of Id* strip, by Brant Parker and Johnny Hart, February 27, 1966. For "wine" read "grant," for "King" read "foundation," and for "sage" read "poet" or "painter." Here is "theater of the absurd" put to proper didactic use, instead of an isolated formalistic cult.

49. It is perhaps superfluous to illustrate this 1962
Head—Red and Yellow by Roy Lichtenstein (Albright-Knox Art Gallery, Buffalo) except as a reminder that "pop" art only did with insolent obvious-
ness what all Fine Art had been doing for a century
past—borrowing forms invented by social necessity
from the Low Arts, ripping them out of functional
context and making Precious Objects of them to tit-
illate connoisseurs' increasingly jaded whims. As a
matter of fact, this particular form was itself borrowed by comic-strip artists of the 1930s from movies
—if you look at a typical suspense strip of the 1930s
(or now) with motion pictures in mind, you will at
once recognize the same pattern of alternating close-
ups, panoramas, full-stages, and so forth.

50. ASPECTS OF ANIMATED CARTOONS

(a) Frame from 1908 animated cartoon by Emile Cohl (1857–1933), who between 1908 and 1918 made over a hundred such. As a pupil of cartoonist André Gill in the 1870s (71c) and himself a fashionable photographer in the 1880s, Cohl's career is a good example of continuity of evolution in the Low Arts.

(b) This frame from *Ichabod Crane* in the 1940s typifies Walt Disney's all too frequent tendency to neglect animated cartoons' full potentialities for fantasy by attempting to make his work "artistic"; in despite of his medium here and elsewhere, he essentially follows the Hogarthian tradition of narrative easel painting —e.g., compare this format with John Quidor's illustration of the same subject a century before (31a).

(c) Typical frame from one of Jay Ward's *Rocky and Bullwinkle* (Rocket J. Squirrel and Bullwinkle the Moose) television cartoons. To meet new demands for mass production and a new mass audience, animated-cartoon makers revert to their medium's stick-figure origins.

51. FROM EASEL TO SCREEN

Still from Edwin S. Porter's *Uncle Tom's Cabin*, 1903. A. Nicholas Vardac in *Stage to Screen* (Cambridge, Mass., 1949) has aptly pointed out how closely sets for this particular movie paralleled William Brady's 1901 stage play of Harriet Beecher Stowe's novel; how the idea of movie versions of popular books descended directly from the vogue for stage versions of them (Dickens's were especial favorites) from the 1860s on; how many devices developed in staging melodramas led directly to Porter's cinematic syntax. But as Vardac's own illustrations of advertisements for plays show, their basic concept of stage arrangement derived from illustrative paintings and prints. The general format of both Porter's movie and Brady's play is anticipated in numerous Currier & Ives illustrations of *Uncle Tom's Cabin* from the 1850s; and the particular effect here is curiously reminiscent of the way angels are represented in Doré's woodcuts.

52. FINE ART ORIGINS OF THE EUROPEAN MOTION PICTURE

(a) George Méliès's *Hydrothérapie fantastique* or *The Doctor's Secret* of 1908 derives from Fine Art like James Ensor's proto-Dada, with touches of Art Nouveau (note shapes of test tubes and bottles, for example)—clumsily, to be sure (the proper medium for such a theme would be an animated cartoon, of course), but just as plainly as American films draw on the Low Arts.

(b) Louis Mercanton's four-reel *Queen Elizabeth* of 1912 is essentially a series of 19th-century paintings brought to life—here the divine Sarah Bernhardt emotes, and in a moment will crash to the cushions and expire in a final scene exactly reproducing Paul Delaroche's painting of *The Death of Queen Elizabeth* from the 1840s.

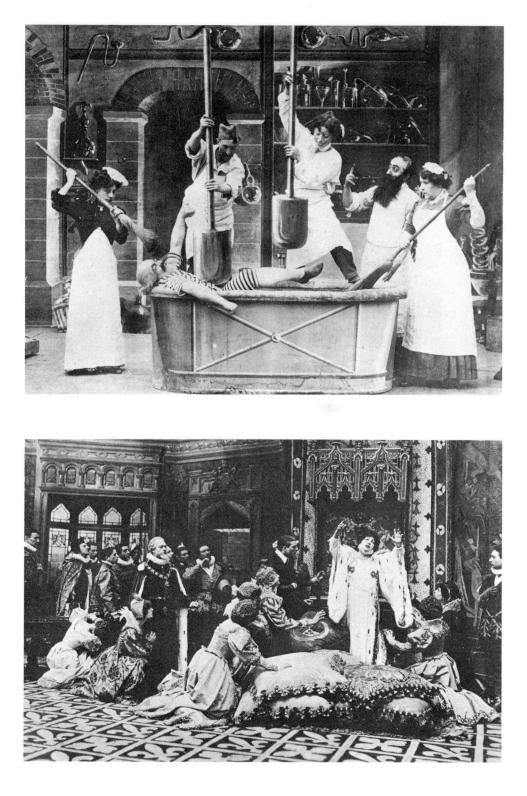

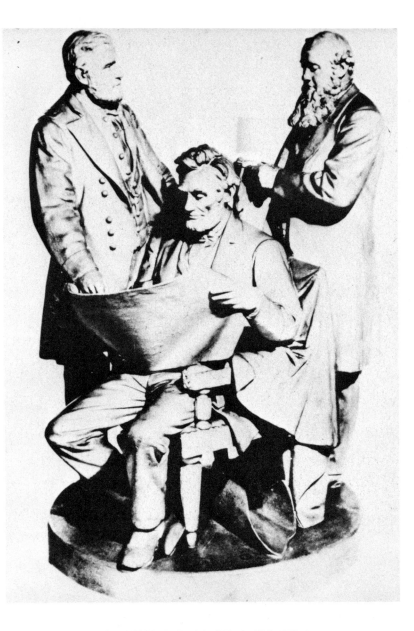

53. *THE BIRTH OF A NATION*

(a) D. W. Griffith's great popular reputation was
made with *The Birth of a Nation* in 1915, which consistently drew on Low Art sources—for instance,
Griffith's scene of Lincoln drafting the Emancipation
Proclamation was essentially this Rogers group of the
1860s, *Council of War,* brought to life.

(b) Griffith made good use of Civil War battle photographs by Brady, Gardner, and others.

54. SOURCES OF SUCCESS:

AMERICAN MOVIES OF THE 1920s

(a) This still from *Tol'able David* (with Richard Barthelmess, directed by Henry King for First National, 1921) exemplifies the basic appeal of that film—the same romantic image of youth facing the world's promise and challenge that is central to so much American illustration.

(b) Many learned critics have analyzed the popularity of Charlie Chaplin's tramp, tracing it to the 18th-century Comédie Italienne, Picasso's harlequins, and so forth. But in fact it is simply the old *Happy Hooligan* tradition of the Low Arts (43c) translated to the screen. When he combined with it the *Yellow Kid* slum-dweller tradition (43a) as here in this 1920 scene from *The Kid* (with Jackie Coogan, First National), audience approval was sure.

55. FROM ROMANTIC TO REALISTIC SEX

(a) Until the 1930s American sex queens were wildly romantic figures; here Theda Bara lives up to her anagram—"Arab death" —in a scene from *Cleopatra* (Fox, 1917). If it looks quaint, that is of course because it was drawn from "quaint" 19th-century paintings—the gestures imitate Egyptian reliefs, and the poses Pharaonic cult statues; but then everybody assumed such a character to be romantically unlike real life.

(b) A change begins around 1930, when Marlene Dietrich and Gary Cooper acted this scene in *Morocco* (Paramount, Joseph von Sternberg). Though the casbah setting and plot are romantically remote from ordinary life (and the last scene wildly so, as Dietrich tramps off into the desert after her legionnaire), still the character is supposed to be believable—Dietrich came to American movies from the "realistic" tradition of European Fine Art movies. Later sexpots like Jean Harlow or Marilyn Monroe were regularly put in "realistic" domestic settings, a practice creating new and disastrous personal problems when they were expected to live up to such an image in private life.

(c) By the late 1940s and -50s, Fine Art "realism" had taken over the sex theme in movies, with sad results summed up in this cartoon by Sempé in the Paris *Exprès* for June 1965: while intellectual and mate exult, "That must be a good one," the audience streams miserably out from another of Ingmar Bergman's gruesomely literal depictions of lust.

"Ça doit être bien . . ."

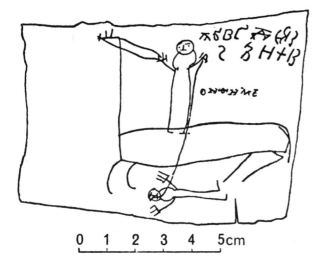

(a) Child's drawing on birchbark found on the fifteenth level of excavations at Novgorod, representing mounted man thrusting lance into an enemy, with word "Onfim" and beginning of Russian alphabet. M. W. Thompson in *Novgorod the Great* (1967) comments. "A modern child might have put a cowboy hat on the figure and a revolver in his hand, but the spirit of the daydream would no doubt be similar in both cases"—i.e., it is an image of conviction, meant not so much to be seen by any spectator as to give reality to an idea in the maker's mind.

0 1 2 3 4 5cm

56. IDEOLOGICAL ARTS OF CONVICTION AND PERSUASION

(b) Drawing of a bison, painted around a rock boss at Altamira in prehistoric times. Made more to confirm a reality than to be seen, it was for all intents and purposes invisible. The origin of such a painting is undoubtedly in three-dimensional "primeval naturalism," here reduced to two dimensions (except for vestigial third supplied by the boss), hence the deceptively "naturalistic modeling."

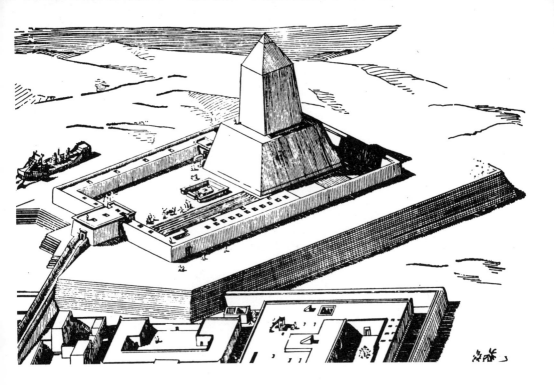

(c) Obelisk and sun temple at Heliopolis, 5th dynasty Egypt, drawn by E. Baldwin Smith for his *Egyptian Architecture as Cultural Expression* (Boston, 1938). Smith's is one of the best of all demonstrations of how architectural forms originate and function to embody ideas, essentially shaped neither by aesthetics nor structure.

(d) This famous 1st-century A.D. satire on Christian belief, "Alexamenos Worshiping His God," one of several *graffiti* uncovered during excavations on the Palatine Hill in Rome in 1857 and preserved in the Collegio Romano, is among the rare survivals of this kind of persuasive art from historic times; in the nature of things most of it vanishes without trace within days or weeks.

57. MEDIEVAL ARTS OF ARCHITECTURAL CONVICTION AND PERSUASION

(a) Spire of the Sainte-Chapelle, Paris, built in the reign (1226–1270) and under the personal supervision of Saint Louis of France to contain a relic of Christ's crown of thorns. Here atop a structure which Robert Branner has shown to be quite literally a large-scale reliquary is a symbol which, like hieroglyphs covering Eyyptian temples top to bottom, Byzantine dome mosaics, or cave paintings, was hardly visible, but simply stated convictions—the royal lilies of France and the crown of thorns together proclaiming Louis the "most Christian King" of France.

(b) Comparably typical of later ideological art is this
early-16th-century tomb of Marguerite d'Autriche in the
church of Brou à Bourg (Ain). By this period the whole
political and social structure of the medieval world is under
severe strain, and as with Egyptian New Kingdom and
Roman Imperial monuments, statements of the old verities
—in this case, the feudal family and its ordained place in
society—are made with hysterical elaboration, obviously
made to be seen and to impress. Typical, too, is the self-
consciousness manifest in its tendency to archaism—note
especially the Romanesque columns and arches supporting
the bier.

58. TRADITIONAL
LOW ART PRINTS

(a) Print of Saint Andrew from an engraved metal plate, c. 1500. Descended from shrine souvenirs, intended for devotional purposes, it carries conviction only to those already convinced—i.e., the symbolism of the cross, the walled garden, meditation in the heavenly city, and so forth, is meaningful only to those already believing it; it will not convert anyone. Both in theory and in practice, such a print functions as a painting, using this medium for reasons of economy, not because it does anything painting could not—a Low Art version of the kind of High Art represented in 57b.

(b) Romeyn de Hooghe, *Intake of the Roman Clergy*, c. 1685. Still less a "cartoon" than an etched painting—i.e., embodying beliefs so widely held as to be convictions within the society for which it was made (here the idea of Papal venery, in Calvinist Holland). This Dutch tradition, passing to Hogarth, inhibited him from developing full potential of prints as a medium for persuasion.

59. ARTS OF REFORMATION PERSUASION

(a) *The Papal Ass at Rome*, c. 1520. Despite its polemic purpose, such a print is still a variant of painting, for these forms are not caricatures invented to persuade individuals but adaptations of the traditional iconography used by painters for centuries to represent the Anti-Christ described in Revelation.

(b) *Stoning of the Pope by the Four Evangelists*, anonymous early-16th-century Italian painting now in Hampton Court Palace, apparently brought to London by Henry VIII. Paintings like this and the much more famous *Four Evangelists* by Albrecht Dürer at Nuremberg show how at this period painting was still the normal medium for all social uses, but also show its limitations— a print would have done the job here much better, for painting is not essentially a good medium for polemic persuasion.

(c) *Luther, Catherine von Bora, and "family"* (of Reformers), c. 1580. Though still showing some influence from painting in its complexity, the print by this time is unmistakably developing characteristics and functions of its own. The idea of a fat man wheeling his paunch goes back to a German print of *The Toper* (c. 1510) and is employed *mutatis mutandis* in a 1635 French print of General Galas during the wars of the League.

Guil: Marshall Sculpsit

60. THE PRINT AS A POLITICAL WEAPON IN ENGLAND

(a) The famous *Eikon Basilike* ("Sacred Image of the King") print of Charles I at prayer. Like the palace of Whitehall by Inigo Jones and the painted ceiling commissioned from Rubens for it, this was an attempt by Charles I, possibly with his personal collaboration, to create a symbol of hereditary authority ("A King is responsible *for* his people, not *to* them," he said on the scaffold)—a print used in the old way as a more easily distributed form of painting (very like shrine souvenir prints in function (58a).

(b) *The Scots Holding Their Yovng Kinges Nose to ye Grinstone,* Parliamentarian satire on Charles I's folly in relying on a Scottish army for support in his quarrel with the Long Parliament—a very different image of "the majesty that doth hedge a king," without any vestigial suggestions of painting, single-mindedly dedicated to polemic persuasion.

(c) *The Sturdy Beggar,* 1757 print satirizing Stephen Fox's securing his sons a lucrative sinecure held by Bubb Doddington, presumably for political favors. Cromwell's victory in the Civil War fatally weakened the principle of hereditary authority represented by Charles I, and despite the Restoration of 1660, it was repudiated throughout wider and wider sections of society thereafter. Cartoons like this reflect how old social foundations dissolved and new families rose to power.

61. THREE IMAGES OF HEAVEN ON EARTH

(a) Sir William Orpen: *The Signing of Peace, Versailles 1919*. London, Imperial War Museum. Somewhere it seems we have seen pictures like this before—and so we have. With its twelve saintly figures on one side of the table and the villain isolated opposite, it is traditional Last Supper iconography—Clemenceau, Wilson, and Lloyd George playing a Trinity, German delegates Müller and Bell a double Judas; the background with its triple arches and palatial splendor combines Leonardo's and Paolo Veronese's *Last Suppers*. Ironic is the cartouche inscription "Le Roy Gouverne"; neither God the Father nor any hereditary monarch rules here, but the Sovereign People, whose eternal happiness through Political Democracy has now been assured.

(b) Most World's Fairs have involved intrinsic symbolism, and Expo '67 in Montreal was no exception. In this particular pilgrimage shrine the second phase of human perfectibility was emphasized. Steel, glass, and concrete are the materials exalted—products of that Applied Science which was to have assured Economic Democracy, as capitalism was to have assured the political Eden of the first phase. Habitat '67, seen here, is a vision of socialist egality with every human in his identical cube (some, perhaps, like Inner Party apartments in Orwell's *Nineteen Eighty-Four,* a trifle more identical than others); behind it rises the pavilion extolling Man the Visionary; in front sits Copernicus, apostolic father of this new world.

(c) Here again in this 1967 hippie poster for "Dance Light Show, Underground Rock" is the millennial vision of Man the Good and Happy. The old political and socialist democrats look square indeed beside these flower children; for in this third phase of mystic faith, Heaven on earth is populated by beings of Rousseauan innocence and guileless equality—the *Eloi* foreseen in Wells's *Time Machine.* Its Art Nouveauish forms are appropriate, for in that era this most irrational of all the visions grows.

South End Forever.

North End Forever.

Extraordinary VERSES on *POPE-NIGHT*.

Or, A Commemoration of the *Fifth of November*, giving a History of the Attempt, made by the *Papishes*, to blow up KING and PARLIAMENT, A. D. 1588. Together with some Account of the *POPE* himself, and his Wife *JOAN*; with several other Things worthy of Notice, too tedious to mention.

1 **H**UZZA! brave Boys, behold the *Pope*,
   Pretender and *Old-Nick*;
   How they together lay their Heads,
   To plot a poison Trick?
2. To blow up KING and PARLIAMENT
   To Flitters, rent and torn:
—— *Oh! blund'ring Poet, since the Plot,*
   Was this Pretender born.——

15. If that his *deeden* Self could see
   Himself so turn'd to Fun:
In Rage He'd tear out His *Pope's Eyes*,
   And scratch his Rev'rend Bum.
16. He'd kick his tripple Crown about,
   And weary of his Life,
He'd *curse* the Rabble, and away
   He'd run to tell his *Wife.*

62. OLD AND NEW RELIGIONS IN AMERICA

A WARM PLACE — HELL.

On brave *RESCINDERS!* to yon *yawning Cell*,
SEVENTEEN such *Miscreants* sure will *settle Hell*;
There puny *Villains* damn'd for petty Sin:
On such distinguish'd *SCOUNDRELS* gaze and grin:
The out done *DEVIL* will resign his *Sway*,
He never curs'd his *MILLIONS* in *a day.*

WHILE *gasping Freedom waits her future Fate*,
   And Commerce sickens with the sick'ning State;
   What Tennes, Mentor, Judas, more than Fiend,
   Their Country's last Resort wou'd vote RESCIND?
Cou'd Hope, cou'd Fear, cou'd weighty Cudgels maul,
A very Camel to relinquish all?
And shall the Hero, Sage, and Prophet say,
To *save our* RIGHTS, *we shou'd them all betray.*
Resign, RESCIND, submit to sov'reign Will,

(a) *Pope-Night Parade, broadside* printed in Boston, 1768.

(b) Broadside on the Massachusetts Rescinders, engraved by Paul Revere, printed in Boston, 1768. Though coming from the same year and place, and in similar media, these two broadsides depend on radically different frames of reference—the one on a traditional view of religion providing ethical values to the State, the other on the State providing ethical values to religion.

216

63. IMAGES OF AMERICAN CONVICTION

(a) Thousand-dollar bill issued by the Bank of the United States, 1844. Stability of both bank and nation is proclaimed in the classical forms of the bank building and icons of the Founders—Franklin, Penn, and so forth.

(b) The 1926 Astor Column in Portland, Oregon. As the great stone heads on Mount Rushmore are a late and grandiose variant of earlier Founders' icons on coins, bills, and public portraits, so this is a late and grandiose variant of the symbolic classical architecture of the early Republic. Its immediate prototype was the much simpler Washington Monument in Baltimore (1814–1829); its ultimate inspirations the Column of Trajan in Rome and symbolic Freemasonry columns (c).

THE PILLARS OF

WISDOM, STRENGTH AND BEAUTY.

217

64. THE CARTOON AS AN ART OF CONVICTION

James Gillray, *Promis'd Horrors of the French Invasion,* October
20, 1796. Like the French in 1940, the British in the 1790s woke
up to the fact that personal freedom, however incomplete, still
means freedom from being arbitrarily picked off streets and
carted to torture chambers or forced-labor camps. So Gillray
abandons his early radical attacks on upper-class follies (cf. *The
Restless Art,* p. 102) to forge a weapon for rallying national
spirit. Here patriotic warning is combined with satire of Brookes's
Club radicals who mindlessly applaud a revolution threatening
all their liberties. By the early 1800s Gillray's transformation was
complete, and his cartoons were dedicated to making symbols of
continuity around which a stable society could be built.

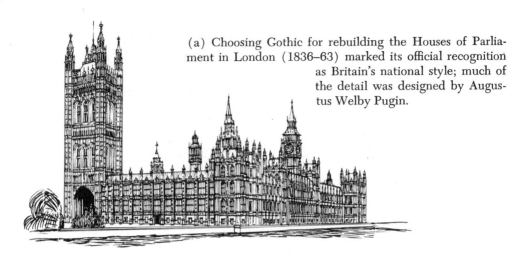

(a) Choosing Gothic for rebuilding the Houses of Parliament in London (1836–63) marked its official recognition as Britain's national style; much of the detail was designed by Augustus Welby Pugin.

65. THE BRITISH NATIONAL STYLE

(b) For the next three or four decades Gothic decoration was all the rage. Pugin bitterly assailed much of it, castigating such desk accessories, andirons, lamps as these illustrated in his *True Principles of Pointed or Christian Architecture* (1841) as "Brummagem Gothic"—products of "those inexhaustible mines of bad taste," Birmingham and Sheffield. Such decoration being essentially intended to create symbols of national conviction and not to recreate the Middle Ages, Pugin's criticism not only was irrelevant but led directly to that principle of Reality which ultimately destroyed the arts of decoration.

PUNCH OFFICE, 85, FLEET STREET.
AND SOLD BY ALL BOOKSELLERS AND NEWSMEN.

(c) Richard Doyle's design for *Punch's* cover, first drawn in 1844 and reworked for the January 9, 1849, issue—and thereafter standard for over a century—was a typical assemblage of Gothic bric-a-brac, creating a national symbol entirely appropriate to the new kind of "official" cartoon *Punch* was evolving.

THIS IS THE BOY WHO CHALKED UP "NO POPERY!"—AND THEN RAN AWAY!

66. FROM PERSUASION TO CONVICTION IN *PUNCH* CARTOONS

PUNCH'S ILLUSTRATIONS TO SHAKSPEARE.

" Is all our travail turn'd to this effect ?
After the slaughter of so many peers,
So many captains, gentlemen, and soldiers,
That in this quarrel have been overthrown,
And sold their bodies for their country's benefit,
Shall we at last conclude effeminate peace ?"
Henry VI., Part 1

(a) Though from the beginning *Punch* was never as radical as *Charivari* in France, its early cartoons showed many vestigial survivals of 18th-century social caricature, as in this famous satire on Lord John Russell by John Leech in 1849; significantly, however, the attack is not on class privilege, but on deviation from the English *via media* in Church and State policy.

(b) John Tenniel's comment on Crimean peace negotiations, in "Punch's Illustrations to Shakespeare," April 12, 1856, exhibits a whimsical national medievalism comparable to such contemporary illustration as à Beckett's only half-facetious *Comic History of England* (1848). It was work like this that attracted Lewis Carroll's attention to Tenniel.

67.

PUNCH'S
SOCIAL
CARTOONS

THE TIME-HONOURED BRITISH THREAT

Indignant Anglo-Saxon (to Provincial French Innkeeper, who is bowing his thanks for the final settlement of his exorbitant and much-disputed account). "Oh, oui, Mossoo! pour le matière de ça, je PAYE! Mais juste vous regardez ICI, mon Ami! et juste—vous—marquez—mes—MOTS! Je PAYE—MAIS JE METTE LE DANS LA 'TIMES'!"

(a) Typical of George Du Maurier's ability to essentialize British upper-class manners and mores is *The Time-Honoured British Threat* (1871)—strong and (more or less) silent Englishman contrasted with the stereotyped Frenchman, counterpart of the comics' *Alphonse and Gaston* (43b).

(b) Chivalry and fashions of the middle class guyed together by their greatest satirist, in a cartoon from John Leech's *Pictures of Life and Character from the Collection of Mr. Punch* (London, 1860); also a reminder of rural survivals even in the biggest British cities of the 1850s.

Youth, "YOU NEEDN'T BE AFRAID, MA'AM. STAND BEHIND ME!"

68. GERMAN

POLITICAL CARTOONING

(a) Franz von Pocci plays a gentle game of *lèse-majesté* in this 1806 water-color cartoon with "citizens of Munich honoring Burgomaster Steindorf" (note, incidentally, early collage technique, a distant harbinger of Schwitters).

(b) Olaf Gulbransson plays a gentle game of *lèse-majesté* in this 1909 cartoon from *Simplicissimus* with the Kaiser on army maneuvers: "His Majesty explains the enemy positions to Prince Ludwig of Bavaria."

69. AMERICAN
POLITICAL CARTOONS
AFTER THE CIVIL WAR

(a) Thomas Nast, satire on "Boss" Tweed's position after the election of November 9, 1871, in *Harper's Weekly*. Typical of Nast's style (the resemblance to Tenniel, whence he also derived his animal symbolism, is obvious), of his cleverness (the usual diamond stickpin becomes a cameo on Tweed's paunch) and of his basic assumption—Tweed's crime, like Revere's "Rescinders" (62b) is not so much personal as political sin, against the Sacred Republic. Appropriately, therefore, the cartoon is modeled on New York painter John Vanderlyn's *Marius on the Ruins of Carthage* (1807), product of the times when Roman heroes and architecture symbolized the republican ideal.

"WHAT ARE YOU LAUGHING AT? TO THE VICTOR BELONG THE SPOILS"

(b) John T. McCutcheon, cartoons in the *Chicago Record-Herald* (L.) before (March 27, 1902) and (R.) after (April 2, 1902) the election of "Bathhouse John" Coughlin in Chicago. In a very different manner from Nast's earnestness, McCutcheon lightheartedly admits his bets on this particular game of politics were wrong. In the figures of Coughlin's cronies, note the ancestors of Augustus R. Mutt.

(a) Lithograph by Alexandre Decamps satirizing Charles X as *le pieu monarque,* an artificial creation with no roots in "the people" (1830).

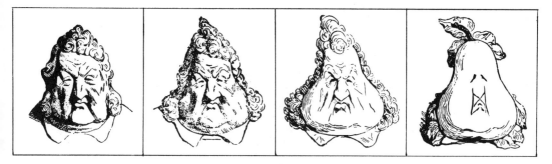

(b) One of the innumerable satires of Louis Philippe as a "pear-head." This one a wood block by Charles Philipon in *Charivari*, 1834.

70. CARTOON IMAGES OF THE RULERS OF FRANCE

(c) "A Nightmare of Mr. Bismarck's," lithograph by Honoré Daumier from an 1870 *Actualités*. Bismarck too is satirized as "out of touch with the people," but not so much as the social satirists of France were out of touch with the *actualités* of history and government, as the events of 1871 proved.

71. THE WICKED FRENCH BOURGEOISIE

(a) Henri Monnier's *Sketch for a Monument to Monsieur Prudhomme*, c. 1835, typical of the strawmen cartoonists erected to throw bricks at (from J. F. F. Champfleury, *Histoire de la Caricature*, Paris, 1865).

(b) A typical intimation of luxurious "bourgeois decadence" by Gavarni, from *Baliverneries parisiennes*, ii, 1846. Top-hatted *galant* simpering, "My dear lady . . . so sweet . . . a little kiss . . . for God's sake . . ." gets the contemptuous retort: "Your father had me already this morning. . . ."

(c) André Gill, leading cartoonist after the Commune, satirizes Gustave Doré in this 1878 cartoon from *Eclipse* for his "bourgeois" energy, efficiency, and—what is worse—his "bourgeois" popularity.

72. GERMAN
SOCIAL CARTOONING

(a) Drawing from *The Sketchbook of Heinrich Kley*, published by Albert Langen (*Simplicissimus*'s founder), 1904. The technique is reminiscent of Grandville, and many ideas anticipate Disney (who may well have drawn the elephants and crocodiles in *Fantasia* from Kley) but the basic Marxist implications of a degenerating possessing class (*Verelendung*) are more sinister than funny.

(b) One of Heinrich Zille's innumerable sketches of that *Lumpenproletariat* who, reaching the depth of misery at the moment ruling-class degeneracy is complete, will inherit the Marxian earth at its *Zusammenbruch*. But as a Low Artist Zille is close enough to life to know (unlike Kollwicz, who borrowed heavily from him) that the Working Class like any other is made up of human beings, who are not always sacred and are sometimes laughable—just because he is not dealing in some transcendental Reality of Fine Art, Zille is both truer to real life and more effective.

"Mummy, Fritz is all wet!"—"Keep'm in the sun, so he'll dry!"

73. ENGLISH

SOCIAL CARTOONING

(a) The *Lumpenproletariat* in England, from Phil May's *Guttersnipes* (London, 1896).

(b) Max Beerbohm, *The Rare, the Rather Awful Visits of Albert Edward, Prince of Wales, to Windsor Castle.* Typical of Beerbohm's deceptively simple style of drawing, his near-private jokes (few at the time would know how "Bertie" and his mother got on), his gentle reminders that the British upper class was not all it seemed.

(a) In this *Punch* cartoon on Hitler's success at Munich (*Bluff and Iron:* The Old Chancellor: "Not my methods exactly, but you seem to have nearly the same success"), Bernard Partridge carried on both the style and the attitudes of Tenniel (Sept. 21, 1938).

(b) David Low comments on Hitler's aggressions of the 1930s in a very different style—and by the objective standards of judgment possible in the Low Arts, very much more effectively.

74. OLD AND NEW STYLE ENGLISH POLITICAL CARTOONS IN THE 1930s

"HOW MUCH WILL YOU GIVE ME NOT TO KICK YOUR PANTS FOR, SAY, TWENTY-FIVE YEARS?"
(1936)

"Yes, Willie, this is a rubber toy to amuse you and Teddy. It represents the Working Classes. See how Papa pulls its leg."

75. SOCIAL CONSCIOUSNESS IN THE AMERICAN CARTOON

(a) A 1900 cartoon by Frederick Burr Opper against "the Trusts." Willie (McKinley), Teddy (Roosevelt), and nursemaid Mark Hanna, McKinley's manager in the 1900 election campaign.

(b) Cartoon by Art Young in *The Masses*, 1912. Closer perhaps to Zille than any other contemporary, Young frequently showed the same sort of sardonic humor, though moral indignation has overcome it here.

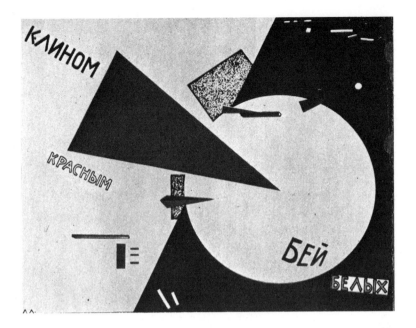

76. FROM FINE ART TO LOW ART IN RUSSIAN POSTERS

(a) Louis Lissitzky's 1919 poster *Strike the Whites with Red Bayonets,* issued by the "Political Department of the Western [Polish] Front," conformed to the spiritual Realities in Fine Art enunciated by Wassily Kandinsky, but unfortunately not to the more practical functions of persuasion it was supposed to serve.

(b) By 1920 Russian rulers had been forced to adopt the embattled capitalist states' favorite kind of direct psychological hard-sell recruiting poster: "Have *you* volunteered?" this pointing finger demands, as Kitchener's and Uncle Sam's had earlier, for other causes.

77. SOCIALIST ARTS
OF PERSUASION
AND CONVICTION

(a) To illustrate the Holy Spirit of Socialism, Walter Crane in this cover from 1903 employs a combination of Christian angel and Greek *nike* figure; his Holy Worker is, of course, descended from creations of Géricault, Blake, and Courbet.

ОРУЖИЕМ МЫ ДОБИЛИ ВРАГА
ТРУДОМ МЫ ДОБУДЕМ ХЛЕБ
ВСЕ ЗА РАБОТУ ТОВАРИЩИ

(b) By the mid-1920s, when Nikolai Kogout made this poster, Soviet power was established, but still wobbly from the attempt to make socialism work, with resultant famine. Half persuasive, half expressing established conviction, the Holy Worker is on his feet, declaring "With weapons we got the enemy, with labor we'll get our bread. Everyone to work, comrades."

(c) Thanks to abandoning attempts at governing on the principle that men are naturally noble and selfless, and reverting to ancient institutions disguised under fashionable labels, the Soviet State achieved enough stability to repel Hitler's invading armies; here on Mamayev Hill at Volgograd (Stalingrad) is the monument to that achievement—the Holy Worker and Genius of Socialism from persuasive posters of the 1890s translated into graven images of established conviction.

wer jemand hie der gern welt lernen dütsch schriben vnd lesen vß dem aller
kürtzisten grundt den jeman erdencken kan do durch ein jeder der vor nit ein
büchstaben kan der mag kürtzlich vnd bald begriffen ein grundt do durch er
mag von jm selber lernen sin schuld vff schriben vnd lesen vnd wer es
nit gelernnen kan so vngeschickt were Den will ich vm nut vnd ver-
geben gelert haben vnd gantz nut von jm zu lon nemen er syg
wer er well burger ouch handtwerckß gesellen frowen vnd ju-
nckfrouwen wer sin bedarff Der kum har jn der wirt drüwlich
gelert vm ein zimlichen lon Aber die jungen knaben vnd meit-
lin noch den fronuasten wie gewonheyt ist Anno m cccc xvi

78. TRADITIONAL ADVERTISING

(a) Tempera painting on oak panel describing and illustrating a school to teach reading and writing in German, by Hans Holbein the Younger, 1516. Kunstmuseum, Basel.

(b) Advertisement in *The London Graphic* for 1900 describing and illustrating invalid equipment. Exactly the same principle of simple presentation of goods and services available as in Holbein's painting four centuries before.

(c) Late 19th-century signs made to identify a butcher's stall in Baltimore and a jeweler's shop in Vermont. Shelburne Museum, Vermont. Each about 2½ feet high. Signs like these identified shops, stalls and taverns for hundreds, perhaps thousands of years past. In them was an origin of the brand name (cf. 79a).

235

79. THE COMPELLING SYMBOL

(a) Cigar band advertising Bully Brand Cigars c. 1870. ("Bully": "very good"—a favorite slang word of Theodore Roosevelt's; also "bullfrog," get it?) Cigar bands represented one of the last survivals of 18th-century chapbook woodcut technique—and so illustrate the link between traditional advertising by simple image (78c) and compelling symbol.

(b) Advertisements by H. S. Marks (L., 1889) and Phil May (R., 1900) for Pears' Soap, very well illustrating how such campaigns plastered a single word or phrase all over the world, in every conceivable place—sky signs, hotel rooms, and (here inadvertently) on South Sea islands. Nor was this entirely a joke; advertising was indeed a major factor in transmitting Western ideas elsewhere in the world (and vice versa, for the Japanese prints so admired by Fine Art connoisseurs in the later 19th century were essentially a kind of advertisement in their homeland, and came to the West as wrapping on parcels).

(c) This store at a crossroads outside Agassiz, British Columbia, illustrates how compelling symbols tended to cancel each other out (screaming scarlet set against screaming orange, etc.) and so encouraged development of more "personal" kinds of advertising).

THE BIRTH OF CIVILIZATION — A MESSAGE FROM THE SEA ※

A SKY-SIGN REFLECTED BY MOONLIGHT.

PEARS' SOAP.

PEARS' SOAP

CORDON HOTELS PEARS' SOAP ONLY USED IN THESE HOTELS

Oh dear! Day And Night!

NIAGARA CORN STARCH.

Pure and Sweet

CONS. & CO. BUFFALO, N.Y.

80. ASSOCIATED IMAGERY OF PERSUASION

Use Acme Soap

Why, the foam is bringing him up !

(a) In this Niagara Corn Starch trade card from the 1870s the association of "pure and sweet" is plain enough.

(b) Somewhat more complicated but still intelligible is the association here; in this third of a series of four (trade cards often came in photo-comic-strip sequences), the little boy has fallen in the well while carrying home a bar of Acme Soap (how? why? no matter) and "Why, the foam is bringing him up!" Moral, still spelled out: "Use Acme Soap!"

(c) The association here is a bit more far-fetched—if you buy an Estey Organ from Bailey's Music Shop in Burlington, Vermont (which distributed this card in the 1880s), it seems unlikely that your Vermont home would come to resemble the harem where this lady is performing—but then again, it might . . .

(d) In this Five Brothers Plug Tobacco advertising card, the association has a Dadaist irrationality; only the sort of mind that rejoiced in puns like this (tale: tail; cities: sittees, get it?) could understand the connection—perhaps.

(a) A primitive kind of hard sell is represented by this mobile kiosk advertising the last state lottery in England in 1826; while the actual text was simply informative, the idea of having someone shout it out is a remote ancestor of the "few words from our sponsor" on television (as is the barker's spiel at fairs).

(b) By the 1890s a new psychological note is beginning to creep in, as here—"You ought to have this product, because if you don't you won't be beautiful." But it is still hardly more intrusive than the advertisements Samuel Johnson complained of in 1759.

THE KEYNOTE OF CREATION–CHANGE!!

'Oh! ever thus from childhood's hour,
I've seen my fondest hopes decay;
I never loved a tree, or flower,
But 'twas the first to fade away.

I never nursed a dear gazelle
To glad me with its soft black eye,
But when it came to know me well,
And love me, it would pass away.'—*Moore.*

Sᴏᴍᴇᴛʜɪɴɢ ᴀᴘᴘᴀʟʟɪɴɢ!

Mᴀʟᴀʀɪᴀʟ ꜰᴇᴠᴇʀ!

'Wʜᴀᴛ ɪs ᴛᴇɴ ᴛʜᴏᴜsᴀɴᴅ ᴛɪᴍᴇs ᴍᴏʀᴇ ᴛᴇʀʀɪʙʟᴇ ᴛʜᴀɴ ʀᴇᴠᴏʟᴜᴛɪᴏɴ ᴏʀ ᴡᴀʀ?

Oᴜᴛʀᴀɢᴇᴅ ɴᴀᴛᴜʀᴇ!

Sʜᴇ ᴋɪʟʟs, ᴀɴᴅ ᴋɪʟʟs, ᴀɴᴅ ɪs ɴᴇᴠᴇʀ ᴛɪʀᴇᴅ ᴏꜰ ᴋɪʟʟɪɴɢ, ᴛɪʟʟ sʜᴇ ʜᴀs ᴛᴀᴜɢʜᴛ ᴍᴀɴ ᴛʜᴇ ᴛᴇʀʀɪʙʟᴇ ʟᴇssᴏɴ ʜᴇ ɪs sᴏ sʟᴏᴡ ᴛᴏ ʟᴇᴀʀɴ—ᴛʜᴀᴛ ɴᴀᴛᴜʀᴇ ɪs ᴏɴʟʏ ᴄᴏɴQᴜᴇʀᴇᴅ ʙʏ ᴏʙᴇʏɪɴɢ ʜᴇʀ.

Mᴀɴ ʜᴀs ʜɪs ᴄᴏᴜʀᴛᴇsɪᴇs ɪɴ ʀᴇᴠᴏʟᴜᴛɪᴏɴ ᴀɴᴅ ᴡᴀʀ.

Hᴇ sᴘᴀʀᴇs ᴛʜᴇ ᴡᴏᴍᴀɴ ᴀɴᴅ ᴄʜɪʟᴅ.

Bᴜᴛ ɴᴀᴛᴜʀᴇ ɪs ꜰɪᴇʀᴄᴇ ᴡʜᴇɴ sʜᴇ ɪs ᴏꜰꜰᴇɴᴅᴇᴅ. Sʜᴇ sᴘᴀʀᴇs ɴᴇɪᴛʜᴇʀ ᴡᴏᴍᴀɴ ɴᴏʀ ᴄʜɪʟᴅ. Sʜᴇ ʜᴀs ɴᴏ ᴘɪᴛʏ, ꜰᴏʀ sᴏᴍᴇ ᴀᴡꜰᴜʟ, ʙᴜᴛ ᴍᴏsᴛ ɢᴏᴏᴅ ʀᴇᴀsᴏɴ.'— *Kingsley.*

'Fᴏᴜʀ ᴍɪʟʟɪᴏɴ ᴘᴇʀsᴏɴs ᴅɪᴇ ᴀɴɴᴜᴀʟʟʏ ᴏꜰ ꜰᴇᴠᴇʀ, ᴘʀɪɴᴄɪᴘᴀʟʟʏ ᴍᴀʟᴀʀɪᴀʟ, ɪɴ ʙʀɪᴛɪsʜ ɪɴᴅɪᴀ ᴀʟᴏɴᴇ, and if we take into consideration the numerous other dependencies situated in such ᴜɴʟᴏᴠᴀʙʟᴇ ᴘʟᴀᴄᴇs ᴀs ᴛʜᴇ ɢᴏʟᴅ ᴄᴏᴀsᴛ, ᴛʜᴇ sᴛʀᴀɪᴛs sᴇᴛᴛʟᴇᴍᴇɴᴛs, ɴᴇᴡ ɢᴜɪɴᴇᴀ, ʙʀɪᴛɪsʜ ɢᴜɪᴀɴᴀ, ʜᴏɴᴅᴜʀᴀs, ᴀɴᴅ ᴛʜᴇ ᴡᴇsᴛ ɪɴᴅɪᴇs, ᴛʜᴇ ᴛᴏᴛᴀʟ ᴘᴏᴘᴜʟᴀᴛɪᴏɴ sᴛʀᴜᴄᴋ ᴅᴏᴡɴ ʏᴇᴀʀ ʙʏ ʏᴇᴀʀ ʙʏ ᴍᴏʀᴇ ᴏʀ ʟᴇss ᴘʀᴇᴠᴇɴᴛᴀʙʟᴇ ꜰᴇᴠᴇʀ ᴍᴜsᴛ ʙᴇ sᴏᴍᴇᴛʜɪɴɢ ᴀᴘᴘᴀʟʟɪɴɢ!'—*Observer.*

PLATO MEDITATING ON IMMORTALITY BEFORE SOCRATES, THE BUTTERFLY, SKULL AND POPPY, ABOUT 450 B.C.

The Head of Plato is from an Ancient Marble Bust, discovered in Greece, now in the Museum at Rome.

Iᴍᴘᴏʀᴛᴀɴᴛ ᴛᴏ ᴛʀᴀᴠᴇʟʟᴇʀs.—"We have for the last four years used ENO'S 'FRUIT SALT' during several important survey expeditions in the Malay Peninsula, Siam, and Cambodia, and have undoubtedly derived very great benefit from it. In one instance only was one of our party attacked with fever withont it, and have also recommended it to others.—Yours truly, Commander A. J. Lᴏꜰᴛᴜs, F.R.G.S., his Siamese Majesty's Hydrographer, E. C. Dᴀᴠɪᴅsᴏɴ, Superintendent Siamese Government Telegraphs, Baugkok, Siam, May, 1883."

during that period, and that happened after our supply of ENO'S 'FRUIT SALT' had run out. When making long marches under the powerful rays of a vertical sun, or travelling through swampy districts, we have used ENO'S 'FRUIT SALT' two or three times a day, in the following manner and proportions:—At daybreak two teaspoonfuls mixed with the juice of a raw lime, and a little sugar in a tumbler of water; shortly afterwards a light meal of tea or coffee, bread and fruit; about mid-day one small spoonful with raw lime-juice and water; and before retiring for the night another teaspoonful in water. ENO'S 'FRUIT SALT' used as aforesaid acts as a gentle aperient, keeps the blood cool and healthy, and wards off fever. We have pleasure in voluntarily testifying to the value of ENO'S 'FRUIT SALT,' and our firm belief in its efficacy. We never go into the jungle withont it, and have also recommended it to others.

Tʜᴇʀᴇ ɪs ɴᴏ ᴅᴏᴜʙᴛ ᴛʜᴀᴛ ᴡʜᴇʀᴇ ENO'S 'FRUIT SALT' has been taken in the earliest stages of a disease it has in innumerable instances prevented a serious illness. The effect of ENO'S 'FRUIT SALT' on any disordered or feverish condition is simply marvellous. It is, in fact, nature's own remedy, and an unsurpassed one,

240

(d) A World War I psychological hard-sell poster in Britain, curiously echoing the theme of David's *Oath of the Horatii* (*The Restless Art,* p. 21). Appeals to duty through shame and fear like this blanketed whole countries, and created a kind of mass hypnosis. The immediate results of such advertising were impressive; the long-range results, disastrous—four decades of magazine, radio, and television hard sell on the same principles, numbing all capacity for belief, and ultimately a generation trained to see the whole world as one gigantic put-on.

(c-*left*) The immense change begins around 1900, with advertisements like this: essentially, "If you don't use our product you are rejecting the wisdom of the ages, and killing yourself"— strong medicine indeed; acid to dissolve all sense of values.

(e-*right*) Typical advertisement from a 1933 magazine. Extravagant promises, extravagant hopes, extravagant fears, ensuring that each successive generation will be just a little less sure of what basic values may be, just a little less capable of logical thought, just a little more convinced that the world is cheating it.

e

Why No One Asked Her To Dance

Marvelous Prescription Conquers Bad Breath At The SOURCE. Doesn't Just Cover It Up For A Few Hours Like Lots Of Treatments.

a beautiful girl of charming figure and personality finds herself unpopular—ced to dances or the movies the second l because of offensive breath.

ow nothing is quite so repulsive and the pitiful victim is unaware she But how well her acquaintances how they dread meeting her!

Be Sensible—Treat This Condition Scientifically

an't expect to get rid of tainted breath highly-touted preparations of an un-: nature—remedies which you must very day to protect yourself and which er up bad breath for a few hours—

nust get at the Cause. 9 out of 10 ually come from a gassy, sour, acid and there's one prescription, known y to many reputable physicians, which come this trouble and do it quickly little cost.

Simply take a teaspoonful of Bisurated Magnesia in a glass of water after each meal.

Bisurated Magnesia immediately starts to purify, cleanse and sweeten the stomach—it puts disordered stomachs in fine, healthy condition and keeps them that way—that's why it's one of the best treatments you can buy from any druggist (no prescription cost) to keep foul breath away for good.

Not only does offensive breath disappear but also dull headaches, acidity, gas pains, bloat, dizzy and bilious spells, indigestion, nervousness and sleeplessness. A healthy stomach means a life of longer years—it means YOUTH lasts longer!

A few days' faithful treatment with Bisurated Magnesia and you'll agree with thousands of other grateful folks who benefited after everything else failed, "An Anti-acid par excellence—nothing better to put vigor and healthy activity into weak, sickly stomachs."

Bisurated Magnesia
Corrects Stomach Acidity--Always Works

ROMAN DRAYNEFLETE

82. Five scenes from Osbert Lancaster's *There'll Always be a Drayneflete* (Boston, 1950). In each successive age costumes and architecture change but life goes on—temple, tavern, town hall, gateway each in their place ("the basic patterns of institutional relatedness that make up the State and traditionally pro- vide most of the occasions for meaningful archi‑ tecture," in Norris Kelly Smith's words); squir‑ and priest, soldiers, drunks, nobles each i theirs. But in the last picture, everything is di‑ ferent—"Drayneflete of the Future" is a visio‑ of Heaven on earth, with all things made new‑ that it is not likely to descend soon is implie‑ throughout Lancaster's brilliant satire.

IMMEDIATELY AFTER THE NORMAN CONQUEST

DRAYNEFLETE AT THE END OF THE SEVENTEENTH CENTURY

TWENTIETH-CENTURY DRAYNEFLETE

243

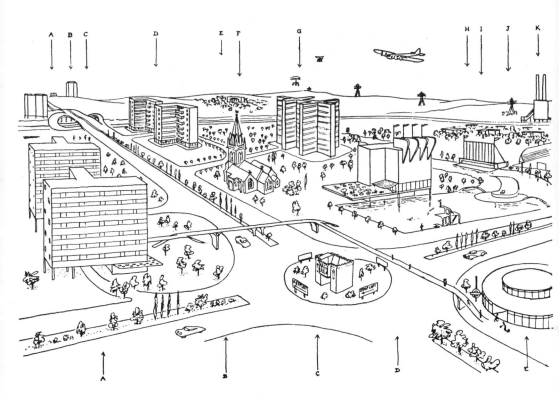

THE DRAYNEFLETE OF TOMORROW

Key to Illustration

Top : A. Cultural Monument scheduled under National Trust ('Poet's Corner'). B. Gasometer. C. Clover-leaf crossing and bridge. D. Communal Housing Block. E. Lunatic Asylum and Littlehampton Memorial Park. F. Cultural Monument scheduled under National Trust. G. Municipal Offices including Community Centre, Psychiatric Clinic, Crèche and Helicopter Landing-strip on the roof. H. Housing Estate for higher-income brackets. I. Communal Sports Centre, Yacht Club, and Football Ground. J. Floating Concert Hall for audience of 2,500 and full symphony orchestra. K. Power Station.

Bottom : A. Communal Housing Blocks. B. High-level Pedestrian roadbridge. C. Cultural Monument scheduled under National Trust. D. People's Restaurant, Swimming Club, Bathing Pool, Cinema and Amenities Centre. E. Underground Station.

II

CHANGING PATTERNS
AND NEW ARTS OF ILLUSTRATION
IN THE 1890s

IN THE COURSE of the 1890s, the traditional pattern of High and Low arts of illustration that had been maintained since 1750—or from that matter, since the beginning of art history—abruptly dissolved. Illustrative easel painting began to decline noticeably and rapidly, in both quality and quantity, and by 1920 had to all practical intents and purposes disappeared. So did illustration of adult books for mass markets; in its place a Fine Art of Illustration appeared, concerned with limited editions of expensive books for connoisseurs. Illustration for mass-market magazines, children's and youth books flourished, and indeed some of its greatest examples come from the years 1890–1930; but in contrast to the preceding period, it was typically done by professional book and magazine illustrators, artists who considered their work to be something quite different from and fundamentally unrelated to the Art of painting.

It would be easy, and conventional, to explain all these developments as simply manifestations of the triumph of Fine Art—to say that as more and more enlightened people perceived the superior merits of Cézanne, Gauguin, and Picasso, illustrative painting naturally disappeared; that "commercial" illustrators were naturally recognized as different from and inferior to those painters who were discovering truths of society and Realities of form; that among these Realities the illustrational form was one which Fine Artists would naturally explore for its own sake sooner or later. Related to this explanation is the idea that romanticism "lost its appeal" in the 20th century, no longer expressed the "spirit of the time," and died out; 19th-century illustration, being incorrigibly romantic, necessarily died out too. But this is too simple, and not at all what happened.

In fact, narrative pictures did not disappear; they simply began to move. With illustrative paintings in mind, look at early movies from 1900 to 1920, and you will see that "moving pictures" is quite literally what they are. The art of narrative pictures is not dead, only transferred into a new medium where, with vastly expanded range, it has flourished more vigorously than ever. Heroic epics, domestic conversation pieces, dramatized history, every category of illustrative painting can be found in the movie (as distinguished from the "Art film") to this day. Or consider comic strips; they likewise are illustrative pictures set in sequence and so in motion. Book illustration for adults was similarly transferred to new media. One was the half-tone photographic illustration perfected in the 1880s and proliferating in the new mass-circulation newspapers of the 1890s. Magazines and motion pictures took over some of this function also.

Illustration has not disappeared; only the kinds of art that illustrate have changed. Neither has romanticism died; in those new forms of illustration it flourishes still. It is an absurd view of history that predicates a set of fixed periods through which humanity passes once and forever. Romanticism is a permanent part of the human condition—so inherent to human nature, in fact, that all sorts of people make it their business to be continually warning against it as "escapism." It is continually provoking

> uneasiness in those who, for whatever reason, wish to keep us wholly imprisoned in the present conflict. That perhaps is why people are so ready with the charge of "escape." I never fully understood it until my friend Professor Tolkien asked me the very simple question, "What class of men would you expect to be most preoccupied with, and most hostile to, the idea of escape?" and gave the obvious answer: jailers. . . . Fascists, as well as Communists, are jailers; both would assure us that the proper study of prisoners is prison. [C. S. Lewis, "On Science Fiction," *Of Other Worlds*, London, 1966, p. 67]

So teachers of painting are forever telling their charges never to escape, but to be always exposing, protesting, crying havoc; and orthodox art historians complete the job, boxing us all into darkest Zeitgeistheim by explaining how "good" artists always work in "the spirit of their times," how "romantic escape" is not "our spirit," and therefore how "bad" and "backward" is any tendency to indulge in it. Why? Because, as Lewis continues, there is

> perhaps this truth behind it: that those who brood much on the remote past or future, or stare long at the night sky, are less likely than others to be ardent or orthodox partisans.

And by 1900 the pattern familiar ever since had been established, in illustration as in all other arts—instead of the traditional High and Low forms, there were living Low Arts of illustration—movies, comics, children's and adolescents' and magazine illustration—and a dead Fine Art of Illustration addressed to artists and connoisseurs, needing all the ardent and orthodox partisans it can recruit.

1. *Fine Art Illustration: William Morris and the "Art Book"*

To all intents and purposes, the "art book" was invented in England, by William Morris (1834–1896). It was the last great artistic interest of Morris's life, developing towards the end of that same decade of the 1880s in which he was preoccupied with socialist agitation. While his first experiments in typography were going on, in fact, he was also busy writing his utopian socialist romance *News From Nowhere*, which appeared serially in *The Commonweal* during 1890 and was the second major art book to be published by his Kelmscott Press, following *The Story of the Glittering Plain* (1891) by only a few months (**36a**). This concurrence is not fortuitous. Both the subject matter and the form of *News From Nowhere* manifest Morris's final retreat into a mystical dream of the coming Heaven on earth from what, after the decay of his marriage, had come more and more to seem the vexing world of time, history, and refractory fact.

Morris's utopia, unlike many others, makes little pretense of presenting some working, functional plan for achieving the ideal society it describes; as Philip Henderson pointed out, it simply presupposes the operation of some magical force miraculously bringing about

> the final stage of communism in which the State, we are told, will wither away. "We are for the withering away of the State," said Stalin at the 16th Party Congress, adding with a certain grim humor, perhaps, "To keep on developing State power in order to prepare for the withering away of State power; that is the Marxist formula." So far . . . we have yet to see any body of men, corrupted by almost unlimited power over their victims, voluntarily relinquishing that power and so in effect signing their own death warrants. [*William Morris*, London, 1967, p. 329]

Complementing this concept is Morris's illustration, which makes no pretense at working function either. It was not intended to elucidate or help sell books, but existed simply as an end in itself, as illustration for the sake of illustration alone. So far from making his books more readable, it made them less so. Like all Fine Art, it involved a retrogression to obsolete forms, to early Renaissance book-printing still based by mimesis on medieval manuscript tradition, and so reversed three centuries of progress towards clear legible typography (**36b**). Where Tenniel or Cruikshank or Richter fused pictures with text to make both clearer and more meaningful, Morris buried the text in ornamental illustrative forms;* and so far from helping sell books, Morris's illustration put his books financially quite beyond any possible mass market, for it also involved a retrogression to obsolete techniques long discarded on economic grounds. Not content merely to revive the 15th-century Venetian type of Nicolas Jenson (Golden, used in his 1892 *Golden Legend*) and the Gothic type of early German printers (*Troy* and the smaller Chaucer used for the Kelmscott *Works of Geoffrey Chaucer*), Morris had to revive their practices of setting it by hand and adding decorated initials separately; he even insisted on their kind of handmade paper dried over hand-molded wires to produce textural irregularities.

It seems a strange way to end a career begun on the principle of reviving "honest" expression of materials and structure in decorative arts; but in fact, given Morris's premises, some such ending was inevitable. For Morris's dedication was not to Beauty, but to Reality. His art was the counterpart to H. H. Richardson's architecture and Manet's painting in the same generation—that is to say, premised on and addressed to a visionary world of the artist's own making, not the world of here and now; from this everything else follows.

Morris began as a Gothic Revivalist; but whereas medieval forms had earlier been admired for their associations with Christianity, Morris advocated them because he felt art had grown more honestly and naturally out of the Realities of life in the Middle Ages than later. It followed logically, one might have supposed, that if medieval forms were good art because they grew out of medieval Realities of life, then good art now must begin with forms growing out of present Realities. But Morris's logic was different. He argued that the way to create good art was to make forms *as if* medieval Realities still obtained. And such art, once created, would by some osmosis generate the Realities it embodied. If the Artist would only

---

* Even if you make the unfair comparison of Morris's luxurious editions with cheap Victorian mass-produceed books, this is *still* true.

Forget the snorting steam and piston-stroke,
Forget the spreading of the hideous town;
Think rather of the pack-horse on the down,
And dream of London, small and white and clean,
The clear Thames borded by its gardens green,

then somehow *The Earthly Paradise* that he here describes (1868–70)
would in fact appear. This is all very familiar. When Morris defies
Addison's dictum that the "arts are to deduce their laws and rules from
the general sense and taste of mankind," and says instead that the
general sense and taste are in effect to be deduced from the laws and
rules of art, he is hardly alone. So Jacques Louis David made the
world conform to his neoclassical art; so Courbet posed himself in his
Studio as the Leader who teaches mankind to see truth. So later the
men of Versailles would create a treaty that would have been perfect if
only mankind were different from what all experience and history
showed them to be. It is not logic, but religion, that guides Morris—
the religion of the irreligious, the compulsive illusion of a heavenly
kingdom on earth that logic and no precedent can ever shake. And
so he came in the end, inevitably, to art illustration and *News From
Nowhere.*

And inevitably, once reach the point of divorcing forms
from use and all the principles and attitudes of Fine Art come into
effect. If the public finds Morris's books too esoteric and too high-
priced; if, so far from being the vanguard of a great revival of Good
Book-Making, his Kelmscott Press interests only a few like-minded
dilettantes, that is not at all (in his mind) because his books have no
practical function, but solely because public taste has been "corrupted"
by capitalism. Morris fully shared what Cesar Graña in *Bohemians
Versus Bourgeois* calls the "hatred and fear with which Baudelaire,
Stendhal, Flaubert and others looked on the emerging forces of 19th-
century life—science, technology, and the demands for material well-
being." To him it was entirely because of these wicked forces, because
"bourgeois life is not condusive to the creation of Art," that art like his
was no longer patronized by the great or appreciated by the masses as
in medieval times. It never seemed to occur to Morris that, whereas
medieval monks in their scriptoria were producing something as useful
to their society as the work of airplane designers in ours or railway
builders in his, and so needed no "patron," his work was a hobby that
had to be subsidized; that whereas 15th-century editions of Chaucer
were produced for people who wanted to read the *Canterbury Tales,*

his *Chaucer* had no function except to be a Work of Art. Chaucer's poems were to Morris's art books what apples were to Cézanne or sunflowers to Van Gogh—motifs, excuses for form rather than its cause. Morris not only refused to recognize that medieval forms were as dead as any others once their function was lost; he refused to recognize what illustration is all about.

The first principle of traditional illustration was fidelity to a text. Artists did not invent their own subject matter; they gave form to subject matter already determined. This was as true of Michelangelo illustrating subjects on the Sistine ceiling worked out by the Papal theologian Marco Vigerio, or the Master of Olympia craving an iconographical program worked out by some great Greek dramatist, as it was of Tenniel illustrating *Alice* or Richter illustrating student *lieder*. Illustration existed because of the text; it followed that "good" or "bad" forms of illustration were judged by fitness for that function. But once assume that illustration exists for its own sake, that texts are a mere jumping-off point for the Artist's imagination, and you have no possible grounds for calling some illustrations "better" than others. That is simply a matter of what a given connoisseur prefers.

Morris happened to prefer early Renaissance or late medieval illustrative forms, and by example and precept imposed his taste on a number of followers. Closest to him was Walter Crane (1845–1915), in whose career evolution of the art book can be traced in microcosm. Beginning as a minor painter in the later Pre-Raphaelite orbit, he became a major illustrator of children's stories (forty *Toy Books* alone between 1865 and 1876); then, under Morris's influence, a socialist aesthete, creating all sorts of elegantly Art Nouveauish posters and pamphlet-cartoons (**77a**); finally, a pretentiously stylized illustrator of delux "prestige" Shakespeare editions. In America, Morris's example was taken up and vulgarly exaggerated by Elbert Hubbard (1856–1915) with his medieval airs ("Fra Elbertus"), his scrapbook wisdom, and his Roycroft Shop at East Aurora, New York, churning out deluxe editions of classics in the Morris manner. From Morris's art books to the sinuous line and exotic dilettantism of Art Nouveau was just a step; it was taken first by Aubrey Beardsley (1872–1898) best known for his prurient illustrations to Oscar Wilde's *Salome* (*The Restless Art*, p. 245) and the elegant decadence of the *Yellow Book*, and Will Bradley (1868–1962), known for his posters; thereafter by a host of Art Illustrators playing variants on the Morris-Art-Nouveau-

objet-d'art game: Harry Clarke (1890–1931), Eric Gill (1882–1940), Norman Lindsay (b. 1879), John Austen. . . .

But of course Morris's taste for sinuous line forms of late medieval derivation was only a personal preference; other Art Illustrators could (and did) prefer different forms, with just as much (or little) reason. And so in the late 1880s and -90s all sorts of long-obsolete illustrative forms and printing techniques began to be revived and made Precious Objects for Exhibition in art books. In France, Auguste Lepère (1849–1918) began reviving the flat black wood-block technique that had died out with chapbooks in the 18th century, and it soon became a fad among advance-guard painters, beginning with Emile Bernard (1868–1941), Gauguin, and the Pont-Aven "primitives." German Expressionists, too, found it entrancing and made much of it—Ernst Barlach (1870–1938), Franz Masereel (b. 1889), Nolde, Munch, Schmidt-Rotluff, all experimented with "pure woodcut form." Later on Picasso, Matisse, Maillol, and Rouault demonstrated their versatility by throwing off a woodcut or two:

> Dunoyer de Ségonzac has influenced a great number of young illustrators. Ségonzac's drawings must be prized for themselves. To the chagrin of some authors and publishers, his illustrations usually have little relation to the printed page. His vivacious line full of intense feeling decorates the text by masterly inference."
> [Howard Simon, *500 Years of Art & Illustration*, 1942, p. 220]

Needless to say, such an activity has nothing to do with any art of illustration in the proper sense; it is simply the Fine Art of painting pursed by other means (**37a–d**). The same applies to the revival of lithography and other ancient techniques embodied in fancy productions by The Overbrook Press, the Limited Editions Club, and all the rest from Stephen Gorden and Rockwell Kent, Elfriede Abbe and Arthur Szyk—all so elegant, so clever, so contrived, so dead. They need not detain us. The only question about Fine Art Illustration that concerns any study of the living, Unchanging Arts, is why it appeared so suddenly in the 1890s. The basic reason, of course, is technological.

2. *New Mechanical Techniques of Mass Illustration*

Not only was adult book illustration in general being made a minor field by competition from movies and comics in the 1890s, but in the 1890s two radically new methods of reproduction were appearing that made all earlier illustrative forms economically obsolete. The search for means to make reproductions without any intervention by a human draftsman was over at long last. It had begun in the 1850s, when in France Firmin Gillot (1820–1872) had invented a process of making autographic relief etchings (gillotypes) which would take the place of wood blocks for book and magazine illustration, and in England Bolton sensitized the surface of a boxwood block so that a print could be photographed on it instead of being drawn by hand. It continued in the 1870s, when photographic transference of line drawings to zinc plates was developed by Gillot's son to produce photographic line cuts, which became common in the 1880s. But all these processes still required the services of an engraver. In the late 1870s and -80s experimenters everywhere began trying to eliminate him by devising some method of breaking the printing surface into points from which a relief could automatically be made: Max Jaffé in Vienna made cross-line halftone engravings using a screen of bolting cloth in 1877; Joseph Swan of London (1828–1914), something similar in 1879 by turning his single-line screen during exposure. Georg Meissenbach of Munich (1841–1912) and William B. Woodbury of New York (1834–1885) patented comparable processes in the 1880s. Frederick E. Ives (1856–1937) of Philadelphia fastened two single-line glass screens to make a cross screen about 1885. Finally in 1893 Max Levy (1857–1926) developed the first commercially practical way of making halftone screens. Now printing surfaces could be made from photographs directly without intervention from either draftsman or engraver.

In an article written in 1928 ("Photography and the Modern Point of View . . . ," *Metropolitan Museum Studies,* I, 1, pp. 16–24), William M. Ivins speculated that this development of automatic reproductive processes was almost as important a milestone in the history of art as the original invention of photography, for it meant that art historians could now compare works of art from many scattered places with an ease, speed, and objectivity impossible before. He also suggested that "release from the tyranny of the imitative requirements" of print-making and illustration encouraged a new "artistic freedom"—i.e., departure from naturalistic appearance, conventional laws of perspective, and so forth. But of course, this sort of "artistic freedom" in fact had begun long before, and as we pointed out in the preceding chapter on photography, its so-called "retreat from likeness" was not a retreat *from* photographic literalism, but *into* it. The real influence of this new process was on the art book, for by making all the old techniques of woodcut and lithography economically obsolete, by cutting them loose from social function, it made them available and attractive to the Fine Artist. Now that woodcuts and lithographs no longer had any use, Fine Artists could use them freely without fear of criticism on objective grounds of misuse, or indeed on any other. Or in other words, the moment they died, they became Fine Art (**37a, b, c**). And of course, they also ceased to be living arts of illustration; those were going on elsewhere.

3. *Professional Illustrative Arts, 1890–1930*

Though the High Art of easel-painted illustration and the Low Art of adult book illustration both died out after 1890, a Low Art of illustration for children's books and magazines flourished for another generation or two—indeed, the period from 1890 to 1930 includes some of the most famous names in the history of all illustration, who at first sight seem to be carrying on its tradition with conspicuous success. But on closer analysis, significant divergences appear.

To begin with, instead of their art being modeled on a High Art of illustrative painting, it follows precedents in earlier Low illustration. Thus, for instance, Cruikshank is plainly the inspiration for Kate Greenaway (1846–1901), Alfred Kubin (1877–1959), Ernest H. Shepard (b. 1879) and Rex Whistler (1905–1944). Tenniel, Arthur Hughes, and Dicky Doyle furnish the combination of romantic and whimsical elements characteristic of Arthur Rackham (1867–1939), Edmund Sullivan (1869–1933), W. Heath Robinson (1872–1944), Edmund Dulac (1882–1953), and Beatrix Potter (1866–1943). The Brandywine School of southeastern Pennsylvania and Delaware, led by Newell Convers (N. C.) Wyeth (1882–1945) (**38b**), Stanley Arthurs (1877–1951) and Frank Schoonover (1877–1963) depends on precedents set by the last generation of truly traditional illustrators—the generation of Howard Pyle (1853–1911) (**38a**), Edwin Austin Abbey (1852–1911) and Edward Windsor Kemble (1861–1933) (**35a**)—who had drawn on the High Art of Homer, Eakins, and the late Romantics. John R. Neill, second illustrator of L. Frank Baum's Oz books, draws on the first, W. W. Denslow (1856–1915) (**38c**). And leading magazine illustrators of the period, like James Montgomery Flagg (1877–1960) and Norman Rockwell (b. 1894), draw partly on Pyle and Wyeth, partly on the Low Art interpretations by Charles Dana Gibson (1867–1944) of Sargent's High Art style.

The reason they draw on Low Art precedent is obvious enough; once High Art Illustration begins to die out, they have no alternative. Two results follow. The first is that they are professional illustrators in a new narrow sense; where earlier Low Artists through their associations with High Art were related to the whole tradition of Western art generally, they are concerned only with a sharply defined segment of it. And the second is that, by a curious yet logical paradox, they made a quasi-High Art out of mass-oriented illustration (39a). It is no accident either that so many of these illustrators characteristically wrote or compiled books of their own (*The Arthur Rackham Fairy Book*, Howard and Katherine Pyle's *Wonder Clock*, Will Bradley's *Peter Poodle*, Beatrix Potter's *Tales*, and so forth) or that, whereas we look in vain for large collections of the originals from which Tenniel or Doré or Richter's book illustrations were made, originals by these "professionals" have been commonly collected and frequently exhibited. The most striking example of this tendency is the collection of Pyle and N. C. Wyeth originals in the Delaware Art Center in Wilmington, hung in perpetuity by terms of bequest (cf. **38b**); but of course its culmination is in the status achieved by the illustrations of Norman Rockwell and N. C. Wyeth's son, Andrew Wyeth (b. 1917).

4. *Norman Rockwell, Andrew Wyeth, and the Persistence of Romantic Illustration*

It was commonly said in the 1930s and -40s that Norman Rockwell was the most popular artist in the United States; in the 1950s and -60s Andrew Wyeth was more or less officially confirmed in that distinction. Needless to say, no such estimate of them prevails among Fine Artists. Andrew Wyeth is accorded some grudging recognition because of the "psychological Realities" his paintings are said (by some) to reveal; but to orthodox Fine Art apologists Rockwell's paintings are in the same category as Joyce Kilmer's *Trees*—the kind of horrible example bright young intellectuals begin classes in Art Appreciation with, something so safely and easily jeered at that rapport is established at once.

By their standards Rockwell is not a painter at all—he is a fossil, an artist entirely traditional in theory and practice accidentally intruding into a century Fine Artists claim for their own. Concerned only to amuse, inform, or please, he shows no interest in their concept of Reality. Rockwell does not invent subject matter in the sense that

Courbet or Gauguin or Picasso invented theirs; his subject matter is in essence dictated to him by public demand. Hence its extraordinary consistency (or, in Fine Art terms, "unoriginality"). From his first *Saturday Evening Post* covers in 1916 to his latest work of the 1960s, his basic themes remain unaltered: carefree, high-spirited, "normal" boys and girls; hard-working providers and devoted homemakers; kind friends and close families—in a word, healthy and sane people in a happy world. Of course, this world is no personal invention or private fantasy of his own. Rockwell's subject matter simply perpetuates in 20th-century clothes and context the mental and moral atmosphere of E. W. Kemble's illustrations for *Huckleberry Finn* and Joel Chandler Harris's *Uncle Remus* stories, of N. C. Wyeth's illustrations to *Heidi, The Yearling, Scottish Chiefs, The Last of the Mohicans, King Arthur, The Oregon Trail;* of Homer and Eakins, of Bingham and Mount.

Rockwell depicts, in other words, neither Realities that exist in this world now, nor visionary Realities belonging to another world, but images of this world here and now as it ought to be—as all older artists traditionally did. And he creates them, furthermore, by their traditional process of abstraction and selection from nature and from the works of preceding artists. When, for example, Rockwell modeled his rugged figure of "Rosie the Riveter" for a 1943 *Post* cover (**39b**) on Michelangelo's prophet Isaiah on the Sistine ceiling, he was only following Reynolds's precedent in *Sarah Siddons as the Tragic Muse* (*The Restless Art,* p. 11) and the traditional principle of creating "noble human forms in noble action" by judicious abstraction from nature and selection of appropriate prototypes. This is by no means to put Rockwell beyond criticism, however. It means only that he should be criticized on the right grounds.

Most criticism of painting like Rockwell's begins with the assumption that what chiefly appeals to the public is its "naturalism," and proceeds to argue that if only the public were educated to "appreciate abstract art" Rockwell's art would have nothing to offer. This is absurd. Rockwell's paintings are admired not for their forms but for their content. They are romantic paintings; it is their romanticism that pleases; and all criticism must start from there. We could all agree, for example, that compared to Bingham or Homer, Richter or Delacroix or Doré, Rockwell's is in general not very high-level romanticism. We could go further and argue that the romanticism of his *Four Freedoms* of 1942 in particular is feeble and inappropriate; that a simple Vermont mechanic speaking up in the Arlington Town Meeting has no proper relevance to the Freedom of Speech in modern industrialized society; that Freedom from Fear needs some image deeper than two middle-class Vermont parents tucking their children into bed. But surely it takes no great powers of perception to realize this, and to explain the immense appeal of these paintings—perhaps the most popular ever done in the United States—in terms of public bathos is fatuous. Actually, the reason is simply that the public was offered no choice. It was not a case of preferring Rockwell's images of the Four Freedoms over some other, higher embodiments; the choice was Rockwell or nothing.

That the public would have chosen more effectively romantic paintings than Rockwell's, given a chance, was demonstrated in the 1950s and -60s by the immense popularity of Andrew Wyeth's work, particularly by the extraordinary success of his exhibition in Philadelphia in the fall of 1966. Dr. Edgar Preston Richardson, who wrote an introduction for the catalogue of that show, was kind enough to send a copy to me on the West Coast, and with it a letter commenting on the huge crowds it drew. "People are hungry," he wrote, "for an art that speaks to them." Precisely. These crowds were not drawn by Wyeth's "magic realism," but by the pleasure his subject matter afforded; they came because he, unlike Fine Artists, offered them something besides unwanted and unneeded disquisitions on all the dismal Realities, great or petty, of 20th-century life—because Wyeth's, like Rockwell's, was art performing its ancient function of making life somehow more bearable, somehow happier. It spoke of a different kind of world, a world of such permanent appeal to everyone that even as hardheaded a man as George Orwell longed for it:

> What's the use of saying that one oughtn't to be sentimental about "before the war"? [Which is, of course, a romantic image of something better than anything actually existing then.] I *am* sentimental about it. So are you. . . . People then had something that we haven't got now. . . . they didn't think of the future as something to be terrified of. It isn't that life was softer then than now. Actually, it was harder. People on the whole worked harder, lived less comfortably, and died more painfully. . . . And yet people had in those days a feeling of security . . . of continuity. . . . whatever might happen to themselves, things would go on as they'd known them. . . . their way of life would continue. . . . They didn't feel the ground they stood on shifting under their feet. . . . Forever and ever decent God-fearing women would cook Yorkshire pudding and apple dumplings on enormous coal ranges, wear woollen underclothes

and sleep on feathers, make plum jam in July and pickles in October, and read *Hilda's Home Companion* in the afternoons, with the flies buzzing round, in a sort of cosy little underworld of stewed tea, bad legs, and happy endings. . . . [*Coming Up for Air*, 1939, Ch. 10]

Wherever art has spoken to this kind of romantic longing, it has been alive. Such, for instance, is the appeal of most ordinary movies—Westerns, love stories, spy and gangster adventures; they all show life as it ought to be. Such too is the appeal of the great children's "classics" of the earlier 20th century. Surely L. Frank Baum's Oz books owe their popularity neither to his prose style (which is execrable) nor to any particular excellence in Denslow's or Neill's illustrations, but to the romantic allegory of the good life they embody—not, again, any life actually lived (for one reaches Oz only through metaphorical death by tornado or shipwreck) but life as one viscerally feels it ought to be (Oz is in fact an Eden, except that here the serpent is cast out). That too is the kind of life inherent in Hugh Lofting's Doctor Dolittle books and A. A. Milne's Winnie-the-Pooh books, and that too is the secret of their appeal.

All these represent concepts of art antithetical to all Fine Art stands for, and since 1940 Fine Artists have moved in on the children's book field and virtually put an end to it. The modern children's illustrated book has become a model of everything "real child art" should have, with the single exception of appeal to children. That is to say, it pleases connoisseurs of "good child art," but not children—for, all Fine Art theory to the contrary, children do not in fact like child art, whether their own (which they are forever trying to "improve") or arty adults' imitations—as anyone who has read to small children must soon discover. Advance-guard children's books are, then, as useless as every other kind of Fine Art. But it no longer matters, for the whole medium has become obsolete anyway. Children's book illustration has fallen into the hands of Fine Artists for the same reason adult book illustration did thirty or forty years before; it has been technologically superseded by other media—comics, movies, animated cartoons, in which the traditional art of illustration lives on, and in which its ancient social functions are still being served.

III

ILLUSTRATION IN MOVING MEDIA

1. *Moving Pictures: Common Origins of Comic Strips and Movies*

IN ONE SENSE, something like comic strips has existed since the beginning of art history, in the sequences of pictures that wind around Trajan's Column, parade over walls of Egyptian temples and Chinese tombs, in the Bayeux tapestry and the bronze doors of baptisteries, in cathedral windows and chapbook pages. And something like movies has been inherent equally long in plays and pantomimes and in arts based on them, like the Holy Sepulcher series in Constance Cathedral, Claus Sluter's Well of Moses at Dijon, or Hogarth's narrative prints. By 1800 such narrative sequences had become well established in the Low Arts; a particularly good example is the series of *Tours of Doctor Syntax* illustrated by Thomas Rowlandson (1756–1827) between 1810 and 1815—or, more exactly, "texted" by William Combe (1741–1823), for, in fact, Rowlandson did the drawings first and Combe wrote verses accompanying them to order (**40b**). But between this traditional kind of picture-storytelling in the early 19th century and the comic strip proper, there is one great difference—the principle of sequential movement. Whereas each of Rowlandson's drawings, like Hogarth's narrative prints and all their predecessors, is still essentially a single episode and so as self-contained as a painting, each picture in the comic strip of the 1890s is as incomplete without the others as any single still on a reel of motion-picture film. The comic strip put pictures into motion, just as movies did; and the two processes developed side by side throughout the 19th century.

While some experimenters were putting strips of pictures on revolving drums and otherwise making them move mechanically, others were devising strips of pictures that moved graphically. Among the first was Rodolphe Toepffer (1788–1846) of Geneva, with his "pictorial literature," in which various adventures (*Histoire de M. Jabot,* 1833; *Histoire de M. Crépin,* 1837; *Histoire de M. Vieux Bois,* 1837; *Le Docteur Festus,* 1840) were related in short sequences each concerned with a single episode (**41a**). Toepffer's innovations were followed by Heinrich Hoffmann-Donner (1809–1894), whose fantastically successful *Struwwelpeter* (Frankfort, 1845, republished as *Slovenly Peter* in London, 1848, New York, 1850, and in fact still in print) spread it around the world; further developed by Gustave Doré in his lithographed series *The Labors of Hercules* (1847); and perfected by Wilhelm Busch (1832–1908) in the 1860s and -70s. The results were remarkable. Doré anticipated by almost forty years Fine Artists' attempts to represent successive moments of "stopped action," and the photographers' (which the Fine Artists were imitating) by almost thirty (**41b**). Busch was comparably far ahead (**41c, 42a**). By the end of the 1860s he had not only multiplied pictures of successive moments of episodes to a point where for all intents and purposes they need only have been put on transparent paper to become animated film strips; he had also multiplied successive moments within a single picture to the point reached in painting only with Cubism in the early 1900s (e.g., *A New Year's Concert* from *Fliegende Blätter* for 1865/66, republished as *The Virtuoso* in *Münchener Bilderbogen,* 1868) and anticipated Expressionist principles by the same stretch of time (e.g., *Herr und Frau Knopp,* 1876; *die Haarbeutel,* 1877).

By the 1880s such storytelling devices were common in comic art—illustrators Arthur B. Frost (1851–1928) and T. L. Sullivant used them regularly for humorous anecdote in American magazines, for instance (**42b**—and thence to both comic strips and motion pictures was only a short jump (**42c**). By the 1890s both were appearing, strikingly similar to each other—as a comparison of the first minute-or-two movies, like *Washday Troubles* (1895) or *Baby's Breakfast* (1895) by Auguste and Louis Lumière (1862–1954 and 1864–1948) with early comics will make plain.

They also had the same sort of audience. Both were essentially created by and for the first generation coming to maturity fifteen or twenty years after introduction of universal public education in most Western countries around the 1870s. Without these new masses of people educated just enough to read, publishers like Hearst and Pulitzer would have had no market for their cheap daily newspapers, and no incentive to put entertainment like comic strips into them. And without audiences able to read captions, motion pictures could never

259

have evolved from curiosities at country fairs into vehicles for telling complex stories. Conversely, of course, it was their potential market that stimulated all the mechanical inventions of the 1880s that made cheap newspapers and motion pictures economically and technologically feasible—high-speed presses and cheap paper from woodpulp, new automatic halftone photographic reproduction, rotogravure (invented by Karel Vaclav Klič, 1841–1926), celluloid film, portable movie cameras, electric-lit projectors. It follows that both comics and motion pictures were in their inception entirely Low Arts for the masses, displacing other Low Arts like Currier & Ives prints, cheap illustrated books for adults, burlesque and repertory stage entertainment, as they in turn had displaced copperplates and chapbooks, miracle plays and Punch-and-Judy shows.

It follows that, given such a half-literate matrix, these first comics appealed to and manifested much in common with preliterate, nonverbal mentalities known from medieval, archaic Greek, and other eras of history. That is why later comics seemed to a critic like Hellmut Lehmann-Haupt so deplorable a retrogression from the "animation" of earlier ones:

> In twentieth-century America animated drawing has once more slipped back into the limbo of "illegitimacy." . . . I am unable to explain why this should have happened. . . . Current attempts . . . lack true animation. . . . The speech balloon in its current elaboration interferes with the basic simplicity of animated drawing. . . . ["Animated Drawing," *Illustrators of Children's Books 1744–1945*, Boston, 1947, pp. 212–14]

And that too is the root of Marshall McLuhan's theory (in *Gutenberg Galaxy*, 1962) that movies (along with radio and television) are involving and promulgating a new kind of mentality which will displace the old verbal categories and processes of thought.

Both go wrong, I think, in premising their argument on the common assumption that such Low Arts are taking their direction and forms from advance-guard painting. McLuhan in particular refers constantly to painters pioneering the new vision, and electronic arts spreading it through all levels of society in accordance with the painters' lead. Facts refute any such premise. In this case as in every other, new forms produced in Low Arts to satisfy social needs were copied later by Fine Artists as ends in themselves. Specifically, preliterate and nonverbal forms were not invented by Dada, Surrealist, or related advance-guard painters, but were in fact borrowed by them from the Low Arts of photography, motion pictures and comics, where they had appeared decades earlier. It follows that, so far from growing out of or manifesting some deep and widespread change in modes of perceiving Reality within Western society, the appearance of these forms in Fine Art meant just the opposite—that they had been discarded by Low Arts as irrelevant to social needs and were now subjective Realities relevant only to painting; for it is the nature of Fine Art never to adopt forms with living functions, only those whose function has been lost. And historically that is just what happened. Comics and movies, so far from steadily spreading a nonverbal and preliterate habit of thought throughout society, steadily shed it, as Lehmann-Haupt was quite acute enough to recognize. What his premises inhibited him from seeing was the reason—that "animated form" was not a matter of choice for Low artists, something they could keep or lose at will like a painter choosing a new "style," but dictated by the function of their art in society. Hence if comics (and movies) became less "animated," less preliterate and nonverbal, it was because their public demanded, and imposed on them, an ever more literate, articulate, and rational form of communication. Like the history of all living arts, theirs is not the record of adopting and discarding purposeless forms at tastemakers' whims, but of the development and perfecting of forms for set purposes understood by artist and public in common.

2. *Maturing of the Comic-Strip Form, 1890–1910*

Who first perfected the comic-strip form is as pointless to argue as who first perfected Romanesque vaults or Byzantine mosaics or Greek amphora. Like all living art, it appeared not on individual whim but in response to given demand under given conditions. All that can certainly be said is that circumstances favored its appearance during the 1890s in the United States, where heavy lower-class immigration combined with higher average wages and a more systematic public education system to create a larger market for new mass media than elsewhere. Among its pioneers four were outstanding: Richard Felton Outcault (1863–1928), creator first of the *Yellow Kid* (*Hogan's Alley*) in Joseph Pulitzer's New York World (February 16, 1896), later of *Little Mose* (1901) and *Buster Brown and Tige* (1902) in the New York *Herald;* Rudolph Dirks (1878–1968), creator of *The Katzen-*

jammer Kids on the model of Wilhelm Busch's *Max und Moritz*,* New York *Sunday Journal* (December 12, 1897); James Swinnerton (b. 1875), whose protocomic *Little Bears and Tigers* appeared in the San Francisco *Examiner* as early as 1892, but whose major contribution was *Little Jimmy*, begun in 1905; and Frederick Burr Opper (1857–1937), creator of *Happy Hooligan* (1899) and *Alphonse and Gaston* (1903).

Among them, these four introduced all the major elements of the modern comic strip (**43a, b, c**). Outcault and Opper developed the principle of continuing characters appearing regularly with distinctive and predictable personalities like those in plays or novels, that readers could "make friends" and identify with. A systematic format of sequential picture boxes was first tried experimentally by Outcault, used regularly first by Dirks, and refined by Opper and Swinnerton, whose *Happy Hooligan* and *Little Jimmy* finally rid comics of all the extraneous stage properties inherited from the older cartoon-print tradition and concentrated on figures alone. Outcault began the practice of having characters' speeches carry the burden of meaning with little or no reliance on captions below; Dirks of consistently putting these speeches in balloons (balloons themselves being an old invention, of course); and Swinnerton introduced the principle of consistent left-to-right sequence of balloons for coherent reading of dialogue. Distinctive dialectal or slangy speech was first used by the *Yellow Kid* and *The Katzenjammers*.

All these innovations, of course, were steps away from pure nonverbal animation towards a more precise and literary form of communication, and this development was consummated by Harry Conway (Bud) Fisher (1884–1954), who coordinated all these diverse principles into one consistent pattern and so created the first completely mature comic strip, *Mutt and Jeff*, introduced in the San Francisco *Chronicle* for November 15, 1907 (**44a**).

3. Mutt and Jeff: *The First Classic Comic Strip*

Mutt and Jeff was the first comic with boxes consistently arranged in a strip instead of square or rectangular groups; the first to appear on a regular six-days-a-week basis; the first to have a drawing

---

* Max and Moritz have always been assumed to be the Katzenjammers' prototypes; yet I own one of Reinecke's *Münchener Bilderbogen* as early or earlier, featuring characters who not only look more like the Katzenjammers than Max and Moritz do, but are named Hans and Fritz and are drawn in a style extraordinarily like the early Dirks's.

style consciously appropriate to the medium (flying globules of exaggerated sweat indicating violent exertion or anxiety, stars indicating pain, dotted lines from eyes to observed objects, all were essentially Fisher's invention); the first to identify characters with particular slang phrases (beginning his career as a sports illustrator, Fisher made Mutt originally a race-track tout and from his argot phrases like "fall guy," "piker," and "get his goat" passed into the language). *Mutt and Jeff* was also the first comic whose characters grew. As the strip shifted its home base—to the San Francisco *Examiner* in 1908, to the New York *American* in 1909, to the New York *World* in 1915—so its characters shifted their locale; from hanging around race tracks Mutt moved to gymnasia, meeting Jeff as a boxer there in 1909 and becoming a promoter, which led to a short-lived fortune in 1910, marriage to Mrs. Mutt, and thenceforward steady progress towards domestic respectability (if hardly felicity). By 1910 Fisher's development of novellike characters was emphasized by his producing the first "comic book," a collection of *Mutt and Jeff* strips (which sold well but, curiously enough, had no successors for eighteen years to come), and confirmed in 1915 when he won a major lawsuit restraining Hearst from imitating *Mutt and Jeff* as he had *The Katzenjammers,* on grounds that Fisher's characters were a literary creation and not a "property" like Dirks's. Such a "literary" development ended any early existentialist potentialities in the comic-strip form, of course. It also was what enabled Fisher to create the first comic-strip classic.

By definition, a "classic" is anything demonstrably the best of its kind; a classic in art is a creation that comprehends, embraces, and supersedes all art of similar kind and purpose, as Michelangelo's Sistine ceiling comprehended and surpassed the achievements of Masaccio, Giotto, and the Romanesque vault of Saint-Sernin, or the Master of Olympia all earlier Greek temples. It is in this traditional sense that *Mutt and Jeff* was the classic among early comic strips, for it comprehended and surpassed all the most characteristic creations of the first twenty years.

All early comic strips by their nature were creations and reflections of lower-middle-class American culture in the two decades before World War I altered it forever, and so have much in common. All manifest in varying degrees a characteristic taste for violence and crude horseplay, descending from frontier saloons and burlesque stage routines, that finds flying brickbats and black eyes and "gag" dialogue with puns for punch lines irresistibly funny; an isolationist mentality originating in America's long colonial years, that populates the nonwhite-native-born-American world with comical stereotypes of mono-cled Englishmen, pugnacious Irishmen who live on corned beef and cabbage and call their daughters Bridget, superstitious Negroes de-voted to Ole Massa, debonair Frenchmen adept at love-making, dumb Swedes whose mates are all called Katrinka, Germans by turns fat, furious, and philosophizing, and so on; and above all, an unshakable conviction that despite all contrary appearances America really still is an Eden where men can get along without working if they choose, and where all opportunities lie open to everybody. What distinguished *Mutt and Jeff* was not that Fisher's themes were different, but that he handled the same themes better, more comprehensively, with intima-tions of universality. Consider, for one example, Augustus R. Mutt in his first half-dozen years' existence as an embodiment of the old American ideal of Adamite idleness, compared with typical contempo-raries. Where they are specific, he is a universal type. *Happy Hooligan* is a bum. The *Yellow Kid* is an outcast. Jiggs is a post-Civil War and mauve-decade type of *nouveau riche*. But Mutt is a broad symbol of the freedom a bounteous land makes possible. Though he never toils, he never starves. Though he never wins at the track, he always finds money to make more bets somehow. For his endless follies there is no retribution. Here then is a true descendant of the image earlier embodied in lounging Brother Jonathan, in Bingham's gamblers and jolly flatboatmen, in Mount's contented idlers—a universal symbol of the new American man, freed from the primeval curse of work, at ease in Eden.

4. Krazy Kat: *Klassic Kultural Expression of the 1920s*

In 1917 Bud Fisher put Mutt and Jeff into the Army; though duly demobilized in 1919, they were never the same again. Subtly, steadily, *Mutt and Jeff* shifted from burlesque to domestic situation comedy. An era had ended, and Fisher was quite acute enough to realize it. Not that he claimed gifts of inspired insight enabling him to discover and reveal the spirit of the times, of course; it was simply that public demand and attitudes were shifting, and he changed accordingly. Indeed, only in restrospect would sociologists be able to analyze exactly what was going on and define it, like C. Wright Mills in *White Collar: The American Middle Classes* (1951), as "white-collar" work and outlook supplanting "blue-collar" as the lower-middle-class norm. "By their rise to numerical importance," Mills wrote, "the white-collar people" not only confounded Marxist predictions that the division between capitalists and proletariat would grow steadily sharper, but "transformed the tang and feel of the American experience. They carry, in a most revealing way, many of those psychological themes that characterize our epoch."

It is typical of the confusions generated by the 20th-century concept of Fine Art that Mills went on to wonder why such a major sociological change seemed to have had so little effect on American art or literature. For this is absurd. If once you turn from the Fine Arts of painting or literature in the 1920s, which were indeed almost entirely preoccupied with talking about themselves, to those arts with living functions in society, you find that white-collar life, fears, and fantasies constitute by far the largest part of their subject matter from 1920 to 1945. This is true of popular novels, magazine stories, and their illustrations. It is true of movies. And it is especially noticeable in comics; what happened to *Mutt and Jeff* was characteristic of almost all.

The old proletarian world of the early comics simply faded out in the early 1920s. A few stubborn holdouts remained, such as *Moon Mullins* in his loud checked suit (à la Mutt) and retinue of prewar characters—Uncle Willie in long woollen drop-seated underwear, Aunt Mamie with tattooed forearm, Kayo in his derby hat (a latter-day *Yellow Kid*) and Lord Plushbottom, the monocled silly-ass Englishmen. But they were fossils, like the comic postcards in Orwell's famous essay on "The Art of Donald McGill":

> A whole category of humour, integral to our literature [and High Art] until 1800 or thereabouts, has dwindled down to these ill-drawn post cards, leading a barely legal existence in cheap stationers' windows. The corner of the human heart that they speak for might easily manifest itself in worse forms, and I for one should be sorry to see them vanish. [*Dickens, Dali and Others*, 1946]

Now the mainstream of comic-strip art was represented by the "domestic idyll" acted out by Nebbs and Gumps, Willetts and Wallets, Toots and Caspar and Little Buttercup, Dagwood and Blondie and Baby Dumpling.

What was so appealing about such domestic-idyll strips? It could be argued that they embodied vestigial survivals of atavistic folk humor, and certainly prototypes for mismatched pairs of domineering wives and meek husbands like Andy and Min Gump, Toots and Caspar, or Mr. and Mrs. Mutt could be found in Chaucer and Boccaccio, while *Our Boarding House* with Amos and Martha Hoople might be seen as a faint reincarnation of the Southwark tavern where fat Falstaff bragged and cadged his keep from Mistress Quickley; but this is a tenuous case at best. Even shakier is the notion of some "delighted recognition of the realities of ordinary life" that one commentator suggested. It is hard to imagine why any white-collar reader would enjoy reminders of the fact that he was condemned to be

> never as independent as the farmer used to be, nor as hopeful of the main chance as the businessman . . . always somebody's man, the corporation's, the government's, the army's . . . the man who does not rise . . . the dependent employee whose advent has paralleled the decline of the independent individual and the rise of the little man in the American mind. [Mills, *White Collar*, p. 203]

No; what these strips provided was just the opposite—an escape from Realities into the old American dream of a life untrammeled by economic cares, unlimited in its possibilities, infinitely varied in its pleasures. For that is of course the kind of life these strips depict. These happy families have their small troubles and quarrels, to be sure, but nothing fundamentally serious. Nobody ever works very hard; like Bingham's raftsmen and Mount's farmboys, these comic-strip characters always have leisure for fun—even "working girls" like *Winnie Winkle the Breadwinner, Tillie the Toiler,* or *Polly and Her Pals* rarely toil over their typewriters in fact; their appeal derives from the exciting new pleasures emancipation of women has provided. Neither is there much reference to the gnawing insecurities of white-collar life. So Rube Goldberg's fantastic machines can be accepted as hilarious spoofs on impossibly wild ideas for mechanizing industry and automating business instead of some haunting intimation of change threatening all white-collar jobs and security ("don't just stand there, you may be replaced by a button"). So a character like H. T. Webster's Caspar Milquetoast is funny precisely because *The Timid Soul* is taken to be a parody, and never an archetype, of the Typical American Man. The basic assumption behind all these comic strips is that they perform art's old traditional function of representing an ideal world, an idyllic place of retreat from Realities, not an exposure of them. It follows that they could be judged poor, good, or excellent according to how well and imaginatively they carried their function out; and on such grounds George Herriman (1881–1944) was called the greatest comic-strip artist of the 1920s, and *Krazy Kat* the classic of that era (**44b**).

Like his contemporaries, Herriman created a dream world
—except that his was located not in romanticized suburbia but in a
genuine fairyland, the enchanted mesa (pronounced "macey") at
Coconino near Yorba Linda, Arizona, and inhabited not by stereotyped characters like Mom and Pop, Sis and Junior, but by talking
animals. The idea of anthropomorphic animals, of course, was hardly
new. From time immemorial—in early Egypt and Mesopotamia, in
Aesop's fables, in medieval marginalia and tales of Reynard the Fox—
talking animals have been a means of saying things that would sound
seditious or scandalous, ridiculous or platitudinous in the mouths of
human beings, and this is one traditional art nobody could accuse the
20th century of neglecting—the number of talking rabbits alone it has
created is something for a social psychiatrist to explain; Walt Disney
built an empire on Mickey Mouse, and George Orwell attacked one in
Animal Farm. But Herriman's animals were by far the most inge-
niously fantastic, ignoring the trammels of convention in a truly
abandoned way.

The two leading characters, to begin with, are androgynous,
and seem to enjoy all rights and privileges thereto appertaining; here
the mismatched pair familiar from other strips of the period is mismatched to the point of genius. Krazy Kat is infatuated with Ignatz
Mouse (or Meece); so far from reciprocating, the pragmatic Ignatz
despises Krazy for his (or her) romanticism and longs only to "krease
that kat's bean with a brick." Krazy, however, who shares so much
with the Mad Knight of La Mancha, quixotically takes Ignatz's bricks
to be a form of love-making, on the authority of an ancient Egyptian
legend which (unknown to Ignatz) relates how a mouse infatuated
with Kleopatra Kat's beautiful offspring hurled at her (or him) bricks
inscribed with declarations of love. Logically, therefore (from his—or
her—point of view), Krazy resents attempts made by Offissa Pupp
(who plays in Coconino a role rather like the Law at Walden Pond) to
restrain Ignatz from delivering his amorous missives. Offissa Pupp,
however, in turn is infatuated with Krazy . . . And all this is delivered in a wildly poetic dialect, varying with the occasion. Witness,
for instance, Krazy's excursion into the romantic world of the Arts and
Crafts movement:

> *Enter* Krazy, *carrying balls of yarn, hand loom, etc.*
>
> IGNATZ: Balls of yarn, my dear Krazy? Going in for weavery,
> I take it.
>
> KRAZY: You take it right, dollink. I'm about to wiv a febric.

IGNATZ [*scornfully*]: Fancy those foolish fingers fabricating a fabric. Oh the futile foof and fuff of it! A waste of warp, a wanton wear of weft, and woof. Foowy!

PUPP [*defensive as ever*]: You [*to Ignatz*] blow a bombastic blast, my boastful buffoon. . . . Deft fingers will weave as no feckless fate has wove before. . . .

> Last scene. An enormous tapestry in
> solid colors, in the dead center of which,
> embroidered with loving care, a brick.

It's madness, but the result makes Krazy and Ignatz into something far more than another mismatched comic-strip pair; together with their inversions (for of course it is the pragmatic Ignatz that talks poetry and Krazy "the music of the Bronx") they constitute at once a satire and a curiously effective embodiment of those images of basic body-soul dualism that have run through the mainstream of Western culture for centuries past; in them are reincarnated Sancho Panza and Don Quixote, Sam Weller and Mr. Pickwick, Faust and Gretchen, the Fool and King Lear.

Herriman, in short, presented the American dream not only in a new medium but in a new dimension; and he invented appropriately new forms to embody it. His complicated characters were represented as complicated assemblages of front, side, and three-quarter views that curiously resemble Cubist constructions. The fairyland character of his enchanted mesa was similarly expressed by deliberately contrasting backgrounds of white and black areas (or in the color strips, flat geometric patterns) which shifted from box to box so that trees were transformed into shrubs, cabins into churches, cacti into cliffs, from one box to the next in a way reminiscent of Dada exhibitions and Surrealist paintings by Tanguay or Arp. And he broke up and out of the formal lines of his boxes, playing variations on conventional linear spatial organization with an abandon like Giorgio de Chirico's. These resemblances to advance-guard painting have of course been noted, as has the resemblance of Fontaine Fox's distinctive linear style in *Toonerville Trolley* to drawings and prints by German Expressionists like Marc or George Grosz, and Cliff Sterrett's *Polly and Her Pals* to paintings by Léger or to Braque in the same period. On occasion they have been cited as examples of the seminal influence of advance-guard painting on the Low Arts. Rarely if ever has it been noted that all these comic-strip forms *precede* the movements in painting they are supposed to have imitated. Fox's style was mature by 1909 or 1910, Sterrett's around 1914 or -15 (*Polly* began in

1913 as the fashionable "French doll" of the Edwardian age), and while *Krazy Kat* is considered (properly) as the classic of the 1920s, in fact it began in 1910,* and by 1912 at the latest the distinctive forms and character of *Krazy Kat* had been established—far too early for influences from Cubism or any other kind of Fine Art.

If there is any relationship between *Krazy Kat* and advance-guard painting at all, it is surely the other way round—Herriman's creation may well have had some influence on various Dada-derived fads of the 1960s, for that would be about the time normally and consistently required for forms invented by the living Low Arts in response to social function to reappear embalmed by Fine Artists. Despite *Time*'s approving comment in Herriman's obituary for May 8, 1944, that "always he felt very humble towards serious artists," in fact his was a greater creation than most if not all of theirs. A decade that could produce living art like *Krazy Kat* and appreciate the subtleties of John Alden Carpenter's jazz pantomime based on it (performed with great success at Town Hall in New York in 1922) was far from the aesthetic desert conventional Fine Art critics make it out to be.

5. Thimble Theatre, *Classic of the 1930s*

With the Great Depression and its abrupt change in cul-tural climate, the zany and whimsical spirit so classically embodied in *Krazy Kat* rapidly evaporated. In the harsher atmosphere of the 1930s, a different sort of cultural expression was demanded. *Krazy Kat* went on, of course, but increasingly became the cult object for a devoted coterie of admirers, to all intents and purposes a sort of Fine Art for comic-strip connoisseurs. The syndicate decision not to have Herri-man's strip continued by another man after he gave it up in the 1940s involved more than recognition of the distinctiveness of Herriman's creation, it also indicated that by then *Krazy Kat*'s mass appeal had long been lost. Another sort of comic strip had developed that spoke far better to and for the human condition in the 1930s; its classic was *Thimble Theatre*, created by Elie Crisler Segar (1894–1938).

The most obvious change in comics at the end of the 1920s was displacement of the hitherto predominant "gag-a-day" format, where each strip dealt with a single separate and complete episode, by

---

* As a substrip in Herriman's *The Family Upstairs;* cf. Gilbert Seldes, "The Krazy Kat That Walks by Himself," *The Seven Lively Arts*, New York, 1924, p. 209.

"suspense" strips telling protracted stories in a series of successive episodes continuing over weeks and months. Related to it was the equally sudden popularity of comic books and long (twenty- or thirty-minute) animated cartoons: *Tarzan,* first book to tell a story in comic-strip form (drawn by Harold Foster, later creator of *Prince Valiant*), appeared in January 1929, and Disney's first mature animated cartoon story in September 1928, with his large-scale production beginning a year or two later. This sudden popularity is the more striking in that none of these forms was entirely new. A sequence strip called *Desperate Desmond* had appeared as early as 1910; Edgar Rice Burroughs's novel *Tarzan of the Apes* had been a best-seller in 1914, three years after the appearance of *Mutt and Jeff's* first collection of strips in book form had suggested the possibilities of such a medium; and animated cartoons had been telling stories of a sort since 1906. What happened, of course, was that, as always, Low Arts did not develop these new forms until a changing public taste demanded them.

The here-today-gone-tomorrow character of gag-a-day strips and five-minute animated-cartoon antics had perfectly matched a carefree kaleidoscopic succession of fads and phases in popular culture of the 1920s. Now, all at once they came to seem somehow tinny and tinsely. An audience beset by chronic economic depression, unsettled ideologies, vague forebodings of all kinds, demanded a different sort of subject matter. So the "funnies" fade away, and in their place come suspense strips, comic books, animated cartoons, all characteristically, almost compulsively concerned with symbols of power. Superhuman *Tarzan of the Apes,* combining a Noble Savage's stamina with the *savoir-faire* of an English lord, by turns besting alligators in the jungles of Africa and suave villains in the jungles of civilized intrigue was the prototype for a parade of comparable figures throughout the 1930s. Masked marvels and caped crime fighters, fearless adventurers and fabulous spacemen and intrepid investigators crowded the earth in those days. They speak to and for a special mood and human condition: "in every one of those little stucco boxes," muses George Bowling, spokesman for the white-collar worker of the 1930s in Orwell's *Coming Up for Air* (1939), "is some poor bastard who's never free except when he's fast asleep and dreaming that he's got the boss down the bottom of a well and is bunging lumps of coal at him." And in retrospect it is plain why *Thimble Theatre* was the strip that spoke to and for him best, and why Popeye the Sailor was the character he could best identify with.

Popeye was quite literally a creation of the hard times that set in for the white-collar class during 1929. He appeared first on January 29 of that year, in a comic strip that had been entirely undistinguished for ten years past, created by an artist who had been entirely undistinguished even longer. Born in Chester, Illinois, E. C. Segar broke into the comic-strip field on the strength of a correspondence course in cartooning and an acquaintance with Richard Felton Outcault, who got him a job in 1915 with the Chicago *Herald*, drawing *Charlie Chaplin's Comic Capers*. In 1917 he moved to the Chicago *Evening American* to do a strip called *Looping the Loop;* in 1919 he began *Thimble Theatre* for King Features Syndicate in New York. All three were feeble gag-a-day strips, poor imitations of Bud Fisher's *Mutt and Jeff* both in style and content; with *Thimble Theatre* featuring such characters as the Oyl family (Castor, Olive, Cole, and Nana), Ben Zene, and Ham Gravy carrying out comparably uninspired burlesque routines, it is not hard to understand why Segar's was the strip dropped whenever subscribing newspapers needed a bit of extra space. But in 1928 Segar began introducing short suspense sequences, and reader interest picked up. When Popeye appeared and a few days later delivered his first sock to the jaw (of Castor Oyl, in this case, for reneging on an agreement), it picked up even more. Within three years after Segar began to develop his new character in longer and longer sequences, Popeye the Sailor had become a household hero, appearing in advertisements, comic books and animated cartoons everywhere. Everyone could hum his theme song ("I fights to the finish, cause I eats me spinach") and quote his homely maxims ("I yam what I yam, and tha's all I yam"). In 1933 the Chicago *Tribune* commissioned Segar to record his visit to the World's Fair; and in 1937 (crowning glory, perhaps) a life-size painted concrete statue of him by one Julian Sandoval was erected in Crystal City, Texas, to honor "the rejuvenator of the spinach industry in Zavala County." Heady stuff, this. Though a generation knowing Popeye only by debased and vulgarized perpetuations of Segar's creation after his death in 1938 might imagine some character like Batman to be a rival or even (such are the horrific twists of televised fate) superior, in fact in his day Popeye had no superiors and few rivals. His was a unique appeal.

From the very beginning Popeye enjoyed one great and decisive advantage over his array of rival supermen. He was always believable in a way they were not. If C. Wright Mills was correct in suggesting in *White Collar* that

> perhaps the most cherished national images are sentimental
> versions of historical types that no longer exist, if indeed they
> ever did . . . [and the white-collar class's is that] the Ameri-
> can possesses magical independence, homely ingenuity, great
> capacity for work, all of which virtues he attained while strug-
> gling to subdue the vast continent. . . .

then Popeye was an image the white-collar class could identify with completely. Nature had not made him tall, handsome, and preposses- sing like Tarzan or Brick Bradford or Buz Sawyer. Nothing like Superman's or Batman's or Dick Tracy's marvelous scientific props aided him. They went about accompanied by statuesque females with bulging bosoms and tantalizing thighs, but Popeye's companion was, alas! that all-too-common clay, that plank on pipestems, perhaps the most unprepossessing heroine in all literature, Olive Oyl. He was, as opponents frequently pointed out to their eventual chagrin, "an ugly little one-eyed runt" whose powers lay all unsuspected beneath a grotesque anatomy. He had no polished manners and no guile. Wealth occasionally brushed him, but he was too simple and honest to hang onto it. He was full of noble Walter Mittyish plans—now rescuing a fair maiden, now questing for Fountains of Youth, now founding his utopian Great Society of Spinachova. And though somehow his feats and fortunes always seemed to peter out into ridiculously ordinary anticlimaxes, Popeye all the better stood for all those hopelessly put- upon little men who dreamed of turning upon their oppressors and, in defiance of all logic and probability, thrashing them.

And as time went on Popeye became a more and more believable figure. Where at first he drank with impunity from poisoned pools, bounced bullets off his chest, and trounced a succession of apelike monsters and mustachioed villains from the old burlesque stage, he soon began to manifest appealing human weaknesses and to battle far subtler enemies. And the less of a stereotyped superman he came to be, the more closely he came to resemble other, earlier sym- bolic savior figures of history and folk legend—the Greek Hercules or the Biblican Samson, for instance (45a). Deprived of spinach, Popeye was as weak as Samson without hair; as Samson had his Delilah, Popeye had his nemesis in Zexa Peal, the Brutian spy who beguiled him at a crucial moment in his career as Dictipator of Spinachova. Like Hercules, Popeye has a son but no wife; Swee'pea appears as mysteriously as Telephus, the only sure facts about him being that he inherits his father's virtues (consuming immense quantities of spinach and disposing of tormentors with mighty swats from fist or baby bottle as circumstances require) and that Olive Oyl is no more his mother than Deianira. Like Hercules again, Popeye was abandoned in infancy, and when he goes to seek his Pappy finds him on a tropical island, like Zeus on Olympus, surrounded by ministering female natives. . . .

Not, of course, that Segar consciously modeled his hero on historical prototypes. It is simply that life for most people at most times has been largely dull and routine, stultified by intangible forces and stifling circumstances; something like a white-collar class has existed everywhere to some degree; and consequently some figure like Popeye, embodying something like white-collar fears and aspirations, has emanated from all historical cultures. What form it takes will vary with the circumstances and the culture that call it forth. We should not then be surprised to find Popeye the 20th-century successor to Hercules or Samson, for just as any people will get the government it deserves, so will it get an appropriate wish-fulfillment image. And in whichever art form is closest to the popular mind of its age—so, as Hercules was embodied in vase-painting and temple metopes, and Samson in sacred chronicles, Popeye was a creation of the comic strip. And further, we should expect ours to be a more complicated image than those, for ours is a much more complex social situation. So it was; that is the peculiar significance of J. Wellington Wimpy, who first appeared in *Thimble Theatre* as a crooked referee in the great Popeye-Tinearo prizefight of May 5, 1931, and soon became the strip's second major character (**45c**).

Popeye and Wimpy together make up an image compelling and meaningful on at least three levels. They correspond first to the traditional Don Quixote–Sancho Panzo sort of body-soul dualism in general that runs so deep throughout all Western thought—Popeye simple-mindedly daring all dangers and defying all odds to defend his ideals is set off against Wimpy continually, unscrupulously, ineptly scheming for low goals. They are also specifically applicable, believable, and appealing to the white-collar situation in the 1930s. For if Popeye embodies a white-collar dream, Wimpy embodies white-collar reality. If Popeye is how the white-collar worker longs to see himself, Wimpy is what he secretly knows himself to be—prisoner to creature comforts, toadying dissembler, moocher of hamburger crumbs from strong men's tables. And in the deepest sense they represent too those twin extremes of creative independence and conformist mediocrity whose interaction determines the character of any civilization.

To appreciate what Segar did with this symbolic vehicle, one has to read typical long sequences, presently buried in back files of newspapers from the 1930s. They are worth the effort of digging out, for his was a remarkable accomplishment. Better than any of his contemporaries, I think, he solved the basic time-pacing problem inherent in his medium:

> Narrative sequences correspond roughly to the chapters of a picaresque novel: the plot of each is complete in itself but the leading characters are carried over into the next sequence. The usual length of sequences is from forty to sixty installments. They often seem much longer, however, because strip time is so much slower than actual time (I have asked ten faithful readers of *Steve Canyon* how long, according to real time, Pipper and Murphy were marooned on the ice. Almost all the answers ranged between 6 weeks and 3 months, and only one reader gave the correct answer: about 4 weeks) . . . a unique artistic situation, since in novels, plays, and movies, time usually goes much faster for the characters than for the readers. . . .
>
> Like every other art form, the comic strip has certain limitations, at first sight discouraging, which become virtues in the right hands. Probably the most important is that each strip must compete with a good many others for the reader's favor, and at its own peril makes demands on his memory and attention. If an artist is to retain his audience, he must delineate his characters sharply and drive home his point quickly and clearly in strip after strip. [Ignatius Mattingly, "Some Cultural Aspects of Serial Cartoons," *Harper's Magazine*, December 1955, p. 35]

Segar's ability to get the most out of a given situation ringing an extraordinary number of changes on a single theme before moving on, has been rivaled only by Charles Schulz's *Peanuts* in the 1960s, I think; but unlike Schulz, Segar managed to ring these changes within the framework of sequences much longer than usual, containing narratives within narratives. And with this vehicle he created from late 1933 into mid-1937 some of the most extraordinary allegories of his age.

Early in the long "Fountain of Youth" sequence of 1935, for instance (**45d**), a prehistoric monster called Toar is discovered, an apparition from the remote past in whom we may recognize the neo-barbarism then stalking Europe. What to do? Popeye, symbol of traditional virtues and attitudes, is all for seeking out and destroying the monster at once. Wimpy, by contrast, tries sweet reasonableness. "The trouble with Wimpy is," as Popeye once explained to Olive Oyl, "he went to collich onc't, and never got over it"; here he plays the intellectual of the 1930s. With a conventional humanist education reinforced by that pervasive faith in the Natural Goodness of Man typical of our century, he refuses to believe that monsters can exist, preferring instead to assume that all men everywhere are essentially decent and reasonable and so (as Roosevelt wrote in his famous 1938 letter to Adolf Hitler) "All disputes can always be settled at the council table." He insists on treating the monster like anyone else, shakes hands with him cordially, invites him to tea. For a moment, he seems to have put the others to shame by his sophistication. But very soon it develops that Toar really is a monster. He really is capable of destroying everyone and everything. There is in fact no common basis for reaching an understanding with him, and Wimpy flees in panic for his life. Popeye is left to deal with the situation, and he does, in a long and bitter battle that costs him a broken neck; only then is an understanding reached and peace secured. In all of which it takes no great perspicacity to recognize prefigurations of Chamberlain and Churchill, of Munich and the Battle of Britain, and a parallel to the belated realization of intellectuals like Orwell:

> What has kept England on its feet during the past year [1940]?
> . . . chiefly the atavistic emotion of patriotism, the ingrained
> feeling of the English-speaking peoples that they are superior to
> foreigners. For the last twenty years the main object of English
> left-wing intellectuals has been to break this feeling down, and if
> they had succeeded, we might be watching the S.S. men patrol-
> ling the London streets at this moment. ["Wells, Hitler, and the
> World State," *Dickens, Dali and Others*]

Even more complex and pertinent is the allegorical commentary unrolled in Segar's longest sequence, the utopian year-long (1935–36) epic of Spinachova, the new continent that Popeye discovered, colonized, and tried to make into an ideal society where "all me sheeps will be happy." (**45b**) It is a tale of high dreaming fractured on facts: of "sheeps" refusing to fit into slots tidily prepared by benevolent planners; of high resolve to take "from each according to his ability" and give "to each according to his need" breaking down because nobody can determine what abilities and needs each has; of common men coming to their Leader in mobs with "a great idea for winning the war—let's give up"; and above all, of the wiles and woes of liberal statecraft culminating in a final revelation, demonstrated in the war against Brutia, that

the energy that actually shapes the world springs from emotions—racial pride, leader-worship, religious belief, love of
war—which liberal intellectuals mechanically write off as
anachronisms, and which they have usually destroyed so completely in themselves as to have lost all power of action. [*Ibid.*]

E. C. Segar died on October 14, 1938, at the height of that
Munich era whose spirit he had so brilliantly satirized. Insofar as none
of his successors was able to carry on his strip adequately and soon
debased it into mere barbaric buffoonery, it is regrettable that *Thimble
Theatre* was not allowed to die with its creator, as *Krazy Kat* had
been; but probably its days as a classic were over in any event. By the
late 1930s the times were changing again and required another kind of
cultural expression. It was provided by Al Capp (b. 1909) in his strip
Li'l Abner.

6. *Dogpatch, Kentucky: A Classic Allegory of Eden*

When *Li'l Abner* first appeared on August 12, 1935, in the
New York *Daily Mirror*, it was only one more manifestation of a wave
of interest in hillbillies and unsophisticated rural life generally provoked by the Depression, isolationism, and regionalism, a comic-strip
counterpart (by no means unique) to *The Grapes of Wrath* in literature, Grant Wood's *American Gothic* in painting (*The Restless Art*,
p. 391) and the colonial revival in architecture that littered the
countryside with WPA post offices and civic halls in the style of
Samuel McIntire's Salem. Not until the 1940s did Al Capp develop it
into the classic prompting Mattingly's comment that "to find his peer
in richness of invention combined with control over material, one must
go back to Swift or Dante."

Capp's complex and imaginative creation was built, as
traditional art had always been, on a foundation of judicious borrowings from predecessors. Like the enchanted mesa near Coconino,
Arizona, Dogpatch, Kentucky, is a fantasy land where anything may
happen. As hillbillies, Yokums enjoy the same immunities from common convention as talking Katz and Mices (and as fools and grave-
diggers in Shakespearean drama), the same privilege of speaking a
dialect-language of their own that imparts freshness and color to
sentiments trite or pretentious in the mouths of ordinary mortals. From
remoter ancestors like Tenniel's Alice illustrations came Capp's trick of
making oblique topical allusions through caricatures of celebrities

disguised as Dogpatch characters—so we may recognize Calvin Coolidge in the miserly Future Yokum, Winston Churchill in Adorable Jones, Jane Russell (among others) in Moonbeam McSwine. Li'l Abner himself in his golden years drew heavily on the boyish naïveté of Henry Wallace, Roosevelt's third vice-president (1941–1945), chiefly memorable in history—and this is important in the context of Capp's allegory—as the man who in 1948 led a third-party movement pledged to the proposition that Stalin was simply an "agrarian reformer." And from comics like *Thimble Theatre* came the precedent for myth and allegory cast in suspense-sequence form.

Capp's drawing style, however, was much more naturalistic than his classic predecessors', much closer to the "juicy-pen" technique of straight suspense strips like Harold Foster's *Tarzan* and *Prince Valiant*, or Roy Crane's *Buz Sawyer*. Not, I think, that Capp imitated them so much as that they all went back to a common source in the turn-of-the-century illustrative tradition of Howard Pyle, N. C. Wyeth, E. W. Kemble and C. D. Gibson—a matter of some significance, for it suggests the starting point for Capp's distinctive allegory. Where comics of the first three decades spoke primarily to and for a middle-class, white-collar audience, *Li'l Abner's* concern was with the whole Jeffersonian concept of America as a new and different kind of society; it was a comment and allegory on the historic American dream and what was happening to it in the mid-20th century.

Li'l Abner began, to be sure, as a not particularly inspired variant of the Samson-Hercules-Popeye type of white-collar fantasy projection (**46a**), Abner being an elemental type of strong simple hero whose rugged independence is manifested chiefly in resistance to Daisy Mae's charms; Daisy Mae a variant of the girl next door from domestic-idyll strips; and Mammy Yokum an exaggerated but still recognizable version of matriarchal figures like Mrs. Mutt, Maggie, and Martha Hoople. The change began with Capp's development of the two leading support characters in the first few years of the strip. As Mammy Yokum grows steadily stockier and more pugnacious, and Daisy Mae an ever more "bootiful, tremblin' young morsel," each in her way comes to symbolize aspects of the emancipation of women, and by extension, the steady spread of egalitarian ideas through society generally. In Mammy we recognize the new aggressive woman of business appearing in the 1930s. Combining male ruthlessness and female intuition, she not only dominates her home completely—reducing Pappy Yokum to childish insignificance—but also the whole of

Dogpatch, for if ever her fearsome punch fails, she can fall into a trance and call supernatural powers to her aid. As the war years went on and this type of woman (or approximate facsimiles—"Rosie the Riveter" is one, **39b**) became more and more common, traditional male-female relationships inevitably altered. Vanishing were the days when, no matter how browbeaten the white-collar worker might be in his office, he could at least count on being some sort of master in his own household; now he found women not only competing with him everywhere and usurping masculine prerogatives, but at the same time demanding to keep their traditional feminine privileges as well. What then was he to do? Precisely what he did in earlier years when the white-collar corporation structure closed in around him—escape into a fantasy image. And that is the significance of Daisy Mae. Sweet, simple, infinitely amenable, ready to bear any insult from Abner and obey his every whim, she complements the Popeye-type white-collar image of the ruggedly dominant male. With her precocious miniskirt and wispy blouse, she comes straight out of girlie magazines of the period, whose proliferation is directly proportional to female invasion of the working world. The more competitive and competent real women become, the more busily magazines, novels and movies supply a compensatory dream world of googoo-eyed playgirls whose only function (and plainly, only ability) is to be pliant bedmates. Those interested in abstruse research can easily trace the progress of this image in girlie magazines from the 1930s to the present: each decade the playgirls become more naked, more lewd, and the captions more inane, inversely corresponding to the increasing intelligence, drive, and success of women in actual life. But Capp was telling allegorical stories, not making substitute images, and once his symbolical vehicle had been established he soon expanded it to make *Li'l Abner* in the late 1940s and early -50s one great elaborate satire on those promises and dreams of Welfare State Elysiums that were preoccupying all "progressive" minds during and immediately after the War.

Some, to be sure, have seen *Li'l Abner* not as satire on the Welfare State, but as propaganda on its behalf; Mattingly, for one, thought that "Capp manipulates his symbolic apparatus to expound in satirical form the basic doctrine of liberal Christianity," apparently assuming that Capp considered Christianity, socialism, and the Y.M.C.A. all to have the same goal and function of improving life here on earth. And certainly any number of caricatures of "feelthy capitaleests" could be cited romping through those years: Bounder J.

Roundheels the gourmet, General Bullmoose, who lives by "what's good for General Bullmoose is good for the country," the despicable Van Lumps, able and willing to destroy all Dogpatch so that their scion Dumpington might marry Daisy Mae, and so on and on. But the strip is not quite so simple. Consider, for instance, some implications of the long Shmoo sequence (46c), most ambitious of all Capp's Welfare State allegories.

In 1954 there appear in Dogpatch some marvelous creatures called Shmoos, whose chief delight it is to supply human beings with every material want, and who multiply indefinitely. Like the generous American he is, simple-minded Abner natcherly sets out to spread their bounty all over the country, and for a time it seems Utopia is at hand—or Orwell's Animal Farm at least:

> Soon or late the day is coming,
> Tyrant Man shall be o'erthrown,
> Riches more than mind can picture,
> Wheat and barley, oats and hay,
> Clover, beans, and mangel-wurzels
> Shall be ours upon that day. . . .

But then the wicked rich react to protect their privileges and powers; before you know it, the last Shmoo is being exterminated, and everything is on its way back to its usual mizzuble state. Tyrant Man is not o'erthrown, not this time. But soon or late the day is coming. . . . That seems to be the message; or is it?*

Insofar as any deliberate "line" is evident in this story, it is a patent attack on capitalism. Perhaps Capp did incidentally intend it so, though I rather suspect his chief interest was simply to tell a good story that would amuse his audience—that, as they once said of Herriman (in *Newsweek*, May 8, 1944), "delight was his strongest point, in a world where most artists had lost it." But the story raises interesting implications of quite another sort, that Capp can hardly have been unaware of. Supposing the Shmoos had survived, and transformed the world so that Adam need no longer delve nor Eve spin, what then would it be like? It would be like Dogpatch, Kentucky. For that is the kind of life Dogpatchers have always lived—who ever delved or span or was the gentleman there? Dogpatch is in fact the American dream of Eden—and this is the heart of the *Li'l Abner* allegory.

---

* Since this was written, Capp returned to the Shmoo theme in an early-1968 sequence (46d).

Dogpatch is the Jeffersonian vision of every family on its own independent plot of ground: it is inspired accident that Mammy Yokum with her pipe and poke bonnet, Marryin' Sam on his (Methodist) circuit-riding mule, Honest John the (Yankee) trader are all figures straight out of the 18th century. The Dogpatchers are Jefferson's "innocent Americans," living in Arcadian guilelessness and cheerful content, secure in their splendid isolation from the wicked world outside; for them New York and Chicago are what France and England were for Jefferson—"with all their preeminence in science, the one is a den of robbers and the other of pirates," as he wrote to John Adams—and Dogpatchers' visits to the outside world, like outsiders' to Dogpatch, bring only trouble and corruption. This enchanted land of Dogpatch, Kentucky, is an immemorial dream come true:

"The versions of good life as envisaged by both the pious reformer and the atheist leftist, while they differ in minor details, are alike in that this imagined life resembles nothing that has ever been lived but was of old foreseen beyond the grave. In later times, it has been proclaimed but never approached and its principles are at variance with everything we know or can estimate about the behavior of men on this earth. Its perfect form, which is supposed to be the ultimate goal, is complete equality, complete sinlessness—the categories of sin differ but each advocate has his own list of sins that are to cease—complete lack of personal responsibility in the beneficent embrace of the state, whose divine attributes are proclaimed even in the words used to describe it [workers' paradise, utopia, etc.]. And like the Kingdom of Heaven, when once established, this good life is to endure unchanged forever. No evil manipulator can arise within its happy ranks, no outward wickedness can assail it. The reign of Satan will be at an end." [Lawrence Brown, *The Might of the West*, 1963, p. 531]

And in this Eden, what sort of blessed spirits dwell? Well, there are Moonbeam McSwine, Earthquake McGoon, Hairless Joe—lazy, drunken savages fighting, fornicating, frowsting day after happy day. There is Li'l Abner the all-American boy, with a god's physique and a moron's mind. There is Daisy Mae, the all-American girl, full-busted and empty-headed, living only to catch the all-American moron, somehow, some day. For the wisdom of elder generations we are offered Pappy Yokum's whimperings and droolings, Mammy's trances and double whammies. As for the community at large, time and again we observe one overriding principle to prevail—whenever adversity threatens any of its members, abandon him instantly: "Le's go fishin', ah'm tired," all the neighbors agree five minutes after the Yokum cabin has been buried in a landslide. But all enjoy in common the blessings of perfect equality. All Dogpatchers are equal before the law, because there is no law; in learning, for all are ignorant; in skills, for none has any. All Dogpatchers are without sin, for none ever rises to the level of conscious good or evil. All Dogpatchers are free of responsibility, because they have nothing to be responsible for.

7. Comic-Strip Theaters of the Absurd in the 1950s

Al Capp was by no means the only artist so to satirize the American dream, of course. While he was still in art school, Sinclair Lewis's *Arrowsmith* had presented a "100% American town" peopled by

> . . . A. DeWitt Tubbs, Capitola McGurk the Great White Uplifter . . . Dr. Almus Pickerbaugh, dynamic Director of Public Health in Zenith, Booster extraordinary and father of the Healthette Octette—eight strapping girls floridly ranging from Orchid to Gloria. . . . Lewis's use of such comic-strip characters . . . illustrate his contention that America, in seeking to develop a new kind of person, has only turned out new specimens of the grotesque. . . . [D. J. Dooley, *The Art of Sinclair Lewis*, Lincoln, Nebr., 1967]

But what Dooley perceptively called "comic-strip characters" only points up the superior effectiveness of Capp's medium as cultural expression. Lewis wrote as an intellectual satirizing the common man's illusory ideals; Capp's satire grew out of and spoke for the common man's own sense of disillusionment. And as the 1950s went on, two basic shifts of emphasis in *Li'l Abner* recorded how steadily that disillusionment grew.

First came an abandonment of the whole ideal and image of the rugged individualist, dramatized by Li'l Abner's marriage to Daisy Mae in 1951—which effectively put an end to the original ethos of the strip—and implicit in increasingly frequent parodies of the superman theme, of which the archetype was *Fearless Fosdick*, Capp's parody of *Dick Tracy* (46b). And second came an equally significant change in the kind of escape offered readers; instead of fantasy, more and more what *Li'l Abner* offered was simply an escape into the absurd, as characters and situations alike became steadily wilder, more grotesque, more bizarre. Comparable trends had been apparent in a few comics in the early 1940s—in the abject ineffectuality of George Baker's wartime *Sad Sack*, for instance (perpetuated later in Mort Walker's *Beetle Bailey*), or the calculated absurdities of Bill Holman's *Smokey Stover*. In the 1950s they became characteristics common to all the most successful ones.

The "hero" of Walt Kelly's *Pogo* is a possum who wears porkpie hats and likes to smell flowers, and while the outlandish dialects and *mise-en-scene* of Pogofenokee-land may bear some resemblance to Krazy Kat's enchanted mesa and the Great Society of Dogpatch, in fact nothing like *Krazy Kat's* or *Li'l Abner's* basic underlying rationale is apparent; *Pogo's* adventures are less suspense sequences than existentialist episodes.

Plainly, such new directions involved a cathartic reaction to the computerized social-welfarized corporation-organized world that came sharply into conscious focus during the 1950s. What was the point of dreaming about rugged individualism when anyone's entire life history, financial status, marital relations, I.Q. score and compatibility rating spilled out in a pile of cards on some table whenever any official chose to press a computer button? You could not escape into fantasy from a world itself so fantastic; irresponsible absurdity was the only refuge.

This change in comics of the 1950s responded to, mirrored, and measured a far-reaching shift in public mood. An even more significant shift is evidenced in the 1960s, by the enormous popularity of such comics as Charles Schulz's *Peanuts;* Mel Lazarus's *Miss Peach;* *B.C.* and *The Wizard of Id* by Brant Parker and Johnny Hart. For now the comic-strip world seems saner than the real one. In the *Peanuts* strip illustrated (47), Lucy's demand for a life that is "all 'ups' and 'ups' and 'ups' " is not so much fantasy as the traditional American dream; Charley Brown "can't stand it." A *Miss Peach* strip in the fall of 1969 has Ira declaring, "Love is all I really need in life. Love is all anybody needs," and his friends responding, "Right! And we love you, Ira," thereupon shedding floods of hearts over him for three following boxes. "We've got to go now," they say, whereupon he replies, "Thank you for the love," but as he goes off, he reflects, "Now if I could only get rid of my cold, get higher marks, and get my allowance increased . . ."—no Heaven on earth for him, either. Or in the *Wizard of Id* (48) we see that the intellectual-cum-artist who extracts innumerable grants from the Establishment ("More wine for the sage!") only to come up with a pronouncement that "the world is a pork chop" gets rewarded, not with adulative newspaper coverage, rich speaking engagements and a professorship in some university, but with execution. All of which means, I think, the end of the spirit of '76. America may be a great country; it may be a good country to live in; it may still offer opportunity—but it is not a New Eden. The promised *novus ordo seclorum* has not arrived. Americans are not a new kind of men, free from Original Sin, able to perform feats impossible for others living under different institutions. Charley Brown, Ira, the King of Id, the Spook—they are all just types of common humanity. It is no accident at all that comics like these flourished in the same era when older images of American conviction like Roman capitols, the classical Plymouth Rock monument, or the great heads on Mount Rushmore were being superseded by images like the Gateway of the West at St. Louis—grandiose technological achievements, stripped of all specific human meanings or historical associations.

Between comics of the 1950s and -60s and their predecessors there is another significant set of differences. Quite plainly, these later comics are losing any specifically white-collar-class orientation. At the same time, paradoxically, there is a proliferation of new comics aimed at specific kinds of audiences. The appeal of *Pogo*, *Peanuts*, or *The Wizard of Id*—not to mention Jules Feiffer's *Sick Sick Sick*—is limited in a way comics rarely were before. To whole sections of the population they must be fundamentally unintelligible. And a new emphasis on violent animation and exaggerated "sound" effects is now apparent also. All these developments are interrelated reactions to a common situation—beginning in the 1950s, comic strips for the first time faced competition for that lower-middle-class audience which had been their monopoly for so long. By making animated cartoons as available to mass audiences as comics had always been, television transformed what had been the comic strip's poor relative into a formidable rival.

8. *The Moving Comic Strip: Animated Cartoons*

The fact that animated cartoons did not become a truly mass-oriented art until put on television explains much that is otherwise puzzling about their early history.* If we think how Athanasius Kircher published a primitive "magic lantern" device for projecting

---

* Perhaps the best history is Ralph Stephenson, *Animation in the Cinema*, Cranbury, N.J., 1967.

drawings as early as 1640, how many 19th-century experiments in simulating motion involved drawings on moving drums, and how obvious was the combined application of these ideas once celluloid film became available, it could be argued that animated cartoons were the first kind of motion picture. Certainly by 1906 *Gertie the Dinosaur,* Vitagraph's *Funny Phases of Funny Faces,* and Emile Cohl's animations for Gaumont showed their basic technique had been fully mastered everywhere (**50a**). Yet over the next two decades no further significant advances were made. While comics by the 1920s were making predecessors look primitive and naïve, animated cartoons hardly changed at all, so that Pat Sullivan's *Felix the Cat* is hardly distinguishable from *Gertie.* True, animated cartoons were handicapped by having no sound; the inferiority of animated *Mutt and Jeff* cartoons to their comic-strip progenitor demonstrates how essential running dialogue was to the comic strips' effectiveness. But even after sound was introduced in 1928, animated cartoons still did not really compete with comic strips for another twenty years. And the basic reason was, quite simply, that they lacked that discipline which only the demands of a mass audience could provide. For whereas motion pictures proper early became a mass medium in place of illustrated adult books, because they were so much more easily available—it cost far more money and took far more time to buy and read an illustrated book than to spend an evening at the movies ("Have you read the book? No, but I saw the picture . . .")—the reverse applied to animated cartoons; newspapers brought comic strips to a mass audience every day for virtually nothing, but to see animated cartoons you had to go out and buy a ticket. Not until television made it just as easy to sit at home and watch animated "funnies" as to read them in a newspaper would they give comic strips any serious competition; and only then would animated-cartoon makers come under comparable competitive pressures to realize the proper function and utilize all the potentialities of their medium. Of this, the great example is to be found in the work of Walt Disney (1901–1967).

Disney began making animated cartoons in 1923, after a few years' experience as a newspaper cartoonist in Kansas City. For three years he drew *Alice in Cartoonland,* then in 1926 created a character of his own, *Oswald the Rabbit.* Like most animated cartoons of the 1920s, this early work was elemental in concept so that it proved Disney's ultimate good fortune when Central Productions Agency took *Oswald* away from him in 1928 and forced him to strike out on his own. Not only was this the beginning of Walt Disney Enterprises, but by having to build his company around a salable comic-strip character, *Mickey Mouse,* Disney was able to begin overcoming what had been his and his contemporaries' most serious handicap—their confusion between the proper function of animated cartoons and that of movies. Perhaps because both were then made by the same people and in the same way (by separate photographs of drawings for each frame, unlike the later technique), animated-cartoon makers in the 1920s still seemed quite unaware of the basic difference between them. While movies descended on one side from the theater and on the other from Academic easel pictures, and so were inherently romanticizations of actual life, animated cartoons were a kind of comic strip, with even greater natural capacity for pure fantasy, so that "comic-strip effects" grotesque in a naturalistic medium like movies (stunt men crushed under steam rollers springing back to full life and vigor seconds later, say) were the animated cartoon's very essence.

How basic this confusion was, and how long it lasted, is well demonstrated in Disney's career. His two best-known early independent efforts, the short silents *Plane-Crazy* and *Gallopin' Gaucho,* were still very close in spirit to movies. Both were basically satires on current events and interests (*Plane-Crazy* is vaguely related to Lindbergh's flight and fame, while *Gaucho* has a duel sequence of the sort Douglas Fairbanks made famous), and, despite some promising whimsy, neither went much beyond the sort of thing Harold Lloyd or Laurel and Hardy did through trick camera work; much of their success was in fact due to their featuring comic-strip characters Disney had already made popular. Not until Disney's first sound cartoon, *Steamboat Willie* of September 1929, and the *Skeleton Dance* following soon after, did he begin to utilize his medium's natural potentialities for fantasy at all fully; now at last he was creating illustrations (boats that breathe and caper about, skeletons taking themselves apart) no longer related to romantic motion pictures but to the zany, burlesque, fairy-tale worlds of *Mutt and Jeff, Krazy Kat,* the Land of Oz and Carroll's Cheshire cat. To this realm the animated cartoon properly belonged, and along these lines it most consistently flourished.

These were not, unfortunately, the lines Disney most consistently pursued (**50b**). In fact, his animated cartoons of the 1930s and -40s seem almost to have been created by two different people. On the one hand everyone remembers Disney the unrivaled master of fantasy, when he worked entirely in the spirit of his medium and created the gay dance sequence in the Seven Dwarfs' cottage, hilarious variants of old folk humor like Pluto's pause at a hydrant during the mad-dog sequence, the inspired clowning of Goofy and Pluto, and so on.

On the other, we would willingly forget those all too many instances of Disney the Artist trying to "elevate his medium" into something more than a "mere cartoon." His obsession that "serious" music must at all times and places be better than "popular"—which led him to introduce Chopin, Schubert and Mendelssohn backgrounds into his first colored cartoon (*Flowers & Trees*, 1931) instead of the jazz-band Dixie he had used for *Plane-Crazy*, and culminated in the ghastly visual malapropisms marring so much of *Fantasia*—ballet-dancing crocodiles, tutu-skirted elephants, stock stage Chinamen. His rewriting of classic scripts and plots like *Alice* and *Pinocchio,* not to suit the demands of a different medium (which is of course entirely proper and necessary), but to bring them "down to the child's level" (a level on which neither they nor any other great children's books ever were) by stock comedy routines and stale horseplay. His female leads with soupy-syrupy "cultured" voices—Bambi's mother being, alas! an unforgettable example. His vapid "cheery songs," introduced in utter confusion of media, on analogy with Gilbert-and-Sullivan-type light operetta. And above all, his evisceration of classic children's stories to conform with advance-guard ideas of Art Good for Children.

So instead of letting *The Three Little Pigs* (1933) or *The Grasshopper and the Ant* (1934) teach their ancient lessons of prudence, Disney bowdlerizes them in typical 20th-century fashion. No longer do the first two little pigs suffer the consequences of their shortsighted improvidence; instead, they escape to the shelter of their brother's laboriously constructed brick walls, where, refreshed on his hard-won food, they go on capering "Who's Afraid of the Big Bad Wolf" quite as idiotically as before. No longer does the vicious wolf meet his well-deserved end in a vat of boiling water; he only scampers off into the woods, presumably free to terrorize the neighborhood indefinitely. No longer does the frivolous grasshopper starve when summer ends; instead, he appeals to the hard-working ant's overdeveloped social conscience and lives in luxurious idleness all winter too. No longer, that is, does Disney's art have anything to do with the world of the traditional fairy tale, with Grimm or Andersen or Reynard the Fox; still less with the world of traditional romance. This is the world of the liberal intellectual of the 1930s, of economists preaching from-each-according-to-ability-and-to-each-according-to-need-and-we'll-decide-who-gets-what. This Disney, the Fine Artist, has little to do with life or living arts, despite all such efforts as Robin Feild's *Art of Walt Disney* (1933) to prove otherwise. In fact, what influence Disney's artiness had on children's book illustration was largely pernicious, indirectly helping the "arty" Little-Golden-Book rubbish common from the 1930s on to supersede the old Pyle-Wyeth-Shepard tradition.

To find the main line of animated cartoons we need to look around and beside the pretentious Art of Disney edifice at the staple cartoon shorts turned out by and for the major motion-picture studios of the 1930s and -40s, including by no means least Walt Disney Enterprises' own potboilers, which subsidized the financial losses of his more ambitiously artful projects. There, in the *Mickey Mouse* and *Donald Duck* shorts, in *Bugs Bunny*, *Tom and Jerry*, *Tweety and Sylvester*, and *Mr. McGoo*, we find the medium's potentialities for fantasy appropriately utilized, its function properly fulfilled by satisfying the needs of mass audiences in the most direct way without any pretensions to Art. And it is significant that only when Disney followed this main line consistently was he really successful. That is why Disneyland was perhaps the most entirely satisfying and certainly the most financially rewarding of all his enterprises. Had he been content with such a fantastic fun world in all his animated cartoons, his achievements as a master of that medium would have been much greater than they were.

In the 1940s television began to have its great effect on animated cartoons, an effect almost entirely to the good, for the mass audience it created forced cartoons to abandon pretensions to Fine Art once and for all and develop according to principles proper to the medium. First, under the pressure of vastly increased demand for material, the old laborious technique of making separate or substantially different drawings for each and every frame of the reel was abandoned, and with it all vestiges of movie and painted easel-picture technique:

> "The difference between the two cartoon forms," says Joe Barbera . . . "is very easily explained. When we did the *Tom & Jerry* cartoons for MGM we turned out 48 minutes of animation in one year. In TV we are turning out an hour of animation a week. At MGM a complete six-minute cartoon took 17 weeks. In TV a half-hour cartoon, start to finish, takes eight weeks. The difference is . . . there was too much technique in the movie

days, too much time spent in trying to make animal characters move as naturally as real animals. Well, that's not our idea of what a cartoon is supposed to be. A cartoon should have its own personality, its own feeling, its own way of moving." [*TV Guide*, IX, 26, July 1, 1961, p. 15]

Essentially, this meant a return to the original (and proper) stick-figure concept of the medium. Now a single background was made to serve whole sequences, with a few moving parts laid on it to simulate talking or simple action (**50c**); effects of violent motion like crashing and falling were simulated by simply shaking the picture before the camera; correspondingly greater emphasis was laid on distinctive voices and clever dialogue on the sound track. However much intellectual critics lamented sacrificing "artistic qualities" for such economical gimmicks, in fact the medium was so immensely improved by them that animated cartoons of the 1930s began to look as curiously archaic as pre-1914 newsreels, compared to what was being produced by pioneers in the new techniques like Jay Ward (*Fractured Flickers, The Bullwinkle Show*) and the team of William D. (Bill) Hanna and Joe Barbera (*Ruff and Reddy, Huckleberry Hound, Quick-Draw McGraw, The Flintstones*, etc.). Their success was as sudden as it was extraordinary:

> At the beginning of the 1959–60 season there were 27 Western series on the network evening air and no regular cartoon shows, though *Walt Disney Presents* showed occasional cartoons. At the beginning of the 1961–62 season, there will be only 15 Westerns in prime time . . . and seven cartoon shows. [*Ibid.*, pp. 12–16]

In 1957, only a few years before, Hanna and Barbera had been thrown out of work after producing *Tom and Jerry* cartoons since 1937, when "the studio finally decided they were uneconomical"—as, with Disney methods and conception of animated cartoons as a variety of traditional book illustration, they were. The new technique not only made animated cartoons economically feasible, it made them better as well. Not only was its drawing better suited to the medium, but it allowed more genuinely funny dialogue and plots. For one thing, the new cartoons no longer talked down to children. Even though primarily made for showings in the "children's slot" from four to six, they were always pitched a little above the "child's level" so that parents watching over children's shoulders had to explain some of the more sophisticated jokes and topical allusions—just as the sophisticated jokes and topical allusions in *Pooh,* the Oz books, and *Alice* had been explained in generations gone by. Those professional lamenters of the "good old days when children read classics" talked even more nonsense than usual, for animated cartoons of the 1950s and -60s not only exposed children to upper levels of thought quite as much as any of the older "classics," they stimulated children to read those older books. As for the "violence" so often deplored in animated cartoons, surely the nature of the medium made it obvious that they were fantastic, not real, situations; no child was ever inspired to emulate what he saw in the cartoons on TV—and this holds good for the "weirdo" cartoons of the mid-1960s too.* (Emphatically, however, the same could not be said for teen-agers watching the new "art films" coming in during the period.)

9. *American Movies and European Cinema, 1900–1940*

Comics, animated cartoons, and movies all came into being at about the same time and in response to the same general social and technological conditions—that is, when great new mass audiences coincided with new means for putting forms into motion in the 1890s. But whereas comic strips and animated cartoons had Low Art ancestry —mass book illustration, folk theater, puppet shows—movies essentially derived their forms from academic narrative painting, and their content from the legitimate stage. It follows that movies were always inherently the closest to Fine Art. But for a long time this was much less apparent in American than in European movies; the resulting contrast is a principal theme in the history of motion pictures between 1900 and 1940.

---

* Since the above was first written, in the summer of 1967, the original to-do about violence in comics initiated by Dr. Fredric Wertham has immensely increased, and much of it been transferred to "TV violence." From all sides we are told that it has been TV-watching which has "corrupted 'the young,'" which has stimulated crime in the streets, disrespect for law and order, and so forth. Sometimes one gets the impression that violence must have been unknown before the Age of Television. Behind almost all this talk is an assumption that human beings are naturally good, kind, gentle, and benevolent; that to explain "deviant" behavior, therefore, corruption by some agency must be assumed. Only seldom is another possibility even considered—that violence appears in TV programs for the same reason that it has appeared in movies, in books, and in plays at all times and places (*Romeo and Juliet* can hold its own with any TV script in this respect): namely, that man's nature is basically violent, among other things; that violence therefore appeals to him; and that living arts have therefore always provided it. Our ancestors called this state of affairs Original Sin, and believed that the remedy was grace, not censorship.

From the beginning, there was a difference between the kind of paintings and plays drawn on for movies in Europe and in America. In Europe the concept of Fine Art was much further advanced in the 1890s, and mass audiences, because of a consistently lower standard of living, were much smaller. The result was that European movies always tended to be oriented toward an audience of intellectuals with esoteric tastes, the American toward broad appeal to mass audiences. Decade by decade, this pattern can be traced.

If we think of a characteristic example of the first minute-or-so shorts that introduced the new medium in America, something like *Washday Troubles* (1895) is what comes to mind—a fragment from the burlesque stage, a cartoon of the type of Thomas B. Worth's *Darktown Antics* from Currier & Ives put into motion. But in Europe, something like *Baby's Breakfast* (1895) by Auguste and Louis Lumière (1862–1954 and 1864–1948) was conceived as a moving Impressionist painting, a close-up and spontaneous Renoirish slice of life. Most characteristic of American one-reel pictures from the 1903–1908 period are works like *Uncle Tom's Cabin* (1903), Edwin S. Porter's *Great Train Robbery* (1903), *Rescued from an Eagle's Nest* (1907), and the first Westerns, all of them plainly deriving from Low Art sources like Currier & Ives adventure prints, book illustrations, and productions of the old traveling stock companies that toured tank-town circuits. A. Nicholas Vardac's *Stage to Screen* (Cambridge, Mass., 1949) shows how, for instance, Porter's film of *Uncle Tom's Cabin* was taken almost literally from William Brady's stage play of 1901 (**51**). In Europe, films of the sort made by George Méliès (1861–1938) (*Trip to the Moon, Indiarubber Head, The Doctor's Secret* (**52a**) and *World of Toulouse-Lautrec*) were just as plainly drawing on Fine Art sources—Lautrec, proto-Dada art like James Ensor's *Mauvais Médicins,* grand opera.

Then, as movies begin to get longer, we find as the most typical American developments Mary Pickford's sentimental tear-jerkers (e.g., *The New York Hat,* 1912), literal reconstructions of history (*From the Manger to the Cross,* 1911, Sidney Olcott) or dime-novel series (*Adventures of Kathlyn, Perils of Pauline, Exploits of Elaine*). By contrast, *Le Film d'Art* is most typical of Europe. Its object, according to Ernest Lindgren (*Picture History of the Cinema,* London, 1960, p. 16), was "to lift the cinema from a vulgar entertainment to the artistic level of the theatre"; its model, quite plainly, was narrative painting. On seeing *The Assassination of the Duke of Guise,* first specimen of *Le Film d'Art* (1908), with its cast of actors from the Comédie Française and music for the opening especially composed by Saint-Säens, the actor Charles Pathé is supposed to have blurted out emotionally, "Ah, gentlemen, you are indeed our masters!" Anyone who has seen that film will be inclined to doubt the anecdote, but in any event the kind of artist who should properly have said it was not a stage actor but an academic narrative painter, for it was his product that this kind of movie made obsolete. Perhaps the most striking example of putting narrative easel pictures into motion was the French four-reel *Queen Elizabeth* (Louis Mercanton, 1912), starring the famous actress Sarah Bernhardt and based consistently and obviously on a series of Academic narrative paintings of Queen Elizabeth's life from the 1840s by Paul Delaroche (1797–1856) (**52b**). But European studios produced many of them: a Historical Art series from Italy including *The Three Musketeers* (1908), *The Crusades* (1911), and Guazzoni's *Quo Vadis* (1912), Pathé's *Passion Play*, based on Tissot's illustrated Bible, and so on—a whole gallery of easel paintings put in motion. At the same time Scandinavians, led by the Nordisk Company in Denmark, began producing all sorts of "socially conscious" films appealing to intellectuals with their insistence on Reality as the goal of art: *Abyss, In the Hands of Impostors, The White Slave, Sins of the Fathers, In the Grip of Alcohol,* and so forth; Italians followed suit with working-class exposés like *Assunta Spina* (1915).

Such European films pleased professional critics immensely, and have ever since—indeed, a film like *Chelsea Girls* is practically a retake of *In the Grip of Alcohol.* American films did not please them nearly so much, for American film-makers crassly concentrated on pleasing audiences. The result is lamented in every standard history of films:

> Before 1908, Britain and France were the leading centers of the film trade, and in 1910 some 60 to 70 percent of the world's imported films came from Paris. By 1914, however, America was already making a bid for leadership and . . . by 1917 . . . the American film industry stood poised to capture the markets of the world. [Lindgren, *Picture History of the Cinema*]

For this dénoument the same standard reasons are always advanced: interruption of European progress by the Great War (though America was already challenging by 1914); application abroad of "ruthless American business methods" presumably unheard-of among the simple kindly Europeans; bigger budgets, made possible by a large home market, in turn making possible more and more expensive offerings (though Europeans in fact pioneered longer and more elaborate films); "American materialism" (of course) making sordid spoil out "of the importance of money as the key to power, luxury, happiness" (love of money being unknown in Europe); and, above all, "the Hollywood preoccupation with sex" which apparently had some fatal attraction to innocent and otherworldly European audiences. Only occasionally and incidentally is the real reason mentioned, as when Lindgren explains that wartime audiences preferred American movies

> . . . because of their well-constructed stories, their pace, vitality, and their stars. . . . American movies provided escape from the sadness and drabness, the boredom and horror of their daily lives.

In plain language, early American films satisfied audiences far better and far oftener than their European competitors.

And they continued to do so in the 1920s, as the pattern of divergence between American and European films was maintained and intensified.

On the one hand, a whole constellation of brilliant European developments in "cinema art": the Swedish school of Victor Sjöström, Mauritz Stiller and Charles Magnusson, masters of filmcraft for its own sake and of internal dramas of the soul; Expressionist German films like the painter Robert Wiene's *Cabinet of Dr. Caligari* (1919, *The Restless Art*, p. 347), *Secrets of a Soul* (G. W. Pabst, Werner Krauss, 1926), *Metropolis* (Fritz Lang, 1925–26), *Last Laugh* (F. W. Murnau, Emil Jannings, 1924); an "impressionist" school of French film-makers led by Louis Delluc in the early 1920s, and later that decade a "surrealist" school including Man Ray, Fernand Léger (*Ballet Mécanique*, 1923), René Clair (*Entr'Acte*, 1924), inclining increasingly toward Freudianism (Germain Dulac, *La Coquille et le Clergyman;* Salvador Dali, *Un Chien Andalou, L'Age d'Or;* Jean Vigo, *A Propos de Nice*). Their work was just what movies should be, professional critics all agreed—and still do. (Ruth Bronsteen's 1968 *Hippy's Handbook* recommends almost all of them—naturally without indicating their dates, since all were made by people now well over thirty—as among "the greatest films ever made.")

On the other hand, great masses of American films were meanwhile sweeping the world. They, by contrast, pleased critics far less than audiences. Even the innovations of David Wark Griffith

(1875–1948) in selective film-editing and imaginative camera-composing in his 1915 *The Birth of a Nation* (53a) were hard to admire, because the man's politics were so "rightist"; from the beginning, professional Art-film criticism has been oriented toward the principle that a "good" movie must be "left":

> If you read *Sight and Sound,* in which so many films are appraised for the degree of the director's commitment to a social point of view (good if left wing, bad if not) you will discover that in this ideology, location shooting, particularly around working-class locations, is in itself almost a proof of commitment. . . . a film that is stylized or that deals with upper-class characters is somehow "evasive." As a result of this rigid and restrictive critical vocabulary, *Sight and Sound* is becoming monotonous. . . . [Pauline Kael, "Commitment and the Straitjacket." *I Lost It at the Movies,* Boston, 1965, p. 56]

Griffith listened to his critics and made up for his errors with *Intolerance* (1915), first of the American "spectaculars," which in a number of colossal sets directly translated from easel-painted "Academic machines" illustrated an abstract idea of social injustice through complicated interminglings of flashbacks to the fall of Babylon, the Crucifixion, and the St. Bartholomew's Day Massacre. *Intolerance,* like Griffith's later *Broken Blossoms* (1919) and *Orphans of the Storm* (1921) satisfied Art-film critics far better, by leaving out almost all those Low Art elements so marked in *The Birth of a Nation*—visual recalls of Currier & Ives war prints, Mathew B. Brady's photographs, book and magazine illustrations, John Rogers's sculpture (e.g., the Emancipation Proclamation scene); but for the same reason, they satisfied audiences far less, and as a result this first pioneer of American movie epics soon faded out of movie-making.

Cecil B. De Mille (1881–1959), who followed D. W. Griffith's early epic lead (*Joan the Woman,* 1917), did not emulate his later arty turning. For the films of this most successful director of the 1920s, no critical words were too bad: he was a monster who catered to audiences' desires for an escapist dream-world of life or adventure in luxurious and exotic surroundings, who shot scripts condoning the loosening of marital ties beneath superficially moral conclusions and in whose films the workingman as a significant screen figure disappeared. Of course this last, like the kind of movie Art-film critics admired, gives the game away—what they were deploring had nothing basically to do with either morality or aesthetics. It was De Mille's lack of interest in their concept of Art dedicated to Reality that outraged

293

them. He and American film makers like him (e.g., Fred Niblo, *Ben Hur,* 1927, biggest of all spectaculars) apparently did not believe audiences went to movies to be informed about social problems. He imagined they went to be entertained. When it seemed audiences had had enough of themes like *Forbidden Fruit* (1921) or *Adam's Rib* (1923), De Mille switched to religious and moralizing themes like *The Ten Commandments* (1924) and *King of Kings* (1927). And, unkindest cut of all, when these themes palled, American film makers "gambled" on talking movies, and so made all silent films obsolete at just the moment when Europeans had made them into Great Works of Art.

To force audiences to "improve themselves" by attending elevating cinema, Art-film makers in one European country after another succeeded in getting legislation to keep American movies out. But since American movies met so much better the primary condition for success in living arts, providing an art appropriate to their audiences, nothing could keep them out for long. Only the Russians, led by Sergei Eisenstein, Vsevolod Pudovkin and Alexander Dovzhenko, rivaled them, for only they were comparably concerned to please audiences rather than art critics; but they were never serious competition—at first for economic reasons, later because political pressure made them preach at their audiences instead of entertaining them.

For every kind of audience there were American movies on an appropriate level. Appealing to the simplest and most naïve were what Hollywood called C movies. These consisted principally of stereotypes, and consequently have intense historical interest from a sociological point of view. In them, all sorts of bits and fragments of ancient philosophies and legend come welling onto the screen from depths of folk consciousness—images of the Mysterious East and cunning Orientals established in remote ages when rude and simple Franks first met and marveled at the Levant's civilized sophistication; of Gay Paree, dating back to Plantagenet wars and reinforced by generation after generation of English-speaking soldiers in France thereafter; of the Noble Savage in his forests and the Odalisque in her harem. Like the cheap mass-printed and chapbook illustrations from which they are descended, C movies provide rich insight into the stuff of history and the structure of the folk mind.

The basic bread-and-butter American movie audience, like the typical comics reader, was lower-middle-class; it was primarily for this audience that B movies were made. In them we find provided all the symbolic white-collar types familiar from comics of the period—fantasy-satisfying images of lean cowboys and swarthy gangsters, lovers polished or impetuous, seemingly pathetic little men who somehow manage to come out on top in the end, glamour girls with boy friends crowding around, goodhearted prostitutes redeemed by tough-but-tender heroes, and, of course, every possible variant of the domestic idyll (**54a, b**). But between B movies and comics there is one enormous difference—in addition to characters and stories for audiences to identify with, Hollywood also provided stars with separate lives of their own. Naturally this star system was forever being damned as hopelessly "vulgar" by Art-film critics, for whom the whole idea of Artists (i.e., directors, choreographers, scriptwriters) being subordinate to a star and so giving fame instead of getting it was anathema; a cardinal central principle of Fine Art demands that the Artist—Writer, Playwright, or whoever—be always the glorified Creator, never the anonymous servant. Yet in fact the star system was the most powerful single factor in Hollywood's conquest of the world. It provided possibilities for vicarious identification—and so for romantic escape—unrivaled in any other medium. Not only could audiences escape during the few hours their fantasy-doubles were on the screen; they could also continue and intensify their identification during the necessarily long intervals between their favorites' appearances, through movie magazines, newspaper articles, radio interviews, personal appearances. Furthermore, the star system made possible an extraordinary variety of symbolic images—not merely general categories, but special types within them. You could have cowboys of every sort, from strong silent William S. Hart or fancy horseman Tom Mix to singer Roy Rogers; every sort of detective or secret agent, from Edward G. Robinson to Humphrey Bogart; lovers as varied as Rudolph Valentino, Charles Boyer, and Clark Gable. Comic little men might range from sad clowns like Charlie Chaplin through bumbling youths like Harold Lloyd and mad ne'er-do-wells like Buster Keaton to well-meaning fumblers like Laurel and Hardy. Glamour girls tended to be more standardized, and though progress of a sort might be discerned from Theda Bara, whose eyes allegedly burnt holes in blankets, through Jean Harlow and Marilyn Monroe to the current crop of sex queens whose operations on blankets are of quite a different sort, still their basic function remained the same—providing fantasy images not only for men, but also for women who dislike the masculine roles society increasingly thrust upon them.

For middle- and upper-middle-class audiences there were A movies, with quite another sort of appeal. In many ways the 1920s and -30s were even more trying years for the middle and upper-middle classes in America than for lower-middle classes and the proletariat. Not only did they have their economic difficulties, but they had ideological trials as well. The whole Protestant ethic on which these classes had rested for a century was coming under a cloud. On all sides smart and sneering voices were rising to announce that all its traditional principles had been "proved" absurd by one or another of the sciences. This sudden attack bewildered its victims. They knew vaguely that there must be some answer to it, but being unaccustomed to abstract reasoning, they failed to realize that no beliefs whatever could be "proved" in the way sophisticated scoffers demanded, least of all the scoffers' own premises. Knowing instinctively that you cannot use reason as a weapon to disprove reason itself,* but unable to articulate their conviction, they looked blindly for reassurance that somehow they were right, and this the movies provided for them.

Consistently through all this period the Hollywood A movie is premised on an assumption that courage, patriotism, loyalty, integrity, and industry are virtues; that good usually triumphs over evil; that even when it does not, being nobly defeated is better than winning by treachery or deceit. Consistently through this period the same assumption dictates how books shall be translated to the screen: heroic and "gutsy" elements in *All Quiet on the Western Front* or *For Whom the Bell Tolls* (for instance) are emphasized, all but the most inconspicuous aspects of Remarque's or Hemingway's nihilism are quietly shed. And so it remained down to the 1940s. Although throughout all this period attacks by Art-film critics on "Hollywood romanticism" never ceased, they had no visible effect. Tirelessly were Hollywood movies denounced as soporifics encouraging escape from problems instead of work to end them; everlastingly was European cinema extolled for "realistically" doing without romantic stereotypes (except, of course, for Marxist ones); all to no avail. On all levels Hollywood romanticism seemed secure in audience favor, immune from all assault. And then all at once, things changed. Hollywood began producing "Art films."

* Suppose you hear someone following a line of reasoning which concludes, "The world is absurd. Nothing can be knowable." What is the reply? Simply this—"Does that conclusion include what you have just said, or not? And if not, on what grounds do you exempt your own thinking from the futility of everyone else's?" They can't have it both ways.

10. *Television and the Art Film, 1945–1965*

Budd Schulberg's 1941 *What Makes Sammy Run* is the classic exposition of those patterns of organization, attitudes towards movie-making, and conception of what motion pictures are and can do which had dominated American movies for the previous four decades. What it makes clear above all else is that, though on ceremonial occasions lofty orations about "the art of film-making" might be indulged, in fact anything like indulgence towards Fine Art was a high road to ruin. Schulberg's book was essentially a bitter account of how a totally untalented opportunist could shoulder aside and rise to authority over one kind of genuine artist after another—first Julian Blumberg, the "medieval craftsman" writing for the satisfaction of it; then Al Mannheim, with his Renaissance man's delight in mastering his material; finally Sidney Fineman, whose directing at Wide World had pioneered in bringing movies to mature technical form. A number of reasons for Sammy's success are brought out—he is shrewd, brash, daring; he has some ability to spot and use others' skills for his own advantage; he has no moral instincts or sense of fair play to inhibit him. But his main advantage is a total disregard for Art. It is by insinuating to studio owners that Fineman's concern for Good Movies is keeping production costs too high and boring audiences that Sammy ousts Fineman and enjoys his final triumph. And, lest you miss the point, Schulberg relates how after Fineman's dismissal he makes one last simple picture "which turned out to be a unique kind of hit . . . somehow managed to electrify and convince and challenge and entertain . . . without any heavies or comedy reliefs or subplots or sub-sub-plots. . . ." Had he done so earlier, Schulberg implies, Fineman would still have been head of Wide World.

But now all at once Hollywood appeared to renounce the kind of movie Sammy Glick represented. Now all at once it seemed that awareness of Art was what the successful movie maker needed to have above all (**55a, b, c**).

Not every critic has been enchanted with the result. Summarizing the last fifteen years or so, Pauline Kael declared bluntly that "movies are going to pieces; they're disintegrating":

> Movies are being stripped of all the "nonessentials"—that is to say, faces, actions, details, stories, places—everything that makes them entertaining and joyful. They are even being

> stripped of the essentials—light (*The Eclipse*), sound (*The Silence*), and movement in some of the New American Cinema films (there is sure to be one called *Stasis*). [*I Lost It at the Movies*]

By historical analogy, it is not hard to divine what is happening. Movies are turning into Fine Art. They show all the symptoms. This obsession with "essential Realities of the medium" parallels what happened to painting in the dozen years after 1900. Movies—or more exactly Art films, for that is what Pauline Kael is talking about—are disintegrating the way painting disintegrated under Cubism. Art-filmers have begun to repeat the painters' by now familiar claims: only Artists have any right to judge Art; Artists alone should decide what kind of Art the public is offered; forms should be determined and evaluated solely by Artists, without reference to public or patron. And this occurs not only in orthodox advance-guard circles:

> In the old days, the studios ruled Hollywood [even a great star like Chaplin finding it next to impossible to succeed on his own, as his 1936 *Modern Times* proved]. Today the town belongs to the stars. . . . The star often controls the selection of the writer and director. He can hire and fire the producer. He decides on shooting locations. And, of course, he gets top pay . . . sums that would have boggled the imaginations of the prewar stars. They've also won the right to choose their pictures rather than merely taking assignments from a Louie B. Mayer or Harry Cohn. . . . [Peter Bart, *New York Times News Service* article, January 21, 1966]

And as in painting, so now in Art films, the artist left to create Art without any discipline from function flounders in froth:

> Many of the newly independent stars [Bart continues] have turned out to be disastrously bad managers of their own careers and inept judges of movie material. With amazing frequency top actors like Marlon Brando turn up in pictures that prove to be both aesthetic and financial disasters. It is one thing to win creative autonomy but another to use it constructively.

Of course all this is defended by the same old line of apologetics that pronounced advance-guard painting something "higher" than mere comunication or delight, and so beyond "monetary criteria." What we heard before in defense of urinals labeled "R. Mutt," rotting mannequins in taxicabs, and collages of rubbish, we now hear of movies—"Crude technique serves, beautifully, a sensibility based on indiscriminateness, without ideas, beyond negation. . . ."*

And movies in consequence are well on their way to becoming the private art painting has long since been. Antonin Artaud's cry of "BOMBARD THE SENSES," "Keep the Audience Off Guard," may thrill theater theorists, but not audiences. The same is true of Andy Warhol's exercises in existential stupefaction. The first time around, audiences may go away puzzled; the second, bombarded into insensibility; after that, they just go away—and don't come back.

> When movies, the only art which everyone felt free to enjoy and have opinions about, lose their connection with song and dance, drama, and the novel, when they become cinema, which people fear to criticize just as they fear to say what they think of a new piece of music or a new poem or painting, they will become another object of academic study and "appreciation" and will soon be an object of excitement only to practitioners of the "art" [as painting has so long been]. Cinema, I suspect, is going to become so rarified, so private in meaning, and so lacking in audience appeal that in a few years the foundations will be desperately and hopelessly trying to bring it back to life . . . and it will be evidence to your interest in culture and civic responsibility if you go to the movies. [Kael, *I Lost It at the Movies*]

Historical analogy again suggests a reason for this development. According to *TV Guide's* retrospective issue on "Television's First Ten Years" (V, 2, January 12, 1957), the advent of television as a mass entertainment medium dates from 1947. Could we assume that from then on the movie medium became increasingly obsolescent and its forms therefore began turning into Fine Art in accordance with the principle of evolution we have observed in other such cases? *TV Guide's* retrospective vigorously denied it:

> TV is far from just another way to exhibit movies. It is, at its best, a completely unique medium of information and entertainment. . . . It would be preposterous to consider turning all of television . . . over to an industry that is geared for an entirely different type of audience.

And certainly it could be argued not only that television manifestly did not put an end to movie-making, but that movies were in fact improved, much as comics were sharpened in focus and deepened in

---

* Susan Sontag, on Jack Smith's *Flaming Creatures,* in *The Nation,* April 13, 1964.

significance when animated cartoons on television cut into their earlier monopoly of mass audiences for that particular illustrative form. So if a movie like *Doctor Zhivago*, say, has demonstrably greater depth and power than comparable counterparts twenty or thirty years ago, improved technique alone is not responsible; there was simply not the same reason or incentive to cater to a mass audience. These "groundlings" who in earlier decades might have gone to a movie of this type, had their prejudices and tastes been taken into sufficient account, could not now be lured from their TV sets by any artifice, thus freeing the producer to pitch his level considerably higher. Such movies prove that television was far from making their medium obsolete in the sense that photogravure made woodcuts obsolete, for example. Movie forms did not necessarily turn into Fine Art; woodcuts did, because the medium was technologically dead.

But between movies and comics there is this considerable difference—movies are much more expensive to produce. And television *did* cut into the movies' old bread-and-butter audience, very severely. It follows that, in the face of television competition, there was an incentive to find means to make movies pay that did not apply to comics. And this, I think, is the real motive behind the boom in Art films.

Television was fairly restricted; going into homes at all hours of day and night, it had strict censorship. Movies could be freer. If you used the formula "For Adults Only," coupled with the word "Art," the possibilities were limitless. Latent public vulnerability to pornography, sadism, and mindless brutality could be exploited for gain and all sorts of technical (and economical) short cuts excused, simply by talking about cinema Art dedicated to Reality, about "frank," "fearless," "bold," "uninhibited" Facing of Fact. Time-tested weapons to silence old-fashioned objections were ready to hand also. What, for instance, is the answer to the following argument?

> A sophistry may affect the mind, but an obscenity must affect the mind; it is a violence. It may do one of two things equally direct and instinctive; it may shock purity or it may inflame impurity. But in both cases the process is brutal and irrational. A picture or a sentence which shocks sensibility or sharpens sensuality does not offer itself for discussion. It is no more open to argument than a squeaking slate pencil is open to argument, or the choking smell of ether is open to argument. The human victim is drugged—or he is sick. . . . Parallels from other crimes are insolently fallacious. A man reading about a burglary

is not any more likely to commit a burglary. . . . But there is one evil which, by its hold on the imagination (the creative and reproductive part of man) can reproduce itself even by report. We have a right to protect ourselves and especially our top-heavy and groping children against startling and uncivilized appeals to this instinct . . . making them jump like monkeys on a stick. . . . I have no more right to give an unwilling citizen a sexual shock than to give him an electric shock. . . . Pride makes a man a devil, but lust makes him a machine. [G. K. Chesterton, *London Daily News*, 1910, quoted in A. L. Maycock, *The Man Who Was Orthodox*, London, 1961, pp. 121–22]

Very simple; as Orwell observed in the 1930s, you invoke the "benefit of clergy" Fine Artists had invented for themselves:

The artist is to be exempt from the moral laws that are binding on ordinary people. Just pronounce the magic word "Art," and everything is O.K. Rotting corpses with snails crawling over them are O.K.; kicking little girls in the head is O.K.; even a film like *L'Age d'Or* is O.K. . . .

If you say that Dali, though a brilliant draughtsman, is a dirty little scoundrel, you are looked on as a savage. If you say that you don't like rotting corpses, and that people who do like rotting corpses are mentally diseased, it is assumed that you lack the aesthetic sense. [*Dickens, Dali and Others*]

So now, if you say you don't like watching pointlessly detailed exhibitions of rape, murder, incest, dope addiction, or homosexuality, you are informed that you don't understand cinema Art. If you complain about any lack of order, intelligence, amusement, or delight in Art films, you are set down as an escapist, a reactionary in favor of lulling the masses' sense of social Realities, an enemy to enlightenment. If you argue how absurd it is to maintain in one and the same breath that movies need have no more meaning than fugues or ballets, and also that you need to see Art films over and over again to get their full significance, you are advised that unless you are a cinema Artist you have no right to criticize Art films.

What a marvelous invention! Only keep the Artist as a front man, and any conceivable moneygrubbing device is sanctified! Why didn't someone think of this before?

Well, as a matter of fact, someone did; the curious one-eyed alliance between commercial interests and Fine Art goes back a very long way. Nearly four decades ago C. S. Lewis in *The Pilgrim's Regress* (1933) described a 20th-century seeker for meaning in life visiting a colony of "revolutionary intellectuals"—the Clevers—in their town of Eschropolis and being driven out, kicked and "pelted with ordure" for timidly suggesting their Art was less concerned with truth than mere sensation; and how he then limped along a road outside the town and encountered Mr. Mammon, who "owned all the land around those parts. . . ."

> "Where did you get your clothes torn?"
> "I had a quarrel with the Clevers in Eschropolis."
> "Clevers?"
> "Don't you know them?"
> "Never heard of them."
> "You know Eschropolis?"
> "Know it? I *own* Eschropolis."
> "How do you mean?"
> "What do you suppose they live on?"
> "I never thought of that."
> "Every man of them earns his living by writing for me or having shares in my land. I suppose the 'Clevers' is some nonsense they do in their spare time—when they're not beating up tramps. . . ."

Precisely. Fine Artists may be pleased to imagine that through Art films they reveal Reality to the world; but for those who actually control and profit by them, Art films are merely "some nonsense they do in their spare time." They will last only as long as public gullibility; and there are signs the end of that is near—a recent cartoon, for example, has a man reading a movie advertisement to his wife: "Bold! Fearless! Shocking! Faces the Facts!—sounds like a stinker."

In the meantime, to the extent that Art films continue to be produced, they turn audiences over to television by default. For here in television are not only the old movies, but the traditional attitudes. Here the Artist is still subordinate to his audience; here forms are still dictated by function. Consider, for one example, why producer Herb Brodkin's show called (ironically enough) *For the People*, was canceled for lack of audience response. According to *TV Guide* for September 28, 1965, Brodkin maintained that

> "The criticisms of it were commercial criticisms. At its worst, it was head and shoulders above most TV programming. It made people angry. It made people discuss. It raised issues that *needed* to be discussed."

Or in other words, it dealt with Reality. It was Art. No doubt it was, programming officials agreed, but

"People," said one, "are getting tired of seeing the problems they read about on the front pages showing up in entertainment form. I think they want to escape from these problems. . . . Despite what Herb says, *For the People* did not fail because of the time slot. It had *Ed Sullivan* as a lead-in—and *Candid Camera* following it. People who usually stay right through that sequence of programming went to the trouble to switch it off." Commented another:

"This kind of social realism isn't a dramatic form your mass audience will stay with. The social-issue or social-realist shows were successful for a time with the audience because they were new. But the news shows are handling these same issues in spades. . . . There's a lot of righteous indignation around whenever one of these minority-approved shows goes off the air. Well, we have a perfect right to yank any entertainment show that's not doing a job for us. We're out to entertain as many people as possible. The worst thing we can do is bore people, even if we're pleasing a small minority by so doing. Too often, that's exactly what the minority is asking us to do. If someone wants to explore social workers, slum life, criminal psychology, social problems, there are hundreds of other avenues in which to explore these things—news shows, documentaries, and so on."

Documentation; narration; amusement; romantic escape—what is this but simply a listing of the primordial functions of the arts of illustration throughout history? Wherever and however they are performed, there that Unchanging Art lives on.

5

The Unchanging Arts
of Conviction and Persuasion:
Cartoons, Architecture, Advertising

■

I

THE TRADITIONAL ARTS
OF CONVICTION AND PERSUASION

CONVICTION and persuasion are ancient complementary functions of the activity traditionally called art. In any given age arts performing the one have usually looked very different from arts performing the other; forms and media appropriate to proclaim and manifest established beliefs will normally and necessarily not be the same as those designed to persuade people to new or dissident ones. But the two functions are so interrelated that arts serving them cannot properly be considered apart.

1. *The Arts of Conviction in History*

Which function came first in history cannot be known, of course. But on analogy with the art of children, primitives, and prehistoric peoples, conviction is the more likely. All such art begins, apparently, with images intended to carry self-conviction to their makers—tangible symbols, that is, which establish and define things experience has established to be true (**56a, b**). Because the image exists, the truth it embodies exists also in a more convincing and tangible form; so such symbols become means for coping with and controlling the world—whether they represent simple facts like grass being green and skies blue, abstract ideas like the spirits of animals or female fertility, or complicated mythopeoic concepts of father-kings and unseen powers and principalities of the air.

Certainly in historic times arts of conviction have been the more prominent. The reason is that arts with such a function will characteristically be large, showy, and heavy—architectural, most commonly, built to carry weight in both literal and figurative senses, intended to stand as time-defying memorials (**56c**). Enough of them have, that to this category belong the most famous monuments of most eras—the pyramids and Pharaoh statues of Old Kingdom Egypt, the

307

early stupas of India, the fora of Imperial Rome in Antiquity; the Angkor temples and Gothic cathedrals of the Middle Ages; down to the 18th-century classical-style mansions and churches in which the aristocracy of England and America showed forth their pride and power.*

Usually too, though not necessarily, arts of conviction will tend to be ideographic in form. From their function of representing things known rather than seen—generalized mental images instead of views from any particular point of time or space—come the characteristic "primitive" forms of child and folk art, and of decivilized or uncivilized peoples—images composed additively, of parts each conceived separately and exaggerated or diminished to the degree they contribute to ideas in the mind; scale determined by importance in a world of ideas rather than distance from the eye; presentation in a single frontal plane rather than visual three-dimensional space. And the same function of fortifying basic faiths, affirming deep convictions, manifesting truths long held, produces much the same forms in the ideational arts of early civilizations, only grander and more monumental, "primitive" in the original sense of hierarchically impassive, changeless, timeless—the reliefs of Old Kingdom Egypt; the standard of Ur and the stele of Naramsin in early Mesopotamia; Chou bronzes; Byzantine mosaics; the black-figured vases of archaic Greece; the mimetic architectural forms of pyramids and ziggurats, Doric columns and Romanesque towers.

Much ink has been spilled and many typewriter ribbons split marveling at the "masterpieces of art" such monuments allegedly represent. Most if not all this effort has been empty vapor, however, because the one thing you cannot call works like these, or compare them to, is Art in our 20th-century sense of the word. Their function in society and what Fine Art does in ours are entirely different. Yet confusing these functions has been the mistake of all those cyclical historians over the last two hundred years who have buttressed their case for the "decline of the West" on a comparison of the frivolous shifting tides of Art in their own times with the unchanging grandeur

---

* This theme is treated at length in my *Images of American Living: Four Centuries of Architecture and Furniture as Cultural Expression*, Philadelphia, 1964, "Classical America," pp. 115–239, and especially pp. 115–23, 160–63. For a detailed and specific study of a particular example of such symbolism, i.e., the Greek-cross central-plan mausoleum-church of the early 18th century, see my *King Carter's Church*, in University of Victoria Maltwood Museum Studies in Architectural History No. 2, 1969.

of art in early epochs. It has been the mistake too of all those advance-guard apologists who for five generations have been working to restore art to its "primitive vigor"—Morris with his "dream of barbarism flooding the world with beauty," Klee trying to capture the compulsive power of Ravenna's Byzantine mosaics, existentialist philosophers citing the aesthetic purity of primitive arts that are not "about" anything but simply are, that tell no stories but just embody and manifest the basic premises of existence. What they all ignore is that these early monuments were conceived to fulfill their function simply by being *there,* by existing, and so were none of them made to be looked at or admired aesthetically; that, a good many of them, indeed, never could have been seen at all—sealed away forever in caves and tombs, set out of effective sight in vast domes or hypostyle halls; that some were even deliberately made to be destroyed, like the cursing figures ritually smashed by Egyptian Pharaohs, or the wax images of witchcraft. They all ignore too how utilitarian this "art" was, in the most crass sense; what specific, literal, and immediate purposes it served; how utterly different it is from Fine Art made for no other purpose than to be put on exhibition and by definition having no practical function; how inept and pointless is then any comparison between Fine Art and the activity that produced cave paintings, tomb sculptures, Byzantine mosaics, Romanesque churches, primitive idols, how meaningless all conclusions drawn from it. No—if you want to make meaningful comparisons between monuments like these and anything modern, then compare them with those of our arts which serve comparable functions—for we do have them, as we have all the Unchanging Arts still. World's Fairs and skyscrapers, superhighway system and dams, shopping and civic centers with public memorials in them are our equivalent of those ancient monuments made by common consent to serve community needs, carrying compulsive symbolism implicit in their forms. You may still, to be sure, find such a comparison painful. You may think that the ideas embodied in our arts of conviction are shallow and transient compared to what pyramids and temples, cathedrals and tombs embodied in past ages. But this has nothing to do with art. It is the comparison of our one-dimensional civilization, resting all its ultimate hopes in this world and all its interest in man's immediate doings, with societies whose life and works here and now took significance from traditions past and a life in another dimension to come; comparative powers of artistic creativity are not at issue.

2. *The Arts of Persuasion in History*

Characteristically, arts of persuasion take very different forms and media from those of conviction. They are vehicles for doubt, challenge, defiance; they are intended to change or attack ideas, not manifest or perpetuate them. Usually, therefore, they are small in scale, ephemeral in time. Even when not clandestine or subversive, they by definition do not command the central power or major resources of societies or states. They tend to represent the work and outlook of individuals rather than institutions (**56d**).

The probability is that arts of persuasion appeared in history later than arts of conviction, and evolved out of them. At least, most evidence and logic would seem to support such a guess. Alphabetic writing, for example, obviously evolved from pictographs (in China the two never entirely separated); pictographs in turn were stylizations and abstractions from ideational images that carried solipsistic conviction; and even when letters had become something quite distinct from pictures, the magic aura of their origin still hung round them, so that for a long time ideational pictures and sacred texts existed side by side (as in later Egyptian tombs, Mesopotamian steles with pictures of both the god-king and his divine decrees, etc.). And still today the Sacred Word survives in the underground of black magic. But as time went on, the advantages of writing for persuasion, for formulating new ideas, more and more superseded its use in sacred texts, and so writing became the first Great Art of persuasion in history.

We may also guess that the arts of persuasion grew in inverse ratio to the decline of early arts of conviction. All civilizations emerge into history suddenly, with their fundamental ideas and character decisively formed, as if from a long hidden period of gestation, and almost at once the great monuments appear, embodying those ideas and carrying the unmistakable "style" of each civilization forever after. Ancient Egypt is barely out of the prehistoric swamps when its Old Kingdom temples and pyramids appear; ziggurats and mosaicked walls appear with equal suddenness in Mesopotamia; megarons and distinctive pottery in archaic Greece; and every historian has been struck with how abruptly all the most characteristic institutions and artistic attitudes of the West seemed to spring into being in the 10th century. There follows what Toynbee in one of the most useful aspects of his *Study of History* calls a Time of Troubles, when these civilizations disintegrate under attack—Hyksos conquer Egypt and Kassites Mesopotamia, civil war tears the Greek city-states to pieces, the West is rent by schism and dynastic war, and so on. And then there is a period of recovery when the old beliefs are refurbished and embodied in arts of conviction bigger and more magnificent than ever before: colossal New Kingdom temples, overwhelming palaces in Babylon and Nineveh, Roman fora with bombastic triumphal arches, oversize statues of Emperors in 5th-century Greek style, lavishly flamboyant Late Gothic churches (**57b**). But these restored monuments never carry conviction like the old. No matter how grandly stated, Pharaoh's immortality and omnipotence can never be as self-evident or implicitly believed again, nor the gods of Ur, nor the ideals of classical city-states or Latin Christendom; they have an artificial, hysterical quality, a self-consciousness by no means incidentally related to the idea of Fine Art. For in the meantime doubts have arisen, and arts of persuasion been developed to express and spread them. Under the circumstances, such arts must necessarily be humble, obscure, and perishable; in most civilizations almost all we know about them comes from hints in literary texts. Relatively much more has survived from Imperial Rome: election posters and advertising signs from Pompeii, coins with slogans and symbols of contending parties within the state, paintings in Christian catacombs and Mithraic shrines—the matrix for monumental arts of conviction in the future societies of Byzantium and the West, though as yet only a substance of things hoped for by a few. It is from the late medieval West that we know most about the obscure origins of arts of persuasion; that is the peculiar significance of the print in western Europe from the 14th through the 17th centuries.

3. *Origins and Early History of Print-Making in the West*

Like all living arts, prints were so natural and spontaneous a response to social demand that nobody can say precisely how and when the first ones appeared. The general principle of printing was known certainly in the 13th and probably in the 12th century, for Theophilus describes it in *De Diversis Artibus;* but like the technique of oil painting, it apparently remained unemployed until circumstances called for it. These developed in the course of the 14th century, as the intellectual and political consensus of earlier medieval times disintegrated and contending parties, pushing forward increasingly diverse views, began to look for persuasive ways to disseminate them. What was in function the modern advertising poster appeared at Rome in 1347, during the seven-month revolution led by Cola di Rienzi. To propagate his precociously modern fantasy of an ideal state on a populace still intelligent enough to be skeptical, this prototype of the modern visionary demagogue had the walls of Rome painted with all sorts of allegorical figures of Rome, Christendom, Italy, Religion, the Empire, and whatnot. Cola, however, does not seem to have used prints; yet by 1400 prints had become common (though in the nature of things few have survived), and by 1460 woodcut printers were numerous enough to form powerful guilds, Augsburg and Venice being particularly prolific centers.

How arts of persuasion developed from arts of conviction is suggested by the early history of prints. For originally, of course, prints as such were not exclusively or even necessarily concerned with persuasion. Down to around 1450 the commonest kind of prints were pilgrimage souvenirs, colored pictures with identifying title or text cut from a single block, made for distribution at shrines on established pilgrimage routes (58a). Although by the Later Middle Ages what had once been the difficult and dangerous spiritual exercise of pilgrimages to holy places was everywhere becoming a highly organized business, with plotted routes and regular stops and other suitable tourist services—including such souvenirs—still, these prints were quite plainly Low Art versions of High Arts of conviction, cheaper and more easily produced versions of painted and carved altarpieces and memorials in which established belief was proclaimed. The same is obviously true of the block-printed books that developed out of them, like the *Biblia Pauperum* (literally "bibles for poor" preachers who could not afford the expense of manuscript copies) (23a). So too playing cards, which represented perhaps the first secular use of the print technique, took for granted a feudal order of precedence in society and so in effect helped perpetuate it.

Once a technique so much better suited for expression of individual ideas than painting or sculpture became available, its adaptation for purposes of persuasion would seem inevitable. By the mid-15th century ancestors of our political cartoons were beginning to circulate—typical was the famous print made at Ulm around 1470 showing Holy Roman Emperor Frederick III and Pope Paul II as half-naked wrestlers in a political power struggle; then came illustrations in secular books presenting individualistic if not heretical views on established ideas; then commercial advertisements—the earliest being, as might be expected, by a book printer for his books (Gerhard Leeu at Antwerp in 1491, describing his *Melusina* with an accompanying cut for it). This change in function was not yet accompanied by any significant changes in form, however. Until about 1550 print-making remained still in essence a branch of painting, practiced on appropriate occasions for particular purposes both by painters like Schongauer and Dürer and Holbein to serve traditional social functions, and by Fine Artists like Mantegna and Marcantonio Raimondi to exploit special graphic effects for the delectation of connoisseurs.

In fact, as we shall see, throughout all later history prints continued to perform both persuasive and convincing functions as occasion required. If in our minds they tend to be more immediately associated with persuasion, that is primarily because they first took forms distinct from painting while serving primarily for persuasion, in the troubled centuries that followed the Protestant Reformation of 1517.

4. *Evolution of Social and Political Cartoons as Distinctive Arts of Persuasion*

Prints could remain a Low Art variant of the High Art of painting only so long as painting retained its function as an art of conviction—a vehicle for expressing truths in grand and imaginative ways. And for painting to fulfill this function, a stable ideology is essential; as soon as painting has also to persuade in any specific or immediate way, it becomes inadequate (**59b**). Thus, paintings to inspire conviction by dramatic and lucid presentations of contested truths were still being done throughout the 16th and into the 17th centuries—Raphael's implicit defense of the Real Presence in the *Disputà*, Dürer's of Biblical revelation over Church tradition in his Nuremberg altar wings, Michelangelo's of the Church Militant's redemptive work in his *Last Judgment* on the Sistine altar wall, Rubens's altarpiece dramatizing miracles, and so on. But such paintings can only influence spectators already sharing some basic agreement about fundamental truths. Once the Reformation in religion and breakdown of old feudal polities had proceeded so far that all fundamentals were under dispute, attacking and defending them was beyond the effective scope of painting, and so from this point on prints in the form of social and political cartoons had to begin developing independently as separate and distinctive Low Arts.

Naturally enough, the most dramatic examples are prints directly concerned with the Reformation. The earliest ones are clearly related to allegorical paintings and manuscript illuminations, as *The Emperor and the Pope* was earlier—complex allegorical representations of the Pope as a hybrid monster (**59a**), Luther as the devil's bagpipe. But by 1570 a print like *Luther and Catherine von Bora* is clearly evolving on its own; the artist has drawn on many sources, including a famous old German folk print of *The Toper* (c. 1510), to create something uniquely suited to its function and no other; it is not a painting adapted to some other use (**59c**).

The rate at which political and social cartooning develops in any given country naturally depends on the degree of disagreement about fundamental beliefs and of freedom to express it. In Spain, Italy, and Catholic Germany, enough uniformity is imposed by the Counter Reformation and absolute monarchies for painting to persuade still: Tintoretto's *Miracle of St. Mark* may not convert anyone to Catholicism or Velasquez' *Surrender of Breda* convince anyone of Spanish invincibility, but such paintings could effectively reinforce beliefs already held. During the early 17th century religious and civil wars in France provide an environment for satirical prints by Abraham Bosse (1602–1676) on courtly manners and for the protests and exposures of *Miseries of War* by Jacques Callot (1592–1635). But once Louis XIV consolidated his power, painting became the preferred art of persuasion, glorifying the regime with majestic portraits by Rigaud and the grandiose allegories of Lebrun and his Academy. Satire developed rapidly in Holland, where a Protestantism triumphant over Catholic Spain was soon split into Calvinist and Arminian factions, both challenged by early freethinkers; but there too it was still largely done in painting. Many Dutch painters made their reputations as satirists—Jan Steen (1626–1679) and Adriaen van Ostade (1610–1685) were chiefly known for their carousing lower classes, Cornelis Dusart (1660–1704) for his old Jews, and so on; almost all did some, including Rembrandt (his *Ganymede* as a squalling baby is probably the best known), and from Holland the idea of satirical painting spread to Scandinavia, where it survives to this day in a national taste for light humorous water colors. Of course all these painters did etched and engraved prints also; but so strong was the influence of painting that even the most famous Dutch satirical prints, like those of Romeyn de Hooghe (1645–1708) do not begin to exploit the advantages of the medium, and remain essentially etched paintings (**58b**).

314

The result was to leave development of satirical prints for England. There, factions were too violent and conditions too unstable for ideas to be effectively expressed in any other medium. For fifty years Protestant and Catholic parties contended over the religious establishment until defeat of the Spanish Armada settled that question; there followed a century of contest between Puritans and Anglicans over what form a Protestant government shold take, punctuated by a civil war and two revolutions; until 1715 (or even 1745) no principles of Church or State seemed self-evidently acceptable long enough to build a High Art on. Through all this time the arts of political and social cartooning, were without essential rival as means for promoting and refuting ideas, and flourished accordingly (**60a, b, c**).

But at this same moment a new theme appeared that has dominated and determined arts of both conviction and persuasion ever since.

II

THE REVOLUTION IN CONVICTION AND PERSUASION: THREE PHASES: 1750-1960

OVER and over again we have had occasion to refer to that restless drive to establish a Heaven on earth which, preoccupying the last two centuries of Western history, must necessarily be a dominant concern in any study of the living, Unchanging Arts in society.

We have seen how the origins of this religion can be traced back into the Renaissance, and ultimately to anarchic egalitarian movements in the Middle Ages; how as a moving force in history it takes effective form in the years c. 1680–c. 1715, which Paul Hazard so aptly called *La Crise de la conscience européenne* (1935). We have seen how its essential promise and belief in happiness and security necessarily assured here and now on earth is a most ancient notion in itself, only its particular formulation being new, drawn as it has been from a perversion of the medieval ideal of the Kingdom of Heaven.

In describing the rise and rationale of Fine Art, and the High and Low arts of illustration, we have seen how this traditional hope has in effect been upended, so that what was traditionally looked for after death and in another dimension—perfect equality, perfect love among redeemed souls, absolute sinlessness, everlasting peace and immortality—is now promised for the time-space dimensions of our present bodies. In the arts of conviction and persuasion we shall see yet another aspect of this new faith. Since these are the arts most directly concerned with it, attacking and defending the old order, promoting and manifesting the new, they are the arts that best reveal its historic development—and specifically, how this hope has been promulgated, more by logical necessity than conscious design, in three stages. Indeed, neither they nor it can be properly understood without recognizing these three stages or phases for what they were (**61a, b, c**).

The first emphasized political equality—promising that once every individual had an equal vote in determining public policy, all problems would be solved and all institutions transformed; the goal in this stage (roughly c. 1700–c. 1815) was one-head-one-vote franchise, and the opposition, institutions based on hereditary privilege. To this phase belongs 18th-century Freemasonry, openly secularizing Christian ritual in the spirit of John Toland's *Christianity not Mysterious* (1696), training men in its lodges to enjoy political equality on earth as the Church used to train them for angelic equality in Heaven, initiating them by degrees corresponding exactly to baptism, confirmation, and the Eucharist; Rousseau's *Social Contract* (1762) and Montesquieu's *Spirit of the Laws* (1748); David's didactic idealizations of Roman republican virtue in neoclassical paintings, demonstrating how perfectibility on earth is possible. Its chief culmination was the American Revolution of 1776 and the French Revolution of 1789.

Already by 1800, however, a second stage was in evidence—preaching that, since there seemed no more effective equality, no more real happiness, no less sin after these revolutions than before, political equality is not enough; indeed, that it is pointless without economic equality. For another hundred years (roughly 1800–1900) economic equality (i.e., orthodox socialism) was the goal, and the opposition "bourgeois democracy"—i.e., mere political equality. After the 1830 Revolution with its disillusionments, this phase of the faith becomes predominant in France; it sparks the 1848 revolution there, with its twin emphases on romantic nationalism (the state as savior of mankind) and outright class warfare. Eighteen hundred forty-eight is also the year of Karl Marx's *Communist Manifesto*—henceforth the baptismal certificate of most sects in this phase of the religion. Since it is obvious that economic equality cannot be achieved without strong central government, socialist thought becomes steadily more authoritarian, as is already apparent in the 1871 Paris Commune. The climax of this phase is the Bolshevik Revolution of 1917, establishing a theoretical "dictatorship of the proletariat" and the practical dictatorship of Lenin, inherited by Stalin, provoking the antipodal reaction of anti-Communist socialist revolutions in Italy (1922) and Germany (1933).

But already by c. 1900 a third phase of the religion was in evidence, preached by Sorel and Bergson, Freud and Pareto (among others), practiced most obviously by the Anarchists—that neither political nor economic equality will ensure happiness, only equal love among all persons, uninhibited by any formal institutions. Its goal is a State without any institutions at all (an Unstate); its opposition, whatever Establishment happens to be in power—"bourgeois democracy" or "orthodox socialism" (whether Leninist-Stalinist, or Fascist, or British Labour), as the case may be.

To each successive vision obvious objections could be made on grounds of common sense. Meaningful political equality is impossible because opportunity cannot be unlimited; everybody cannot become President. Complete economic equality is impossible because there simply are not resources enough to go around; some people in the world must have less than others, unless everyone is to starve. Social equality is impossible because people are inherently unequal— some are clever with their hands, others with their brains, some with neither; some are born with tall genes, others with short, and some with handicaps. Simply being born into time and history and society means that no two people can ever be exactly equal in ability, in wealth, in status, or in understanding. But in each of the three phases there was a particular instrument, a special *deus ex machina,* that the visionaries confidently counted on to resolve all such difficulties. In the first phase, it was Capitalism. Once get rid of all those feudal regulations and special privileges and patents by which corrupt aristocrats have cornered and controlled the wealth of nations, once allow men

317

free expression of their inherent creativity, and wealth unlimited will flow forth. This was the faith of Voltaire, of Adam Smith, and today of Ayn Rand. In the second phase, it was of course Applied Science that was counted on to perform the miracle and provide riches enough for all to share amply. And in the third phase, it was Applied Psychology; if people are not born equal, they can be made so by proper "conditioning," prenatally if necessary.

To each successive vision obvious objections could also be made on grounds of historical experience. The political and economic and social institutions of European civilization—of all civilizations—result from what Man is now, and has always been throughout history; it would be a disastrously mad gamble, therefore, to restructure them on an unproved and unprovable assumption that he is, or could become, something different. But to this there was an answer too—a model that could be pointed to in proof that such institutions had existed and had worked. In the first phase, that model was the idealized republics of Greece and Rome, whose political institutions were extolled as having made men happier in mind and more independent in spirit than anything Europe had since known. Especially often cited were the writings of apologists for Imperial Rome, whose sycophantic propaganda was swallowed so credulously (for people believe what they want to believe) that historians like Gibbon took for gospel truth their praises of Hadrian's and Marcus Aurelius's tyrannies as the happiest of all human ages. In the second phase, the model varied according to a particular enthusiast's background and circumstances, but usually it was some idealized example of successful collectivized living from very early stages in society, before the corrupting introduction of private property—Israel under the Judges, for example; remote tribesmen in America or Brazil or the South Seas; Teutons during the Great Migrations; certain aspects of early medieval society. In the third phase, the model is simple precivilized man—the childlike innocence of Eden before the Fall (which was interpreted by people like William Blake to mean the appearance of civilized institutions); savage tribes undiscovered and so uncorrupted by the White Man (and so also unknown, of course!); the mythical Arcadia; prehistoric man generally, worshiping the Great Mother in all sexual innocence, covering his caves with animals rendered with pristine clarity of vision.

So it was that whenever a vision faded into the cold light of fact, there was always a position for new visionaries to fall back on.

Have sober historians discredited Greece and Rome as ideal republics? You can still prove an ideal society possible by citing some more remote archaic epoch, safe from their researches. If archaeology and anthropology explode that model in turn, you can retreat to a Garden of Eden myth that defies rational examination. Have capitalists proved no more virtuous than kings? You can switch your hopes to Scientists. And when their promised blessings come mixed with atom bombs and poison gas and pollution, trust to Psychologists for salvation; these new wizards can recondition wicked Scientists along with everyone else.

Now the beauty of this procedure is that each successive failure is not only excusable as irrelevant, but also provides a fresh new enemy to organize agitation around. Cultural anthropologists tell us how the gods of conquered peoples became the demons of their conquerors' religion; so here. That same Capitalism to which visionaries looked for salvation in the 18th century became the most hated of all their enemies in the 19th; and to *their* successors in the 20th century, Applied Science in turn is the god that failed and must be exorcised by fanatical rites in the name of antipollution. The fanaticism and the faith do not have to change, only the enemy to be attacked and the idol to be worshiped.

Consistently through all three phases, then, two kinds of activity are going on simultaneously: (a) attacks on institutions and ideas considered to stand in the way of Man's expressing his natural goodness and realizing his dream of establishing Heaven on earth; and (b) shaping new institutions and formulating new ideas in which the Terrestrial Paradise will take form. Arts in the service of this new religion will therefore have two sorts of function also: (a) to persuade people of the wickedness and falsity of whatever is currently under attack; and (b) to create appropriately convincing visionary images of whatever new perfect world is currently under construction. By these functions (or their reverse on the other side of the issue) the forms of arts of conviction and persuasion have been determined for the past two centuries.

III

POLITICAL DEMOCRACY
AS FAITH AND FACT

1. *Political and Social Cartooning in England, 1700–1800*

IT was in the first, political phase of the new religion that the political and social cartoon as we know it took mature form; historical circumstances, as we have seen, dictated that developments in this medium occurred first in England.

The principal early form of mass-distributed print in England was the broadside, usually a single sheet with text and correlative illustration (sometimes only a crest, at other times more picture than text), printed on a wood block or metal plate as importance warranted. From the early 16th through the 18th centuries such broadsides were officially used for proclamations of royal or parliamentary acts of special relevance to the public. In them, text and pictures alike were formal and flowery; a famous and typical example is the patriotic broadside of the 1620s on Guy Fawkes's plot to burn the Houses of Parliament—clearly a Low Art version of High Baroque, with formal stage, learned quotations in Latin and English, allegorical figures of various kinds, and a complex linking of the defeat of the Spanish Armada with Fawkes's treachery.

But increasingly from the 1550s on, a new kind of broadside began appearing. The Martinist pamphlets are typical; sweeping away all complex Baroque imagery, they hammer straight away at a single idea, using simple and direct language (including the first approximations of inarticulate noises like "ha, ha, ha" and "tsk! tsk!" in written English) and a colloquial debating style, complete with encouraging slangy shouts from an imaginary audience. And they were enormously effective; by the 1640s the masters of this style had become masters of England, and the official broadside of Charles I's execution illustrates it with the same directness, using simple, flat, medieval forms akin to the "plain style" of the Puritans, whose triumph over both Charles I's Baroque theories of kingship and his Baroque tastes in art is here consummated. In this development of forms directly and simply appropriate to function was the seed of political and social cartoons as an art form distinct from painting (**60a, b**).

In the course of the 17th century uses and varieties of the broadsheet multiplied. It spawned the newssheet, which in due course became the newspaper, though curiously enough political cartoons did not begin to appear in that medium until the 19th century. Alongside newspapers, however, broadside "extras" announcing battles, deaths of royalty, spectacular crimes and disasters continued to appear—a direct descendant of them was the first Currier & Ives print, of the steamship *Lexington* disaster in 1840. Some of the more notable of these episodes were collected into chapbooks (i.e., "peddler's books") which continued to be hawked about country districts well into the 18th century, creating and perpetuating a living folklore and repository of social attitudes (**40a**). During the 17th century, too, ballads and satires began to be printed on broadsheets, with appropriate illustrative headings—ancestors of modern sheet music and record covers which still, of course, feature pictures of performers and illustrations intended to sell their works. Edifying funeral verses pinned to palls were introduced in the mid-17th century, and by the early 18th century it was becoming common to print and illustrate accounts of executions with speeches by the condemned deploring their crimes and urging others to eschew them—ancestors of religious tracts.

All this meant an enormous output, so that in the 18th century England became the chief center for print production in Europe. For the years 1720–1800, more than 8000 prints are listed in the British Museum Catalogue of Political and Personal Satires, and clearly in the transitory nature of the medium these survivors can only be a fraction of the total production. At the same time, the broadside proper gradually disappeared, superseded by different kinds of prints specialized for specific function. Media tended to vary according to the social stratum addressed: for middle-class markets the commonest print was taken from a copperplate engraved or etched, which sold in shops for about sixpence, or for a shilling if colored by hand (just as the first medieval prints had been); for upper classes, there were more expensive prints made by the elaborate aquatint or mezzotint techniques; for the lower class, woodcuts made by the old process were still available in chapbooks sold by street hawkers for a penny or two. Forms were comparably dictated by social function. Thus, chapbooks preserved medieval folk forms, essentially; aquatints and mezzotints were characteristically Low Art versions contemporary of High Art, following trends in 18th-century painting at a decade or two of cultural lag; but in copperplates addressed to the middle class, where the ideological battle was fiercest, essentially new forms appropriate to this function were evolved, among them caricature, the grotesque, and dialogue in speech balloons.

All these forms had been known long before, of course. Bernini is usually credited with the invention of caricature in the 17th century, while interest in the grotesque is commonly said to date from Leonardo's physiological studies of deformity a century earlier; but surely these ideas go much further back than that—as early as 1875 Thomas Wright's *History of Caricature and the Grotesque* cited many medieval examples, such as the marginal drawing of an Irishman from a manuscript of Edward I's reign, and another of rich Jews from Norwich on a receipt roll dated 1233. Balloon speech likewise has a long history; its most typical early form is the scrolls so frequently carried by figures on church façades or altarpieces from the Middle Ages. What is new in 18th-century cartoons is the deliberate and systematic use of caricature, the grotesque, and balloon speech for the special function of persuasion, rather than as an adjunct to painting, sculpture, or architecture. It is this combination of older forms used for a new purpose that makes a cartoon like *The Sturdy Beggar*, illustrated here, persuasive art of a kind and to a degree not known before in history (**60c**).

Against this background, and in terms of this social function, the accomplishments and reputation of William Hogarth as a political cartoonist need to be reassessed. Much of that reputation is derived from Hogarth's having been, in 20th-century terms, on the side of the angels—that is, he was an early and zealous propagandist for social change pointed toward the sort of egalitarian society most influential art critics of the 20th century have approved of, using his art to demonstrate how absurd hereditary class privileges were, how a "just society" would reward each according to his need and take from each according to his ability, and so on (**24a**). His prints generally, and especially his sequential series like *The Rake's Progress, Marriage à la Mode*, and *Industry and Idleness* are pictorial counterparts to Voltaire's style of writing—pithy, epigrammatical, propagandizing through overstatements of half truths and speciously selective "realism"; Erich Auerbach's analysis of Voltaire's technique in *Mimesis* (1953) could be applied almost word for word to Hogarth's political cartoons and paintings. But like Voltaire, who essentially remained suspended midway between older High Literature and modern journalese, Hogarth never shook off the influence of Dutch "cartoonists" like Romeyn de Hooghe on whose work he based his early prints, remaining from beginning to end a painter who made satirical prints on occasion, as Steen and Ostade, Dusart and Rembrandt had been. As a High Artist doing illustrative paintings, he for all intents and purposes ignored all the specialized devices appropriate to the persuasive function of political and social cartoons—the speech in balloons, the gross caricature, the concentration on a single idea. His cartoons therefore stand at the head of the line that leads to Courbet's *Burial at Ornans* or Picasso's *Guernica*—to Fine Art convincing only those who are believers already. To find the origins of those explicitly persuasive social and political cartoons that the 19th and 20th centuries knew, we have to look for humbler artisans without Fine Art pretensions, whom art history has largely forgotten. Eighteenth-century America produced some particularly good examples.

2. *Political and Social Cartooning in America, 1700–1800*

Early American prints, like everything else in early America, were strongly medieval in tradition. Explicitly medieval imagery persisted well into the 18th century and even longer—one extraordinary instance is a cut in the *Massachusetts Almanach* for 1774 of the devil coming to claim a wicked man's soul at the hour of death, which can be traced directly back to medieval origins in the legend of *The Three Living and the Three Dead,* and, incidentally, was still to be found in the Currier & Ives repertory in the 1850s (**23a, b, c**).

Traditional medieval imagery used without specific Christian connotations is plentiful, too: devils especially are used in all sorts of situations. And even where no specifically medieval or Christian associations appear, prints still generally see the world and mankind in a traditionally Christian frame of reference, judge men by a moral code ultimately set by transcendental standards, consider individuals rather than collective organizations of ultimate importance, concern themselves with personal vices and virtues rather than acceptable social attitudes. So when silversmith and print maker Nathaniel Hurd of Boston (1730–1777), for example, shows counterfeiters Dr. Seth Hudson and Joshua Howe at the pillory tormented by winged devils, a long accompanying poem makes clear that they deserve punishment not basically for antisocial behavior (as we would put it), but because they are wicked men doomed to Hell and by example perhaps leading others to perdition:

> Now all ye who behold this Sight,
> That ye may get some profit by't,
> . . . Follow my Steps that you may be
> In Time perhaps advanc'd like me
>   [i.e., set up on the pillory]:
> Or, like my fellow Lab'rer How,
> You'l get at least a Post below
>   [i.e., in Hell].

Or again, his print of George III, Pitt, and Wolfe praises them not as National Leaders but as virtuous men: "No Evil and Corrupt Ministers Dare to Approach his Sacred Presence"; "The man resolv'd and steady to his trust, Inflexible to ill, and Obstinately just. . . ."

It follows that in such prints there was a strong element of conviction—that is, they were used as much for stating established beliefs as for persuasion to different views. For example, consider the heading of the broadsheet issued for the 1768 Pope-Night Parade in Boston, illustrated here (62a). The ancestors of the figure on the float were plainly hate figures dragged through medieval streets, like the *grande goule* devil image of Poitiers, the Tarasque of Tarascon, or the wooden effigy of St. Romain's monster burnt annually in the public square of Rouen from Romanesque times until the French Revolution—images, that is, of what was in a given culture considered to be self-evident error; so likewise the print picturing them is intended to reinforce existing established belief, not inculcate new ones.

But from mid-century on, something of new tone and different theme begins to appear in American prints—cartoons explicitly political and explicitly persuasive. Paul Revere (1735–1818) provides some of its best examples. Though well-known as a silversmith and bell founder as well as a print maker, Revere's chief title in American history is "ardent patriot." He belonged to what today would be called an "activist group" dedicated to overthrowing traditional structure of the state and erecting a new one on visionary principles; his dedication to the idea of bringing in Heaven on earth through new political institutions was more than ardent, it was evangelically religious, and this is what gives his cartoons their particular interest. Consider, for example, a print like his "Rescinders" (**62b**). Its imagery is almost as traditional as that of the Pope-Night broadside, published (incredibly enough) in the same year, 1768: devils with pitchforks, Hell represented by the gaping jaws of a leviathan, the whole given local application (as throughout medieval art) by contemporary detail, in this case the cupola of Massachusetts' old Province House, with its famous Indian weather vane. But the whole frame of reference is different. As the accompanying verse makes clear, these seventeen men are not "puny Villains damn'd for petty [i.e., personal] Sin"; their crimes are of a different order. These are the seventeen members of the Massachusetts House of Representatives who voted on June 30, 1768, to obey their King and rescind a resolution which that House had previously passed; so far from being lawless, they had, in terms of the old morality, only done their "bounden duty and service." But men like Revere saw their act in entirely different terms. To him it was wickedness fit to "startle Hell" because he held the vision of a new kind of state in which obedience was owed not to "the powers that be of God"—to hereditary authority—but to the will of that legislative majority of ninety-two House members who had voted not to rescind.

Equation of virtue with following a party line and vice with disobedience to the "people's will" is the kind of temporal morality we in the 20th century know all too well; and Revere's other well-known prints have the same kind of familiarity for us. We know all about "doctored prints" like his famous *Boston Massacre* of 1770, which distorted defense against deliberately incited mob attack into a picture of unprovoked slaughter of innocent civilians; and we are familiar with justifying such deceptions (incidentally including Revere's own theft of the design from Peter Pelham, who charged Revere on March 20, 1770, with robbing him "as truly as if you had plundered me on the highway") on grounds of "higher necessity" to the interests of the state—though we have never yet resolved the inconsistency of justifying deceitful propaganda by appeal to precisely that "majority will" which it was perpetrated to influence.

But to the great public in Revere's time his vision of the state was new and exciting, and the technique of his prints massively effective. To say that we can trace the progress of the Revolution in Revere's prints is not enough; they are also records of the great forces that made the Revolution, by making converts to the new religion whose triumph the Revolution was. Yet with that triumph prints necessarily underwent a great change.

3. *From Persuasive Prints to Architecture of Conviction: Transformations in American Art Forms, 1780–1820*

A great many accounts and collections of early American prints have been published—W. C. Ford's *Massachusetts Broadsides* (1922), William Murrell's *History of American Graphic Humor* (1933–38), *Early New England Printmakers* (Worcester, Mass., 1940), Charles F. Montgomery's *Prints Pertaining to America* (Winterthur, 1964), among others.

Most note that after a final flurry of domestic partisan cartooning in the Federal period, when the two-party system is being evolved with each side castigating the other as heretical deviants from received truth, and Elkhanah Tisdall's *Gerrymander* becomes the first cartoon to add a word to the language, there comes a quiescence. Though the volume of prints does not diminish, nothing particularly new or interesting appears until the Civil War.

Why this should be is not explained; the reason, I think, is the ingrained contemporary habit of thinking about art in terms of forms instead of function. For if you think about the function of prints, it will be obvious why they ceased developing. Their new forms had been evolved primarily for attack and defense in the 18th-century ideological style. Now that style was over. The need is no longer for arts to persuade men of the faith, but to proclaim its established conviction. And for this, other arts are better suited than prints.

Consider, for one example, how the work of Amos Doolittle of Connecticut (1754–1832) changes over three decades. In 1775 we find Doolittle in New Haven, engraving a hortatory memorial to the battle of Lexington and Concord, after participating in it that year. In 1781 his print *America* heralds approaching triumphs of the cause and glorifies its "Patriotic Heroes," saints of the new millennium—before an obelisk inscribed WARREN–MONTGOMERY–WOOSTER–MERCER kneels a furred and feathered American being crowned from the starry heavens with palms of peace. In 1794 a proud *Display of the United States of America* prophesies this new kind of state spreading over all the world, bringing its saving gospel to all peoples. From an art of persuasion, his prints have gradually turned into an art of conviction; and for each of his, there are dozens, hundreds, of parallels: endless iconic prints of Washington and Franklin and the lady America, of the glorious naval victories of 1813 and, finally, of the battle of New Orleans. But plainly, prints are not the most satisfactory sort of commemorative monument. Such a function demands a less ephemeral medium, a more substantial form.

Painting would be more appropriate; and indeed in the Federal period Gilbert Stuart (1755–1828) was only one of many painters to make fortunes turning out life-size portraits of Washington to be hung in ceremonial grandeur in mansions, capitols, and court-houses. Such images of conviction were the chief function of painting in the early Republic, a fact which painters like Charles Willson Peale (1741–1827) realized to their profit, John Vanderlyn (1775–1852) ignored at his peril.

Sculpture serves for conviction even better; and some of the old print forms accordingly are now translated into this solider and more convincing medium. Of this, Masonic symbols provide an excellent example. It is no accident, perhaps, that one of Paul Revere's earliest prints was a Masonic meeting notification form for St. Andrews Lodge, in which Revere became an Entered Apprentice in 1760. For Freemasonry was a prime agent in promoting the new vision in those days. In that Lodge, tradition maintains, plans were laid for campaigns against the Stamp Act, for the Boston Tea Party, and many other activities necessary to turn minority agitation into mass revolution. Masonic symbolic imagery was accordingly persuasive—trowel and square and compass, handgrip and All-Seeing Eye serving as incitements to remind initiates of their charge to build a Kingdom of Heaven here on earth. They were also private, if not secret, to the extent of being chiefly found in Masonic books or regalia, and members' personal possessions. But after the Revolution all this changed. Now Masonic symbols were seen openly and everywhere, in larger and more permanent forms—worked into table tops (16b) and fired into china, carried on tombstones, molded into trivets, emblazoned on buildings.

Obviously, again, the change in form and media corresponds to a change in function—by the time Paul Revere served as Grand Master of the Grand Lodge of Massachusetts in the 1790s, Freemasonry was no longer a solvent of the old order, but a prop for the new; it had ceased to be a proselytizing faith, and become more hereditary in membership, the prerequisite for social and political advancement it would remain until the 20th century. And the more its arts accordingly became instruments for establishing and maintaining conviction, the larger, the solider, the more sculptural they became.

Indeed, as I pointed out in an early article, "Freemasonry and the Neo-Classical Style in America" (*Antiques*, LXXVII, 2, 1960), speculative Freemasonry consistently taught that its ideals of the new and perfect society, the *Novus Ordo Seclorum*, were to be found best embodied in classical, especially Roman, architecture. Architecture is pre-eminently *the* art of conviction:

> According to Nikolaus Pevsner, "a bicycle shed is a building, Lincoln cathedral is a piece of architecture. . . . The term architecture applies only to buildings designed with a view to aesthetic appeal." Zevi [Bruno Zevi, in his article on architecture in *Encyclopedia of World Art*] disputes this, contending, rightly enough, that a bicycle shed may be designed so as to be aesthetically appealing. But would this make it a work of architectural art? I think not, because it would still be unrelated to any area of institutional meaning. Palace, house, tomb, capitol, court, temple, church—these, mainly, are the buildings which stand for the institutionalized patterns of human relatedness that makes possible the endurance of the city, or of society, or of the state; and these have provided almost all the occasions for meaningful architectural art for the past five thousand years. . . .
>
> The uniqueness of architecture lies in the fact that it is *about* the institutional establishment, as the other arts generally are not. . . . A building may be said to be a work of architectural art, then, insofar as it serves as a visual metaphor, declaring in its own form something (though never everything) about the size, permanence, strength, protectiveness, and organizational structure of the institution it stands for (but does not necessarily house). [Norris Kelly Smith, *Frank Lloyd Wright: A Study in Architectural Content*, 1966]

And given the temper of the times, plus the fact that Revere, Jefferson, Washington, and almost every other Revolutionary leader belonged to the Masonic order, there could be little doubt in what general architectural forms the new Republic would manifest its convictions. Only the details remained to be worked out, and this was pre-eminently the work of Thomas Jefferson.

4. *Jefferson's Concept of Classical Revival Architecture as an Art of Conviction*

Thomas Jefferson is best remembered by the world, perhaps, as the author of the Declaration of Independence. But it is a curious fact that the Declaration of Independence, as written, makes no practical sense. As Lawrence Brown has so well pointed out in *The*

Might of the West (1963), "We obviously have life while we live, and the right of men not to have their lives arbitrarily taken from them by other men was hardly a novel proposition at any time in any society," so what possible application can "inalienable right" to "life" have? As for "liberty" and the "pursuit of happiness," they imply each other, and are equally redundant:

> they cannot mean "do whatever you like," for that would be anarchy. If they mean "do whatever does not bother the powerful," that right has always existed . . . if they mean freedom to do what the new government allows but the old government forbade, that is the same thing.

The reason, of course, is that Jefferson is not talking in terms of this world. He is talking in terms of another, visionary one:

> if the verbal images are translated from the deistic jargon of the 18th century back into the theological concepts of the Middle Ages, from an "ideal" condition in this world to a "real" condition in the world to come, they make, and only then make, sense: "We hold these articles of faith to be revealed truth: all souls are created equal and they are endowed by God with certain inalienable rights among which are immortality, free will, and access to grace."

There is a parallel here with Jefferson's architectural ideas. Practically speaking, his idea of building the Virginia state capitol in the form of a Roman temple made no sense either; as I noted in *Images of American Living*, it would be hard to imagine "anything more impractical and inconvenient for meetings of large numbers of people . . . than a box lighted only from the front door, intended to store offerings to some god and never for accommodating people, with a great portico and podium contributing little or no usable space at enormous expense." Nor did Roman temples represent his personal aesthetic taste here and now, which in fact ran to Louis Seize furniture and Adamesque architecture. But convenience in terms of this world, beauty here and now, was not his intention. His concern was with symbolizing another kind of world altogether—that ideal state of political equality which, he was convinced, not only had been conceived by the Romans, but had actually existed in the Roman republic. For him, that ancient republic was proof that his vision of an ideal society on earth could succeed. To build the first new state capitol on the model of a Roman temple was then not a matter of practicality, but a profession of faith, like the Declaration of Independence, that the Revolution had been no matter of petty squabbling over sovereignty but an opportunity to create a kind of state unknown in the world before. To many writers it has seemed surprising that remote America should have been so far ahead of all the world in "taste" as to produce, in Jefferson's capitol, the first monumental example of the neoclassic style in Western civilization. Once realize that the Classical Revival was not a matter of taste but of expressing a transformation of vision into fact, however, and its appearing first in America will be seen as inevitable.

Jefferson's belief in the new vision was passionate enough not only to create a new architecture, but to destroy the social system that had reared him and most other leaders of the Revolution:

> Primogeniture through entail had become common in Virginia among large landholders, who entailed land and slaves with it. This was the basis of the Virginia aristocracy, and it was destroyed by Jefferson through a law abolishing entails. He considered it a major piece of legislation because it . . . broke up the hereditary and high-handed aristocracy, which, by accumulating immense masses of property in simple lines of families, had divided our country into two distinct orders of nobles and plebeians. [Saul Padover, ed., *The Complete Jefferson,* 1943, p. 1295]

To create an appropriate architectural symbol of his convictions, he was quite as ready to sacrifice convenience or aesthetic appeal if necessary. That is why, without a full awareness of its function as an art of conviction, the American Classical Revival architecture that Jefferson promoted can hardly be understood. How many art critics, for example, have deplored the principle of "Victorian eclecticism" Jefferson introduced to architecture, or made unfavorable comparisons of these "poor imitations" with the Great Art of Greece, because they have not understood that these forms were so primarily dictated by a living function in society that all other criteria are fundamentally irrelevant; if classical forms have lost their appeal, it does not mean that they are or were "bad," simply that they no longer function, once the ideas they manifest no longer hold. How many scholars (including myself) have gone astray looking for the origins of Jefferson's forms in "influences" from other forms, because they failed to realize that it is not a question of discovering earlier models with possible practical or aesthetic appeal for Jefferson, but models appropriate for the ideological function he had in mind. The University of Virginia campus at Charlottesville that Jefferson laid out in 1817 is a good case in point.

330

That this campus had symbolic significance is too obvious to be missed; in *Images of American Living* I used it as an example of the variety and depth of Classical Revival symbolism, introducing the whole Victorian architectural tradition. But I did not then realize how completely its function as an image of conviction determined its forms. For example: the single most striking feature of this campus was the contrast its broad "street" lined with uniformly scaled buildings made to the haphazard collections of buildings that had constituted earlier American college campuses. Much has been made of the aesthetic and physically functional aspects of this design, and many ingenious speculations about its probable model. Most of this, however, including a possibility that Latrobe may have supplied ideas for the Rotunda, turns out to be beside the point. Once realize that conviction is its basic function, and it will be clear that what Jefferson was looking for would not necessarily be convenience or beauty or precedents in earlier campuses, but designs that could be made into symbolic embodiments of Heaven brought down to earth. David Daiches in *The Paradox of Scottish Culture* (London, 1964) has pointed out one striking example of such a design in James Craig's conception of Edinburgh's New Town in the 1760s as a deliberately symbolic contrast of Enlightenment order, balance and clarity with the "medieval confusions" of the Old Town's twisted streets and cramped masses of heterogeneous tenements; obviously, it was something like this that Jefferson had in mind. Certainly the same symbolism attached to the wide streets and planned order of L'Enfant's Washington, deliberately intended to be as unique among cities as the American republic was unique among nations, from which descend the distinctive wide streets of American towns laid out in the early 19th century with their classical names—Athens, Syracuse, Troy, Rome. Another possible model was the campus of Union College in Schenectady, New York, laid out in the same open and uniform plan by J. J. Ramée, a young intellectual familiar with advance-guard ideas in France and Germany. These could all have been adapted as images of the conviction Jefferson wished to manifest. But I think he could have got the idea even closer to home. In Lancaster County, Virginia, an area he would have known very well, was what then must have been the famous church built by Robert "King" Carter about 1730—a central-plan building prefaced by a great processional avenue—the same basic plan as the Charlottesville campus. What better parallel to Jefferson's inversion of traditional scholastic verbal imagery in the Declaration than to invert this traditional architectural imagery for his campus, dressing the whole in precise classical forms.* How better express his new faith than to transform the ordered environment of such an 18th-century classical church, intended as a brief foretaste in this chaotic world of the eternal joys of heavenly order promised by the old faith, into the campus of a secular university dedicated to inculcating visions of permanent peace and order promised by a new! During the succeeding century and a half, the need for images of American convictions would prompt adoption of many models far stranger than this (**63a, b, c**).

5. *Diverse Expressions of Conviction in American Architecture, 1820–1960*

Realizing how the primary motivation behind American architectural development was its function as an art of conviction puts American architectural history in a new light. Everyone who knows it, knows how the Roman Revival was superseded by Greek as the reigning favorite c. 1820–1845, how Greek in turn was challenged by Gothic Revival and superseded by Italianate in the 1840s and -50s; how, after a High Victorian picturesque eclectic wave in the 1860s and early -70s, Richardsonian Romanesque swept the country; how out of it on the one hand grew the Arts and Crafts movement of the turn of the 20th century and thence a root of what we call "modern" architecture, on the other the Late Victorian Academic revivals, and especially the "Colonial Revivals" of allegedly 17th- and 18th-century modes of building in New England, Pennsylvania, Virginia, the Spanish Southwest, and so on. But, except for some awareness of the shifting symbolic values that favored Greek over Roman Revival and worked against any widespread popularity for Gothic, this history is generally treated as a sort of parade of "styles," a change of "taste" comparable to what happens in Picasso's painting. Once think in terms of American architecture consistently functioning as an art of conviction, however, and the picture looks very different. You can see that the mixing of styles which begins with Italianate, though it still has ideological implications (the point is discussed in *Images of American Living,* pp. 316–19), could well represent a parallel to the ideological confusions

---

* That B. H. Latrobe is generally credited with suggesting that Jefferson close his campus avenue with the Rotunda does not affect this argument. Had Jefferson not been predisposed to the idea, he would not have accepted the suggestion.

that presaged the Civil War; that architecture of the immediate post-War period does in fact implicitly manifest an ideological breakdown is obvious, and so too is the appeal of Richardsonian Romanesque massiveness and stability in this distracted time (cf. *Images* pp. 337–48; 352–53). That the same functional considerations dictated later changes of style is not readily recognized, however; yet it needs only analysis to become obvious too.

Norris Kelly Smith in his extraordinarily brilliant study of Frank Lloyd Wright (*op. cit.*) has demonstrated to what an overwhelming and hitherto unsuspected degree Wright's architecture was consistently determined by a conscious attempt to create embodiments of the Jeffersonian dream—by its function as an art of conviction, that is. I shall not attempt to recapitulate these arguments here*, but consider rather how the same considerations motivated Wright's great rivals, the Colonial Revivalists, beginning with the famous design for the World's Columbian Exposition of 1893 at Chicago.

What pilgrimage shrines like Santiago, St. Peter's, and Vierzehnheiligen had been to the old religion of the West, world's fairs were to its new vision of Heaven come to earth. In them the new State proclaimed its promises and the new Science its powers; to these Holy Cities believers came to be confirmed in their faith, waverers to be comforted, skeptics to be converted. In them each successive phase of the evolving vision can be traced, from the first, London's Great Exhibition of 1851 in its Crystal Palace, displaying the marvelous creations of Applied Science made possible by free enterprise and political equality, to the last, Expo '67 in Montreal, where the potentialities of Man—collectivized, economically equalized, socially leveled—were paraded (**61b**). And in this light the three American 19th-century fairs have a significance curiously corresponding to dominant architectural styles.

The first American fair was the 1853 exhibition in New York, an imitation of the London Exhibition, ideologically as uncertain as the Italianate style. The second was Philadelphia's 1876 Centennial, a hodgepodge mirroring the confusions of a nation shaken to its ideological foundations by Civil War, a counterpart to High Victorian picturesque eclecticism. The third was very different. This was the 1893 Columbian Exposition in Chicago, *the* great American fair. Its

---

* They are summarized to some extent in my review of Smith's book in *Journal of the Society of Architectural Historians*, XXVIII, 1969, 1; also in my *King Carter's Church, op. cit.*, pp. 30–45.

model was Jefferson's University of Virginia campus—at least, it had the same basic scheme of buildings in several variants of Roman styles lining a broad mall, at the head of which stood a domed Pantheonlike structure; but the differences were so significant as to create a new image altogether. Republican simplicity was smothered in a florid effusion of detail drawn from the later, Imperial Roman times, appropriately enough reflecting the wave of popular enthusiasm for imperial conquest that surprised even those who, within a few years, were promoting the Spanish-American War. Appropriate, too, was the inflation of Charlottesville's modest scale to grandiose dimensions in Chicago, for Jefferson's Arcadia of small farmers living in sturdy independence on their own plots of land bore every year less and less resemblance to a land where more and more people worked for bigger and bigger corporations. Most appropriate of all was the shift from red Virginia brick to the Great White City, for over this fair brooded ghosts of men who in much earlier days tried to reaffirm shaken beliefs and values with the sheer size and splendor of architectural symbols: the builders of Ramses II's temples, of Late Gothic churches, of Trajan's column and Septimius Severus's triumphal arch. It is no accident that the most immediate influence of the Chicago fair was on the design of mighty stations for mightier railroad corporations, or that its most lasting influence was on national monuments. Renewal of L'Enfant's Washington, the Lincoln and Jefferson Memorials, the giant heads of Mount Rushmore, decade by decade they follow one another—in scale grandiose, in form imperial, in color white as death (cf. **63b**). What Luigi Barzini said of the very similar Victor Emmanuel monument to the Risorgimento ideal built in 1911 on Rome's Capitoline Hill applies equally to them:

> The excessive size of the construction, its position, its architecture reveal . . . insecurity. . . . The patriotic minority . . . clearly wanted to celebrate a National Hero to cancel out many of the heroes of the past, a patriot to obliterate all [the] nonpatriotic. . . . The monument is not only the sincere tribute of a grateful people . . . but also the theatrical representaton of such a tribute. [*The Italians*, 1964, pp. 181–82]

Counterpart to these national monuments was and is the Colonial Revival, projecting the same image on a domestic scale—less theatrical, more instinctive, more natural. Indeed, it was not entirely a revival, for when McKim and Stanford White made their famous pilgrimage to New England in search of the "picturesque colonial" after visiting the 1876 Centennial fair, the old vernacular had not fallen entirely out of use there. It also was quite in keeping with the spirit of a reincarnated Rome, for in Rome's later age, too, archaism was nothing new. So writers of the Genteel school, like Bayard Taylor or Thomas Bailey Aldrich, and Colonial Revival architects of every variety sought to recall Gilded Age Americans to the allegedly simpler virtues of John Winthrop, William Penn, or the Mathers.

In terms of orthodox art criticism, the appearance, spread, and tenacious persistence of the Colonial Revival in 20th-century America must surely be among the most remarkable phenomena in the whole history of art. Still during the 1960s, for every one house built in a "modern" style in the United States there were at least twenty, perhaps fifty, built in some variant of the Colonial Revival—Southern, New England, Western Ranch. For every one visitor to museums of contemporary art, there were at least ten to the proliferating "colonial museums"—Williamsburg, Dearborn, Winterthur, Sturbridge, Shelburne, Cooperstown. Despite a barrage of art-appreciation propaganda unparalleled in history extolling the virtues of "modern" architecture and deriding all forms of "imitative" or "illustrative" arts, everywhere banks and office buildings and apartment houses were going up in red brick and white clapboard, with shutters and cupolas and pediments; and speculative builders like Mr. Emilio Capaldi of Wilmington, Delaware, made their fortunes—which depended on accurately gauging public taste—with projects like his Independence Malls, shopping centers consisting of false-front replicas of famous colonial buildings grouped around a false-front replica of Independence Hall. But all this is entirely logical, once we keep the ideological function of architecture as an art of conviction in mind.

No matter how furiously apologists labor to teach appreciation of architecture as an art of pure aesthetic values or expression of the structure, the average American homeowner knows instinctively that this is nonsense, that buildings to be architecture at all must be "about something." And he knows instinctively too that Colonial Revival is the only kind of meaningful architecture being offered him. Feeble though the associations of a barbecue-and-patio Western-style ranch house may be with footloose pioneers pushing intrepidly across the Plains, or Eastern-style Cape Cod cottages with dedicated individualists risking everything for freedom in a new world, still to the inhabitant of Levittown or South Pasadena they are infinitely preferable to coming home to the same sort of impersonal tyrannical glass-steel-and-plastic corporation box that houses him all his working day. No matter how often he is told that it is the Mieses and Breuers and Corbusiers who create "real" architecture, he knows instinctively that what they do is not for him.

6. *The Gothic Revival as an Art of Conviction in Britain*

What the Classical and Colonial Revivals were in American architecture, the Gothic Revival was in British. The difference in form was, as always, dictated by a difference in function—specifically, a difference in the kind and concept of a State whose basic convictions it was to manifest. Just as Classical Revival forms which in the 18th century had been a vehicle of revolutionary vision (among Masons, or in Jacques Louis David's paintings, for example) became the most appropriate forms for expressing American Republican ideals, so what had been the romantic, whimsical, vaguely dissenting "Gothick" of 18th-century England became the chosen vehicle for manifesting the stability of constitutional monarchy as evolved during the same period in Britain (**65a, b, c**).

In 1832 a Reform Bill abolishing "pocket" and "rotten" boroughs deprived the landed British aristocracy of those sure seats which had made 18th-century British parliaments less representative bodies than regular debates among the great families that ruled England. In 1867 a Second Reform Bill doubled the electorate and enfranchised workingmen in towns, and young Robert Cecil foretold a time when the lower classes would dictate all policies by sheer weight of numbers but feel no responsibility for carrying any out, so that "the rich would pay all the taxes and the poor make all the laws." But still, at the end of the 19th century, when he was Prime Minister Lord Salisbury, that time was well in the future, and he headed

> the last government in the Western world to possess all the attributes of aristocracy in working condition. . . . Great Britain was at the zenith of empire . . . and the Cabinet . . . was her superb and resplendent image. Its members represented the greater landowners of the country who had been accustomed to govern for generations. As its superior citizens they felt they owed a duty to the State to guard its interests and manage its affairs. They governed from duty, heritage, and habit—and as they saw it, from right. [Barbara Tuchman, *The Proud Tower*, 1966, p. 6]

336

What had delayed the inevitable was a new national ideal forged in and for Britain in the first decades after Waterloo. Like the new American republic, this ideal State was no longer merely a practical system for preserving orderly conditions of life, but a living thing with a historical personality, promising happiness to all who gave it unconditional allegiance. Unlike the American republic, however, its creation was not conceived as involving a sharp break with the immediate past, but rather a historical process "slowly broadening down from precedent to precedent," as Tennyson put it; not abolishing classes but gradually transforming their function, making monarchs personifications rather than proprietors of the State, considering aristocrats' privileges conditional on services to it.

It followed that where architectural forms revived from the long-lost Roman republic were the natural embodiments of American convictions about their ideal State, the forms that embodied the British ideal would be derived from that Gothic architecture represented in great national monuments like Westminster Abbey and the old Parliament buildings. And appropriately enough, the first great symbol of the new convictions to appear was the new Houses of Parliament in London, built to replace the old ones burnt a year after the first Reform Bill was passed. In them the evolutionary nature of the new ideal was perfectly embodied. Their plans and proportion derived from the 18th-century classical tradition—regular, symmetrical, commensurately ordered; their ornament, from the Middle Ages—designed by that same Augustus W. Pugin (1812–1852) whose life was dedicated to reviving Gothic as the "truly national" style of Britain (65a, b). There followed in due course all over England a wave of church- and cathedral-rebuilding in "truly English" Gothic style appropriate to the role of the Anglican Church as guardian of the ideal State's ethics; and in Scotland, a great Gothic monument arose on Princes Street in Edinburgh to Sir Walter Scott, greatest promoter of the British ideal there. Down to the 1880s, through all vicissitudes of taste, Gothic remained the national British style, its last great monument being George Edmund Street's Law Courts on Fleet Street in London.

But revived Gothic architectural forms were far from the only manifestations of national conviction in 19th-century British art. There was, for instance, a revival of the whole body of Arthurian legend in painting and poetry and music. Just as in the 15th century Malory had presented to an England distracted by the Wars of the Roses an image of the ideal Nation in Camelot and Logres, so now the

337

same image was presented and reinterpreted (perhaps unconsciously) as an antidote to class warfare. And there was yet a third, even more striking—the transformation of political and social cartoons from weapons of persuasion to arts of conviction, complementing the establishment without revolution of a new State, that culminated in *Punch*.

7. *The* Punch *Cartoon as an Art of Conviction*

The transformation began with James Gillray (1757–1815), whose significance in art history I have discussed in *The Restless Art*. In his earlier career Gillray had been a typical 18th-century caricaturist of the Establishment, "feeding like a caterpillar on the green leaf of reputation." He made satires on nobility like *A Peep at Christie's* or *Talley-ho and His Nimeny-Pimeny,* mocking the persons, morals, and tastes of Lord Derby and his inamorata Miss Farren; on royalty, mocking the *Frugal Meal* of Farmer George III and Queen Charlotte, with their salad on the table and their decanter of Aqua Regis, the locked chest full of money beside them, flowers in their empty grate, and an empty cornucopia pictured on their wall. He ridiculed politicians and intellectuals; Berkley and Sturt, rising to Parliament on wealth made in brewing become grotesque sons of Jupiter flying heavenward with beer pots shining starlike in their hands; Samuel Johnson becomes an owl with ass's ears, perched on his *Lives of the Poets,* squinting at the immortal light radiating from volumes by Milton and Pope: *Old Wisdom Blinking at the Stars.* But the French Revolution changed him. Now he takes the side of the Establishment (**64**). Now his mockery is directed at the contrast between visionary promises and Revolutionary performance. Now he extols the virtues of King and Country in print after print. *French Liberty and English Slavery* contrasts a gaunt Jacobin in rags, toeless shoes, and cockaded hat, chewing on a leek and bragging, "Ve svim in de milk unt honey," with an Englishman, so fat he can scarcely get near his roast-beef-laden table, complaining of "this cursed Ministry" with its war taxes "starving us to death." *The Pinnacle of Liberty* is a savage on a flagpole, gloating over murder and riot on the Paris street below (1792). *Her Earlier Profession* suggests how the Emperor of the French first saw his Empress, dancing naked at one of Barras's orgies. George III reappears as the mighty King of Brobdingnag, condescendingly examining a minuscule Napoleon under his spyglass, roaring with laughter at little Gulliver Bonaparte's martial boastings from his toy boat.

Admiral Nelson is no longer the philanderer sailing off from Naples leaving a fat *Dido in Despair* but the hero who serves up platters of fricasseed frigates from Napoleon's navy to a ravenous Johnny Bull. And so on and on. If Dorothy George is right in suggesting (*English Political Caricature*, London, 1960, I, p. 217, fn. 1) that "Gillray would have liked to practise 'high art' as well as burlesque it," the reason is simply that in making his cartoons more an art of conviction supporting an Establishment than persuasion against it, he was serving a kind of function traditional in High Art.

Following Waterloo, Gillray's successors briefly returned to the old sort of satire against the Establishment, but never with anything like the enthusiasm of their counterparts in France. Where the Napoleonic debacle bred disunity in France, Britain's great victory gave rise to a new kind of patriotism. Waterloo, Blenheim, Agincourt, Poitiers, all seemed parts of the same historic national personality, a glorious and divine State that gave stature to the meanest and humblest individual simply by belonging to it. This vision was at its most persuasive in the early years of Victoria's reign. "One has got to read, say, the *Quarterly Review* of the 'thirties," George Orwell wrote, "to know what boasting really is. . . . The one historical fact that is firmly fixed in [Thackeray's] mind is that the English won the battle of Waterloo. . . ."

> Like most Englishmen of his time, he has the curious illusion that the English are larger than other people . . . and therefore he is capable of writing passages like this:
>
> "I say to you that you are better than a Frenchman. I would lay even money that you who are reading this are more than five feet seven in height, and weigh eleven stone; while a Frenchman is five feet four and does not weigh nine. The Frenchman has after his soup a dish of vegetables, where you have one of meat. You are a different and superior animal—a French-beating animal (the history of hundreds of years has shown you to be so)," etc. etc.
>
> ["Charles Dickens," in *Dickens, Dali and Others,* p. 30]

And it is no accident, then, that Thackeray was one of the founders and long-time contributors to *Punch*.

Exactly how and by whom *Punch* was conceived is shrouded in obscure controversy, and matters little; the important thing is that its first issue appeared in July 1841, and its distinctive character very soon thereafter. Though subtitled *The London Chari-*

vari after Charles Philipon's famous satirical magazine in Paris, *Punch* resembled its namesake only briefly in some early rowdiness, and never shared its irreconcilable antagonism to the bourgeoisie at all. Stylistically, the chief early influence on *Punch* cartoons was Cruikshank's illustrations, very apparent in its first cover by Archibald Henning and its second by Phiz (Hablot K. Browne); but thereafter *Punch* rapidly developed a more formal, less spidery style of its own. By 1849, when Richard (Dicky) Doyle designed what was to be *Punch*'s standard cover for the next hundred years, its basic direction was clear (**65c**). This cover was a counterpart to the new Houses of Parliament—classical in balance and symmetry, in detail inspired by the twisted masses of forms and dynamic line patterns of medieval English manuscript illuminations. *Punch*, like the Gothic Revival, was going to be a national institution, a vehible for inculcating a national ideal, and for fifty years it did so, brilliantly; that is the reason why, though competitors came and went—*Tomahawk*, the *Windsor Gazette, Fun, Judy*—none lasted more than a decade or two, while *Punch* seemed to go on forever.

That ideal, like the Church of England's, was a *via media* between extremes; this is the key to understanding *Punch*'s humor, and the distinctive function of *Punch* cartoons. Where arts of persuasion attack dominant ideas and promote new and different ideas, *Punch*'s political and social cartoons do just the opposite. It is always the extremes they attack, and by so doing, they defend and define established convictions. You can see this particularly well in the religious field. *Punch*'s attacks on Roman Catholicism (which led to the resignation in 1850 of Dicky Doyle, a Catholic who was its original chief cartoonist) were consistently motivated by possible threats the Church posed to the existing order of things in England—so its two most famous anti-Catholic satires are John Leech's *Boy Who Ran Away* (1849), on Lord John Russell's failure to make good on promises to resist re-establishment of the Roman Catholic hierarchy in England (**66a**), and John Tenniel's *Putting Out the Light of Modern Civilization* (1867), on Pope Pius II's syllabus of errors condemning habits of mind *Punch* considered props of the English Way of Life. But *Punch* equally ridicules Protestant evangelists like Moody and Sankey, Dissenters like General Booth of the Salvation Army, Scotch Presbyterians and Welsh Methodists, as well as High Church sentiments among Anglicans. Middle-of-the-road Low Church Anglicanism is treated with good-humored guying, no more: "Bishop entertaining

New Curate at dinner: 'I'm afraid you've got a bad egg, Mr. Jones.' 'Oh no, Your Lordship, I assure you. Parts of it are excellent.' " Politically, *Punch* castigated right-wing Conservatives and left-wing Liberals equally; its consistent satire of Disraeli must be explained on grounds that, though Prime Minister of Britain and favorite of Queen Victoria, he was not really a "true Englishman." All foreigners are automatically objects of humor; from its jewel set in a silver sea, *Punch* casts an amused eye at the absurd goings-on across the Channel, and occasionally a reproof at the Americans for boisterous behavior, so unbecoming a people of British descent. Extremes of fashion, extremes of intellect, even extremes of patriotism, all come under the same condemnation.

Punch in fact came to be a school for the nation, inculcating standards appropriate to the national ideal for all classes, beginning at the very top.* For while *Punch* cartoons never attacked the institution of monarchy as such—nothing like the campaign for a republic carried on by such rivals as *Tomahawk* in the 1860s ever appeared in *Punch*—they did attack what appeared deviations from proper British monarchical standards: Prince Albert's pro-German sympathies and interest in business and industry ("Tell me, oh tell me, dearest Albert," implores the young Queen Victoria in an 1845 cartoon during the Railway Bubble scandal, "have *you* any Railway Shares?"); the Prince of Wales's fondness for gambling, high life, and the company of Jewish financiers. They do not attack wealth as such, but wealthy men whose behavior is inappropriate to their class; George Du Maurier's Sir Gorgius Midas is the archetype of this savage but essentially didactic satire, as R. G. G. Price has so ably pointed out in his *History of Punch* (London, 1957, pp. 133–34). Neither do they show the "poor" or "proletariat," but always a "solid" lower and lower-middle class; *Punch* indeed created an image of the British Workingman as the Salt of the Earth—contented, faithful, a bit cynical but always reliable when his country seriously calls, forever ready with drollery or wit in some quaint accent, permanent backdrop to the play of middle- and upper-

---

* And only half-mockingly, for the rest of the world as well. The June 28, 1856, issue, for example, announces complimentary copies of Volume XXVIII being sent to various foreign dignitaries—to Empress Eugénie for her son ("to unfold his rose-bud mind"); to Mr. Pierce (though "for the time being the President defies the influence of all humane letters in the ferocity of his patriotism"); and so on, with "a lively belief that the world will feel the benignant influence of MR. PUNCH's teaching through its civilised and regenerated rules. In the meantime, the Briton will be . . . duly proud . . . that MR. PUNCH as the Schoolmaster, is Abroad. . . ."

class manners and politics going on upstage—that Shaw preserves unalloyed in Alfred the Dustman and his Pygmalion daughter. Their most consistent theme, of course, was the Great Middle Class, truest representatives of the *via media*, whose lives pass as a succession of average happenings in average circumstances; on these typical Britons *Punch* cartoons comment sympathetically, understandingly, even admiringly, as the backbone of the nation.

For each of these areas *Punch* had an outstanding artist. Most famous of them was John Tenniel (1820–1914), who specialized in political life (**66b**). For almost half a century his "Big Cut" represented the considered opinion of *Punch*—for of course, following old tradition preserved in the Low Arts, Tenniel was not expected to invent the subject matter himself, only to give appropriate form to subjects decided upon at a weekly dinner of the *Punch* staff, which as often as not differed from his personal views. Drawing in tight detail with his famous 6H pencil directly on wood blocks, he created one great image after another of the British national ideal: the British Lion, ruling the jungle of lesser beasts without the law—Bengal Tigers, Russian Bears, the Ass of the continental press; the statuesque matron Britannia dominating her slighter sisters Italia, Gallia, Germania; a John Bull whose couth, courage, and comfort made his namesake and ancestor in Gillray's art look like Squire Western; the strong silent Englishman best personified by successive English prime ministers (except for the slightly disreputable Dizzy). Tenniel functioned, in fact, as a kind of Cartoonist Laureate, producing sententious commentary to order for National Occasions (on recovery of the Prince of Wales from pneumonia, on Lincoln's assassination, e.g.), so that nothing could have been more appropriate than his knighthood in 1902. So powerful was his influence that his successors like Linley Sambourne (1844–1910) and Bernard Partridge (1861–1945), F. Carruthers Gould (1844–1925) and William Kerridge Haselden (1872–1953) felt bound to preserve the "Tenniel tradition" for forty years after his death.

George L. P. B. Du Maurier (1834–1896) was *Punch's* great commentator on upper-class life (**67a**), famed for his satires on Sir Gorgius Midas and Art-for-Art's-sake aesthetes, and for his society pictures—slices of life that powerfully influenced modes and manners in the 1870s and -80s not only in Britain but in America, where C. D. Gibson so faithfully imitated them. The British Workingman found his special mirror in the work of Charles Keene (1823–1891). Drunks,

London cabbies, old Cockney ladies, dour Scotchmen and rural sages were his stock in trade. It was inevitable, perhaps, that while Keene was never as highly regarded in the 19th century as Tenniel, Du Maurier, or John Leech, the 20th's pervasive obsession with lower-class life as being somehow more "realistic" would make Keene the most admired; significantly enough, in his own time his reputation on the social-conscious Continent was always higher than at home.

And all *Punch* artists contributed to perfecting an image of the Great British Middle Class. The process began before *Punch,* in Cruikshank's and Phiz's illustrations for Dickens, and especially in the work of Robert Seymour (1798–1836), whose promise as indicated in his *Caricature Gallery,* books of humorous drawings and Hervey's 1835 *Book of Christmas* suggests that but for his early suicide he would have been a leading contributor to *Punch.* As it was, John Leech (1817–1864) provided the first model of middle-class British life for *Punch* cartoons, and to the end of the 19th century *Punch* artists were still essentially following his lead (**67b**). That image survived long enough into the 20th century for George Orwell to give the classic description of it in his study of "Boys' Weeklies":

> There is a cosy fire in the study, and outside the wind is whis-
> tling. The ivy clusters thickly round the old grey stones. The
> King is on his throne and the pound is worth a pound. Over in
> Europe the comic foreigners are jabbering and gesticulating, but
> the grim grey battleships of the British Fleet are steaming up the
> channel and at the outposts of Empire the monocled Englishmen
> are holding the natives at bay. . . . Everything is safe, solid
> and unquestionable. Everything will be the same for ever and
> ever. [*Dickens, Dali and Others,* p. 96]

Punch's cartoons are an art of conviction; all their humor turns on a firm assumption that the English middle class is so sane, solid, and strong that all deviations from that norm are amusing foibles. In them is nothing like that attempt to persuade the world of bourgeois folly, futility and depravity which we shall see in the cartoons being created at this same time by Daumier in France.

All *Punch* artists worked, too, within the framework of a common "*Punch* format" for cartoons. From around 1850 all traces of the droll spidery vignette inheritance from Cruikshank and Phiz rapidly vanish; *Punch* cartoons become much more formally com-posed, more like academic illustrative paintings, and thereafter this format was maintained for fifty years, as consistently as the style of

New Yorker stories or *Time* news reporting in a later era. In part this was because the two leading *Punch* cartoonists at this time had both in fact begun as academic illustrative painters. Leech regularly exhibited pictures at the Royal Academy, while Tenniel had painted illustrative murals for Westminster New Palace and owed his invitation from editor Mark Lemon to join *Punch*'s staff to his illustrations to *Aesop's Fables* having come to eminent contributor Douglas Jerrold's attention at the moment when Dicky Doyle suddenly resigned. In part, too, it was technical; during *Punch*'s early years Gillray's and Cruikshank's practice of making drawings for copperplates was being superseded by drawings made to be carved directly out of hard wood-block ends, which encouraged a tighter, stiffer, more formal style. But the fundamental reason (as always in the Low Arts) was that this form of cartoon better fitted *Punch*'s function. *Punch* was dedicated to supporting and defining the convictions behind a British national idea; for this, monumental and formal images were more appropriate than loose sketches, and the characteristic *Punch* format resulted.

Given the historical background of most European nations, the British national ideal of an evolving historical personality had much broader appeal than the American concept of a brand-new creation, and in consequence imitations of *Punch* proliferated everywhere—among them, *Kladderdasch* in Berlin, *Kikerei* in Vienna, *Figaro* in Zurich, *Strekoza* in Lisbon, even *Nebelspalterin* in St. Petersburg. Italy had two—*Il Fischietto* in Turin (1847) and *Papagallo* in Bologna (1850)—which helped shape the ideal of the Risorgimento away from a republic towards a constitutional monarchy like Britain's. Canada (perhaps inevitably) had *Punch in Canada* by the end of the 1840s and its successor *Grip,* both distinguished by extraordinary provincial feebleness, as J. W. Bengough's *Caricature History of Canadian Politics* (Toronto, 1886) shows.

But the principle of using cartoons to reinforce established convictions was not necessarily tied to constitutional monarchies. Two of the most remarkable examples of it are in fact provided by mid-19th-century cartooning in Germany and the United States.

8. *The Social Cartoon as an Art of Conviction in Germany*

The nineteenth century was a time of momentous political change for Germany, transforming the collection of small kingdoms and duchies and electorates that Napoleon's armies had so easily overrun into that mighty unified power which stood off half the world singlehanded in the war of 1914–18. Yet until *Simplicissimus* in the early 20th century, no German political cartooning ever appeared remotely comparable to the work of Gillray in England, Daumier in France, or Nast in America. Lack of opportunity because of censorship is usually blamed; but in other areas of life Germans managed to circumvent censorship readily enough. Neither was there any lack of talent. In Daniel Chodowiecki (1726–1801) 18th-century German cartooning had as competent a draftsman and print maker as any man of his time. Rodolphe Toepffer (1799–1846), the Genevan professor of aesthetics whose cartoons of manners and aesthetic pretensions were so admired by Goethe, made innovations in technique adapted by Wilhelm Busch (1832–1908) to create the most advanced forms of his time, as we have seen. What was lacking was a genuine burning interest in political activity. Where political reform had been a genuine practical program for achieving Heaven on earth in 18th-century France and America, political fragmentation and Prussian military despotism had made it mere theoretical speculation in Germany; and even when political democracy did briefly become a real possibility during the Revolution of 1848, the intellectuals assembled at Frankfort proposed no more than a timid constitutional monarchy, and were soon overcome for lack of popular support. Thenceforth it was plain that the polity of Germany would be shaped, and the lasting enthusiasm of Germans generally aroused, not by visions of any ideal republican state, but by atavistic loyalties of blood, speech, and war, that the bulk of Germans would be bored by if not actively hostile to the idea of a republic—a fact which Woodrow Wilson ignored to the world's calamity when, imagining that Germans longed for a republic in 1918 as Americans had in 1776, he considered establishment of the Weimar regime to mean certain peace in Europe.

One consequence of immense importance for the history of social cartooning was that class structure in Germany went almost untouched by any of the leveling effected by ideas of political equality operating in France or America. Neither was it leavened by anything like the kind of new blood working into English society throughout the 19th century—Germany had no equivalent to England's sporting Prince of Wales, bringing financiers and actresses into its top circles. If anything, class structure in Germanic lands became even more intricately rigid as time went on.

It follows that what appealed most to Germans was not declarations of independence, bills of rights, or emancipation proclamations, but the apocalyptic vision of a classless state that is Marx's

Communist Manifesto, social-welfare legislation far ahead of other European countries, and ultimately the National Socialist German Workers' Party, combining blood-and-iron nationalism with socialist regimentation into one millennial Reich. It follows too that the German 19th-century cartoon will be primarily concerned with social rather than political themes and, until almost the beginning of the 20th century, will usually be supporting the established order rather than attacking it.

That pattern was set already and characteristically in the work of Franz von Pocci (1807–1876). As master of ceremonies to the court of Ludwig I of Bavaria, Pocci plays the pan-German nationalist, by turns painter, poet, and music maker; his interest in the "Germanic" qualities of drawings and woodcuts of the 15th and 16th centuries prefigured—as usual in the Low Arts—that self-conscious Germanism in the Fine Art of Expressionists and William Worringer three or four decades later. In combining old printed tickets and the like with water colors he anticipated Schwitters by over half a century; his *Self-Portrait in a Feverish Sleep Surrounded by Visions of His Friends* comparably anticipates Ensor. But his cartoons are something else again (**68a**). Here Pocci's concern is almost entirely with social comment made in a style by turns resembling Gillray's or Rowlandson's around 1815, and about an aristocracy-oriented world similar to theirs then. So long vanished is this kind of world even in England that much of the point of Pocci's sort of humor remains obscure to English-speaking peoples—indeed, the characteristic preoccupation of German cartoonists with subject matter incomprehensible to Anglo-Saxons undoubtedly helped foster a common English and American notion that Germans are a humorless people. Furthermore, Pocci is far from critical of his society's rigidity; his cartooning is a record of aristocratic foibles and follies, not agitation for fundamental change—and this too is characteristic of most German 19th-century cartoons. By poking fun at this rigid class structure, they in fact help humanize and so stabilize it.

Directly descended from Pocci is the famous group associated with *Fliegende Blätter* in Munich during the 1860s and -70s: Wilhelm Busch, Adolf Oberländer (1845–1923), Edmund Harburger (1846–1906), and Fritz Steub (1844–1903) among others. As much illustrators as cartoonists, their principal concern was with "Biedermeier culture"—comfortable middle-class bourgeois life; and again, they do not attack it so much as reflect its attitudes and values. Such droll spoofs of the clergy as Busch's *History of St. Anthony* could hardly be construed by anybody as tirades against some "opiate of the people," for example; they might encourage some reform, perhaps, but that is a very different thing from the Marxian attitude of the cartoons of Félicien Rops (1833–1898) on the same theme a generation later, for example. Similarly, there is none of *Charivari's* bitter bite in Busch's sallies at the bourgeoisie (**41c, 42a**). Nothing implies that Max and Moritz would be reformed characters if only the economic inequities that produce class distinctions could be abolished; nothing suggests that Herr Brandtmeier's New Year's Eve drinking is some compulsive compensation for the pressures of capitalist competition; nothing indicates that Busch longs for the millennial day when all the simpletons and shrews and charlatans that caper across his pages will be purged from society and all eccentricities blissfully leveled out for a classless eternity. Quite the opposite; *gemütlichkeit* is prevailing spirit of *Fliegende Blätter*, a deep satisfaction with the existing state of affairs, national and domestic. Hereditary aristocrats manage the State, welfare laws look after the people, *Gott* is *mit uns* all. Such cartoons are in fact quite as much an art working to defend the basic convictions on which the German autocratic state depended as were *Punch's* in defense of the British establishment.

Even more striking was the use of cartoons to defend the new state created by the American Revolution when it was threatened in its Civil War.

9. *The Nast Tradition of Political Cartooning in Defense of American Convictions*

"Fourscore and seven years ago," Abraham Lincoln said in 1863, "our fathers brought forth on this continent a new nation, conceived in liberty, and dedicated to the proposition that all men are created equal. Now we are engaged in a great civil war. . . ." It had all happened with such traumatic suddenness. For decades the American Experiment had seemed to be going so well. America had been the visible proof that Jefferson and the 18th-century visionaries were right; free men from feudal institutions, give them political equality, and see how their natural goodness will be manifest, how instinctively they cooperate, how unselfishly they all work together for the common good. And now all at once free, equal and naturally good men were fighting the bloodiest war in history.

Lincoln had to win that war. If North America were not to become another Europe, with bloody wars breaking out between its several independent States every twenty years or so, the Union had to be reimposed by force. This was a policy of farseeing statesmanship. But in a country ruled by majority votes, farseeing statesmanship cannot be cited in support of policies, for the majority can never comprehend it. Elections are won by candidates with the most enticing visions. The war had therefore to be made into a Cause. Lincoln had somehow to show that while it was a grand and glorious thing to rebel against legally constituted authority in 1776, rebellion against legally constituted authority in 1861 was wicked and criminal. He did so by envisaging the Union much as the Church was envisaged at the councils of Chalcedon and Nicaea, as a sacred creation of generations past—of Patrick Henry and Nathan Hale and George Washington, of Jackson and Webster, Calhoun and Clay—which present generations might add to but never subtract from. In this light Southern secession was not a political act but an attempt at suicide; the Southern seceders were like cancerous cells which had turned in against the living body of the nation history had created, to be cut out in self-preservation. He made the Union, in other words, into an ideal like the British ideal, established by and in history, and this vision is what he called on the North to defend.

To defend it, Lincoln needed more than armies. He needed ideological weapons, immediate in their impact, carrying lasting conviction. In the Revolution American print makers had forged such a weapon, but it was intended for attack on existing institutions, for persuasion to new ideas, useless now. So was the American cartooning that had developed later, such as the humorous weekly called *Yankee Notions*, founded in 1852 on the model of *Punch*. Its chief invention was Brother Jonathan, descended from a character invented by playwright Royall Tyler in 1787, a lank, tuft-bearded individual characteristically propped against a wall, whittling pieces of wood, who clearly represented a counterpart to the kind of characters Mark Twain described lounging about Mississippi River towns, to Bingham's jolly flatboatmen and Mount's fiddlers in the barn—a variant symbol of the American Dream of idyllic idleness, and so the very dream and image that had just been shattered. What Lincoln needed were cartoons that would proclaim American visionary convictions in such a way that men would be moved to defend and preserve them; and when an illustrator working for *Harper's Weekly* began to create such in the

Union cause, Lincoln proclaimed him "our best recruiting sergeant." His name was Thomas Nast (1840–1902).

Nast had come to New York from Germany when he was six. His first love was historical painting, which he studied briefly, but through practical necessity he soon turned to illustration. In 1855, when only fifteen, he was hired by *Leslie's*, one of the new weekly magazines then appearing, and made drawings to illustrate Frank Leslie's various crusades against impure milk, police corruption in Manhattan, and the like. But his early bent was never lost, and when he joined *Harper's* in 1858 he moved farther and farther away from humorous vignettes towards the sort of formally composed illustrative cartoons characteristic of *Punch*. In January 1861 Nast returned from a trip to England (recording the famous Heenan-Sayers prizefight and afterwards something of Garibaldi's campaign in Italy), and once the war broke out, his double-spread political drawings became one of the best-known features in *Harper's*. Their most direct model was the magisterial style of Tenniel's "Big Cuts" for state occasions; their most direct parallels were with the tone of the Gettysburg Address, the Second Inaugural Address, and "The Battle Hymn of the Republic." For they were not persuasions to one view as opposed to another, but affirmations that only one side existed—the high and holy Union, formed by Providence for the redemption of man. In Nast's *Christmas Picture 1862–63*, for instance, the mother and children at prayer on one side and the soldier father in his wintry bivouac on the other both make plain analogy to that earlier Christmas of 1777, after the Revolutionary Cause's military fortunes had been equally low, and Washington knelt to pray in the snows of Valley Forge.

This is a new kind of cartoon in America, impressively effective; by the War's end, Nast is a household name throughout the nation. But in a Union restored by force, the exalted ideal it embodied cannot long be maintained. For a brief while after the War it survives—you can still see something of it in Winslow Homer's great painting of 1866, *Prisoners from the Front* (New York, Metropolitan), in the contrast between Union officers and men with the pale unbending severity of Byzantine angels, or archaic Greek gods, and rebels as unkempt and arrogant as those giants who defy the order of the universe on the great frieze of Pergamum. Thereafter, as the Holy Cause dissolves in a caldron of factions struggling for powers and perquisites, High Artists like Homer withdraw steadily into alienation. Not Nast. He plunges into the fray, using the new kind of cartoon he has forged into a weapon which, while it is still new and unexpected, has devastating power. The technique is simple: impart the aura of a Sacred Cause to all policies approved by Nast and *Harper's;* represent all opposed as rebels and heretics against light and truth.

Nast first pillories Andrew Johnson as a mad Nero martyring Radical Republican saints; a capering tailor; a drunken lord. But Johnson's sins are naught beside Horatio Seymour's; for having the audacity to run for President in 1868 against Ulysses S. Grant, savior of the Union, America's second Washington, Nast pillories Seymour as a poltroon, a traitor, a murderous Lady Macbeth. In 1870–71 Nast turns his weapon on smaller game, closer to home—"Boss" Tweed and his Tammany Hall Ring, who, besides being grafters and machine politicians, enjoy the un-American support of the Catholic church; they appear variously as Falstaff's army of band-legged villains; as incestuous Gertrude and depraved Claudius in the corrupt court of Elsinore; as vultures feasting on the virgin corpse of civic virtue; as freaks distorted in trick mirrors; as bloated monsters (**69a**). By 1872 the Ring is smashed, and a new Presidential election looms. Grant's first four years have been far from outstanding, but for the Republican nominating convention Nast paints a great platform backdrop showing the White House flanked by two pedestals, one empty, the other bearing a figure of Grant with Columbia pointing at it and challenging "Match Him!" And in the campaign that follows, Nast's attacks on Horace Greeley are so savage, so vicious, so merciless, so fanatical that they are widely credited with driving Greeley to mental collapse and death soon afterwards.

Nast's power was at its peak in the early 1870s. These were the years he created the symbols he is best remembered by: the Democratic donkey (1870) and the Republican elephant (1874)—following Tenniel's animal-symbol precedent, of course; the millionaire in evening dress and diamond stickpin (Boss Tweed, 1870–71) that became the bloated capitalist in Art Young's cartoons fifty years later, and is in Soviet cartooning still; and also (in compensation) the potbellied rosy-cheeked red-suited high-booted Santa Claus of modern Christmases (c. 1875). But thereafter his decline in influence was steady. From being the mainstay of *Harper's* he gradually became a liability; in 1888 he finally left it, and when in 1892 his own *Nast's Weekly* failed, he dropped completely from public view.

The reason for this *détente,* according to Nast's biographer Albert Bigelow Paine, was that for him "the times were out of joint.

The public no longer demanded pictorial crusades, but only a pageant of clever burlesque with light hits and mock warfare." True, but for that Nast himself was partly responsible. In each successive campaign he applied the high and holy fervor of a sacred cause to an increasingly partisan end, and the climax came in his attitude to the scandals of Grant's second administration. In attacking the Tweed Ring, Nast had claimed to be motivated solely by moral outrage at graft and corruption, not at all by Tweed's happening to be a powerful figure in the Democratic Party. But when far worse came to light in the Republican camp, Nast's reaction was entirely different—he pilloried those who had exposed it as jackals, foxes, and weasels whose presumptuousness in attacking the Old Lion should be scorned by all right-thinking supporters of the republic (*The Crowning Insult*). Significantly, it was after this episode that Nast's sharp decline in influence began, and nothing he did thereafter improved his case. More and more, his cartoons gave the impression of an evangelist whipping up godly fervor in order to sell chewing gum and soap outside the tent, and ultimately he gave them up and went back to easel painting. Faithful to the end, his last major work was a huge *Lee's Surrender*, painted in 1895 for the Grant shrine at Galena, Illinois.

However, Nast's so debasing the currency of the old faith in a sacred nation above partisanship only sped a process inevitable anyway. Once politics ceased to be a kind of sacred work leading to salvation and became simply the sort of callous conniving it had been in the courts of Louis XIV or Machiavelli's Italy, public enthusiasm for political reform was bound to wane; what was exciting about putting in a new batch of crooks to replace the old? For this reason, and under influences from Europe, crusades for social reform steadily superseded more narrowly political agitation from the 1880s on, as Eric Goldman so convincingly demonstrates in his history of American liberalism, *Rendezvous with Destiny* (1952). The net result was a scarcity of purely political cartoons—their stronghold being in those parts of the country most isolated from European influences, the Midwest and rural towns generally—and that lack of seriousness which Paine deplored—an "if-politics-is-a-game-then-let's-have-some-fun-at-it" attitude. Of this, one famous example was Jay N. "Ding" Darling (1876–1962); faithful supporter of the Republican cause for forty years, best-known perhaps for his long advocacy of Herbert Hoover for president in the 1920s and his courageous support of him against the tides of the early 1930s (recorded in *As Ding Saw Hoover*, 1954). Perhaps the best, however, was John T. McCutcheon (1870–1949), long-time staff cartoonist for the Chicago *Tribune.*

Consider, for example, the contrast between Nast's campaign against the Tweed Ring in New York and McCutcheon's against the machine of "Bathhouse John" Coughlin in Chicago, thirty years later (**69b**). Here is McCutcheon's own account of it, in *Drawn from Memory* (1950, pp. 202–3):

> As the campaign approached its end, the reform elements made a mighty effort and . . . on election morning my cartoon [Chicago *Record-Herald,* March 27, 1902] showed an egg, which conformed fairly well to the architecture of The Bathhouse, being pushed from the top of a high building. The cartoon definitely indicated that The Bathhouse was likely to sustain a profound jar in the future. When the returns were in, he was something over three thousand to the good. It was a mighty victory and necessitated some quick side-stepping on the part of the cartoonist. Next day [actually April 2] I showed The Bathhouse exultantly landing in a net held by his friends, the gang down on the sidewalk.

In technique, McCutcheon was clearly following Nast: the same kind of satirical caricature, the same kind of line drawing, the same ultimate source for both—Humpty Dumpty was a favorite motif of Tenniel's, appearing both in *Punch* cartoons (e.g., the Shah of Turkey, July 20, 1875) and *Through the Looking Glass.* But there is nothing of Nast's fire or fervor. You could never imagine Nast taking defeat in the good-humored spirit of McCutcheon's second cartoon; for him, opponents were never cheerful rogues like these, but monsters of villainy to the end.

Not that McCutcheon was a worse political cartoonist for that. In many ways he was better; he understood, as Nast, with his lingering aspirations toward easel-painted illustration, never fully did, precisely what kind of medium he was using. The definition from McCutcheon's autobiography (p. 203) could hardly be bettered:

> The cartoon differs from any other picture in that the idea alone is the essential requirement, whether it is meant to inform, reform, or solely to amuse. This idea should be brought out with directness and simplicity, in such a way that people will know it is a cartoon and not a work of art. It has little to do with beauty or grace; it has much to do with strength and uniqueness. It is a peculiar form of art for a peculiar purpose, and presupposes the ability to say a thing trenchantly, humorously, or caustically, in terms of line.

The difference between Nast and McCutcheon was not that one was a better artist than another, but that their art reflected fundamentally different concepts of the nature, ultimate importance, and dignity of the political process, its practitioners more commonly Grants than gods; graft and corruption its more or less normal perquisites of success.

And with the change, a quite different kind of cartoon was beginning to appear—attacking the social order Nast and his descendants defended, designed to persuade beholders to radically different points of view. It not only represented another function; it belonged in a different historical phase altogether—to the second, economic phase of the modern world religion.

IV

ECONOMIC EGALITARIANISM
AS FAITH AND FACT

1. *The 19th-Century Attack on "Bourgeois Democracy" and "Victorianism"*

FOR DEVOUT believers in salvation through economic equality, the kind of state manifested and defended in the cartoons of *Punch* and Nast, in Colonial and Classical and Gothic Revival architecture, was "bourgeois democracy"—*the* enemy, an opiate deceiving people into feeling that all was well, when in fact nothing like total equality had yet been achieved. Corollary to it was what could best be called "Victorianism"—the 19th-century spirit of optimism that things were getting better all the time; how could contented people be goaded into revolution? So these became the two prime targets. For attacking Victorianism, the chief weapon was a theoretical attack on "escapist romanticism." By the 1850s a concentrated theoretical attack on Victorianism was underway—i.e., on the kind of visual or literary arts which served to create images of and for bourgeois democracy. To its escapist romanticism, champions of the new religion now opposed their concept of art dedicated to Reality, beginning with Courbet and the pre-Raphaelites (cf. *The Restless Art*).

Against the bourgeois state, however, the chief weapon was the social cartoon, seen at its most typical in Philipon's *Charivari* and the work of Honoré Daumier in France, where the established State was shakiest and attacks on it most violent.

2. *Cartooning in France from* Charivari *to the Commune*

Understand this shifting emphasis of the millenniary vision from political liberty to social equality, and you understand the otherwise puzzling history of French politics in the half century after Waterloo. That Bourbon Louis XVIII, restored in 1814, should be unpopular is understandable enough—he reigns not by the grace of God but by force of foreign arms; and the brother who succeeds him in 1824 as Charles X has no more appeal, for the same reason. But the revolution of 1830 that puts "bourgeois King" Louis Philippe on the throne is a national uprising; why does the intellectuals' discontent continue? Do they want a republic? Apparently not, for when the 1848 Revolution produces one, it lasts only for one election, whereupon France is ruled by an Emperor, Louis Napoleon. Not until the Paris Commune of 1871, when the Communist party seizes power following the Empire's collapse, is the real source of discontent made plain—the agitators have all along been concerned, not with political equality as an end in itself, but as the means to a further revolution dedicated to economic equality.

Understand this history, and you understand the relationship of political to social cartooning in France over the same period. At first it is somewhat confused, and the confusion is compounded by a continuance of David's use of painting for political persuasion: in the 1820s Antoine Jean Baron Gros (1771–1835) is still following David's lead in both style and content, promoting the Napoleonic legend of national heroism, while his pupil Nicolas Charlet (1792–1845) carries the same theme into popular lithographs. Delacroix's *Massacre on Chios* of 1827 and *Liberty Leading the People* of 1830 still represent the old call to destroy feudal barbarism so that political liberty may reign. At the same time the new theme is clearly enunciated by Gericault, whose *Raft of the Medusa* allegorizes the French no longer as noble Romans but as castaways from a ship wrecked by treacherous corruption, and whose lithographs "driving towards the democratization of art" are so praised by Frederick Antal's *Kunstsoziologie*. They point the way; by 1830 the real goal of French reformers is unmistakable in art—attacking, not the aristocracy (knowing 19th-century France only through its Low Arts, it would come as something of a surprise to learn that a French aristocracy had continued to exist), but the class system based on unequal distribution of wealth that they call "bourgeois democracy." And so their chosen medium, the mass-produced social cartoon, is dedicated to one central theme: criticism, satire, and ridicule of the bourgeoisie.

Archetype of his generation of reformers is Charles Philipon (1800–1862), that "little, bilious, bristling, ingenious, insistent man," as Henry James called him in his essay on *Daumier, Caricaturist* (repr. London, 1954), "the breath of whose nostrils was opposition"—opposition to the bourgeoisie and all they stand for. Philipon comes to Paris from Lyon to study painting with Baron Gros, but soon abandons both the medium and the message of this mentor, switching from painting to caricature, and from Gros's old nationalism to socialist agitation for the classless society. As a caricaturist he becomes famous chiefly for his symbol of bourgeois mentality, a pear-shaped head applied particularly to Louis Philippe and soon extended to impute flabby stupidity to the bourgeois class in general (**70b**). Philipon may not actually have invented it—Werner Hoffmann in *Die Karikatur* published an earlier drawing of this symbol by Gros's contemporary Jean Baptiste Isabey (1767–1855) and suggests that the idea was generally "in the air"—but he was the one who popularized it and made it stick. But in any event Philipon's real place in art history is not as practitioner but as patron of French cartooning. In 1830 his Maison Aubert put out a magazine called *Le Caricature,* capitalizing on the new lithographic printing process; it was suppressed in 1835, but *Le Charivari,* which he began publishing in 1832, survived through all political vicissitudes to become the great forum for political and social cartooning in France during the next fifty years. The collection of over 1400 works from his publications that Philipon brought out in 1848 under the title *Le Musée Philipon* included every major figure in the field, and it is through them that Philipon's influence on French history and art is incalculable.

At first cartooning was still quasi-political: Alexandre Decamps (1803–1860) is the great example of it in the 1820s (**70a**). Through his painting teacher, Abel de Pujol, Decamps inherited David's insistence on politically conscious art and his sharp linear forms; they are both evident in his best known cartoon, the *Year of Grace 1830, Fifth of the Glorious Reign*, lampooning Charles X as the quintessential decadent aristocrat, a senile figure muffled in blankets aiming his popgun at a toy rabbit which his valet tows around on a string. But early in the 1830s political agitation as such tapered off; both Decamps and his contemporary Tony Johannot (1803–1852) abandoned it to follow careers as romantic painters—Decamps to acquire a great reputation as a painter of exotic Arab life in the Delacroix manner—and the bulk of cartooning was concerned henceforth with social themes. This was only partly due to government censorship; in the main it was because social equality was becoming the agitators' primary concern. If they could undermine the class structure of France, political reform would follow as a matter of course—and a galaxy of skillful cartoonists bent every effort to this end, in a great variety of ways.

Sulpice Guillaume Chevalier, called Paul Gavarni (1804–1866), was the great master of the killing inference, of the image that compels its conclusions (**71b**). There was nothing overtly seditious about Gavarni's subtle tableaux presenting the foibles of fashionable life; on the surface they are counterparts to Eugène Scribe's facile domestic comedies of manners that filled the Parisian stage in these same years. But the cumulative effect of his work was corrosive. Year after year he played variants of one theme: the contemptible folly and vanity of upper-middle-class bourgeois life (as if it were more contemptible and foolish than other classes). A typical cartoon shows two demimondaines lolling half-dressed on a sofa (anticipating, as Low Art so often does, the Fine Art of Toulouse-Lautrec's brothel pictures decades later), regaling each other with tales of easy conquest. "What fools men are!" they say, referring to their most recent victims—but by inference it is at the whole bourgeoisie that their contempt is aimed and ours invited. There was a reason why the Goncourt brothers should have chosen to write a biography of Gavarni, of all people, in 1873; with the spinsterish shrewdness of their insight into contemporary life, they knew that men like him, more than many far more famous, molded the mind of their era.

Jean Ignace Isidore Gérard, called Grandville (1803–1847), perfected a different and equally deadly mode of attack. His specialty was the absurd image, evolved out of the ancient tradition of grotesque caricature. Instead of the naïve sort of images you find in Reformation caricature, say, with asses' heads and dragons' feet stuck on human bodies, Grandville managed to represent human figures in such a way that they resembled plants or animals or insects, or conversely gave plants and animals and insects the aspects of men. His most effective use of this weapon is seen in the satirical series *Metamorphoses du Jour*, where mockery of bourgeois habits and outlook is all the more poisonous because so well diluted in subtle wit. Later Grandville also turned his talents to book illustration, and applied the absurd image to fables and fairy tales with great effect. That Baudelaire should have praised Grandville's imaginative invention, and the Surrealists acknowledged him as one source of their imagery, was only just—not, we need hardly repeat, because he was unique among Low Artists in providing later Fine Artists with forms, but because of the hard nihilistic strain beneath his light surface pleasantries, and because he similarly used irrationality as a weapon to undermine social stability in the ultimate interests of revolutionary change.

Still another weapon was the stock figure of the bourgeois fool, a sort of straw man to hurl abuse at without fear of reprisal. The chief fame of Henri Monnier (1805–1877) rests on one of these characters, recurring in cartoons and burlesque comedies—"Joseph Prudhomme," a more socially conscious and satirically sophisticated version of Thomas Rowlandson's fatuous Doctor Syntax (**71a**). Another bourgeois goat of the period was "Mayeux," created by Charles Joseph Traviès (1804–1859). Mayeux was more advanced than Joseph Prudhomme or Doctor Syntax both in the technique of caricature and in focused concentration of attack—epitomizing the type of unprincipled "operator" produced by bourgeois politics—and was less a figure of fun than a didactic symbol of corruption aimed at undermining the existing order, a curious transmutation of David's *Horatii*.

3. *Honoré Daumier, Radical Traditionalist*

All these modes of attack were employed in turn, all the achievements of his contemporaries subsumed, in the work of Honoré Daumier (1808–1879), most prolific cartoonist of his age. His first drawing appeared in 1822, and by 1830 he was already publishing lithographs in *Silhouette*. Daumier's *Gargantua* (1831) carried Philipon's pear-head symbol of bourgeois fatuity to new lengths; in fact, this representation of Louis Philippe as a bloated Rabelaisian monster exploiting inequalities of wealth cost Daumier six months in Sainte-Pélagie prison. His picture of bourgeois government as a gross belly in

Le Ventre Legislatif (1833) rivaled Grandville's *Metamorphoses* for inventive imagery of the absurd. The wit of a cartoon like *Le Pacquebot Napoléon*—preposterous little mustachioed Louis Napoleon standing in the old Emperor's tricorn hat, with a decrepit imperial eagle drawing him through a puddle—is as biting as anything by Decamps, and more scathing than contemporary cartoons in *Punch* like Tenniel's meticulous *Eagle in Love*. Joseph Prudhomme and Mayeux had even more versatile counterparts in Daumier's "Ratapoil" and especially "Robert Macaire," who in two series of over a hundred plates each (*Caricaturana* 1836–38, *Robert Macaire* 1840–41) portrayed every sort of corrupt individual produced by the bourgeois economic system: quack doctor, pandering journalist, crooked stock promoter, fake evangelist, degenerate nobleman, all of them full of pompous sentiments extolling the bourgeois Establishment. Daumier's series of *Bons Bourgeois, Moeurs Conjugales, Papas, Philanthropes du Jour, Beaux Jours de la Vie,* and occasional plates on law courts, army, and slums have all the incisive ridicule of Gavarni's satires on bourgeois life, with even wider range. And if Daumier's ordinary work subsumed all his contemporaries', his best demonstrably surpassed theirs, both in exploitation of the textural richness and spontaneity of drawing lithographic techniques had made possible, and in universality of theme (**70c**). The depth and power of imagery in a cartoon like *Rue Tranonain* (1834) made Philipon's or Decamps's attacks on the class system seem trivial witticisms, while beside the ghoulish mockery of a single corpse sprawled amid gaunt ruins that is Daumier's cartoon comment on Louis Napoleon's famous promise *L'Empire, c'est la Paix* (1871), the inventiveness of Grandville or Monnier seems mere light comedy. For Daumier's condemnation of unequally shared suffering springs from love of the poor rather than hatred of the rich—and even when perverted to the ends of a futile faith in Heaven on earth, the old virtue of Christian charity keeps its power to move men's hearts as mean egalitarian envy never can.

From the middle to the end of his life Daumier turned more and more to painting, in preference to cartoons. Given his basic bent of mind, it was inevitable what his theme would be—idealizations of working-class virtues and stolid endurance, executed in monumental generalized forms to contrast with the sketchy ephemeral character of his cartoons on bourgeois folly and fatuity. By general consent, his masterpiece is *Third Class Carriage* (*The Restless Art*, p. 127)—a Holy Family of the new dispensation, a proletarian St. Anne and John the Baptist, a working-class Madonna holding in her arms the new generation whose promised destiny it is to inherit earth. By general consent, the 20th century has come to consider Daumier an Important Figure in French Art. Yet in his own time Daumier was not even the best-known of French cartoonists, let alone a recognized Painter; nor is he classed among the Patriarchs of the modern movement today. In retrospect, it is not hard to see why. First, of course, because while Daumier's paintings were great images of conviction (hence the change of medium, painting being more appropriate to conviction, as prints are for persuasion), they represent Daumier's personal convictions rather than anything shared by society at large in his time. But the same could also be said of Courbet's idealizations of the proletariat —*The Stonebreakers,* for example. The real reason is that the measure of Daumier's greatness was only really demonstrable in terms of the old tradition of art in which forms could be objectively evaluated by fitness for function.

You could say without equivocation that Daumier did superlatively what his best contemporaries only did well; that he was in fact an Old Master in the traditional sense. But in his lifetime the traditional concept of what art is, and the traditional standards for measuring greatness, were being abandoned. In an age when the Artist was increasingly a man out to get fame for himself by personality, gimmicks, and manifestos of theory—Courbet being the prime example—Daumier carried on in the traditional role of giving fame (or infamy, as the case might be) by his work, pseudonymously signing his early cartoons "Rogelin," living in almost total obscurity, selling his cartoons for a few francs apiece, like the craftsmen of the Middle Ages. In an age when artists were proclaiming themselves Seers and Prophets of Reality, Daumier conceived his job as inventing graphic forms for ideas supplied by others. Even Henry James, in his famous essay attempting to prove that Daumier was a great Fine Artist (*Daumier, Caricaturist,* reprinted London, 1954), had to qualify his claim that "Daumier became more and more the political spirit of *Charivari*" with "or at least the political pencil, for M. Philipon . . . is to be credited with a suggestive share in any enterprise in which he had a hand. . . ." While Ynez Ghirardelli in *Daumier: Interpreter of History* (San Francisco, 1940) wrote flatly, "the question was never whether Daumier invented all his captions, but whether he invented any of them; and the best one can say is he may have invented some of the shorter ones." (His most popular character, Robert Macaire, was created by actor-playwright Frédérick Lemaître.)

359

Most heinous of all, in an age when the whole idea of Art was being surrounded by an aura of mystic pretension, Daumier persisted in considering what he did as simply something useful to society. Trained by apprenticeship and observation of past and present art around him rather than in a Fine Art school, he had inherited the attitudes of his mentor Marie Alexandre Lenoir (1762–1839). A minor painter, Lenoir is remembered as the courageous rescuer of historic works of art endangered by revolutionary mobs, who risked personal disaster to preserve them in the Convent of the Petits-Augustins until the fanatical attempt to destroy France's historic past was over, and then presented them to the nation not as a collection of dead Art but as living history—the Musée des Monuments Français. This same sense for living art led Daumier to work in the new medium of lithography—with Nicolas Charlet (1792–1845) and Charles Ramelet (1805–1851), he was one of its pioneers in France—and what was worse for his career, it left him with a lifelong skepticism for all the new pretensions Fine Art was taking on that he expressed in some of his wittiest work: *Classists versus Realists*—gaunt and gawky Greek warrior and stocky saboted peasant battling with maulsticks, brushes and palette-shields over some issue important to nobody but themselves; *Blue-Stockings* and *Bohemians of Paris,* displaying all the fatuous pretensions Fine Artists were claiming; *Ancient History,* deriding the habit of mind that took classical art out of its historical setting and made Precious Objects for Exhibition out of it; *Landscape Painters at Work,* mocking painters who lie about on the grass waiting for proper conditions to conduct their studies of open-air light; *The Critics,* with their battery of adjectives like "creative," "moving," "magnificent," "marvelous," all utterly meaningless when divorced from any functional reference. Daumier was not only acute, he was prophetic. As early as 1839 his *Saltimbanques* shows a full appreciation of the circus that was going on: here, as mountebanks in a sideshow, are such specimens of the New Artists as Jules Gabriel Janin, feeble novelist and fearsome critic of the *Journal des Débats;* sculptor David d'Angers, celebrated for the gimmick of pedimental figures in modern dress on the Pantheon in Paris; Paul Delaroche, Victor Hugo, and Hector Berlioz, types of publicity-hungry "professional romantics" in painting, literature, music.

Not that all this made Daumier himself any less of a great artist. To say that Daumier did not invent his own subjects no more denies the greatness of his pictorial forms than Michelangelo's or

Raphael's greatness is denied by the discovery that their iconographical programs for the Sistine ceiling and the Stanza della Segnatura were worked out by a Franciscan theologian named Marco Vigerio; to say that Daumier did not "take Art seriously" in the Fine Art sense is no more than could have been said of them. But it did make recognition almost impossible for him. To the mighty Establishment that Fine Art had become by the 1840s and -50s in France, Daumier was a standing rebuke; nor could he be any more fundamentally acceptable to the immensely more powerful and world-wide Fine Art Establishment of our own time. True, the orthodoxy supported by that Establishment has now changed. Now the ideal it imposes on its faithful is a compound of subjective Reality, nonobjective form, and anarchist principles, instead of the historical anecdote and Renaissance classical style of Daumier's day. But it is if anything even more antagonistic to any notion of recognizing an artist whose forms and media are dictated by social needs and function. It follows the tradition of Courbet, who so contemptuously ignored the very idea of anyone or anything dictating to *him,* the Seer, the Artist, what he should do or be. That anyone professing to be an Artist should sit in a garret scrawling out lithographs for the commercial press at a penny apiece—what a revolting suggestion!—it would be as bad as imagining that some comic-strip doodler who draws for a syndicate could be an Artist!

So Daumier lived his life in obscurity, last of the Old Masters in France. With him the old tradition in French painting came to an end. And more; with him France's great era of social cartooning came to an end also. For if he lived long enough to see the final turning away from all objectivity and everything he cared about in painting with the advent of Post-Impressionism, he also lived long enough to see the first great disillusionment with the faith he had worked for so long—to see the collapse of bourgeois order followed not by any Heaven on earth but the bloody anarchy of the Paris Commune. Those with eyes to see, saw; and thenceforth the messianic fervor of French cartooning was gone. There were plenty of able cartoonists in later 19th-century France—André Gill (1840–1885) with his gnomelike capering figures (**71c**); Jean Louis Forain (1852–1931) following Gavarni's lead in content and social Impressionism in style; Emmanuel Poiré, called Caran d'Ache (1858–1909), a Gallic version of Wilhelm Busch; but all were infected with Fine Art formalism, more concerned with style than functional effectiveness. There was also a rash of late 19th-century humorous periodicals—*Gil Blas, Le Rire,*

L'Assiette au Beurre, La Vie Parisienne; but increasingly their surpass-
ing concern was with petty political squabblings among splinter
parties and maneuverings of pressure groups—even the Dreyfus Affair
was pursued less primarily from human concern for Dreyfus's fate or
abstract justice than for factional advantage in power struggles among
parties in the Third Republic, one among which was now a Socialist
Party abandoning its goal of transforming society in practice (though
not yet in theory) to become merely one more contender for privilege
within the state. Real fervor remained only where practical results
from theories of social equality had not yet been experienced, where
Heaven could be promised without any embarrassing debacles from
the real world to explain away: in Germany, England and America
during the twenty years before 1914.

4. *The Social Cartoon as an Art of Protest and Marxist Persuasion in Germany, 1890–1933*

No social legislation, no degree of national pride and satisfaction can suppress indefinitely the vision of classless paradise sweeping the 19th-century Western world, and toward the end of the
century a new spirit is manifest in German cartoons. Its leading vehicle
is another Munich humorous journal, *Simplicissimus,* founded by
Albert Langen (1869–1909) in 1896. Around *Simplicissimus* revolved a
galaxy of famous artists, whose distinctive variants of a common style
based on strong patterns and sinuous line influenced German Fine Art
for decades, anticipating Klee and Beckmann, Expressionist before
Munch or Barlach, Surrealist before Ensor or Dali: Thomas Theodor
Heine (1867–1948), cofounder of the magazine; Eduard Thöny
(1866–1950); Bruno Paul (1874–1960); Rudolf Wilke (1873–1909);
Olaf Gulbransson (1873–1958); Karl Arnold (b. 1883). Equally distinctive was the character of *Simplicissimus*'s satire (**68b**). Because the
magazine was suspended in 1898 and its editors forced into temporary
Swiss exile after a special number devoted to Kaiser Wilhelm II's visit
to the Holy Land, some writers (e.g., Eugen Roth, *Simplicissimus,*
Hannover, 1954) talk as if it were an organ of political commentary
and persuasion like *Punch* or *Harper's* or *Charivari.* But in fact true
political cartoons in *Simplicissimus* were rare, invariably mild, and
mostly late, like the famous 1932 anti-Nazi cartoon of an elderly
German retorting to Nazi youths bawling their Wake-Up-Germany
slogan under his window: "Wake up? I haven't been able to sleep

since 1914." In no respect was *Simplicissimus* more typically German than in the basically, overwhelmingly, and consistently social rather than political concern of its cartoons. Even the famous censorship of 1898 was provoked not by anything like a campaign in favor of a republic or a constitutional monarchy; it was simply a case of *lèse-majesté*, of cats impertinently looking at kings. *Simplicissimus*'s cartoons are typically German too in turning on subtleties of class privilege and distinction only partly intelligible to foreigners, and undoubtedly (being the highbrow magazine it was) to many Germans as well. *Simplicissimus*'s attacks on the existing order had the same curious air of parade-ground maneuvers, rather than warfare in bloody earnest, that distinguished German Socialism generally. It is not in *Simplicissimus* but in the work of independent free-lance artists that real dedication to class warfare is to be found. Among them two are outstanding: Heinrich Zille (1858–1929) and Heinrich Kley (1863– c. 1945).

Zille and Kley complement each other like scissor blades (**72a, b**). Between them they summarize in pictorial form *Verelendung und Zusammenbruch,* the two infallible signs of an approaching apocalyptic end to traditional society preached in the gospel according to Marx. As the Master prophesied it, capitalism inexorably destroys itself, because its system cannot prevent the possessing classes from coming to possess more and more, while the workers lose everything. Wealth corrupts, and absolute wealth corrupts absolutely, so that as the rich get richer their degeneracy becomes steadily more complete, until finally their moral fiber disintegrates utterly and they lose all will to defend themselves—this is *Zusammenbruch,* the dogma of capitalist collapse; and this is the theme of Heinrich Kley. But at the same time, as the workers become poorer, they lose all sense of identity with the existing order, realize they "have nothing to lose but their chains" and rise in desperate and irresistible revolt to sweep their enervated oppressors away—this is *Verelendung,* the dogma of progressive pauperization presaging the revolution; and this is the theme of Heinrich Zille.

Heinrich Kley was the great mirror of what Edmund Taylor called "the gathering Wagnerian murk" of upper-class German culture in the years before the Great War. He began as a painter, progressing so far as to get an official commission for two murals in Baden-Baden with the grand-operatic titles *Consecration of the Roman Altar to Mercury* and *Kaiser Wilhelm's First Walk;* but he soon switched to free-lance cartooning, and for thirty years his cartoons appeared in various places all over Germany. His consistent subject was the social commentary familiar for the past century in German cartooning, but his way of handling it was quite different. Ostensibly he dealt with conventional upper-class life—balls, charities, banquets, outings, promenades, operas—in the conventional upper-class Academic Impressionist style of the period; Kley's themes and juicy pen-and-ink technique remind an American of C. D. Gibson. But there was nothing conventional about his interpretations. Under Kley's pen all these superficially innocent activities undergo a sinister metamorphosis. Eligible tuxedoed bachelors turn into leering satyrs; elegantly coiffured debutantes become lascivious bacchantes; matrons' gowns dissolve to reveal hideous sagging nakedness; demonic animals—crocodiles, elephants, tigers—caress them indiscriminately in slithering embrace, and over everything morbid fascination with bestiality hangs like a coprophagous cloud (**72a**).

In the 1920s and -30s it became fashionable for Fine Artists to "expose" the Realities of decadent life with self-conscious Freudian imagery, and much was made by critics of the discovery that Edvard Munch and the Brücke group in Dresden had been doing something like this even before 1914. But for effective imagery none came close to Kley, who predated them all. Kley's bestiary was the pictorial counterpart to written records of life at the Wilhelmine court: the neurotic eagle of a Kaiser oscillating between bombast and funk; the homosexual sybaritic lizard that was "Phili," Prince Eulenburg; the molelike Baron Holstein, harbinger of Martin Bormann; the Machiavellian tiger von Bülow; the elephantine court favorite Count Hulsen-Haseler, who at the age of fifty-six died of a heart attack after cavorting around the Kaiser's hunting lodge dressed in a ballerina's tutu; syphilitic satyrs like Archduke Otto of Austria. Here was *Zusammenbruch* for all to see.

Heinrich Zille satirized the same "barbarism lit by neon" (as Karl Kraus called it), but at the other end of the social scale. *Verelendung* was his theme; his concern not counts and hunting lodges but the slums and back alleys of Germany's industrial cities. After a brief start painting Fine Art genre, Zille spent forty years depicting a world of blowsy whores and squalid derelicts, of chamber pots and drunks in gutters, of vagrant-ridden doss houses and diaper-laden tenements where the funniest thing that ever happens is to watch a half-grown girl squatting in the corner of a vacant lot (**72b**).

There the *Lumpenproletariat* was sullenly breeding, dead to any life of mind or spirit, waiting for the demagogue who would put them in uniform and bring them onto the stage of history. And he was there, sullenly waiting his moment; Zille might well have drawn him. For the young Hitler, as Hanisch the tramp described him in Vienna, was Zille's kind of subject: "in a long black shabby overcoat which hung down to his ankles and which had been given him by a Hungarian Jewish old clothes-dealer . . . greasy black derby which he wore the year round . . . matted hair. . . ."* On Zille's seventieth birthday party in 1928, his Berlin friends sang him a song that ended: *"Keiner hat in diesen Länden, So wie er ein Volk verstanden."* That Zille knew the German lower classes well no one doubted; but at least one man believed he understood the German people better: almost exactly ten years later, on his fiftieth birthday in 1938, Adolf Hitler announced to a secret meeting of his generals his intention to begin Germany's war of conquest without delay, while he was still at his physical peak, "for no individual will ever again understand the people of Germany, or enjoy their confidence, as I do now . . ." (William L. Shirer, *Rise and Fall of the Third Reich,* 1960, p. 935).

Though Hitler and Zille studied in the same school, the lessons they took were very different. Zille firmly believed that by exposing proletarian misery he would encourage discontent that would ultimately bring the whole existing order crashing down. Hitler worked with the same short-range object:

> The original slogan of revolutionary Nazism, the slogan which had inspired the déclassés and the propertyless, the outcasts and casualties of society who had made Nazism before the Junkers and generals, industrialists and civil servants joined it . . . the authentic voice of Nazism uninhibited . . . which Rauschning had heard, with timid aristocratic dismay, ringing suddenly out among the tea-cups, the cream buns, the cuckoo-clocks and Bavarian bric-a-brac of the original Berchtesgaden . . . was the doctrine of class war, of permanent revolution, of purposeless but gleeful destruction of life and property and all those values of civilization. . . . [H. R. Trevor-Roper, *The Last Days of Hitler,* 1947, pp. 46–47]

But whereas Zille, like all adherents of the Enlightenment religion in all its phases, expected that, once wicked bourgeois institutions had collapsed, mankind's natural goodness would infallibly be manifest in a new paradisial social order, Hitler saw much further. He realized

---

* Alan Bullock, *Hitler,* 1938, p. 8.

that all the people working against the established system were in fact parasitical on it; that the "Wandering Birds" who went about prewar Germany with uncut hair and unkempt beards carrying guitars and smelling flowers were as utterly dependent on industrial prosperity and the welfare state that Bismarck had initiated as are their beatnik and hippie counterparts in the 1950s and -60s; that the Dadaists and social protesters of the 1920s lived only on sufferance of a working population who despised and resented them as drones; that the more dissatisfaction they fostered, the more welcome a New and stronger Order would be; that, in fact, all these people worked in the ultimate interests of National Socialism. And so it was. As the French intellectuals who had worked to destroy monarchical France got the guillotine and Napoleon for their reward, the German anarchist intellectuals got concentration camps and the Third Reich. Not, of course, that they were entirely disappointed in the end. For, in the dying months of Hitler's empire,

> The horrors of bombardment now acquired a new significance for the exultant Dr. Goebbels; they were instruments not of fearful but of sanitary destruction, and he welcomed them. "The bomb-terror," he gloated, "spares the dwellings of neither rich nor poor; before the labour offices of total war the last class barriers have had to go down." "Under the debris of our shattered cities," echoed the German Press, "the last so-called achievements of the middle-class nineteenth century have been finally buried." . . . There is no mistaking his jubilation. [Trevor-Roper, *op. cit.*, p. 47]

So the old socialist ideal of equality was finally realized. Junkers and middle class, peasants and workers and capitalists, all were brought down in one common bloody ruin.

This object lesson came too late to benefit England, however. There the same Enlightenment religion bloomed after 1945 into its Welfare State, with the inevitable collapse soon following—a history that cartoons all too well record.

5. *New Jerusalem Builders in English Cartooning, 1890–1945*

In retrospect, the 1890s were a turning point for Britain. This was the decade of Queen Victoria's Diamond Jubilee, apogee of the island's imperial power, and the last decade of John Tenniel, whose cartoons so admirably chronicled it (he retired from *Punch* at the end of 1900). It was also the decade when British statesmen began to realize that their nation was no longer self-evidently strong enough to stand in splendid isolation and began to cast about for alliances with one of the European powers, leaning first toward Germany, ultimately settling for France.

In this decade fundamental changes began in cartooning, too. Most obvious was the technical shift from wood block to halftone for reproduction. It began in advertising, as we shall see; in *Punch,* the first examples appeared during 1892. Though the halftone process was vastly more complicated—involving photography through a close-lined screen, a papier-mâché mold made from the resulting dotted plate and a metal cylinder made from that—its effect was to permit unheard-of freedom and accuracy in reproduction, and the most immediate result was the appearance of a basically new kind of cartoon. Instead of quasi-illustrative drawings with lengthy captions, the trend was to simplified drawings that were more or less self-explanatory in themselves; captions were reduced to a few words or a line, or eliminated altogether, so that an essentially different quality of visual experience was established with the reader. With the new technique came a new trend in subject matter; its two chief exponents are the plebeian Phil May (1864–1903) and the patrician Max Beerbohm (1872–1956).

May began as an *enfant terrible* political cartoonist for three years (1886–88) in Sydney, Australia, with caustic commentary on British colonial policy generally and the revered Queen Victoria in particular; but his lasting reputation was made in Britain with disturbing depictions of slum life (73a). May was the British counterpart to Heinrich Zille. He developed a style—*Guttersnipes* is the most mature example—in some ways resembling Zille's, though with a characteristically English emphasis more on nervous line than textural effects (cf. 79b); his content, too, had a typically English reticence, condemning more by implication than brute record. Beerbohm, by contrast, was a British Kley, at least to the extent that his work had the same distinctive stylization (an early contributor to Aubrey Beardsley's *Yellow Book,* Beerbohm always retained a vaguely Art Nouveau character), and the same mocking presentation of upper-class manners and mores as absurd, decadent, and unsubstantial. England's portly heir apparent, the naughty boy who has to stand in a corner during *The Rare, the Rather Awful Visits of Albert Edward, Prince of Wales, to Windsor Castle* (73b), leads a whole gallery of aristocrats parading through Beerbohm's books in reedy forms and ridiculous light—*Cari-*

367

catures of 25 Gentlemen (1896), *The Poets' Corner* (1904), *Second Childhood of John Bull* (1911), *Fifty Caricatures* (1913) . . . In other ways he differed. "Max's wit," David Low remarked in his *Autobiography* (London, 1956), "was sometimes so cultured in derivation and so local in application as to make his caricatures almost private." Only someone aware of the pretentiousness of poems like "Sail, sail thy best, ship of Democracy" could fully appreciate the absurdity of Beerbohm's *Walt Whitman Inciting the American Eagle to Soar* (from *The Poets' Corner*), with its sage in suspenders capering before a seedy, sullen, suspicious eagle on its perch; only someone aware of the cult of George Bernard Shaw, but not sharing it, would be amused by Beerbohm's band of horn-rimmed intellectuals burning incense into the philosopher's gigantic nostrils with the caption, "And calls himself a non-smoker!" (from *Observations*, 1925); only someone with historical perspective would understand Beerbohm's *Tale of Three Nations* from *Things Old and New* (1923). And nobody could ever imagine Kley saying what Low records of Beerbohm: " 'It must be awful to be a slave to skill,' said he, shuddering delicately . . . he so avoided academic form that his imatators came to believe that all that was needed to become a cartoonist was not to be able to draw."

Now also more direct attacks on the whole British social system and incitements to revolution appear. Those by Walter Crane (1845–1915) are perhaps the best-known; more or less led into social protest by his attachment to William Morris, Crane produced cartoons in an elegant pre-Raphaelite-cum-Kelmscott-Press style filled with elegant angels blowing trumpets of doom and immaculate working-men in tidy smocks and noble expressions that were much admired by Fine Art critics but probably had proportionately little effect (77a). More powerful were the cartoons of Will Dyson (1883–1938), less pre-Raphaelite and more Phil Mayish in style, less Ruskinian and more Marxist in content.

After a brief interval of wartime euphoria between 1914–1918, all these trends were focused in the work of one man, David Low (1891–1963), a master of the cartoon as persuasive weapon rivaled perhaps only by Daumier.

Low only occasionally worked for *Punch*. After making a great reputation in his native Australia with his wartime satires of intransigent Premier "Billy" Hughes in the Melbourne *Bulletin,* he was invited to be regular cartoonist for the London *Star* (1919–1927), and his greatest works were done for Lord Beaverbrook's *Evening Stand-*

ard (1927–1950). The shift from Australia to England coincided with a change from an original meticulous linear style in Tenniel's tradition (Linley Sambourne was probably the immediate model) to broad pencil and brush strokes reminiscent of Daumier. Low also shed the whole *Punch* paraphernalia of allegorical goddesses and John Bulls and German eagles to concentrate on simple figures drawn in broad caricature. Like Daumier's, Low's deep and abiding concern was always social reform, and this was at once his strength and his weakness. It enabled him to penetrate the façade of British parliamentarians in the 1920s and -30s and reveal them for what they were. Possibly no Western country ever had such an unbroken succession of political imbeciles as the prime ministers of Britain from Lloyd George to Neville Chamberlain, and Low flayed them all. Who can forget his skitterish little imp of a Lloyd George ("Lloyd George changes his mind as often as his shirt—probably oftener," as a contemporary said), his faceless and phlegmatic Stanley Baldwin, disguising vacuity of mind behind a mask of impassive profundity, his owlish Chamberlain, stalking smugly to ruin?

At the same time, it prevented his seeing why such people were in power, for he shared the same obsession with social transformation that blinded intellectuals everywhere to the practical necessities of politics. The lunatic side of Hitler he saw plainly enough, embodying it in a capering little figure with fluttering forelock out of comic opera; that Hitler was also a dangerous criminal he recognized only intermittently; that force alone could stop this criminal lunatic who controlled the second strongest nation on earth he admitted far too late. In 1933, the year Hitler came to power, Low published his famous *Disarmament Conference* cartoon of a weeping crocodile telling a crowd of sheep, "My friends, we have failed. We just couldn't control your warlike passions"; plainly he prefers Labour's charges of conniving armament makers to the official explanation that "alarming international developments" forced the conference to disband.

And so it goes year after year. He castigates the folly of leaders who fail to stand up to the dictators: Eden, Litvinov, Daladier cowering in a corner while a prancing Hitler sneers, "How much will you give me not to kick your pants for, say, twenty-five years?" (**74b**); Chamberlain and Eden facing into an icebox with the sage admonition, "We must keep a cool head," while Mussolini and Hitler smirk behind them and set fire to their coattails. But he is equally opposed to any measures involving counterforce. Low's cartoons ardently support an alliance of menaced nations for collective security; just as ardently, he denounces all proposals for arming any of its members. Churchill and his small band of Tories urging rearmament appear in a 1936 cartoon as thugs lurking in sinister shadows, threats to peace as great as Hitler. Anyone suggesting that now may not be the ideal time to press for shorter work weeks and heavy taxes on industry is a "Colonel Blimp," the walrus-mustached figure Low borrowed from Tenniel's White Knight in *Through the Looking Glass* and made into his most effective satirical vehicle—though if we look back now at precisely what Colonel Blimp was advocating, he oftener than not resembles the Fool in *King Lear,* called crazy for talking sense in a world full of fools, knaves, and dreamers. Low, like Britain generally begins to wake up only after Hitler breaks the Munich pact and annexes Czechoslovakia late in 1938; finally cartoons appear urging resistance by force. But it is all far too late. Low's cartoon on the Soviet-German pact of June 1939—his most famous single work—representing Stalin and Hitler exchanging greetings over the corpse of Poland ("The scum of the earth, I believe?" "The bloody assassin of the workers, I presume?") is in effect the first of his war cartoons. But not until the great German victories of the early War does Low really abandon the idea that everything would soon be all right if "people everywhere" would just rise to demonstrate their "love of peace."

Not that Low's political naïveté ever detracted from his effectiveness as a persuasive artist in the years he cartooned regularly for the *Standard;* why should it? Low Artists are not to be judged on their revelations of Reality; that is not their business. They are to be judged on how effectively they give visual form to ideas supplied them; and by this standard Low ranks among the greatest, for his embodiment of public opinion through the 1920s and -30s was unrivaled. It could be fairly argued that his most famous war cartoons, like *The Angels of Peace Descend on Belgium* (1940) or *This Is Where We Came In* (1945) match and may well surpass Daumier's cartoons on the Franco-Prussian war. Just, too, is the comparison of Low's role in World War II to Gillray's in Napoleonic times.

But conversely, after Low went independent in 1950 and set himself up as a seer and inspired commentator, his art declined. As his *Autobiography* makes clear, he carries over into the 1950s that naïve faith of the 1920s which inspired his only half-jesting *Ideal Cabinet* of 1926 with George Bernard Shaw prime minister and H. G. Wells minister of education; he has worked too long for a socialized

Britain to admit that it has not brought the Millennium any closer. Far into the Welfare State he mocks, with horrific flashbacks to Depression bread lines, those Blimps who imagine that "planning would sap enterprise and initiative . . . weaken self-reliance and self-respect . . . the best qualities of the British people," ignores the apathy and irresponsibility and collapsing power and influence of a nation "sinking giggling into the sea," and, with floods surging on all sides, goes on preaching the need for irrigation. By the 1960s he was far out of touch with the national temper, and his knighthood in 1962, like Partridge's in 1926, was a tribute to vanished powers.

6. *Some Born More Equal: Social and Class Cartooning in America, 1890–1960*

It was not until the mid-1880s that social cartoons in the European sense began to appear with any frequency in America. According to official dogma, they should not have appeared at all, for in the 1880s (and long after, as we have seen manifest in the Columbian Exposition of 1893, the Lincoln and Jefferson Memorials, the Mount Rushmore collossi and the Colonial Revival generally) America was proclaimed still to be that new nation brought forth in 1776 and dedicated to the proposition that all its citizens were equal members of a classless republic. Human nature being what it is, there had in fact been "high society" of a sort from the Republic's earliest days on; but until the Civil War it was broadly true that American class structure was fluid, that the shirt-sleeves-to-shirt-sleeves-in-three-generations rhythm of rising and falling fortunes had some foundation in fact. In the years after the Civil War, however, this older pattern began fading into myth. Rags-to-riches stories were still common enough, for the country's natural resources seemed inexhaustible; but instances of rags-to-riches-to-rags became fewer. As new family fortunes were made they tended now to merge with old ones by marriage—Booth Tarkington's *Magnificent Ambersons* (1918) describes the process admirably in a literary counterpart to the betrothal scene of Hogarth's 18th-century *Marriage à la Mode*—and so all of a sudden in the late 1880s it was plain that a permanent American upper class was taking form, almost as rigid and perhaps even more privileged than any in Europe.

Every aspect of American life manifests the change. You can see it in architecture, when individualistic Italianate and High Victorian Picturesque Eclectic creations are suddenly superseded by

the Late Victorian academic "revival of the revivals," as a new aristocracy self-consciously appropriates forms suitably manifesting its establishment—French lords' castles along the Loire, Tudor courtiers' half-
timbered mansions, princely palaces of the Italian Renaissance, and
not least, the old colonial aristocracy's Georgian mansions from Virginia, Philadelphia, and Boston. But the change is most strikingly
manifested in American cartoons, beginning with the generation represented by Frederick Burr Opper (1857–1937).

Opper's debt to Nast in technique and form is plain;
equally plain is the great difference in spirit between them, apparent
from the beginning. Opper's first published work, an 1876 cartoon in
Wild Oats mocking Nast's anti-Catholic phobia, sets the tone. Nast
was anti-Catholic not primarily on religious grounds, but because he
believed that the corrupt political machines appearing in his day drew
their strength from bloc voting by Catholic immigrants under Church
dictation, and that the way to attack these machines was to expose the
Church's connivance in them; his anti-Catholicism, that is, was premised on the simple direct political thought of prewar America, the ideal
of government by the unprejudiced votes of free and equal citizens. To
Opper's generation such thinking seemed anachronistic futility. In his
experience, elections were won not by influencing individual voters but
by appealing to broad segments of society en masse, by directing
organized pressure groups. From beginning to end Opper thinks in
terms of such abstract social forces. His two early comic-strip creations
are typical (**43b, c**). *Happy Hooligan* and *Alphonse and Gaston* are
not so much individuals with personal characteristics as stock images
drawn from the folk mind; compare *Hooligan* with the Duke and
Dauphin in *Huckleberry Finn,* for instance, and you see that, while
Twain's are plausibly real people with distinctive reactions to plausibly
real situations, *Hooligan*'s actions are as predictable as the burlesque
comedian's pie in the eye—and could you imagine ever meeting
Alphonse and Gaston in real life? The great body of social cartoons he
did as chief cartoonist for *Puck*, from 1881 to 1899, are likewise concerned with types more than individuals. He was the ideal illustrator
for *Bill Nye's History of the United States* (1894) and *Mr. Dooley's
Philosophy* (1900) by Finley Peter Dunne (1867–1936) because these
two humorists also are examples of "old-philosopher" types responding in an invariably predictable way to every situation. And this same
attitude informs Opper's political cartoons of the first Roosevelt era.

Opper's best-known political cartoons are the two series devoted (if that is the word) to William McKinley: "Willie and Poppa" and "Willie and Teddie" (**75a**). In the first, McKinley appears as a tiny puppet doing tricks on command from a bloated top-hatted figure immediately recognizable as the descendant of Nast's Boss Tweed. But unlike its prototype, this is not the cartoon of an individual, but of a social force or class; it represents an abstraction called "the Trusts." McKinley is not really an individual either; what Opper castigates is not a wicked man like Nast's Andrew Johnson, or a fool like Nast's Horace Greeley, but the abstract symbol of a government controlled by vested economic interests. Theodore Roosevelt as McKinley's vice-president cuts the same sort of figure: a cowboy-puppet on a little cockhorse, "Teddie" like "Willie" is a plaything of the Trusts. And though Opper's attitude toward Roosevelt later changed from criticism to admiration, his way of representing men as abstractions did not. For Opper, Roosevelt was never an individual with personal idiosyncrasies as Grant had been for Nast or Napoleon for Gillray; always he remained to some extent a symbolic type—in this later case, of the Responsible Aristocrat, exemplar of How the Upper Class Should Behave toward the Lower.

In the work of Opper's slightly younger contemporaries Charles Dana Gibson (1867–1944) and Art Young (1866–1943), all vestiges of the Nast political tradition disappear. They are social cartoonists in the full European sense. Parallels are obvious: Gibson as satirist of the upper classes and Young as proletariat protagonist are to some extent counterparts to Kley and Zille in Germany, Beerbohm and Phil May in Britain. But differences that make them characteristically American are plain.

In the cartoons Gibson drew from 1885 to 1905 as chief cartoonist for the old *Life* (founded 1883 by John Ames Mitchell) and *Judge* (founded 1881)—the very appearance of such class magazines was a sign of the times—upper-class society is often enough shown in what is, to say the least, an unkind light: shallow, vain, overbearing, foolish. He ridicules without mercy the kind of snobbery represented by socialite arbiter Ward McAllister (a favorite butt of his), *nouveau-riche* affection of aristocratic airs, or infatuation with titles acquired by marriage to foreign nobility. But rarely if ever is there anything like Kley's implication that all upper-class life is some monstrous obscenity, or Beerbohm's collective characterization of aristocrats as decadent freaks. Quite the contrary; Gibson's approach is essentially didactic. It

373

is as if he had taken to heart Edwin L. Godkin's famous descriptions in the *Nation* during the 1870s of the American rich as

> a gaudy stream of bespangled, belaced, and beruffled bar-
> barians. . . . Who knows how to be rich in America? . . . To
> be rich properly indeed is a fine art. . . . It requires cultivation,
> imagination, and character. . . .

and used his cartoons to show them how to behave, refining manners inherited from the old raw Molly Brown mine-field and Captain Gardner windjammer days by providing proper "types" for emulation. Essentially Gibson's attitude to the American upper classes was the same as Du Maurier's to the English in *Punch;* even before he met Du Maurier on a trip to England in 1888, Gibson had adopted his Aca- demic Impressionist drawing style, and with it he created dicactic images even more influential.

First and most successful of them was the "Gibson Girl," a type of ideal young woman created in 1890 (*The Restless Art,* p. 229). Its impact, in those days before movies and television, was truly ex- traordinary. Found, according to Gibson's biographer Fairfax Downey (*Portrait of an Era,* 1936), all over the world—"in the palace of the last Czar of Russia after his exile and death, in cabins on the Klondike, palm-leaf huts in Central America, Tokyo shop windows and the cabooses of American trains"—the Gibson Girl influenced the posture, hairdos, dress, and corsets of a whole generation of women. Almost as influential was the Gibson Man, who shortly followed. His shorn hair and shaven chin (and a Gillette Safety Razor advertising campaign equating beards with "barbarism") were credited with establishing a standard "clean-cut look" incumbent on executive pyramid climbers in big American corporations ever since. Gibson's types also helped along emancipation of women, for when Gibson Girls and Gibson Men swimming, bicycling, and playing golf or tennis together indicated upper-class approval of women's moving out of the home, mass exodus soon followed.

One reason for the difference in attitude between Gibson and Kley or Beerbohm was certainly that Gibson had upper-class connections himself. His was a good New England family, and his artistic associations (he originally intended to be a painter) were with upper-class painters like Saint-Gaudens, Kenyon Cox, William Merritt Chase, Blashfield and Sargent. But there was a more basic reason: American society was sounder. There was nothing in America com- parable to the socialist agitation that so embittered class relations in

Europe. Determined attempts had been made to import the European notion of permanent class warfare into the United States ever since the Civil War, but as Eric Goldman has pointed out in *Rendezvous with Destiny*, none had ever really caught on. Characteristic American reformers simply wanted the rich to behave decently and stop monopolizing opportunity; as Goldman describes Thorstein Veblen, for example, he was "much more deeply offended by the competitive extravagance of the rich than by the poverty of an exploited working class." It followed that what Downey describes as Gibson's "simple universal themes: 'Youth and Beauty, Honor and Decency and Dignity, Love Conquers All, Money Isn't Everything'" did not strike his contemporaries as hypocritical. In the 1880s and -90s it still seemed reasonable to talk about each class raising its standards of civilization and material welfare, everybody behaving a little more decently, and the world so becoming a more decent place to live in. And Gibson's kind of approach to social problems may well have been sounder and saner than what enlightened intellectuals have advocated since. Certainly it could hardly have been more futile.

The same difference in basic attitude distinguishes Art Young's cartoons (**75b**) from Zille's or May's. Young was a Socialist, to be sure, with the fanaticism of a convert. After many years of conventional political cartooning and news illustration in Chicago and the West, he suddenly appeared on the New York scene in 1911 as coeditor and chief cartoonist of *The Masses*, ran on the Socialist ticket for the New York State Assembly in 1913 and the Senate in 1918, and flailed capitalism in line and word. In his cartoons capitalism is a huge bloated monster (an image sired by Opper's Trusts out of Nast's Boss Tweed), swilling down tureens of caviar on the edge of a precipice; a miser clutching hoarded money bags as monkeys hoard coconuts (*From Jungle to Civilization*); a whorehouse where *Freedom of the Press* is kept—this famous 1912 cartoon brought him a lawsuit from Associated Press; an orchestra of demons playing dance tunes on cannons and machine guns for clergy, press, politicians and patriots— this comment on American motives for entering the Great War, *Having Their Fling*, jailed him in 1917.

But Young will not stoop, as Zille and May do, to portraying the exploited proletariat as bestial creatures for propagandistic effect. Like the Ash Can painters with whom he had connections— Sloan, Luks, and the rest—he always portrayed the poor with dignity. Typical is his famous cartoon of the two slum urchins gazing up at the tiny patch of night sky visible between their tenement walls: "Chee, Annie! Lookit the stars—thick as bedbugs!" These are not Zille's sub-human animals, these are human beings, with human reactions and human potential. And though he despises the bourgeoisie, he is never blindly vindictive. A political cartoon like *Eyes Right*, which portrays Roosevelt's Bull Moose candidacy as a streetwalker blandishing Taft's regimented delegates on their way to the 1912 Republican convention, is not the doctrinaire "plague on both your houses" of British Labour; it is the American attitude of a Samuel Gompers, working for reform within the system, defying all pressures to form a separate Labor Party. Most typical of how Young tempers savagery with sympathy is his *Inferno* series (1933); the poor businessmen put through their paces by capitalist devils are more objects of pity than damnation, just as Sinclair Lewis's *Babbitt* by the end of the book has dwindled from an agent of the system to its victim, plaintively telling his son, "I never in all my life did anything I really wanted." Essentially, you could say of Art Young what Orwell said of Dickens:

> Behind the page . . . I see . . . the face of a man . . . laughing, with a touch of anger in his laughter, but no triumph, no malignity. It is the face of a man who is always fighting against something, but who fights in the open and is not frightened, the face of a man who is *generously angry*—in other words . . . a free intelligence, a type hated with equal hatred by all the smelly little orthodoxies which are now contending for our souls. [*Dickens, Dali and Others*]

World War I and its aftermath made such a position untenable. Idealism generally was discredited. European ideas of all kinds were suspect, and socialism especially so because it came to be associated in the public mind with "bolshevism" and an uncritical assumption that "what's good for the U.S.S.R. is good for the U.S." Young went on publishing cartoons, and some of his best-known date from the 1920s, like the two bums on a park bench reading from a newspaper that "we made 185 million dollars out of the world war"; the two huge policemen dragging off an insignificant little man for "overthrowing the government"; the smart young thing shocking her dowager mother with, "Mother, when you were a girl, didn't you find it a bore to be a virgin?" But it was not until the Depression brought a wave of renewed interest in the "old radicals" generally that Young's cartoons—like Wright's and Sullivan's architecture—again attracted wide attention. Five books date from those years: *Trees at Night*

(1927), *On My Way* (1928), *Art Young's Inferno* (1933), *The Best of Art Young* (1936), and *Art Young: His Life and Times* (1939). Yet though social skepticism had revived, idealism had not; in the 1930s Young's cartoons figured more as a period revival than a persuasive force.

The basic reason was, of course, that socialism, from the broad point of view, was no longer a new, subversive, visionary movement; it had been established as official doctrine by one of the world's major powers. What it now needed were arts of conviction, to manifest its established beliefs.

7. From Poster to Pravda: Arts of Socialist Conviction, 1917–1960

Bertrand de Juvenal's *On Power,* studying the revolutions in 17th-century England, 18th-century America and France, and 20th-century Russia, concluded that in every case, once the upheaval subsided, the historic character of each state reappeared essentially as before, except that the powers of its central government were vastly increased. Cromwell's England pursued the same policies as Elizabeth's, only far more effectively. Life in the thirteen colonies had been free and optimistic before the Revolution; it remained so afterwards, but instead of a weak central government in London growing steadily weaker, there was a strong central government in Washington growing steadily stronger. Bourbon France had been an authoritarian state with an aggressive foreign policy; Napoleonic France was the same, only far more so. Czarist Russia was a police state threatening all the Balkans and Slavic Europe; Soviet Russia was a police state which in thirty years overran them all.

But though these revolutions failed to transform life, they did transform the arts of persuasion that served them. We have already seen how the Classical Revival art which in Jacques Louis David's early painting had been a weapon of revolutionary persuasion was adopted by both Jefferson in America and Napoleon in France as a compelling symbol of the New Order, and so completely changed its character; and how the 18th-century cartoon of social criticism was transformed into *Punch*'s didactic art of Establishment conviction following the "Quiet Revolution" of the 1830s in Britain. But official Soviet art is the most striking example of all.

Probably the most cogent and illuminating account of how official Soviet art theory evolved is to be found in Donald Drew Egbert's *Socialism and American Art* (Princeton, 1967 ed., pp. 49–85). It is an involved Byzantine story, superficially of almost incomprehensible intricacy. What is the rationale of all these shifts and reverses of party line; advance-guardists one day pampered and the next castigated as the "infantile disorder of Leftism"; the same architecture successively labeled Leftist, Rightist, formalist, bourgeois; Picasso simultaneously an ardent and propagandistically invaluable member of the Communist Party and chief exemplar of an art proscribed in the Soviet Union? Once grasp the principle of art forms' being determined by their function for persuasion or conviction, and it is all quite simple. With the Revolution established, what was now demanded of artists was no longer weapons of attack, but bulwarks of defense—images of those convictions on which the new state rested (**76a, b**). Hence "socialist realism" in painting—images to inspire confidence in the courage and resolution and infallibility of Soviet leaders, faith in emergence of the "new Soviet man" happy and sinless as promised (**77b**), instead of Kandinsky's elfin spiritualism or Malevich's exercises in nihilistic logic. Hence the solid somber bulk of Lenin's shrine in Moscow's Red Square, or Dmitrov's in Bucharest, instead of the airy constructivism of Tatlin's proposed monument to the Third International. Hence the marble stairs and platforms, the severe and stolid giants of the Stalingrad memorial (**77c**), instead of the spatial fantasies of Moholy-Nagy and Gabo. Once grasp the principle, and the origin of these forms will be plain, too.

There is a current assumption that Soviet art is really nothing but a very *retardataire* version of the Fine Arts of the West. Typical is James H. Billington's brief and passing observation, in the course of a massive analysis of Soviet culture, that

> All of the enforced artistic styles of the Stalin era—the photographic posters, the symphonies of socialism, the propagandistic novels, and the staccato civic poetry—appear as distorted vulgarizations of the predominant styles of the 1860's. [*The Icon and the Axe*, 1966, p. 534]

But if, instead of dismissing it with the curt contempt of Fine Art convention, you take the trouble to look at Soviet art at all objectively, no connection with Fine Art past or present can be made out. In *The Restless Art* (pp. 363–68) I suggested the essential difference that whereas Fine Art is solipsistic, totalitarian art rests on the very different—indeed, opposite—basis of collective solipsism. And its origins are patently different, too. So far from being based on any study of advance-guard art in Paris during the 1860s, the forms of Soviet official art—and of other Communist countries later—are quite plainly adaptations of various Low Arts of the West. Most influential of all has been 19th-century advertising.

On the great mausoleum in Red Square one single hypnotic word "Lenin" is carved, as the single hypnotic word "Holloway" was once painted on market places and mountainsides. Massed marchers bearing their great banners inscribed with Marxist icons and Maoist mottos follow paths trod by sandwich-board carriers of the 1840s. Colossal portraits of Lenin and Castro have their precedent in the great outdoor billboards of the 1870s and -80s. For the stylistic origins of the gigantic goddess crowning the Stalingrad battlefield, look no further than the avenging angel of socialism who rescues the oppressed workingman from all his foes, on posters of the 1890s and early 1900s, like Crane's (**77a**).

So history repeated itself. As when political democracy became an Establishment, so when socialism was established: forms originating in ephemeral arts of persuasion were transformed into images of conviction in the heavier and more permanent media of sculpture and architecture.

But of course arts of socialist conviction have not been limited to the U.S.S.R. They appear everywhere that social democracy became the established goal of State policy—which was, for all intents and purposes, in every major Western nation. That socialism was established in them without revolution, and often not even in name, is irrelevant as far as its expression in the arts is concerned.

In Western architecture, the pre-eminent expression of socialist conviction has been the so-called "International Style." True, its exponents have customarily talked as if their enthusiasm for "pure" creations of steel, glass, and concrete were solely a matter of aesthetic taste. But in fact the real reason for the appeal of such materials—none of them particularly attractive by any objective standards—was that they were conspicuous products of that Applied Science which was to have been the means for realizing economic democracy, just as Capitalism earlier had been relied upon to realize political democracy.

Since pre-1914 Germany had the fastest-developing heavy industry and the most advanced welfare programs in Europe, it is no accident that the most striking and conscious presentiments of this new architecture appeared at the 1914 Werkbund Exhibition at Cologne. There Bruno Taut exhibited his Monument to Iron—a 20th-century Sainte-Chapelle, its shape reminiscent of a medieval reliquary and in fact symbolically functioning as a shrine to the new faith in Heavy Industry as the redeemer of mankind. There Walter Gropius exhibited his Model Factory, a steel-and-glass cathedral complete with towered façade, where the saved were meant to gather in sacramental labor under the coming new dispensation; when Gropius took charge of his famous Bauhaus art school in 1919, he made a cathedral its emblem. In 1923 Gropius designed one of the 1920s' most famous works of architecture, the glittering steel, glass, and concrete Bauhaus building at Dessau; and at the same time he drew almost identical plans for an (unbuilt) International Philosophical Academy. This concurrence is not fortuitous, nor was it merely a result of consistent aesthetic principles. Rather it expressed Gropius's conviction that the Bauhaus was not an "art school" at all in the old sense of a place where students went to *do* things like painting pictures or designing furniture or studying architecture, but a place where students went to *become* a particular sort of people, imbued with a new outlook, prepared to go forth and transform the world according to the New Vision. Students went to the Bauhaus, in fact, for much the same reasons as postulants in times past entered monasteries, less to learn than to become something—and just as medieval monasteries with their massive walls and rich ornament and clustered towers were images of the Heavenly Jerusalem, so the Bauhaus imaged the coming New Jerusalem on earth, when Applied Science in the Service of Society would end capitalist drabness and surround men everywhere with creations of shimmering glass, glinting steel, and glowing concrete.

In the middle years of the 1920s visions were being spun in Paris too by Le Corbusier, with his plans for ideal cities whence all the old untidy individualism of private enterprise building had been swept away and replaced by soaring high rises set in public parks, where every citizen had his allotted cubic footage of living space carefully calculated by master planners, and so could look forward to blissful order now and forevermore. And there were others—most, like Corbusier's, paper plans only. But as time went on, cities and public buildings increasingly began to draw on the ideas they promoted, until by the late 1940s, these dreams were becoming realities everywhere. That this process coincided with the growth and development of Welfare States is no accident, of course; such architecture expressed the convictions on which they were being based. Between the impeccably neat steel-and-glass-and-concrete United Nations slabs in New York and the haphazard jumble of skyscrapers behind it there was in the late 1940s the same contrast as between the Old and New Towns of Edinburgh in the 1820s; and it expressed similar aspirations—a break with an old order, creation of a New.

By the 1950s that New Order could be seen everywhere—in primly planned New Towns all over Europe, like rebuilt Rotterdam or atomic-run Farsta outside Stockholm; in their counterparts, the developer-built and mass-produced new suburbs of American cities; in the spanking new neon-and-plastic shopping centers that serviced them; and above all, in World's Fairs. Just as the realized vision of political equality and beneficent Capitalism had its pilgrimage shrines in World's Fairs like the Great Exhibition of 1851 or the Columbian Exposition of 1893, so the realized vision of economic equality and beneficent Applied Science had its great expression in 20th-century fairs like Chicago's in 1933, New York's in 1949, and a climax at Expo '67 in Montreal. There the awed faithful could wander through streets of pavilions extolling the wonderful world Economic Man had created for himself, and there he could see still greater marvels planned for the future, like Habitat '67—a huge block of concrete cells, looking like a cross between Navaho cliff dwellings and a comb constructed by crazed bees, where presumably would sleep rude descendants of megalopolis "each in his narrow cell forever laid" (61b).

That this was and is an art of socialist conviction, let no one doubt. Simpletons there are, to be sure, who run about squalling that Capitalism still survives—for after all, are not the stores in the new shopping centers still in private hands? are not the glittering office blocks still managed by big corporations? is it not discriminatory and elitist for moneyed people to rent apartments in Habitat '67 when such miseries are not available to the poor? But such dim-witted commentators can be ignored; to anyone with eyes to see, it is obvious that in every Western country nothing like free capitalism has survived. Businesses remain in private hands simply because their services must be provided by somebody, and it is easier for the State to let private individuals do the work and then confiscate their profits by taxation, than to have Government run them directly; had this kind of capitalism not so conveniently existed, socialist States would have to invent it, as indeed the Soviets have done. And like its counterpart in Russia, this Western architecture of socialist conviction took its forms from

Low Arts of the previous century. If you want to find the origins of the International Style, you need to go no further than the 19th century's great engineers and speculative builders of railways and bridges—men like Thomas Brassey (1805–1870), Donald Smith (Lord Strathcona, 1820–1914), and John Roebling (1806–1869). Though the persuasive power of these men's work was recognized by many (John Ruskin was moved to extraordinary flights of fancy by the sight of a steam engine), they were no more considered "artists" than cartoonists were; in their own day they were called "Master Builders" precisely to distinguish what they did from the Art of Architecture. That modern critics should have been so fond of calling Gropius, Miës, and Corbusier the Master Builders of the 20th century is a recognition, all the more apt because unconscious, of the fact that the art of conviction they created drew its inspiration not from the formalism of Fine Art but from the living Low Arts.

So in the 1960s Great Societies, Welfare States, New Orders were all creating their splendid images of realized conviction. But unkind fate! like the Irishman whose horse died just when he had taught it to go indefinitely without food, so at the very moment of triumph, the whole enterprise came unglued:

> The students here [said Malcolm Muggeridge in his 1967 speech of resignation as Rector of the University of Edinburgh] as in other universities, are the ultimate beneficiaries under our welfare system. They are supposed to be the spearhead of progress, flattered and paid for by their admiring seniors, an elite who will happily and audaciously carry the torch of progress into a glorious future opening before them. . . . All is prepared for a marvellous release of youthful creativity. We await the great works of art, the high-spirited venturing into new fields of perception and understanding. And what do we get? The resort of any old slobbering debauchee everywhere in the world at any time—dope and bed. . . .

What went wrong? Nothing that had not been wrong with this vision from the beginning, and had been made indeed plain for all to see even in the architecture that expressed it:

> Writing in Paris in the early 1920s, as a lonely, unapproachable, zealous enthusiast, almost as isolated from the ongoing life of the world around him as if he had been imprisoned on the Island of Patmos, Le Corbusier was plainly inspired with an apocalyptic fervor that was in many ways like that of St. John. Having lately seen the angels pour out their vials of wrath upon the nations

assembled on the Plain of Armageddon, he felt even more acutely than did the Dada artists that the old order was utterly corrupt, chaotic, and doomed, and he looked forward to there being installed a New Epoch, a New Age, sustained by and suffused with a New Spirit and uncontaminated by anything out of the past. According to John, "He that sat upon the throne said, Behold, I make all things new"—and that is precisely the declaration that Le Corbusier so passionately desired to make to the fallen world in which he found himself. Like the first-century authors of the "Books of the Secrets of Enoch" and of the "Apocalypse of Baruch," Le Corbusier was obsessed with the necessity of purging the world of all things corruptible and of preparing it for the reign of incorruptibility. One of the most striking characteristics of his brave new city is its complete imperviousness to decay—and one takes it for granted that its citizens are as incorruptible as are its buildings.

Le Corbusier reveals his apocalyptic stance most directly, I believe, in his use of perspective vista. So, too, with John—to a degree that makes him unique among Biblical writers. "And there came unto me one of the seven angels," he tells us, "and he carried me away in the spirit to a great and high mountain, and showed me that great city, the holy Jerusalem, descending out of heaven from God, having the glory of God; and her light was like unto a stone most precious, even like a jasper stone, clear as crystal." Time and again Le Corbusier speaks of how the glass-walled, crystalline buildings of his *Ville Radieuse,* his Radiant City, will stand glittering in the sunlight (for it is inconceivable that there should be any night here—or any fog or wintry rain or smoke-pall or industrial smog); and time and again he imagines himself to be standing in some high place, looking out over his immense city, "with the nations of the saved walking in the light of it." For unlike Wright, he had no Chosen People, any more than had John: he longed to install his New Jerusalem, the *Ville Classée,* in all the nations of the earth.

Not only will there be no night here; "there will be no death, neither sorrow nor crying, neither shall there be any more pain": there are no cemeteries, no mausoleums, no monuments to the dead; there are no homes for the aged, no hospitals, no orphanages, no insane asylums, no houses of correction, no jails—"for the former things have passed away." "And I saw no temple therein," John reports, "for the Lord God Almighty and the Lamb are the temple of it." So it is with the *Ville Moderne:* there are no churches, no synagogues, no lodge halls, no buildings that can be associated with business corporations; there are no private homes; there are no subsidiary institutions of any kind, for the City itself provides the one basis for binding together all men, who will live here without sin and in timeless harmony with one another, beyond the reach even of death. For Le Corbusier, as earlier for Auguste Comte, the Age of Science, bringing with it the totally engineered environment, was to be final age, when ignorance and darkness would be forever dispelled and when history would cease.

Well, how has it worked out? Where do we stand today? No one surely knows, of course; but I think it fair to say that the defenders of the cause of Modern Architecture are at this point in much the same position as were the early Christians who had finally to reconcile themselves to the near-certainty that the Second Coming was not imminent after all and that history was going to go on for an indefinitely long period of time; or they are in the position of the Spiritual Franciscans who in the 1250s were convinced by the prophecies of Joachim of Floris and of Gerard of Borgo San Donnino that the Age of the Holy Spirit was going to be inaugurated in the year 1260—and who then had to learn to live with the fact that it did not happen as they had been led to expect. History continued. So, too, with Comte's third and final Age of Science. That New Age with which every modern architect has habitually associated the word "clean" has turned out to be anything but clean. Instead, we are throwing up 800,000,000 tons of pollution into the atmosphere every year, and we are learning to live with kinds of dirtiness in war, in urban life, and in the arts that make the period of the 1920s seem, by comparison, not chaotic in the least but curiously innocent. The desert has not blossomed like the rose; instead, new deserts of rubbish and of dead cars spreading all around us. After the disappointment of 1260, Gerard of Borgo San Donnino was imprisoned for life on charges of heresy. It is too late now for us to imprison the Founding Fathers of modern architecture, for they are all dead; but perhaps we would do well at least to raise some question as to whether or not we have been following false prophets. [Norris Kelly Smith, *"Millenary Folly: The Failure of an Eschatology"* in *On Art & Architecture in the Modern World*, University of Victoria Studies of History in the Arts, No. 4, 1970.]

This could have been the time for some serious re-evaluation of the premises underlying Western thought, action, and politics for the past two hundred years. This could have been a time to recall a saying by someone, whose name slips the memory, about man not living by bread alone. This could have been a time to reopen the question of whether man is in fact good by nature, and to remember that if he is not, all talk about transforming earth into Heaven is mad. But nothing like that happened. Instead, history began repeating itself. Not the goal, but the means were shifted. If economic democracy proved no more of a panacea than political democracy, then, all the wise sheep concluded, the reason must be that people are still not equal enough. Social democracy is the answer—a Just Society, where justice will mean not that everybody gets what he deserves or earns, but where everybody gets the same regardless of what he does. All remaining distinctions between persons must be broken down. Every individual must become absolutely equal to every other individual, as the angels are in Heaven. Love is the answer—love as it was in pre-civilized ages, pure interpersonal relations untrammeled by caste or creed or convention; love as it was in the Garden of Eden. On, then, to the third phase of the revolution; on to "Universal Love."

V

SORCERER'S APPRENTICE: THE ARTS OF ADVERTISING IN THE SERVICE OF UNIVERSAL LOVE

THE VISION of a world freed not only from political and economic inequality, but from social inequality as well, where nothing like vertical master-and-men relationships would exist, was always inherent in the whole concept of naturally good beings creating a Heaven on earth. It is implicit already in Rousseau's "noble savage" myth. It permeates the art of William Blake (1757–1827)—an art not only based on systematic and deliberate rejection of all authority restricting expression of that godlike genius of Imagination which he assumed every individual to possess in equal measure, but also filled with recurring variants on that image of primeval Garden-of-Eden innocence which was and remains the central justifying image of this whole last phase of the movement (cf. *The Restless Art*, pp. 55–59). Early 19th-century Romantics gave it clearly recognizable form. Their delight in contemplation of individuals lost in wild nature, of open boats on storm-tossed seas, of wanderings through misty moonlight, of the terror and carnage of battles long ago, stems from their conviction that both man and nature are naturally good, indivisible, and equal. In this early Romantic period too, the characteristic internal contradictions of the movement became evident—men can now take such pleasure in Nature's awesome power precisely and only because advancing technology has rendered those terrors remote from actuality (cf. *The Restless Art*, pp. 44–46, 81). So in the next, mid-19th-century phase, when the movement becomes "realistic" and "primitivism" is no longer a remote ideal but something to be realized here and now, Thoreau can affect the life of "natural man" by Walden Pond secure in the knowledge that any time he needs to, he can trot over to Mrs. Emerson's for a nice cup of hot tea—just as in our own times the hippie's shiny Yamaha stands parked outside his simple pad, in case he needs to escape the System via Interstate 5.

With the third, later-19th-century generation, anarchism proper appears as the inevitable outgrowth of such a view of life. In this era political anarchists make the most headlines—shaggy fanatics who try to bring in the Millennium by assassinating rulers of every kind in a systematic way, and do indeed succeed in killing quite a few presidents, queens, czars, and suchlike. But philosophical anarchists were by far the most numerous. These people's anarchism was at least logical, in that it was a matter of private conviction rather than social agitation. Believers in the New Art propounded by Courbet gravitate to them by instinct and convention both; by the 1880s it was as obligatory for a good "modern artist" to be a philosophical anarchist as it had been for a good republican to be a Freemason in the 1780s. As Donald Drew Egbert has pointed out, almost every single figure of any consequence in the "modern movement" between 1880 and 1940 was an anarchist of some persuasion.* Van Gogh is one typical example; that all his later paintings should essentially be portraits of himself (cf. *The Restless Art*, pp. 271–73) is from the anarchist point of view, entirely logical—every individual being an absolutely unique entity, his perception depends on no authority but his own. Gauguin provides an ever better demonstration. In his person he was the archetypal anarchist—shaggy hair, drooping mustache, dress fashionably imitating working-class clothing, his whole life-style anticipating the "hip" world by eighty years. His art shows plainly the evolution from romantic naturalism (in his early Sunday-painter and Pont-Aven days) to self-conscious primitivism centered on the Garden-of-Eden theme

---

* "The Idea of 'Avant-Garde' in Art and Politics," reprinted in *On Arts and Society*, University of Victoria Studies of History in the Arts, No. 3, 1970.

of primeval innocence (cf. *The Restless Art,* pp. 283–86). Die Brücke, Der Blaue Reiter, Nolde, Klee—they all fall into this pattern.

But all such works are essentially private. Insofar as they had any relation to the traditional functions of the activity called "art," they were images of private conviction, by specific definition of their makers, without relation to society at large.

"Modern painting," then, did not constitute the persuasive art of his third phase of the Enlightenment religion. What did? Was there a persuasive art dedicated to destroying that logic upon which a vertically structured society must depend? Was there a persuasive art dedicated to attacking that Practical Reason which takes the existence of some kind of authority and discipline in human affairs for granted, as self-evidently necessary? Was there a persuasive art dedicated to deriding and degrading any suggestion of that innate superiority and inferiority among men which modern cant calls "elitism"?

There was indeed. It went—and still goes—under the name of "advertising." But it is a true and traditional art form, nonetheless, and if it changed its character and scope vastly during the 19th and 20th centuries, after surviving essentially unchanged in form for millennia, that was simply because it now had a new mission, a new urgency. Advertising is not a reflection of the state of the public mind; it sets out to create the public mind itself. However inadvertently, its function is to prepare for the New Dispensation, to bring in total social equality.

1. *The Beginnings of Advertising*

At the beginning of the 19th century, most advertising still basically consisted of announcements. It had for centuries (**78a, b, c,**). Something like advertisements can be found in all sorts of earlier times and places: the papyrus from Thebes in New Kingdom Egypt offering reward for return of an escaped slave that has been called the first "poster"; Caesar's *Acta Diurna* put up in the Roman Forum; the painted vines and animals identifying Pompeian taverns and butcher shops; Gerhard Leeu's book blurb at Antwerp in 1491, whence were descended the signboards and trade cards of 18th-century shop-keepers, merchants, and craftsmen. They provide interesting enough examples of Low Art dependent on High Art trends for forms and character—in cabinet makers' trade cards you can trace the evolution of taste from Baroque through Rococo to Adamesque especially well—

but they remain essentially announcements of what is available where and from whom, and no more. And so they still were as the 19th century opened.

For the literate classes, there were complex announcements —descriptions of merchandise, theater bills, and the like; for the poor (most of whom were still illiterate), simple words or symbols, like signboards for taverns and inns with pictures of "The Blue Fox," "Key and Chain," and so forth. Sometimes the two were combined in traveling kiosks drawn through the streets, accompanied by criers reading out their notices for any unable to do so. As newspapers multiplied, reproduction techniques improved and literacy levels rose, such simple advertisements became proportionately fewer, but plenty could still be seen down to the end of the century. The chief change in them was content. At the beginning of the century, they were largely concerned with advertising staples—groceries, furnishings, supplies, labor of all kinds; at its end, with small luxuries: bicycles, organs, corsets, cameras, washers. In itself, this change reflects no more than the steadily rising standard of living and available leisure made possible by the Industrial Revolution, and is principally interesting as cultural expression. But with the change in what was advertised came also a change in how it was advertised.

This change had begun—as so many characteristically "modern" phenomena began—in the mid-18th century, with the appearance of "advertisements," in the literal sense of "turn-and-looks," that tried to influence actions and stimulate desires by deliberately playing on human hopes and fears. Among the earliest examples were the political cards produced by Matthew Darley, "artist, printseller, drawing-master and designer of chinoiserie decorations and furniture" (as Dorothy George describes him in *English Political Caricature* (London, 1960, I, pp. 115ff.) and his wife Mary, "also an artist and printseller." They were clearly the ancestors of the "scare" election posters and campaigns describing the awful consequences of electing one party and the paradisial delights in store once the other is in power. Medical advertisements of the same sort had appeared even earlier, promising instant relief from affliction and marvelous well-being for all using touted preparations or devices, misery and early death for those neglecting their opportunity—the classic, perhaps, is Dr. Graham's Celestial Bed, which couples could rent "for the propagation of Beings, rational and far stronger and more beautiful in mental as well as physical endowments than the present puny, feeble and nonsensical race of Christians."* It was this increasing practice of what Samuel Johnson called "gaining attention by magnificence of promises, and by eloquence sometimes sublime and sometimes pathetic" that inspired his famous observation in the *Idler* in 1759 that "the trade of advertising is now so near to perfection that it is not easy to propose any improvement"—and his concern that, "as every art ought to be exercised in due subordination to the public good, I cannot but propose it as a moral question to these masters of the public ear, whether they do not sometimes play too wantonly with our passions?"

It was only during the 19th century, however, that the new principle Johnson so perspicaciously recognized, and the ill he boded for it, were realized. Advertising then became more and more a matter not merely of telling you where and at what price you could get what you needed, but of persuading you that you ought to have things, that you had a right to own what the advertiser had to sell. It was an ominous development.

2. *Development of the Repetitive Compulsive Symbol*

The technique developed in three successive stages as the century went on. First came the repetitive compulsive symbol (**79a, b, c**). It originated in response to conditions in the transitional period between assembly-line production of mass luxury goods, and introduction of compulsory education enabling the masses to read advertising copy—that is, roughly between 1830 and 1860. Reasoned appeals to buyers' discrimination being useless, it followed that the best way to sell goods or services to the mass market was to keep a few simple words—brand names especially—so continuously before the public eye that they would eventually sink into the subconscious as. self-evident facts, accepted without question. Posting handbills with one or two simple words or phrases was one common early way of achieving this end, and from the late 1820s through the 1860s the walls of city buildings were everywhere plastered with them; every night hundreds of bills were pasted up, most of them (fortunately enough) on top of those put up the night before, and a good percentage—significantly

---

* Perhaps the best account of the career of James Graham, who, as the spiritual ancestor of P. T. Barnum, the modern television commercial, and much else besides, deserves some recognition from posterity, is to be found in William Connor Sydney, *England and the English in the Eighteenth Century*, Edinburgh, 1891, I, pp. 317–25.

indicative of the audience addressed—upside down. Sandwich boards were also used; the term was coined by Dickens, and you can see "sandwich men" walking up Hampstead Hill in the background of Ford Madox Brown's *Work* as examples of the useless sort of labor castigated by Thomas Carlyle, who stands to the right in front of them in that picture (*The Restless Art,* p. 151). Carlyle was in fact more alive than most of his contemporaries to the significance of the new art of advertising, and in his *Past and Present* left a classic description of the new technique as practiced by the "hatter in the Strand of London" who in the 1830s,

> instead of making better felt-hats than another, mounts a huge lath-and-plaster Hat, seven feet high, upon wheels, sends a man to drive it through the streets. . . . He has not attempted to *make* better hats . . . but his whole industry is turned to *persuade* us that he has done so. . . .

But it was in the 1840s that this technique was perfected, and its two most famous practitioners appear: Phineas T. Barnum (1810–1891) in America and Thomas Holloway (1800–1883) in Britain.

Barnum's career began in 1835 when he bought and exhibited in Philadelphia a Negro slave named Joice Heth, supposed to be 116 years old and first owned by George Washington's father. For this first campaign he wrote fairly long and complicated advertisements, but by 1841, when he acquired the American Museum of New York, he had mastered the technique that made him famous. This is the way he advertises his first show in the newspapers:

VISION OF THE HOURIS
VISION OF THE HOURIS
VISION OF THE HOURIS
A Tableau of 850 Men,
Women, and Children
CLAD IN SUITS OF SILVER ARMOUR
CLAD IN SUITS OF SILVER ARMOUR
CLAD IN SUITS OF SILVER ARMOUR

and thereafter he never looks back. Decade after decade he perfects the formula; through banners, bands, transparencies, by any and every means, he hammers a few simple words into people's heads, and eventually works it into the famous seven-step philosophy of advertising described in his autobiography:

> The reader of a newspaper does not see the first insertion of an ordinary advertisement; the second insertion he sees, but does

not read; the third insertion he reads; the fourth insertion, he looks at the price; the fifth insertion he speaks of it to his wife; the sixth insertion he is ready to purchase; and the seventh insertion he purchases. [W. R. Browne, ed., *Barnum's Own Story*, 1927]

Across the Atlantic Thomas Holloway is making another fortune with the same technique. The pill that he concocts in 1838 is no better and no worse than many another in this medically unsophisticated time; the difference is that he does not waste advertising money with elaborate descriptions of what it will do compared to any rivals, but simply plasters London with the simple words "Holloway's Pills" in hopes that when people want a pill for any ailment, they will buy his. They do. By 1842 he is already spending the equivalent of $50,000 a year on advertising, blanketing England; by 1852, half a million, covering the world. Holloway's name

> assaulted the eye on every wall in London; it was to be found in the ill-printed newspapers of China, India, and Peru; once it screamed from the Great Pyramid. But it failed to find its way into the pages of Dickens, who refused an offer of £1,000 for a "puff." [E. S. Turner, *The Shocking History of Advertising*, 1953, p. 87]

Barnum and Holloway set an alluring example, that others were quick to appreciate. The compulsive symbol principle was a major factor in the success of packaged name brands. In contrast to the older practice of retailers' ladling out milk into customers' containers, weighing out quantities of their own tobacco mixtures, slicing off hunks of bread from big loaves or cuts of meat from carcasses hung in the windows, more and more products were offered in neat and uniform packages prepared by a wholesale manufacturer—first milk (in the 1850s by Nestlé in Switzerland, Borden in the United States), then solid extract of beef (1860s, Liebig Extract of Meat Company, parent of Oxo), fluid extract (Bovril, 1884), packaged meat products (Swift, Armour), pickles and preserves (Heinz, 1880s), mass-produced bread (Hōvis, 1880s), cocoa (Fry's, Cadbury's), innumerable brands of soap, cigars, and soon everything packageable at all. The practice was advocated as more convenient (which it was) and more healthful (which followed less logically); but its chief advantage was in ease of advertising. Instead of dealing with customers who had some idea of quality from personally inspecting and choosing among products, the advertiser could now sell simply by repeating slogans.

Like Holloway's Pills or Barnum's freaks, names and distinctive package designs could be so dinned into the public mind that they would buy as a conditioned reflex, without comparing or (as time went on) even remembering how to make comparisons. The ideal was a public that would ask for a brand name instead of a product—that would demand three bars of "Pears'" (soap) (**79b**) or a bottle of "Oxo." Some few actually achieved this advertiser's Valhalla; in the effort to reach it, the rest defaced the world. The high point of compulsive repetition in advertising came in the 1890s, a moment in history when, as E. S. Turner recounts,

> A Gothenburg margarine factory had painted its slogans on the walls of the fiords, right up into the Arctic Circle. The rock faces of the Thousand Islands of the St. Lawrence were hideously daubed with slogans for stove polish and tooth powder. Out of the Mississippi rose letters twenty feet high testifying to the virtues of a chewing tobacco. Voyagers on the River Hudson at night were regaled, whether they liked it or not, by endless billboards on the banks, picked out for their benefit by the ship's roving searchlight. Every other rock in the canyons of Nevada was disfigured. In Europe, on one of the loveliest bends of the River Reuss a giant boulder had been painted brown, with a chocolate firm's name on it. High on the Rigi were enormous gilt letters advertising a hotel. Even the remote hills of the Sudan carried slogans for soap . . . an enormous billboard looked down on Niagara Falls. [*The Shocking History of Advertising*]

In this decade also you could see advertisements for pills, blacking, and watches projected onto Nelson's Column and the pillars of the National Gallery in Trafalgar Square at night, Pears' Soap advertised on British postage stamps, and a light ale on the Union Jack; in New York, Times Square had already begun to be what one later critic later called "the most beautiful sight in the world—if only you couldn't read." Thereafter the worst outdoor excesses of the technique were over (though not, of course, its use—it is still the commonest one in political elections, for instance). Lovers of natural scenery and conservatives banded together in the S.C.A.P.A.—Society for Checking Abuses in Public Advertising—to good effect; egregious horrors like the huge sign advertising oats on the White Cliffs of Dover gradually disappear (though not entirely, for still in the 1960s the magnificent view from Dufferin Terrace in Quebec is dominated by the name of a brand of flour screaming in neon from the South Shore). Unfortunately, however, this was far from an unconditional triumph for good taste and sense. In many ways it was more like finding your house free of mice because rats have driven them out. The repetitive symbol declined at least as much because newer and ultimately even more noxious techniques had in the meantime been perfected.

3. *Advertising by Irrational Association*

More than anything else, probably, it was brand-name packaging that stimulated the next major development—advertising by irrational association. Since most early packaged goods were staples like milk and meat and tobacco, their advertising had to be aimed at the broadest mass market, and the symbols chosen to identify them had to appeal to the lowest common denominator of taste. Most were more or less obvious descendants of the kind of signs that used to advertise taverns and inns and shops—the Nestlé cow's head or the Heinz pickle, for example—and in both design and technique were related to the old broadsides and chapbooks (probably the last commercial usage of 18th-century-type woodcuts was for cigar bands (**79a**)). But it soon became apparent that on this level the compulsive symbol alone was not enough. With rival products all using it, its effect was lost (**79c**), and yet elaborate written texts proclaiming superior virtues had little effect either, for the kind of people to whom they were addressed read little if at all. The answer was association of ideas. Exactly what evil fairy first hit upon this principle cannot be known; but certainly it was beginning to appear with frequency by the end of the 1870s.

Some of its best early examples are the advertising or trade cards that were commonly tucked into packaged products or given away at counters, consisting of a colored lithographed picture with the product's name worked into or printed over it (**80a, b, c, d**). Unlike earlier advertising where the picture represents the product, however, here it was usually a picture of something else entirely. Accompanying the picture of a fat contented baby you may have a brand name for canned milk, for instance; a jovial fiddler may carry the name of a chewing tobacco; a sailing ship in the sunset, some laxative; a happy family scene, scrubbing boards. The advertiser does not say that feeding babies X's milk will make them fat and contented, that chewing tobacco will make parties more convivial, laxatives promote serenity of mind, or Y's washboard improve family life; he hopes the public will draw that conclusion by irrationally associating the two images.

393

The technique is to persuade by insinuation alone. Never say anything positive; rely entirely on the audience's inferring relationships, transferring ideas from one image to another.

Once established, the principle of association offered infinite scope for variation. Historians of art will recognize one of them in the collage technique that became such a fad among painters in the early 1900s; but of course this is only one more of the innumerable instances of Fine Art's borrowing a form from the Low Arts, ripping it out of functional context, and making a Precious Object for Exhibition out of it—the living form had long since developed far beyond such simple beginnings. Decades before Dada, advertisers had discovered the inherent potentialities of irrelevant puns and irrational humor, for instance, using them to imply that manufacturers with such wit surely must have a good product—Harry Furniss's tramp writing to Pears', "Two years ago I used your soap, since when I have used no other," is probably the most famous example. They had also discovered the value of testimonials from well-known people; merely picturing an actress or duke beside a product, without even a suggestion of their using it, was enough to spur sales. They had discovered, in short, "the beauty of irrationality"—the more irrational an association of ideas, the more effective it is likely in fact to be. It followed that, so far from attempting to establish logical connections of thought, the trick is to discourage logical thought altogether. The successful advertisement is one that makes an irrational association instantaneously, before customers have any time to reflect; therefore avoid complicated images that may provoke thought, and concentrate on simple broad shapes that can be taken in at a single glance. That is the rationale of the poster, which by the 1880s was superseding both advertising cards and the older handbills.

Among the first to recognize the function of broad, simple, uncomplicated images in the new advertising was a Parisian named Jules Chéret (1836–1932), who began his career in the 1850s making simple black-and-white handbills to paste on walls. In 1858 he began experimenting with bills in three colors, and from 1859 to 1866 was in London learning the then new technique of color lithography. The results appeared on his return to Paris, with the 1867 poster of Sarah Bernhardt that made him famous—a broad-patterned, simple image that was an instant success. Similar posters followed at once, and already in the 1870s people were talking about Chéret's having transformed the boulevards of Paris into "art galleries." In 1881 Chéret formed his own poster factory in Paris, and from it came posters by thousands; in 1896 alone he made 882. As "father of the modern poster" he has a museum to himself, the Musée Chéret in Nice.

From Chéret there are three lines of descent. First, the workaday poster, frankly intended to sell and persuade; Dudley Hardy (1867–1922) was a famous early practitioner, and almost all outdoor billboards are later examples, including the posters all governments use for recruiting (most typical are the "I Want You" posters of World War I, with accusing fingers pointed at "shirkers" by Uncle Sam, Kitchener, Czar Nicholas or whoever), exhortations against littering, against setting forest fires, against discrimination, and so forth and so forth; in them, irrational association is everywhere the primary principle.

Second, the practice of "art in advertising," proceeding from a premise that it is good public relations to "elevate the tone" of one's product by associating it with an "art-gallery world" which is allegedly above sordid mercantile considerations. In this even more obviously irrational category belong such famous early examples as the 1887 reproduction of Sir John Millais's *Bubbles* and Sir Edwin Landseer's doggy pictures, elevating the associations of Pears' Soap and pet food; the sort of thing extolled in the 1920s by W. Shaw Sparrow's *Advertising and British Art* (1924)—exquisite drawings of Arthurian legend pasted on walls with a tactful mention of a British railway beneath, historic depictions of Old London with Johnny Walker unobtrusively striding through them, and, in our own time, the practice of commissioning pictures from celebrated artists to manifest otherwise unsuspected cultural sensibilities animating manufacturers of diamond jewelry, corrugated boxes, and tin cans.

And third, of course, the "art poster" proper. Here Toulouse-Lautrec (1864–1901) is the great hero, advance-guard apologists having seized on him as proof that Fine Artists could be useful in society after all; this lead was followed by a host including Aubrey Beardsley, "the Beggarstaff Brothers" (James Pryde and William Nicholson), and Edward Penfield, down to the psychedelic poster-tasters of the 1960s, with the inevitable result that the Fine Art poster soon became something of interest only to Fine Artists, made as a Precious Object for erudite critics to analyze and Museums to put on Exhibition. Picasso's dove-of-peace poster in the late 1940s is the best example of the genre, plainly recalling the kind of posters advance-guard painters made in the early days of the Russian Revolution before Lenin threw them out and insisted on persuasive posters of the Chéret-Hardy sort that would speak to someone besides art critics.

4. *The Psychological Hard Sell*

Of course, the early appearance of art posters was clear indication how very briefly the poster remained a major advertising form—they became Fine Art, that is, because they were becoming technologically obsolete. Already in the 1890s the great bulk of advertising was shifting from outdoor forms like posters to the indoor form of newspaper and magazine advertisements—a development essentially dictated by the new advertising technique itself, which by its nature was primarily responsible for a dramatic rise in sheer numbers of newspapers and magazines published from the late 1880s on. There were other factors: a new technique for manufacture of cheap paper from wood pulp; universal public education providing a mass reading public; but it was a sudden immense increase in revenues from advertising that started the whole process. The old simple kind of announcement could be inserted in a relatively small space, and the compulsive symbol could be effective with barely more, but the associative image had to be big to be effective. Furthermore, it had to be broad and simple; this discouraged the old detailed woodcuts and stimulated development of process prints which began to appear in the late 1880s, whence they were taken over into general printing in the -90s. But process prints in turn led to printing from cylinders, which vastly increased the speed of printing generally, and so made mass media even cheaper. And the cheaper they became, the more profitable it became to use them for advertising.

It was a great spiral, which resulted by the early 1890s in far more advertising than ever before in history. Compare one of Hearst's or Pulitzer's newspapers in the 1890s with papers of the Civil War period, or Edward Bok's *Ladies' Home Journal* (founded 1901) with *Harper's Weekly* or *Leslie's* in the 1870s, and you will be struck with the difference—where the earlier publications are mostly text with a few advertisements inserted at front and back, the later ones are literally laced through with advertisements. This meant a public exposed day and night to persuasion of a new irrational sort. Nor was that all. For as advertisers more and more used media that entered the home, they inevitably aimed more and more directly at individuals rather than people en masse. And so to the compulsive symbol and the associated idea succeeded a third kind of advertising, the direct "hard sell" by psychological appeal (**81a, b, c, d, e**).

Not, of course, that the older forms disappeared. Both went on, and you can see them to this day everywhere—pictures of sultry women alongside brand names of gin or hair tonic and implications that such delights go naturally together; invitations to live like brawny he-men in the wilds or nightclubbing celebrities by sharing their alleged preferences in cigarettes, and so on. But from the 1890s on there was an increasing percentage of advertisements of the more direct kind, with an ever greater influence on shaping public mentality.

Though the new technique had been developed empirically well before 1900, it was the sometime director of the Psychological Laboratory at Northwestern University outside Chicago, Walter Dill Scott (1869–1955), who fostered, formulated, and made it into a "science." In books like *The Psychology of Advertising* (1908) and *Influencing Men in Business* (1911), and in lectures and consultations all over the world, he hammered his message home: advertisers should "appeal to ruling interests and motives . . . the desire to be healthy, to hoard, to possess, to wear smart clothes, to get something for nothing, to be like the more privileged and successful classes." Or in plainest language, base advertising on envy and shame. Suggest not so much how happy people will be with your product, as how miserable and empty life will be without it.

In the years before 1914 the new technique was employed chiefly to make necessities out of what had originally been luxuries, like automobiles and flush toilets; and since many of these things did in fact make life more comfortable, it could be defended (and of course, vigorously was) as a civilizing influence. That it also stimulated a herd mentality, covertly working to enforce conformity (the razor manufacturers' campaign to make beards synonymous with senility and barbarism, mustaches with villainous intentions, is a good example), was less noticeable. With World War I such comfortable illusions were stripped away, and the Frankenstein that had been created began to stalk in earnest. Psychological advertising was among the mightiest weapons that prolonged the slaughter, imputing perversion and poltroonery to anyone not absolutely believing or unhesitatingly carrying out every government policy and program—a technique all the more essential as the cause and ultimate purpose of the War became increasingly cloudy and incomprehensible. A famous example from those years is the British recruiting poster picturing the humiliation of a man who had not been "in it" asked by his children in after days "Daddy, what did *you* do in the Great War?"—an appeal neither to reason (for it makes no attempt to justify the War) nor yet to patriotism (as in earlier posters about "doing your bit"), but entirely to what Dr. Johnson once described as base irrational shame: "Sir, every man secretly thinks the less of himself for never having been a soldier."

So blessed and tried in conflict, the new advertising blossomed on a fantastic scale in the 1920s and -30s (**81e**). All restraints vanished. Every conceivable human frailty and vice was played upon with consummate conscienceless skill. Envy, greed, lust, fear, pride, even sloth were all called in to sell products neither needed nor wanted. Timid protests raised by logic or common sense at some particularly abominable excess were shouted down: prosperity demands productions of goods without end, and social justice sharing them without limit, so that advertising supports both; then let nothing and nobody inhibit the advertiser, Who only doeth marvelous works. Are there people who don't like you? That is the worst disaster to befall a human being. Everybody naturally loves everybody else all the time, so obviously it must be that your armpits stink, or your clothes are inappropriate, or your teeth are bad, or you drive a cheap car, or your house is unfashionably furnished, or you're serving the wrong kind of soft drink, or your grammar is bad, or there's dandruff in your hair. Quote from our scrapbook; take our piano lessons, buy our car, our beer, our mouthwash, our shampoo, our foot powder. But never be content when you get it; it's your right always to have everything everyone else has.

5. *Television Advertising: Preparations for* Nineteen Eighty-Four

In the late 1940s the volume of advertising in magazines and newspapers began to slack off, and with it, the number of publications themselves; as dramatically as they multiplied in the 1890s, they began folding up one by one. No sudden resurgence of sanity was responsible, unfortunately. Quite the opposite—a new and far more seductive medium had appeared: television advertising, combining the techniques of irrational association with hard-sell psychology, to the advantage of both.

It had long been plain that irrational association could be effected on motion-picture screens better than anywhere else; as early as 1915 D. W. Griffith's *Birth of a Nation* proved how naturally an audience would connect one movie image with its immediate predecessor—show a full shot of a grieving woman and then a close-up of clenched hands, and no audience doubts either that they are her hands or that they are clenched in grief; show a soldier firing a rifle and then a man falling in the street, and everyone assumes that the one shot the other. But until the advent of television, motion-picture technique could be employed for irrational-association advertising only to a limited extent, because audiences in motion-picture theaters assumed that they had paid to be entertained, not to be cajoled into buying things. Advertising before movies was resented as uncalled-for, and theater owners who tried much of it found that they lost more business than the advertising was worth to them. Television completely changed this situation. In television, as in radio, it was assumed that the entertainment had been paid for by a sponsor, who therefore had a right to speak; that to hear tunes an audience must expect to first "listen to a few words" from whoever paid the piper. And television advertising had this further enormous advantage over both radio and media like newspapers or billboards—instead of appealing only through the ear, or only through the eye, it could intrude on both senses at once, with an impact far more powerful and far more immediate than ever before. Television in fact realized what to earlier generations of advertisers would have seemed the utopian dream of being able to employ irrational association of ideas in direct psychological hard-selling; it quite literally put the public at their mercy.

From television advertising, neither taste nor age afforded refuge. Commercials impartially interrupted symphony concerts and situation comedies, animated cartoons and cowboy reruns and Shakespearean festivals. Night and day, year by year, they conditioned most of the human race; and by the 1960s results were becoming apparent. How much the Affluent Age owed to increased purchasing stimulated by television advertising would be hard to say. But there can be no doubt that television advertising played a major part in that "credibility gap"—that endemic contempt for law, distrust of education, suspicion of ethics generally—which rapidly grew to threaten the very fabric of society. Why? Because for seven decades advertising had been relentlessly pulling at those seams of reason, logic, and mutual trust which alone held American (or any other) society together, each successive form of it being more powerful than the last; and television has consummated the process. Television advertising was social dynamite, pure and plain.

I don't mean simply that advertising in general has been one of the most corrosive forces at work to destroy capitalism and encourage egalitarian fantasies, though this irony is perhaps obvious. Never were socialists like the Webbs or Bernard Shaw wider of the mark than in their railings against advertising as a "capitalist tool," for its actual influence on society has been just the opposite. Unceasingly, decade after decade, with ever more subtle and irresistible means, advertising has worked to keep a shimmering paradise of material happiness before Everyman's eyes. For generation after generation, advertising has inculcated the conviction that everyone has an equal right to everything. Of course, if that were all, people could (and do) argue that advertising is ultimately a Good Thing, working however inadvertently toward a more just society. But it is not so much the ends advertising has been devoted to as its means of attaining them that have been so poisonous—and particularly the twin techniques employed on television. The kind of mentality they foster could support no civilized society at all. They fit people for one kind of world only, the world of *Nineteen Eighty-Four*.

Consider first the attack on reason. Compulsively repetitive symbols, illogically associated images, psychological hard sell, all are designed to discourage reasoned thought, and each more effectively than the last. Their whole object is to produce minds conditioned to respond to stimuli like Pavlov's dogs. Such a mentality might conceivably be defended as necessary preparation for Heaven on earth—all the Enlightenment religions fundamentally depend on leaps of faith, on a belief in man's natural goodness and sinlessness and kindness which never has been supported by any evidence or logic whatsoever, whence it presumably follows that any agency working to destroy reasoned thought works in favor of some kind of brave new world. But not in fact. In fact, for a society of robots responding automatically to symbols, leaping mindlessly to associate one idea with another, moved to instant action by plays on shame and fear, only one kind of social organization is possible—Big Brother's superstate.

Or consider the consequences of consistently deriding any idea of intrinsic excellence, as advertising does with its insistence that all men can be successful, all women desirable, all children equally popular with their peers, if only they will buy this and use that; that anybody can be elected to any office with the proper "television technique." What kind of world must it be where no natural superiority of mind or body is ever acknowledged, where dedicated study is never rewarded and industrious application counts for nothing; where everything is leveled to the lowest common denominator? That, too, has already been described:

> In our world there will be no emotions except fear, rage, triumph, and self-abasement. . . . There will be no art, no literature, no science. . . . There will be no distinction between beauty and ugliness. There will be no curiosity, no enjoyment of the process of life.

It is attacks on mutual trust that lead to *Nineteen Eighty-Four,* to the "exact opposite of the stupid hedonistic utopias that the old reformers [and the television advertisers] imagined," where "no one dares trust a wife or a child or a friend any longer." For teaching people to think themselves miserable without new cars and fur coats and Caribbean cruises, disguising the fact that everything cannot be available for everybody and could never guarantee happiness even if it were, implying therefore that there must be some monstrous force in the world frustrating people's enjoyment of what should rightfully be theirs, is to inculcate a mentality requisite for the Two Minute Hate. And the mindless assumption that all life is somehow a cheat breeds a mistrust of the very possibility of any disinterested truth or unaffected sincerity; and that is the prerequisite for every totalitarian system. For it is axiomatic that in freely and rationally organized societies, relations between individuals will be governed primarily by trust and mutual confidence; and conversely, the more irrational and tyrannical a society is, the more completely isolated each individual must be from his fellows, the more necessarily ruled by force and fear. Without trust there can be no freedom; and so it is by destroying capacity for trust that advertising does its deepest evil in our world.

Advertising necessarily involves lying—deliberately, consciously, consistently. All beers cannot be the one best, all cigarettes cannot be mildest, all soap powders cannot get clothes cleanest, all joys cannot consist in abundance of possessions; but advertisers must pretend they can. The result is a world awash in oceans of lies. In earlier generations, people learned this fact late enough in life to be able to devise little rafts of personal integrity for keeping sanity and trust afloat. But from the late 1940s on, complete immersion in lies began at birth, so that people grow up never knowing anything else.

Before ever children can think, let alone read, they are taught distrust as a permanent condition of life. It may begin on the Christmas Day they discover their new doll or gun or game is not at all what weeks of pre-Christmas advertising on television so confidently, so sincerely, so disarmingly told and pictured it; it may begin any number of ways. But however begun, there is no end. From childhood, when the miserably cheap little toy delivered in the morning's mail is compared with those glowing promises on the box top sent off so trustingly weeks before, to adolescence, when the billboards ask "In these bewildered times, where shall a man turn to replenish the wells of his courage, to repair the walls of his faith?" and reply: "*Beer,*" everything precious or noble or idealistic in life is systematically exploited and defiled. Science is a trick to sell things, a gimmick for measuring nicotine content, for proving that one pill dissolves in stomachs faster than another, creams take hair off legs better than razor blades (or vice versa), sprays keep armpits fresher than roll-ons. All feeling for history is aborted, for in advertising "the past" means "the worthless"—nothing is so utterly without value as last year's model car or refrigerator or television, unless it be the old product before TCP or CQD or GOK was added to it (it is no accident that it has been during this Advertising Era that the word "primitive" lost its Johnsonian sense of "simple," "dignified," "venerable," "uncorrupted"—in which sense the Pre-Raphaelites understood "primitive" Italian art as late as the 1860s—and acquired its modern pejorative connotation of "crude," "awkward" and "inferior"). No more admirable training for a job in *Nineteen Eighty-Four*'s Ministry of Truth could be devised.

6. *Advertising and the "Crisis in Credibility"*

Every organ in the body has the capacity to develop antibodies for repelling hostile organisms; eye, ear, and mind are no exception. And so, growing up in an environment filled day and night with the din of competing advertisers' devious deceits, we all have developed an ability to close off our senses that would have astonished our ancestors, and is rarely recognized even by ourselves. Wittingly or not, we have all come to resemble the two little men who in one famous cartoon stand outside a theater marquee covered with advertisements for the Stupendous, Colossal, Unforgettable, Thrill-of-a-Lifetime movie going on within, and wonder, "Do you suppose it's worth seeing?" All of us have learned to drive along highways lined with signs shrieking at us with every allure science and art and psychology can devise, and never notice any of them. All of us can to some extent "filter out" television commercials from our conscious minds. In this way we survive after a fashion; but it is a poor way to live. For in shutting our senses to lies, we also deaden them to truths. Conditioned to disregard all signboards, we may miss the one that says, "Bridge Out Just Ahead." From disbelief in many things it is no great step to disbelief in most, and then all. Meaninglessness can become a normal condition of life. And there are many indications that it already has.

Anyone who has had much to do with students in the last half-dozen years can testify that the one common denominator running across the "new" generation is a paranoid fear of the put-on, an unwillingness to believe the best, or see sincerity, in anyone or anything. Fine Artists, eagerly searching for Realities to reveal, have made much of the resultant pervasive sense of meaninglessness, with "paintings" consisting of plaster bags and sandpiles, sculpture of trash, and most obviously, the "new" theater:

> Either God exists and perfection on earth is not required, or God does not exist and human life can be perfected. . . . But if God does not exist (contrary to Plato), and if wisdom cannot be realized (contrary to Hegel), then the madmen, the criminals and dope addicts are as reasonable as the philosophers, and even more reasonable insofar as they do not attempt to philosophize. [Lionel Abel, "So Who's Not Mad? On *Marat/Sade* and Nihilism," in Irving Howe, ed., *The Radical Imagination*, 1967, p. 156.]

But of course such arts are not responsible for the spiritual vacuity they allegedly reveal; Fine Art is far too out of touch with society to be responsible for anything. As a matter of fact, put-ons in Fine Art only represent the last in a continuing series of Fine Art forms and attitudes borrowed from advertising. Flat simple shapes borrowed from advertising posters for Art Nouveau designs; associated images borrowed from mid-19th-century advertisements in collages and synthetic Cubism and Dada; Barnum's and Holloway's compulsive symbols appropriated by Klee; Al Held's obvious imitations of the effects of outdoor billboards—the list is almost endless ("Imagine how marvelous [Held's 12' x 56'] *Greek Garden* would look in an international airport," *Newsweek* for January 29, 1968, quotes a museum director as saying; well, quite a few similar works line the approaches to every airport already).

403

Insofar as all this has any serious significance beyond another demonstration that Fine Art has invented no new forms since the 1870s, it is no more than a competition among several different sorts of Artists to control the Sorcerer's Apprentice for their own advantage.

For the real source of the restless malaise afflicting the late 1960s, we need to look farther back, and deeper.

6

Conclusions and Implications

∎

I

CONCLUSIONS:
UNCHANGING ARTS
AND UNCHANGING HISTORY

SOCIAL CRITICS of all kinds are fond of citing the swampy jungles of television advertising as an indictment of "American democracy." But you can blame American democracy for greed and fear and similar failings so evidently common to human beings in every time and place and condition only if you sincerely believe that changing laws or institutions or economic systems can or ought to change basic human nature. And if you believe that, not only will you find the old visionary promises of American life denied in television; you will find *all* the visionary promises of the last two centuries denied in *all* the Unchanging Arts.

At the close of the 1960s, three superstates dominate the world's political landscape. Each is the product of a revolution supposed by its protagonists to transform human life on earth. There is the United States, product of the 1776 Revolution against hereditary authority and dedicated to the proposition that all men are created politically equal; there is the Soviet Union, product of the 1917 Revolution against bourgeois capitalism and committed to belief in a "new Soviet man" emerging from economic equality; and there is China. What the long-drawn-out Chinese Revolution was against is plain—its protagonists revile bourgeois capitalism and Soviet Communism alike. What it is for cannot be so easily discerned; but those Westerners well disposed to it may be right in calling it yet another attempt to realize Heaven on earth—this time by promoting what could best be called a state of angelic selflessness through environmental conditioning. Are these successive visions about to become reality at last? Not according to anything that can be read in the Unchanging Arts.

We have seen, for instance, how the convictions behind the American Revolution were architecturally embodied in a series of styles beginning with the Classical Revivals and presently represented in the Colonial Revival; and we have seen how feeble an expression of conviction the Colonial Revival has become. We have seen how American convictions were also supported by cartooning, in the days of Thomas Nast. Is there any modern-day equivalent? If there is, *The New Yorker* magazine represents it—and what an image it projects! As begun in 1925 by Harold Ross (1892–1951), *The New Yorker* was conscientiously daring. Possibly as a reaction to his immediately preceding job as assistant editor of the *American Legion Weekly* from 1921 to 1923, Ross originally put "Not for the Old Lady from Dubuque" on his masthead, and ever since, the magazine's cartoons have maintained a deliberately irreverent tone. It runs through all their different styles and themes as a leitmotiv—Helen Hokinson's corseted clubwomen concerned over "what shall we do with Russia?," Charles Addams's monsters haunting General Grant mansions; Richard Taylor's stylized drawings of high jinks in the café set; Peter Arno's broadly brushed bloods and fillies in naughty situations; George Price's zany slices of life in New York; James Thurber's Freudian variations on Beerbohm; and so on. But, quite obviously, beneath this flimsy veneer *The New Yorker* has long been a bastion of the American upper-middle class, in the same sense that Pocci and Busch were bastions of the 19th-century German social system—by poking innocuous fun at the manners and mores of American life, they humanize and present it in a sympathetic light. And the Establishment image that they project is essentially disillusioned. American life is never going to be fundamentally different from life anywhere else. Take what amusement the passing show offers, but expect no radical changes in the playbill. Resign yourself. The only exception in Ross's tenure of *The New Yorker* was when the New York Central Railroad in 1942 began broadcasting advertisements over loudspeakers in the waiting room of Grand Central Station, and he threw all his magazine's resources into a campaign against them. Otherwise, no involvement. No agitation. No crusades.

So much for the new kind of life promised through political equality. Economic equality has done no better. Apart from the dreary stereotyped images of Lenin, happy workers, contented peasants that represent the New Soviet Man, its chief manifestations perhaps are in British social cartooning from the 1900s on.

Some of this cartooning appears in *Punch*, which since the 1950s has been supporting the Socialist establishment in much the same way it did the 19th-century British ideal. The period of transition was long and painful, however; during World War I, the transformation by Bruce Bairnsfather (1888–1959) of the salt-of-the-earth British workingman into Old Bill the stoical trench veteran, and the evocations of Tenniel's grand manner by Bernard Partridge (1861–1945) (74a) were so successful that it took thirty years of increasing irrelevance and absurdity for *Punch* finally to abandon the disintegrating 19th-century rational ideal in favor of themes and format more appropriate to the Welfare State. So the new kind of cartoon originated elsewhere, among independents, the most effective of them being Osbert Lancaster (b. 1908).

Associate of the Royal Institute of British Architects and an accomplished stage designer, Lancaster made his first reputation as an erudite satirist of architectural modes and manners—*Progress at Pelvis Bay* (1936), *Pillar to Post* (1938), *Homes Sweet Homes* (1938); and though since 1939 he has been regular cartoonist for Beaverbrook's *Daily Express,* his most effective single work was the satire on a typical English town history, *There'll Always Be a Drayneflete,* published in 1960 (82). Here what his *Express* cartoons (collected as *Signs of the Times* in 1961) only hint at is set forth plainly. *Drayneflete* is the counterpart in social cartooning to Orwell's *Animal Farm.* Who, in *Animal Farm,* represents Orwell's own mature point of view? Not the intellectual pigs, who in the end themselves come to embody all the evils egalitarian socialism was supposed to end forever. Surely not the willing worker Boxer, too stupid to learn more than four letters of the alphabet at one time. Even less the dogs who police any state indifferently, or the bleating masses of sheep. Clearly it is Benjamin, the donkey, who is intelligent enough to read, who can understand the principles of the Revolution, but who yet maintains that "animal nature" never changes and despite all the new institutions life will remain very much the same. It was Orwell's fate to realize finally, after a lifetime's dedication to egalitarian socialism, that it could never work, that the world of time and history is and was what it is and always has been because human beings are what they are. *Drayneflete* says the same in the form of social cartooning.

Between *Drayneflete* and its obvious 1936 predecessor *Progress at Pelvis Bay,* there is the same difference as between *Animal Farm* and Orwell's 1936 *Road to Wigan Pier*—the earlier trickle of hope that despite human perversity things could improve has evaporated. As age succeeds age, *Drayneflete's* buildings and costumes change; successive rulers bring one new creed and vision after another, but the essence of life alters not at all. Nor, we may be sure, will it change in that glittering Wellsian vision of Science and Technology triumphant which is "Drayneflete of the Future"; this is satire, not prophecy. It is no accident that Lancaster illustrated C. Northcote Parkinson's *The Law and the Profits* (1960), for beneath the surface sparkle of Lancaster's wit, like Parkinson's, is a deep well of resignation. Whatever Lancaster's private views, his work mirrors that profound apathy which visitors to Britain in the 1960s everywhere found so pervasive and so appalling.

Not, alas, that Heaven on earth has finally been discredited. Far from it. There are those who construe developments in Cuba to mean that all educational systems, sexual codes, and corporate hierarchies premised on human beings' needing some form of coercion to work together are about to melt away. There are those who imagine that a new world of heavenly love and brotherhood on earth is about to appear in the New China. Many of them believed the same of Russia thirty years ago; for this is the third phase of the same millennial faith, as powerful as its predecessors.

And in architecture there are plain evidences of something going on comparable to what happened in the 1920s—the formulation (self-contradictory though it may be) of an architecture expressing the convictions of an anarchist Establishment! For example, if you consider late works of Corbusier like the chapel at Ronchamp, or buildings like the chapel at Brasilia, or the "New Brutalism" generally, you will see that what they all have in common is a deliberate and unmistakable primitivistic imagery. The Ronchamp Chapel looks, when you stop to think about it, either like a great megalithic dolmen from 3rd-millennium Brittany, or like one of the houses in Bedrock where TV's *Flintstones* live (and it is the more significant, in that this form does not derive from the properties of poured concrete). The chapel in Brasilia resembles nothing so much as a gigantic wigwam or a hut made of tree branches—an enormous version of a primeval round house. "New Brutalism" specializes in sophisticated reproductions of the cave- and cliff-dwellings of our prehistoric (and precivilized, of course!) ancestors.

But all of this is even less plausible to rational beings than the visions gone before. For the fact is that to establish each successive revolutionary social order force has been required, and in each case more and sooner than in the last. The reason should be obvious. Each successive vision has rested on an increasingly false concept of the real nature of human life. Insofar as men can be made equal at all, it requires less force to establish and maintain some kind of political equality than economic; imposing selfless love would require the most violence of all ("It's an act of love to Kill a Cop," as Mr. Rubin put it), for here we are up against what the old theologians used to call the sin of Pride, the most deep-set human fault of all.

Whatever real strength each successive revolution has had has been derivative.

"It would have been a profound shock," wrote Lawrence Brown in *The Might of the West,* "for the liberal Jefferson had he discovered behind his great preamble not the togaed ghost of Tiberius Gracchus but the black-robed schoolmen of the Gothic Ages." That the American Revolution created a great nation was due, not to any visions of a *novus ordo seclorum,* but to the stability of traditional values and concepts written into the American Constitution—had its framers really believed men were naturally good, they would hardly have provided so many checks and balances against abuse of power. Similarly, when the *Handbook of Leninism-Marxism* speaks of "the struggle of the working class and the Communists. . . . being waged for the highest and noblest ideal. . . ." it derives concepts of what is "high" and "noble" necessarily from a value system outside itself— from the same ultimate source, that is. Flower children and self-criticism-session leaders live off remnants of the spirit that moved Christian monks of old. Whence comes an answer to the question most art historians have been asked at one time or another, What do you imagine art will look like in the future? From this study we can answer categorically, nothing like what is conventionally called art now. Precisely what its forms may be no one can guess; but its principles will be those of the Unchanging Arts, just as the principles on which societies rest are the unchanging truths about human nature and life. The return to them will be a real revolution.

II

IMPLICATIONS:
REVOLUTION IN ART AND HISTORY

THIS BOOK is the second of a three-part study of art and history. The basic premise of this study is that the activity currently called Art differs in ends, means, and social function from what was thought of as art in the past, and that people calling themselves Artists today no more than go through the same motions as people known as artists in history, since what they do or claim to do in and for society is in fact fundamentally different.

The precise nature of this change, and how and why it occurred, was analyzed in *The Restless Art,* the first volume in this study. This present book pursues the question, if painting no longer performs its traditional functions of substitute image-making, beautification, illustration, conviction and persuasion, what activities do?—so it is concerned with the history and cultural expression of photography, commercial design, such forms of illustration as movies and comics, and such arts of conviction and persuasion as political and social cartoons, ideographic architecture, advertising, and the like. But there are implications far beyond present-day art forms.

1. *The Teaching of Studio Arts*

Most North American colleges and universities have departments of art where painting and drawing are taught, and usually design and crafts of some kind as well. The rationale for offering such courses is universities' traditional function and obligation to pass on human heritages of ideas, skills, and knowledge—they teach art on the same essential grounds that they teach physics, geography, classics, or history. But what if this Art (i.e., the kind of painting, drawing and design usually offered) is not in fact concerned with any heritage of

412

ideas, skills, or knowledge? What if it is an activity so personal in significance and so subjective in practice as not to be teachable in any meaningful sense at all? Then surely curriculum revisions are in order. In Europe they are already under way. In May 1967 I visited ten leading art schools in Britain, Scandinavia, and Germany, to study their offerings in connection with establishing a Studio/Visual-Arts program at the University of Victoria; and in every case I found painting and its allied activities being de-emphasized, in favor of programs in photography, commercial design, commercial illustration, and the like. Not that any value judgment is necessarily being passed on the worth of the aesthetic experience and creative act involved in what is called painting, compared to arts with more direct social relationships and implications; it is simply that painting as now understood has become unteachable. Once a student grasps the essential principle (and that will not take long, however abstrusely ponderous its formulations), nothing more can possibly be taught him. It follows that traditional art schools based on aesthetic experience and creative act have lost any real reason for existence. They survive, in fact, only in inverse ratio to the spread of the concept of painting as an entirely self-justifying activity divorced from all social connotations; we may therefore expect to see North American art schools changing in the next ten years as European art schools have been changing in the last ten.*

2. Collecting Policies and Practice in Museums and Galleries

Museums and galleries commonly collect "art of all periods," on an assumption that Greek vases and Buddhist sculptures and Trecento altarpieces all were produced by essentially the same processes and motivations as Cézanne's paintings and Brancusi's sculpture and Oldenberg's plaster hamburgers. But what if they were not? Then this principle of collecting is absurd. For which of the grounds for collecting historic art also justify collecting what Fine Artists produce today? Not Beauty, certainly. Ever since *avant-garde* artists in Courbet's time abjured Beauty as their goal in favor of investigating Realities of various sorts, Beauty has not been their direct concern, and is rarely now even a by-product of their activities. Still less intrinsic

* See the complete report, published as "Art Schools Abroad," *College Art Journal*, XXIX, 2, 1969, pp. 209ff.

worth—by its nature what we call Art is ephemeral, the transient records of aesthetic experience or experiment for its own sake, at best possessing no more than the artificial value of rare postage stamps; least of all, value for historic record. By their own definition the Reality Fine Artists concern themselves with is so subjective and personal as to be divorced from social interests and concerns and therefore deliberately removed from the stream of history. There can be in fact only one justification for museums collecting today's Fine Art, and that is to "encourage Art." For along with complete independence, Fine Artists have also achieved complete unemployability.

Doing nothing society wants done, all their functions now taken over by commercial designers and cartoonists and the like, Fine Artists would in the normal course of events be vanishing as completely as carriage makers or fighting-cock breeders—as in fact they did in Russia under Lenin, and are doing in China. What keeps them alive in the West? Welfare, ultimately, but disguised in various ways. Some live off patrons—as one wealthy man's hobby is salmon fishing in Scotland and another's to photograph hummingbirds, so others again keep stables of Fine Artists for amusement, flattery, and (if the art market is played adroitly) even profit. But such patrons are in chronically short supply, even in this Affluent Age. Other Fine Artists live by teaching, especially on the college level. But quite apart from the question whether theirs is an activity "teachable" in any meaningful sense, there is an obvious limit to the numbers so supportable. No matter how rapidly college art departments expand, the supply of young painters they turn out must inevitably be far in excess of any possible reabsorption of the products; Fine Artists cannot live indefinitely like the fabled Chinese taking in each other's washing. Ultimately, in fact, all that college teaching of art accomplishes is to inflate the number of unemployed and unemployable painters beyond all hope and reason.

There remain museums and galleries willing to buy Fine Artists' work. The pressure on them to "collect modern" is accordingly enormous. And it will grow more so as long as museums continue to recognize no difference between historic art and what is called Art now. For then they can have no grounds for refusing to allot more and more of yearly budgets to supporting Fine Artists, less and less for attempting to fulfill their traditional functions as archives of a certain kind of historic records, repositories for cherishing the achievements of the past. In the end they must become more or less openly welfare

414

agencies existing to feed hungry painters—as many for all intents and purposes are already.

There is really only one remedy: recognize Fine Art for what it is, and frame policy accordingly: *Never acquire anything deliberately made for a museum.* Restrict collecting to objects that originally had some use other than to be put on Exhibition, that hence have some measurable value and ascertainable place in history.

This means not only "historic art"; it also means things like machines and cans and bottles and comic strips and calendars. Institutions like the Ford Museum in Dearborn are the true "museums of modern art."*

3. *The Study of Art History*

Most universities and colleges in the past have commonly considered art history and studio arts together, as branches of the same discipline. Customarily they have been put into a single department. This arrangement has always had the practical effect of forcing art history to carry a studio-arts program on its back; since studio teachers habitually maintain that they cannot handle more than fifteen or twenty students per class, and usually demand fewer, studio programs are usually paid for by overcrowded classes in art history. That burden has hitherto been justified on an assumption that what art historians are concerned with is the same thing artists do now. Once upon a time—broadly, before about 1850—that may have been so. But what if that is so no longer? Then such an arrangement makes no theoretical sense; you might as well say that since both Political Science and Domestic Science have "Science" in their titles, they should be taught together—in the Department of Physics, say! Then there is no advantage in art historians having practical experience of the present-day practice of Art, whether by association with Artists or by actually taking studio courses themselves. Worse—and of the greatest importance for art history—there are decided and crucial disadvantages in assuming that they should; not merely in practical terms, but in potential distortion of the whole discipline. For if a student comes to imagine that Picasso and Pollock were the same kind of people or doing same kind of thing as Perugino or Phidias, he properly understands none of them. Unless art historians realize that

* See further "Museums and Living Art," *Museum News*, Oct. 1969, p. 9.

415

their discipline has no fundamental connection with the present-day practice of Fine Arts, they will not see that it is in fact a social science—that its proper and natural academic relationship is with history, history of science, history of literature (Erich Auerbach's sort, not criticism or appreciation), theology, linguistics, and some aspects of psychology. And without grasping what kind of discipline art history fundamentally is, its full potentials for revealing the past go unnoticed.

4. New Premises for Art History

Most of what is currently thought, said, and done about art is premised on an implicit assumption that art in ancient Egypt or Tang China or medieval Europe was essentially the same kind of activity as Art in 20th-century Paris or New York. It is taken for granted that galleries and museums exhibit Sumerian or South Seas or Baroque art along with Dada or Pop Art, and so imply that all are products of the same intellectual and cultural processes. It is taken for granted that standard surveys of the "history of art" begin with the caveman and end with Picasso, inviting mutual comparisons among these "artists." Such books, indeed, often point out how entirely new and different from anything in the past "modern art" is; but no implication is drawn. *Yet if what was called art in the past not merely looks different from what is called Art now, but is an activity wholly different in its ends and social function, then most of what is currently being thought, said, and done about "art" is meaningless to the point of absurdity.* The whole field of "art history" needs to be rethought and restructured.

Not only has a contemporary concept of Art been mistakenly transposed into past ages when that concept was unknown, but contemporary categorizations of Arts as "major" and "minor," "utilitarian" and "Fine," have been likewise transposed into past ages. Such categorizations of historic art are, if possible, even more absurd, and have hopelessly distorted "art-historical" judgment, both in general and in specifics.

We think of art essentially as a leisure and luxury activity, a by-product of affluence, an "extra" which enlightened patrons choose to support. But in earlier ages, art was a necessity. Society depended for its cohesion and very operation upon the images of conviction, the visual communication, the persuasion, and so forth that it provided. Art was not icing on a cake, it was itself the cake. The forms that it took proceeded from necessity in the first instance, and not from "genius" or "sensitivity"; the artist was not someone who discovered or proclaimed new truths, but one who gave visual form to ideas given him.

And specifically: because *we* make a distinction between "major" arts (e.g., architecture, sculpture, painting), and "minor" arts (e.g., ceramics, jewelry, furniture, embroidery, decoration, etc.), art history conventionally assumes all peoples in the past did likewise. It therefore considers 5th-century Greeks, say, superior "artistically" to 5th-century Etruscans or Scythians, because these latter people had no such "major" arts of architecture and sculpture as the Greeks. But this is invalid. Since the whole concept of "art" in our sense was unknown in 5th-century Greece, or anywhere else, since historically, art never existed as an independent, self-justifying activity in our sense but always grew out of social need, such comparisons of one culture's "art" with another's are totally meaningless. Valid judgment can be properly made only by comparing how given forms perform comparable functions, not on the basis of forms in themselves.

On such a basis, it will be apparent that we cannot dismiss Scythian or Etruscan art as inferior to 5th-century Greek art because the forms are different; we need to evaluate each form in terms of its particular use. When we do, we find that degrees of excellence can be ascertained in the first two quite comparable to the last.

Similarly, we shall not make the mistake of thinking that Scythian metalwork or Etruscan terracottas or Chinese bronze or jade mirrors of the 5th-century B.C. were necessarily inferior to Greek temples or statues of marble, because in the 20th century the former are "minor" arts and the latter "major." We shall find that each has its own excellences, each performed comparably important functions in its own society, none is inferior.

History must be structured horizontally and universally, not vertically and selectively, if it is to be properly understood.

The line-of-progress organization followed in conventional art history—from Egypt to Greece to Rome to Middle Ages to Renaissance to Us—is meaningless and misleading. Past generations did not live their lives with remote posterity—Us—in mind; neither was it the goal of "artistic development" in earlier centuries to introduce "modern painting" to 20th-century students.

To be intelligible, history must be structured in successive epochs, considering what was going on all over the world in each. And each epoch must be studied on its own terms, not in relationship to what was to follow, nor by comparison with some standard of excellence set in any one. Fifth-century Greek sculpture is worth studying not because it was the perfection of 6th-century trends, nor because it was "superior" to 4th-century sculpture, and still less because it set a "standard" not reached by Persians or Chinese or whoever; it is to be studied because it was the embodiment of ideas and aspirations of human beings at a particular moment in time—and time, like mankind, is indivisible, so that in studying it we study ourselves.

Of course, the idea of approaching history horizontally is hardly new. I do not believe, however, that it has ever been done systematically. Because, once it is done, one fact becomes inescapably plain:

At any given epoch in history, the evidence of historic art (as here defined) suggests essential and meaningful similarities in underlying premises of thought, institutions, and ideas all over the world.

Century by century, generation by generation, we see similar ideas successively seizing men's minds, being revealed and perpetuated in their artifacts.

Instead of the conventional historical image of ripples of "influence" spreading from a single source, you find that history looks more like a field strewn with seeds, each growing in a somewhat different way depending on the kind of ground it finds. Where do these seeds, these successive new ideas and attitudes, come from? This, the climax and ultimately important meaning of this whole study, I shall leave for the third and last volume.

PICTURE CREDITS

PICTURE CREDITS

19a. Courtesy Chrysler Corporation.
  b. Courtesy Chrysler Corporation.
20. Author's collection.
21. Courtesy Newark (Del.) *Weekly.*
22a. Courtesy Florida Southern College, Lakeland.
  b. Courtesy Chinese Village Restaurant, Victoria, B.C. Photo by Robin Clarke.
24b. Collection of the Philadelphia Museum of Art. Photo by A. J. Wyatt, staff photographer.
30a. Staatliche Kunstsammlungen, Dresden.
31a. Sleepy Hollow Restorations, Tarrytown, N.Y.
  b. Everson Museum of Art, Syracuse, N.Y.
32a. City Art Museum of Saint Louis.
  b. New York State Historical Association, Cooperstown.
33a. Robert Hull Fleming Museum, The University of Vermont, Burlington. Photo by author.
34a. The Metropolitan Museum of Art, Alfred N. Punnett Fund and Gift of George D. Pratt, 1934.
  b. The Metropolitan Museum of Art, Wolfe Fund, 1906.
35b. Montana Historical Society.
37d. Author's collection.
38b. Collection of the University of Delaware, courtesy Elbert F. Chance.
39a. Photo courtesy New York Public Library.
48. By permission of John Hart and Publishers-Hall Syndicate.
49. Albright-Knox Art Gallery, Buffalo, N.Y., Gift of Seymour H. Knox.
50c. Jay Ward Productions, Inc.
51, 52a, 52b, 53b, 54a, 54b, 55a, 55b. Museum of Modern Art/Film Stills Archive.
55a. Courtesy of Twentieth Century-Fox Film Corporation.
55b. Courtesy of Universal Pictures.
55c. *L'Exprès de Paris.*
56b. Direccion General del Turismo, Archivo Fotografico, Madrid.
57a. Ministère de la Jeunesse des Arts et des Lettres, Service de l'Information à l'Etranger.
  b. Archives du Touring Club de France.
59a. From E. Fuchs, *Karikatur der europäischen Völker.*
  b. Hampton Court Palace. Copyright reserved.
  c. From E. Fuchs, *Karikatur der europäischen Völker.*
60a. The Curators of the Bodleian Library, Oxford.
  c. The Trustees of the British Museum, London.
61a. By courtesy of the Trustees of the Imperial War Museum, London.
  b. Office Municipale du Tourisme, Ville de Montréal.
62a. Library of Congress, Washington.
  b. American Antiquarian Society, Worcester, Mass.
63b. Oregon State Highway Travel Division.
74a. © *Punch.* Reproduced by permission.
  b. David Low cartoon by arrangement with the Trustees and the London *Evening Standard.*
77c. Novosti Press Agency. Courtesy USSR Embassy, Ottawa.
78a. Oeffentliche Kunstsammlung, Basel.
  b. Courtesy of the Shelburne Museum, Shelburne, Vt.
79a. From A. D. Faber, *Smokers, Segars and Stickers,* Century House, Watkins Glen, N.Y., 1949.
  c. Photo by author.

INDEX

Indexes make strange bedfellows—Cruikshank and Cubism, Tolkien and *Tom and Jerry*, Woodrow Wilson and J. Wellington Wimpy, *Batman* and Baudelaire, and so on indefinitely. Yet these juxtapositions are not altogether accidental. Besides suggesting the scope and range of what is called "art" in this book, they also demonstrate its fundamental contention that those arts which perform the unchanging traditional functions of historic arts in the past are those most closely in touch with life in the present.

A small "q" before a page number indicates a quotation.

INDEX